Men of Empire

The Johns Hopkins University Studies in Historical and Political Science
127th Series (2009)

1. Monique O'Connell, *Men of Empire: Power and Negotiation in Venice's Maritime State*

2. Morag Martin, *Selling Beauty: Cosmetics, Commerce, and French Society, 1750–1830*

Men of Empire

POWER AND NEGOTIATION IN VENICE'S MARITIME STATE

Monique O'Connell

The Johns Hopkins University Press
Baltimore

This book was brought to publication with the generous assistance of the Gladys Krieble Delmas Foundation.

Printed in the United States of America on acid-free paper
2 4 6 8 9 7 5 3 1

The Johns Hopkins University Press
2715 North Charles Street
Baltimore, Maryland 21218-4363
www.press.jhu.edu

Library of Congress Cataloging-in-Publication Data

O'Connell, Monique, 1974–
Men of empire : power and negotiation in Venice's maritime state / Monique O'Connell.
p. cm. — (The Johns Hopkins University studies in historical and political science; 127th ser., no. 1)
Includes bibliographical references and index.
ISBN 978-0-8018-9145-8 (hardcover : alk. paper)
1. Venice (Italy)—History. 2. Venice (Italy)—Colonies—Administration. 3. Venice (Italy)—Territories and possessions—Politics and government. 4. Justice, Administration of—Italy—Venice—Territories and possessions.
I. Title.
DG677.85.O25 2009
945'.31107—dc22 2008031489

A catalog record for this book is available from the British Library.

CONTENTS

ACKNOWLEDGMENTS

During the course of this project, I have accumulated debts of gratitude to numerous institutions and individuals, and it is a pleasure to now acknowledge their help and support. I spent many years in the Venetian state archives and other libraries, research time which was made possible by a number of generous grants. The Jacob K. Javits Foundation and the Gladys Krieble Delmas Foundation offered me over two years of residence in Venice. Subsequent funds from the Stanford University Introduction to the Humanities research leave program, Wake Forest University's William C. Archie Fund for Faculty Excellence, the National Endowment for the Humanities, and the Renaissance Society of America allowed further trips to archives and libraries in the United Kingdom, Italy, Croatia, and Greece. I would not have been able to complete this book without the concentrated writing time offered by a year-long research leave from Wake Forest University and a fellowship at Harvard University's Villa I Tatti Center for Renaissance Studies, an ideal environment for study and contemplation.

I have been very fortunate to be surrounded by a wonderful community of scholars and friends in both Italy and America. At the Archivio di Stato in Venice, Michela dal Borgo and Claudia Salmini have opened many doors. Anthony Molho, James Grubb, Dennis Romano, Benjamin Arbel, John Law, Sally McKee, Holly Hurlburt, Josko Belamarić, and Deborah Howard have all asked great questions both in and out of the Venetian archives. Many people have provided rich and valuable commentary on this work. Stanley Chojnacki, Paula Findlen, Tamara Griggs, Robert Lerner, Michael Hughes, Holly Hurlburt, Carl Petry, and Stephen Vella all read drafts of the work in its various stages and offered helpful suggestions; Eric Dursteler read and commented on a penultimate draft of the manuscript. Edward Muir has been an ideal mentor, helping me find sources of funding and providing a constant source of constructive criticism, encouragement, and advice throughout this project's long gestation, and I am grateful for his exacting and insightful remarks on several drafts of the work.

Special thanks are due to my "Venetian family," Feruccio, Margit, Francesca, and Caroline De Stefani. Their friendship and hospitality has made Venice seem like a second home to me, and they have cheerfully helped me solve many of the difficulties and crises I faced while living abroad. I am profoundly grateful to them for their many kindnesses.

I have had the opportunity to present pieces of this work at numerous conferences and seminars and received rich and stimulating commentary that have much improved the manuscript. The feedback I received at the Folger Shakespeare Library Seminar "Artifice and Authenticity: The Ambiguities of Early Modern Venice," in spring 2003 and at the Venice International University seminar "Trade, Colonies, and Intercultural Contacts in the Venetian World" in spring 2004 was particularly valuable and I thank all the participants and organizers. My colleagues in the history department at Wake Forest University have also offered stimulating reflections, and students in my courses over the years have asked a number of very direct questions that have consistently forced me to clarify my ideas and their expression.

I must thank my coauthors on the *Rulers of Venice* database project, Benjamin Kohl and Andrea Mozzato. Andrea has solved countless knotty paleography and linguistic problems for me with unstinting patience, and Ben has been the most supportive senior colleague imaginable. Thanks are due as well to the interlibrary loan staffs at Northwestern, Stanford, and Wake Forest universities, who over the past decade have procured a remarkable number of obscure books and articles. I am also grateful to Mary Pendergraft and Robert Ulery, Jr., of the classics department at Wake Forest University for their cheerful willingness to untangle Latin puzzles for me. Henry Y. K. Tom has asked pointed and constructively critical questions as he guided this book to completion with extraordinary patience, and the manuscript is much improved because of his involvement. Bill Nelson produced the maps for the book.

Final thanks go to my parents, Jeanne and Edward O'Connell, who have supported me in countless ways over the years. This study is dedicated to them not only for their financial and moral support throughout my education but for teaching me to follow my own path and their unfailing belief in me as I did.

NOTE ON PROPER NAMES AND DATES

The geographical range of this book is wide; this presents difficulties with medieval and modern place names as well as with personal names. Furthermore, during the period under consideration, the names of cities and territories often changed along with political boundaries. In order to preserve some sort of consistency, I have used the Italian versions of place names, with the exception of places generally familiar to an Anglophone audience (e.g., Athens, Cyprus). I have noted variant place names at appropriate points in the text and in appendix A.

Much of the data on officeholding in this book comes from the database *Rulers of Venice*, ed. Andrea Mozzato, Benjamin G. Kohl, and Monique O'Connell. At the time this manuscript went to the publisher, the database was in a final editing stage at the Renaissance Society of America but not yet available to the public, and I have used a beta version of that database in preparing this volume. The database standardizes the spelling of personal names in order to make computerized searching possible, and I have therefore used the Italian versions of personal names when referring to Venetian patricians. This standardization imposes a regularity on individual names that did not exist at the time, where, for example, the same individual might be referred to in different documents as Zuan, Zuanne, Giovanni, Iohannes, or Iannis. In the text, I have tried to strike a balance between clarity and consistency and the linguistic diversity of the eastern Mediterranean.

The Venetian year began in March; I have modernized all dates.

Introduction

Venice's commercial maritime empire was a fluid one, its islands, port cities, and hinterlands connected by the sea lanes where ships plied the waters of the Adriatic and eastern Mediterranean. The administration of this empire was also "written on water," in that its political structure was based on negotiation, contestation, collaboration, and accommodation.[1] Venice was not alone in its practices of power. Historians of a wide variety of early modern empires—from the Spanish Americas to the Ottoman-Chinese frontier—have found the idea of negotiation a useful way to approach the dynamics of dominance in early modern empires, as it allows a discussion of the reach of empire's influence without overstating the degree of dominion states actually exercised over the territories they claimed to rule.[2] This negotiation occurred on both an individual and institutional level, between rulers and ruled and between central and peripheral forms of control. The bargaining that took place between state and society, or between elites that directed state action and local political actors, was clearly asymmetrical, with the balance of power firmly on the side of the state and its military force.

The state's coercive abilities, however, were tempered by "control that was exercised mainly over narrow bands, or corridors, of territory and over enclaves of various sizes and situations."[3] This was certainly the case in the Venetian empire, where fragmented geography and political differentiation led to a fragile and often interrupted institutional control over territories. Venetian power was centered in the cities and towns and faded as one moved into the countryside. It was in this context that Venetian elites negotiated with their subjects, both on a communal and an individual level.

The size and reach of Venice's empire certainly cannot—and could not—compete with other iterations of empire in the early modern period. While Spain, Portugal, and Britain reached out into new worlds, Venice's commercial empire remained firmly at the center of the old.[4] But while the territory it ruled was perhaps less exotic and the distances involved smaller, the Venetian state faced many of the same problems of governance in its Mediterranean territories that Iberian and Northern European states experienced in the Atlantic and Indian oceans. Venetian administration in the Adriatic and Aegean had to overcome problems of distance and communication and the religious, ethnic, and linguistic diversity of the subjects over whom it ruled. Within this context of distance and diversity, the Venetian state and Venetian administrators struggled to strike a workable balance between local and central powers.

Unlike most other early modern empires, Venice was not a monarchy but a republic, something that introduced a separate set of structural challenges. States led by a monarch were able to unify old and new possessions through the person of the monarch, creating what J. H. Elliott has described as a "composite state."[5] The disparate parts of these empires were thus drawn into a larger political community while retaining some degree of internal autonomy. Royally appointed officials, acting as representatives of the monarch, embodied this union on a local level. Venice, however, was ruled not by a king but by councils; its ruling elite's loyalty was aimed not to a monarch or to a dynasty but to the city itself and to the collective body of patricians and institutions that governed it. The difference in ideological motivation was matched by the practical function of appointment—royal officials were appointed to serve at the pleasure of the monarch, and many imperial officials in the Americas and the Indies created semiprivate dynasties and power bases through their continued holding of administrative posts.[6] Venetian administrators, in contrast, were elected by councils to serve for terms of about two years, meaning that the administrators were, in theory at least, responsible to a collective public—as embodied in Venetian councils—rather than an individual ruler. Venice is thus unusual in the degree of tension between public and private in the governance of its empire.

This book is an examination of the role these administrators played in the creation and maintenance of Venetian empire. These men, collectively called rectors (*rettori*), were at the center of a three-way negotiation between the Venetian state and its imperial subjects. Charged with putting Venetian state policies into practice, the Venetian rector played an essential mediating role, acting as the main face of Venetian rule for subjects and as the primary conduit of information, demands, and requests to and from the city. Rectors themselves, however, came to the job already enmeshed in the hundreds of kinship, friendship, and commercial alliances that bound the Venetian patriciate together. Many extended their networks of kinship and of clientage while abroad, forming both temporary and more permanent alliances with residents of Venice's maritime domains. These relationships blurred the distinction between a governor's public role and private actions, an ambiguity that had both beneficial and detrimental effects on the maritime empire's overall stability.

The experience of the Venetian patrician Girolamo di Mosé Venier, elected count of Spalato (Split) on the Dalmatian coast in 1484, provides an example of the complications, opportunities, and tensions that surrounded Venice's administrators of empire in practice. The Venetian council that elected Venier intended for him to remain in the position for thirty-two months, but before he had served his full term, he was recalled to Venice and asked to defend himself against charges brought by the syndic of the Levant, Andrea da Pesaro, a state inspector in charge of investigating Venetian officials in the maritime empire. According to Da Pesaro's report to the Senate, Venier had caused "murmuring and indignation in this city and confusion among the subjects."[7] Da Pesaro's accusations against Venier were convincing enough to have the Senate recall the count from his post. Once Venier returned to Venice, Da Pesaro was unable to make his charges stick when the case came before the Senate, and Venier was not convicted. The prolific Venetian diarist Marino Sanudo's account of events in the city implied that Venier's victory was due to legal maneuvering rather than genuine innocence, writing that Da Pesaro "remained undone, and was roundly outwitted."[8]

The fact that Venier was brought before the Venetian Senate to face charges that he had governed badly was not in itself unusual; he was one of thousands of Venetian patricians sent to govern in the republic's maritime empire and one of hundreds who were later accused of malfeasance. What is unusual is that some of his private papers and correspondence have survived, offering a rare window onto the web of personal ties and private interests that animated Venice's administration of its maritime empire. While the official record does not spell out the exact charges brought against Venier, his correspondence demonstrates that the controversy centered on the election of a town doctor that had taken place in the communal council of Spalato on April 24, 1485.[9] As was part of his duty as a Venetian count, Venier presided over the assembly, at which a Spalatine citizen, Ser Doimo de Papalibus, stood and extolled Master Gabriele de Malvasia de Brixia, the current town doctor. Ser Doimo suggested that Master Gabriele be reappointed to the position for another year, an idea Venier praised and which the council voted in favor of forty-seven to seven. Venier's correspondence shows that he maintained connections after he left office with numerous Spalatine citizens, and among this group of business associates and clients was Ser Doimo de Papalibus. Furthermore, Venier left 60 gold ducats in his will to Master Gabriele. Together, these relationships imply that Gabriele's reelection as town doctor might not have been the result of spontaneous acclamation. Rather, the general outrage in Spalato came from the collaboration between the count and one of the town's leading citizens to reelect a friend of theirs. By the fall of 1486, their complaints had reached Da Pesaro, who demanded an investigation into what he termed Venier's "innovations."[10] Venier successfully defended himself in the Senate and returned in the summer of 1487 to his post in Spalato, where he engaged in a vigorous letter-writing campaign to recover his salary from the months he had been in Venice.

Venier, together with his brothers Mosé and Zuan-Francesco, was a merchant as well as an officeholder in the Venetian republic, as were many of his contemporaries. The Venier brothers' letters show them to have had strong commercial interests in the maritime empire; notably in the town of Modon (Modone), on the southern tip of the Peloponnesus, but also including the Cretan city of Rettimo (Rethimno), the Dalmatian city of Zara (Zadar), and Lepanto (Navpaktos) on the Gulf of Corinth. At the time Venier was count in Spalato, all of these cities were also under Venetian rule, part of the republic's maritime empire, which stretched down the eastern coast of the Adriatic and on to the Mediterranean islands of Crete, Cyprus, and Negroponte. As a complement to their commercial concerns, the men of this particular branch of the Venier family had a strong interest in offices that touched on the administration of maritime commerce and of maritime cities. Girolamo's grandfather, Biagio, was himself a syndic of the Levant (1441); his father, Mosé di Biagio, was a counselor in Negroponte (1439); Girolamo's brother Mosé was *podestà* of Cervia (1482) and *podestà* of Mestre (1490); and Zuan-Francesco was commander of a Venetian galley (1493). His uncle, Marco di Biagio, was the Venetian consul in Tunis (1463) and captain of Crete (1482), immediately before Girolamo's term in Spalato. Two members of the larger Venier clan had recently served in Spalato as well—Andrea as count (1461) and Lorenzo di Pietro as castellan (1473). The distinct pattern of specialization in maritime officeholding fits with the Venier interest in overseas trade. Some family members acted as merchants and others as public officials, and all were in a position to cooperate should family interests be at stake.

The Venier family's exploitation of public office for commercial interest was in no way unusual among the Venetian patriciate. The eminent historian Frederic C. Lane characterized Venice's maritime domains as an "empire of naval bases," maintained in large part to support the interests of the merchant patrician oligarchy, which benefited from collective regulation and protection for the fleets of galleys that plied the waters of the Mediterranean, carrying precious metals and woolens from Northern Europe to Damascus, Alexandria, and Constantinople and returning with spices and silks for European nobilities. Lane saw the roots of modern capitalism in Venice's commercial practices and the roots of republicanism in its government, although in both arenas he presented individual initiative as tempered by collective state control.[11] Venetian economic policies and governmental initiatives were often aimed at maximizing the patriciate's collective profits.[12] For instance, Hocquet's monumental work on the salt trade has shown that the state's control of salt production and its sale subsidized both the government and the long-distance voyages of the merchant fleet, to the benefit of the patricians who directed both enterprises.[13] It was in the administration of the state-run galley fleets that individual economic interest and public office most obviously intertwined. The galleys themselves, constructed at the Venetian arsenal, remained public property, and the right to outfit these galleys was auctioned among Venetian patricians on a yearly basis.[14] In the later fifteenth and sixteenth century, control over the state-run galleys was concentrated in the hands of an even more restricted number of families, and Doumerc and Judde de Larivière have argued that the disruption of the tenuous balance between public and private interests was in part to blame for the 1530 collapse of the state-run galley system.[15] The intertwined connections between family and state, the economic and the political, public and private interest were thus at the heart of Venetian state and society.

The rhythms of the Venetian commercial and military galleys regulated the life of the empire, connecting the territories to one another as well as to Venice, and providing a way for goods and people to move from one to another. Venetians did not view their overseas domains in purely economic terms, however; the city's possession and maintenance of a maritime empire was a point of pride and an essential part of Venetian self-representation. The fifteenth century saw a shift in the character of the Venetian maritime state, from a disparate conglomeration of territories acquired for primarily commercial reasons to a more centralized and regularized group of territories that had a political as well as an economic importance. In Senate deliberations, legislators regularly referred to the twin motives of "profit and honor."[16] The commercial aspects of this empire provided Venice with a powerful economy and a structure of transnational connections that led, in some places, to formal political dominion, and in others to a more informal economic hegemony.[17] Where Venice exercised formal political dominion, it created an empire of administrators as well as merchants. In other words, the commercial network that crisscrossed the Venetian maritime state had to be supported by a political enterprise, by government institutions and a network of Venetian power built, maintained, and exploited by Venetian castellans and treasurers as much as by merchants or galley captains.

These administrators of Venice's empire were at the intersection of the changing dynamics between state and family, commerce and government. As count of Spalato, Venier was sent to protect Venetian profit and honor by administering justice and ruling in Venice's name. In practice, his interactions with both Venetian and Spalatine individuals and institutions were much more complicated than his commission indicated. Elected in Venice's Great Council, Venier presided over Spalato's communal council in his role as count. Accused of wrongdoing by another Venetian elected official, Venier turned to professional advocates, Michele Pensaben and Bernardino Grasso, to argue his case before the Venetian Senate, scoring a personal victory and a return to his public role as the count of Spalato. After leaving office, Venier remained connected to at least four Spalatine citizens through business relationships. He then appeared before the ducal counselors to petition for the remainder of his salary and corresponded with subsequent counts of Spalato over the money he claimed was owed to him from the town's treasury.[18] Looking at Venier's letters and petitions, his personal interests were virtually indistinguishable from his actions as a representative of the Venetian state. The Venetian state, in the person of the state inquisitor Andrea da Pesaro, was determined to disentangle the two, bringing Venier to trial over having exercised too much influence on behalf of a client. Venier's eventual acquittal, and Sanudo's judgment that he had "outwitted" the prosecutor, points to the deep tension between public and private actions, between institutional procedures and extra-institutional connections, at the heart of Venice's imperial administration.

A Venetian patrician's ability to navigate the often serpentine paths of Venetian legislation and justice could be a great help to an individual subject or to a community as a whole. By exerting extra-institutional influence, a number of Venetian governors acted as advocates for interest groups within the empire, providing a way to balance local and imperial interests and to resolve local conflicts without resorting to violence. As in the case of Venier, many Venetian rectors remained involved in the affairs of the territory they had administered after their term of office was over and they had returned to Venice. Venetian judicial and legislative institutions regularly turned to former officials when an appeal or a question touching that territory arose. Rectors could also act as advocates for individual subjects in Venice. Venier's correspondence with Spalatines after he left office offers a rare glimpse into the way these informal, personal contacts were maintained. Venier had lent money to Luca di Balistarius and received regular payments on the debt through 1498. Venier used Girolamo Cambio, a Spalatine citizen and member of a Florentine banking family, as his agent—Cambio collected money on Venier's behalf, managed the house Venier bought or leased in the city, and sold an ox and some wheat from property Venier owned nearby. Two other Spalatines, Giovanni Arneri and Antonio Xagrovich, also collected money and acted on Venier's behalf in the city. These connections speak to the wide range of extra-institutional transactions that could occur between Venetian patrician officials and imperial subjects.

But both the Venetian state and many of its subjects were suspicious of, if not openly hostile to, the governor's position at the nexus of state power and personal influence. The state sent inspectors like Da Pesaro to act as a counterweight to the rector's influence, and the resulting trials for malfeasance struck an often uneasy balance between public and private interests. Some rectors were convicted and punished for actions that were detrimental to the good of the state as a whole; others, like Venier, were not found guilty; still others were not prosecuted at all. Ultimately, the system functioned—through both informal negotiation and formal judicial proceedings—to offer increased possibilities to certain segments of local communities at the same time that it restricted others' horizons.[19]

The town of Spalato, where Venier served his time in office, was one of a mosaic of fortified towns, islands, inland castles, and waterways that together created Venetian dominion over a large swath of the eastern Mediterranean in the fifteenth century. The fragmentary nature of this liquid empire was captured neatly by a young Florentine named Cristoforo Buondelmonti, who in 1421 described his travels around the eastern Mediterranean in an *Isolario,* the first example of this particular type of geographical treatise.[20] Buondelmonti's *Liber Insularum Archipelagi* devotes a separate page to each of the many islands he sailed past or visited, dividing the eastern Mediterranean into discrete chunks rather than a single connected space. In Buondelmonti's vision, the eastern Mediterranean was marked by its Greek and Roman imperial past as well as its Christian present, and his depictions of the classical ruins, fortifications, and churches reflected the religious and the antiquarian interests of the Italian Renaissance. The region was familiar to many of Buondelmonti's contemporaries because of the intensive trade networks in spices, silks, and precious metals that linked its shores; it was also notorious as a site of religious conflict, where Latin Christian crusaders clashed first with Muslims and then with Orthodox Christians. And although this was certainly not his aim, Buondelmonti also traced the corridors of power in Venice's maritime domains, highlighting its piecemeal and interrupted nature. As with many other early modern imperial states, Venetian power and institutional control cannot be understood as a block of static influence; rather, it flowed along particular pathways and collected in urban centers of exchange, leaving blurred boundaries and uneven gaps.[21] The Venetian state exercised an umbrella of influence over the eastern Mediterranean through the economic reach of its merchants and the military power of its fleet as well as through the political power of its directly ruled territories. Venetian diplomacy extended this umbrella to client rulers in the Aegean islands and on the peripheries of the Dalmatian cities.

While the shadow of Venetian influence was wide, this book is focused only on the places where Venice ruled directly. This approach excludes the Venetian "trading nations" in Constantinople, Alexandria, and Damascus as well as the numerous small islands and territories ruled by Venetian families or by clients under Venetian protection, such as the islands of Amorgos, Santorini, and Andros. The Istrian peninsula, suspended between *terraferma* and maritime regions, is also excluded, as is the independent republic of Ragusa/Dubrovnik.[22] The geographical focus of the book is on the Venetian-ruled towns of the eastern Adriatic, now part of Croatia and Albania; on the Ionian island of Corfu; the Peloponnesian towns of Coron and Modon; and the islands of Crete and Negroponte, now part of Greece; as well as Cyprus. This approach focuses its attention on the centers of Venetian power in cities and towns; Venice's relationships with clients on the peripheries of Venetian control were certainly important in the construction and maintenance of imperial influence, but this project is focused on rectors and their role in the administrative practices of empire.

This book furthermore restricts its focus to a "long" fifteenth century, the time of Venice's greatest territorial expansion. It begins in 1380, at the close of the fourth war with Genoa (1378–1381), a moment that marks Venice's beginning of recovery from the crises of the mid-fourteenth century. It ends in 1540, at the end of Venice's fourth war with the Ottomans (1537–1540) and a decade after the conclusion of the war of Cambrai (1509–1529) on the mainland. This period includes Venice's massive expansion onto both the mainland and into maritime territories and the establishment of administrative and judicial structures to rule over these territories. It also includes the pressures brought to bear on Venice's empire by the Ottoman state's expansion into the same region but precedes the era of greatest conflict between Christian/Spanish and Muslim/Ottoman forces.

Venice was not alone in its outward expansion in the fifteenth century; many other Italian city-states were creating regional states out of the formerly independent towns and villages of their *contado* during the late fourteenth and fifteenth centuries. As Venice turned east to the Ionian islands, Albania, and Dalmatia, Florence took Arezzo (1384), Montepulciano (1390), Pisa (1406), Cortona (1411), and Livorno (1411).[23] The Milanese state, under Gian Galeazzo Visconti, also took a number of cities in the Po River valley in this period, an expansionist effort ended only by Visconti's death in 1402. Venice itself moved west as well as east in this period, taking Vicenza, Feltre, and Belluno (1404), Rovigo, Verona, and Padova (1405), Udine (1420), Brescia (1426), and Bergamo (1428). The historian Giorgio Chittolini's model of regional states has been influential in interpreting the dynamics of territorial consolidation and state formation in north-central Italy; he highlights the central role ties of kinship, faction, patronage, and clientage played in shaping political strategies and institutions, complicating simple divisions between public and private power.[24]

Scholars of the Venetian mainland state have followed Chittolini's lead in emphasizing the tensions, contradictions, and inconsistencies in Venetian rule on the mainland.[25] Ventura's influential study of Venetian *terraferma* rule pointed to the conquest, exploitation, abuse of justice, and the unwillingness of the Venetian aristocracy to share power.[26] Cozzi's view of Venetian practices of territorial rule focused on the importance of judicial structures in mediating between rulers and ruled, a perspective that Viggiano's synthetic study *Governanti e Governati* expanded upon by arguing for the importance of multiple legal jurisdictions in the "negotiation, contestation, and accommodation" between local and central magistracies.[27] Studies by Grubb, Law, Knapton, and Muir of individual cities on the *terraferma* have demonstrated that within this overarching framework, Venetian rule in each locality was carefully adjusted to local circumstances, creating a "composite" or "federal" state structure.[28] There are significant similarities between Venice's rule in its mainland and its maritime territories—notably its jurisdictional complexity, institutional structure, and reliance on negotiation, contestation, and accommodation in the day-to-day practice of rule. As was the case on the mainland, Venetian maritime administrators worked in concert with civic councils composed of local elites. In both the mainland and maritime cases, these councils provided a structure for regional self-government, but recently Papadia-Lala's important work on councils in Greek-speaking Venetian territories has highlighted the degree to which maritime civic councils also channeled religious and ethnic identities into stable social categories through the inclusion or exclusion of various groups from civic life.[29]

Where the Venetian maritime state differs from both its mainland counterpart and from Milanese and Florentine regional states is in its geographic, religious, and cultural diversity. In fact, the distances and diversity of Venice's dominion were matched only by its main rival, Genoa. But while the Genoese presence in Chios, Kaffa, and Pera was primarily driven by family and individual initiative, Venice's overseas domains remained closely controlled and governed by the Venetian state.[30] Subjects of Venice's maritime empire spoke Greek, Slavic, Croatian, and Albanian as well as Italian.[31] The two main religious identities in the Venetian maritime state were Latin Christian and Greek Orthodox; small Jewish communities existed in many of the port towns as well. In general, the Dalmatian and Albanian coastal cities followed the Latin rite while the Ionian islands, the Peloponnesus, Crete, and Cyprus adhered to the Orthodox rite. A further complication in religious identity was introduced by attempts to mend the Schism between Eastern and Western Christianity. At the Council of Ferrara/Florence (1437–1439), a group of Orthodox clergy, led by the Byzantine emperor John VIII Palaiologos, accepted the council's compromise on several theological issues in return for promises of military aid against the Ottomans, but the union was rejected by many Greeks. Within Venetian territory, Venice's official support for Unionist clergy exacerbated Greek resentment of Venice's restrictive religious policies toward the Orthodox clergy.

The division between different religious identities breaks down even further when one looks closely at questions of ethnicity and identity in each particular locale. The Venetian republic and its domains, located at the boundary between East and West and the Latin Christian, Greek Orthodox, and Muslim worlds, has proved to be a fertile ground for scholars' investigations of questions of ethnicity, identity, coexistence and cooperation.[32] McKee's work on Crete shows that many officially "Latin" individuals had Greek family members, left bequests to Greek churches, and spoke Greek at home, complicating the easy distinction between the two groups.[33] She argues that part of Venetian state formation was aimed at producing clearly delineated ethnic identities of "Latin" and "Greek" on the island but that these categories did not reflect islanders' lived experience of identity, which was nuanced not only by religion and language but by economic, legal, and social status as well as by gender. Dursteler's *Venetians in Constantinople* proposes a more "ample, fluid view of community and identity" through a study of the Venetian nation in the sixteenth- and seventeenth-century Ottoman capital, examining the components that structured Venetian-Ottoman cooperation and coexistence.[34] In the Dalmatian context, the question is framed in less overly religious terms, focusing instead on the divisions and symbiosis between Latinate and Slavic cultures.[35]

Braudel looked to Venice's convoys that plied the Mediterranean seasonally as evidence of the structural unity that underlay the sea as a whole.[36] Over the past thirty years, scholars have increasingly used Venice's far-flung merchant network and trading enclaves as a starting point for a broader examination of cultural exchange. The study of interchange of ideas and individuals as well as materials has been influenced by the wider interest in questions of Mediterranean unity and identity, a debate reinvigorated by the 2000 publication of Horden and Purcell's *A Corrupting Sea,* and questions of diversity and crosscultural contact have moved to the center of Venetian studies in recent years.[37] Contemporary scholars' focus on multiculturalism and interaction between different linguistic and cultural groups is a move away from the national historical traditions—Italian, Greek, and Yugoslav and then Croatian—that dominated studies of the region in the twentieth century. For Greek historians working in the nineteenth and early twentieth century, the history of the "Venetocrazia," or the Greek-speaking lands under Latin rule, was tied up with emerging definitions of Greek nationhood and territorial and cultural unity.[38] Italian-language scholarship in the first part of the twentieth century was conditioned by the rise of fascism and renewed imperial claims to what Mussolini termed "Mare Nostra," and the history of Venetian territorial domination in Dalmatia and the Aegean played an important role in the articulation of renewed Italian claims to domination in the Adriatic.[39] As Ivetić has argued in a penetrating analysis of Italian-language scholarship on Dalmatia, from the 1920s to the 1960s, the history of Venice itself was increasingly studied by a "cosmopolitan community of specialists," while the history of the *stato da mar* was left to Croatian and Greek scholars as part of their national histories.[40]

In the second half of the twentieth century, struggles over colonization and economic exploitation became the primary lens of analysis for the maritime state. One of the most synthetic works on the region, Thiriet's 1954 study *La Romanie Vénitienne au Moyen Age. Le Développement et l'exploitation du domaine colonial vénitien* focused on the way Venice benefited from its overseas colonies in the Greek-speaking parts of the empire. In the late 1980s and 1990s, three edited volumes under the direction of Michel Balard and Alain Ducellier reinvigorated the debate over comparative colonizations in the medieval world, bringing to light the many continuities and similarities between medieval Italian and Iberian colonization efforts in the Mediterranean and later colonizing ventures in the Atlantic.[41] Over the past decade, the Istituto Ellenico di Studi Bizantini e Postbizantini in Venice, under the direction of Chryssa Maltezou, has sponsored a number of significant conferences and publications that brought together an international community of scholars to examine the maritime state from diverse scholarly perspectives. The publications resulting from these meetings, including *Venezia e Creta, Byzantina e Franco-Grecia, Ricci e Poveri, Italia-Grecia,* and *Venezia e le Isole Ionie,* both promote scholarly exchange and present the latest research on economic exchange, cultural coexistence and synthesis, and tensions and conflicts resulting from Venetian domination.

Scholars engaged with this literature are coming to agree that the medieval and early modern Mediterranean cannot be understood as a contest between two or even three political and cultural monoliths, but instead as a constant and competitive negotiation among multiple and shifting political authorities. This book offers a way of understanding the Venetian interactions in the Mediterranean as one based on a more fluid type of negotiation—neither binary conflict between Christianity and Islam, nor utopian cooperation among different ethnic and religious groups, but one where cooperation and conflict existed in constant tension. The core argument of this study is that the Venetian state relied on negotiations conducted through patronage, family connections, and the judicial system to bridge the gaps of geographic separation, local and regional particularism, and multiple languages and legal traditions in its maritime state. In this nexus of state power and personal influence, the state officials Venice sent played a crucial role in both presenting the Venetian state as a dominant power and in creating these extra-institutional connections between Venice and its maritime dominions. The empire was certainly not run on negotiation and collaboration alone: military force played an important role as well, and the threat of compulsion lurked in the background of all interactions between rulers and ruled. Venice's Renaissance empire was characterized by an evolving combination of military force and negotiations for loyalty along the increasingly contested Venetian-Ottoman frontier.

This study also argues that rather than being the model of Venetian rule overseas, Crete was an exception, in large part because it was a colonial society. Unlike its practice in Dalmatia and Corfu, Venice sent colonists to the island who established deep military, cultural, and economic roots there; this state-sponsored colonization was augmented by individual migration. The Venetian state gave these thirteenth-century colonists land grants, called fiefs. The descendants of these settlers, the Veneto-Cretan patriciate, intermarried with the indigenous population while at the same time retaining ties to Venetian society. McKee's study of Cretan society in the fourteenth century has elegantly and exhaustively demonstrated the near-impossibility of pulling apart the composite ethnic and cultural identities that resulted from the coexistence and intermarriage between elite and common Greek Cretans and Latin Venetians.[42] In terms of administration, the presence of a colonial settler elite with one foot on Crete and the other in Venice influenced the Venetian officials' interactions with the island's inhabitants, as they could rely on a much more stable, dense, and deeply rooted network of connections to create extra-institutional ties between island and metropole.

The fifteenth-century Venetian acquisition of territory is the subject of the book's first chapter. Beginning in the late fourteenth century, the increasing competition from the Ottoman state for direct control of the Balkans pushed the Venetians to consolidate their informal influence over the region and to defend the territories essential to their security. By examining the circumstances by which Venice acquired Corfu, Durazzo, Argos and Nauplion, Zara, and Cyprus, the chapter argues that Venice's expansion was based on a combination of diplomacy, military action, inheritance, purchase, and voluntary submission. It also argues that Venice actively campaigned for these communities' loyalty, creating and propagating an idea of Venetian rule as just, stable, and able to offer protection from both Ottoman incursions and internal dissent.

Chapter 2 describes the framework and structure of Venetian maritime administration in the fifteenth century. An examination of the careers of the men elected to maritime office reveals that individuals and families deliberately developed specialties in maritime officeholding, returning repeatedly to the same posts or regions. This specialization created significant tension within the Venetian patriciate as a whole, leading to protests over the monopolization of office by the few in the Great Council. In response, the council added new maritime offices in 1442 and in 1450, but the more important offices within the maritime state continued to go to a restricted number of experienced individuals. This pattern complicates the picture of officeholding presented by Donald Queller, who saw many of the territorial offices as part of a large welfare scheme to support the lesser nobility.[43] In fact, officeholding patterns demonstrate that only the newly created, less important positions were reserved for needy patricians; many maritime offices were difficult to obtain and very prestigious. The reasons behind this specialization in particular locales were not simply skill-based or institutional but relied on the networks of association governors and families built up outside of Venice.

Chapter 3 examines the relationship between public duty and private interest in the practice of maritime office, finding a significant tension between state ideology and patrician practice. Legislation regularly forbade rectors from coming into close contact with their subjects or stepping outside their public role as a Venetian representative; governors just as regularly associated with those over whom they ruled, creating long-term connections to the territory through marriage ties, commercial exchanges, and property holding. The significance of these conflicting expectations is not that Venetian patricians failed to live up to their own myths but rather that the Venetian ideology of public services existed in continuous tension with the practices of private network building.

Chapter 4 looks at one of the most important institutional connections between center and periphery: the judicial system. The idea of justice loomed large in Venetian representations of its imperial prerogatives; the Venetian state carefully defended the *arbitrum,* or individual judgment, of Venetian judges, and Venice's claims to legitimacy rested in part on its ability to provide social order, stability, and an effective means of dispute resolution. The judicial appeals presented to Venetian courts demonstrate the way in which Venice presented itself as an impartial arbiter of local conflicts and that ultimately Venetian rule—formal judicial proceedings combined with the possibility of multiple appeals—formed a kind of ongoing negotiation with subject communities. On a local level, the Venetian judicial system gave both elite and common residents the opportunity to pursue their claims and articulate their grievances in a space controlled by Venetian interests, while cases appealed to the central Venetian magistracies were generally, but not always, from elites who were already connected to the Venetian regime in other ways. While it was certainly more difficult for nonelite subjects to access Venetian justice, it was not impossible, and Venetian subjects were able to exploit the jurisdictional complexity of the Venetian judicial system. This type of legal structure provided the framework for negotiation in a number of early modern empires; Benton has argued that in the fifteenth and sixteenth centuries colonial societies in the Iberian Americas, Islamic Africa, Christian Europe, and the Indian Ocean were all characterized by jurisdictional legal complexity, providing a way for rulers and ruled to play out their differences.[44] The Venetian judicial system was similarly structured, and its jurisdictional complexity was a powerful and flexible tool for negotiation between different interests in the Venetian empire.

In addition to its judicial system, Venice relied on formal petitions from its subject communities and an extensive system of state patronage to create a network of connections that stretched across the empire. Chapter 5 examines the way the Venetian state used these special favors, pardons, or privileges, collectively called *grazie,* to promote state interests among clients seeking favors or advancement and to respond to unrest within the empire. Governors played a central role in the state's granting of these *grazie,* which were both a source of Venetian influence and of conflict. There were frequent protests from local communities that Venice or its governors were abusing their rights of appointment and bypassing the regulations which governed eligibility and access to office on a local level. Venice's policy in response to these complaints was one of outward flexibility and accommodation, and a less obvious insistence on its own right of nomination and election to key posts within local administrations.

A crucial part of Venetian officials' role as governors was to mediate between center and periphery, and the networks of private influence and patronage they constructed often helped them to accomplish this goal. Both the Venetian state and segments of the local population resisted rectors' attempts to benefit themselves and their local collaborators during their time in office. Prosecutions against rectors accused of malfeasance or improper behavior in office reflect these different interests in limiting rectors' power. Chapter 6 examines the system of denunciation and investigation that led to these prosecutions. Rectors were most often charged with acting against "God, justice, and the honor of our dominion," reflecting the state's concern for its reputation and institutions, or with causing "scandal and murmuring," reflecting a kind of popular protest. The prosecutions did draw an unwritten and very flexible line between acceptable and unacceptable official behavior, a line that was worked out in the trials of former rectors. On a local level, these officials left in their wake not only the memory of public scandal but deep resentments and bitter grievances against Venetian representatives, and they thus placed significant strain on Venice's institutions of empire.

In the early sixteenth century, war and economic difficulty placed Venice's system of governance under a great deal of pressure. Chapter 7 examines the way Venice's traditional mechanisms of compromise and negotiation frayed and snapped in the maritime state in the wake of the crisis of the League of Cambrai. Three decades of the high taxation that accompanied almost constant war on land and sea, combined with raids from Ottoman pirates and bandits that drained the maritime territories of agricultural and human resources, created conditions that were ripe for rebellion and protest. This chapter analyzes two popular uprisings in the first decades of the sixteenth century. The urban uprising at Lesina (Hvar), from 1510 to 1514, and the rural revolt on western Crete, from 1523 to 1529, both show the limits of coercive power and the deeply rooted structures of appeal in Venice's imperial system. The chapter also looks at the role the Venetian state and Venetian rectors played in both causing and reacting to the popular unrest in these two cases, finding that military solutions were nuanced by a reliance on negotiation and appeal. The rebellions at Lesina and Canea were not isolated incidents but signaled a much larger change in the position of Venice's maritime empire. Venice sank astronomical sums into the defense of its remaining cities and towns, creating a military stalemate on its borders. The state's instructions to its officials in the sixteenth century increasingly emphasized the necessity of not provoking its Ottoman neighbors and protecting Venice's hard-won peace, indicating the fragility of Venetian empire in the later sixteenth and seventeenth centuries.

ONE

The Shape of Empire

Every Ascension Day, Venice marries the sea in a ritual called the *sponsalio.* In the fifteenth and sixteenth centuries, the Venetian doge traveled in the *Bucintoro,* the ceremonial barge of the Venetian republic, to a point directly in front of San Nicolò on the Lido, where he dropped a gold ring into the waters of the Adriatic saying, "We espouse thee, O sea, as a sign of true and perpetual dominion."[1] The clear message of this ritual is that Venice was meant to rule the sea, in particular the Adriatic, and that its maritime empire was in some way a natural outgrowth of its privileged position on the water. The idea of the integral connection between Venice and the sea was ensconced in the well-known "myth of Venice" and was accompanied by deliberately crafted rhetoric suggesting that not only was Venice the natural lord of the seas but Venetian rule was benevolent, almost philanthropic in nature.[2]

When looking at the territories that Venice conquered and ruled in the eastern Mediterranean, past historiography has at times echoed this laudatory assessment of Venetian imperial ambitions. Cessi, for example, wrote in *Storia della Repubblica di Venezia* that "Venice did not intend to embark upon a policy of military conquest in Dalmatia and extend its possessions to Slavonia . . . the renewed Venetian effort in Dalmatia was inspired by a high and noble ideal—tranquility, neutrality, and peace."[3] Later scholars abandoned the rhetoric of neutrality and peace but still provided explanations that suggest Venetian empire building was forced on the city, either by circumstance or by competition from other powers, such as the Genoese. For instance, when discussing the Venetian acquisition of Crete, Thiriet has argued that the Venetian government had not originally intended to colonize the island as completely as it did but was forced into doing so by the Greek rebellions and Genoese competition.[4] Borsari also pointed to Genoese competition as a factor that pushed Venice toward a more complete colonization of the island.[5] The implication of explanations like these is the idea that

Venice was not aiming to create an empire but that it ended up with one because of circumstance.

Venetian empire was neither accidental nor philanthropic. The Venetian government actively worked to acquire and control territories beneficial to its own interests: to control the material and human resources of the Adriatic and Aegean in order to protect Venetian shipping and to bring honor and glory to the city. Venice acquired the territories that made up its maritime domains using a variety of methods, ranging from purchase to inheritance to military conquest to diplomacy; the one common factor in Venetian acquisition of empire was the long-term, patient, and deliberate strategizing that created opportunities for imperial expansion.

Roots of Dominion: The Thirteenth and Fourteenth Centuries

The roots of Venice's domination of territories in the Adriatic, as well as the beginnings of its imperial ideology, began with Doge Pietro II Orsoleo's triumphal journey down the Adriatic in the year 1000, during which he defeated the Narentine and Croatian pirates and established Venetian overlordship of the Gulf.[6] In the early thirteenth century, Venice used the opportunity presented by the Fourth Crusade to consolidate its control in the upper Adriatic and expand its influence into the lower Adriatic and the Aegean, at a time when many other Latin Christian powers were also imposing their rule by force on the Greek-speaking, Orthodox populations.[7] The Venetian fleet that transported the crusaders to Constantinople reasserted Venetian control over Zara and the other towns on the Dalmatian coast, and the treaty that governed the division of the Byzantine empire after the fall of Constantinople in 1204 awarded Venice the western half of the Balkan peninsula, key Aegean islands, and a swath of land from Adrianople to Gallipoli, near Constantinople.[8] Many of these territorial awards were due to Doge Enrico Dandolo's skillful maneuvering in the aftermath of the Fourth Crusade.[9] His successor, Doge Pietro Ziani, encouraged individual Venetians to independently conquer Greek islands, and by 1212, the Sanudo family ruled in the Duchy of Naxos, the Ghisi family in Tinos and Mykonos, Marco Dandolo in Andros, Leonardo Foscolo in Anaphe, Marco Venier in Cerigo, Iacopo Barozzi in Santorini, and Iacopo Viaro in Cerigotto.[10] The men who participated in these private colonizations were both Venetian citizens and vassals of the Latin emperor in Constantinople, and in practice they exercised a great deal of independence in ruling what they had conquered. Over the next centuries, Venice continued to claim the islands as part of its sphere of influence and its rulers as part of its citizenry;

Venice's practical influence on these islands, however, fell far short of sovereign control.

Much of the territory awarded in the partition of 1204 passed out of Venetian hands as quickly as it had passed in. A Venetian fleet commanded by Renier Dandolo and Ruggero Premarin took possession of Corfu, Modon, and Coron in 1206, and Venice leased Corfu to ten Venetian nobles and their heirs in return for an annual payment and special privileges for Venetian merchants.[11] Venice dispatched rectors and laid down ceremonial conventions for Coron, Modon, and Durazzo, but by 1214 both Durazzo and Corfu were in the hands of Michael Doukas, the despot of Epiros. Doge Dandolo's shrewd diplomacy in Constantinople was not wasted; Venice did establish lasting regimes in Crete, Modon, and Coron, while the Venetian *bailo* on Negroponte shared control of the island with three Latin lords.

In the case of Crete, not included in the treaty of partition with the other crusaders, Venice first purchased Boniface of Monferrat's claim and then battled for physical control of the island, first with the Genoese adventurer Enrico Pescatore and then with the Cretans themselves, who did not want to give up the de facto independence they had enjoyed under the late Byzantine empire.[12] Venice treated Crete differently than its other dependencies from the very beginning. Venice instituted a system of direct rule, modeled on the government in the city itself, and gave more attention to administration in Crete than was the case in Coron, Modon, or Negroponte.[13] The metropole replaced the local nobles with its own settlers, introduced Venetian law, eliminated the Greek Orthodox religious hierarchy, and imposed a Latin clerical hierarchy. The waves of military colonists from Venice, who received confiscated land, or fiefs, in return for military service, were followed by further immigration, creating a Venetian society in miniature in the island's port cities.[14] Crete was certainly not the only place in the *stato da mar* where Venetian nobles and citizens owned landed estates, nor was it the only place where Venetian landholding was described in terms of feudalism.[15] Crete was different, however, in the extent and the longevity of Venetian landholding as well as in Venice's treatment of the local elite. Venice initially planned to exclude the Greek Cretan aristocracy completely from the sociopolitical system of the island, but a number of these noble families led revolts against Venetian rule in the thirteenth century, compelling Venice to recognize their lands and privileges.[16] This recognition was granted only to the families that had rebelled, not to the entire Greek Cretan nobility, a situation that contrasts with Venice's later practice in other places of granting rights and privileges to communities or nobilities as a whole.

BLACK SEA
N
Venice
Zara
Sebenico
Spalato
Ragusa
ADRIATIC SEA
Rome
Durazzo
Constantinople
Thessalonica
Butrinto
Corfu
Parga
AEGEAN SEA
Negroponte
Lepanto
Cefalonia
Patras
Tinos
IONIAN SEA
Zante
Argos
Mykonos
Egina
Nauplion
Malvasia
Modon
Coron
Cerigo
Rettimo
Canea
Candia
Rhodes
Sitia
Sfakia
CRETE
Nicosia
Famagusta
CYPRUS
0 100 200 mi
0 100 200 300 km
MEDITERRANEAN SEA
Jerusalem
Alexandria

Venice's commitment to external expansion was sorely tested in the fourteenth century, a difficult one for Venice itself as well as for its nascent empire. In addition to the ravages of the 1348 plague, Venice fought two long and costly wars against the Genoese, from 1350 to 1355 and 1378 to 1381. A drawn-out conflict with Hungary from 1344 to 1358 ended in defeat for Venice, and in the peace treaty Venice ceded its territories from the Gulf of Quarnaro to Durazzo.[17] The loss of Dalmatia was a serious blow: Venice lost its control of the Dalmatian salt markets and access to the overland routes of the Balkans, as well as the sheltered ports and manpower for the fleets. Outside of the Adriatic, Venice faced another grave challenge to its maritime supremacy in the eastern Mediterranean when Crete, the lynchpin of Venetian dominion in the Aegean, rebelled in 1363–1365.[18] In 1363, a group of discontented Veneto-Cretan feudatories joined with Greek citizens of Candia, imprisoned the Venetian duke of the island, and raised the flag of San Tito, the local patron saint. Venice was forced to send a large and costly mercenary army to suppress the revolt. Despite these challenges, by the end of the fourteenth century Venice had overcome the threat of losing Crete and defeated the Genoese fleet in 1381, within sight of the lagoon.[19]

Age of Expansion: The Fifteenth Century

The situation in the eastern Mediterranean had shifted by the late fourteenth and early fifteenth century, opening a second window of opportunity for Venetian expansion. Many of the powers that might have hoped to unify the region were in retreat, or their interest was engaged elsewhere. The Catalans, who had been a commercial, political, and military force in the region, were retreating as their attention was drawn westward.[20] Hungary, which had been a dominant force in the Balkans under King Louis in the fourteenth century, was internally divided by questions of succession to the throne, making it difficult for the kingdom to act aggressively toward its neighbors. On the Italian peninsula, Milan and Florence were at war, and the Roman papacy was weakened by the Great Schism, turning these cities' attention away from the eastern Mediterranean as well.

In contrast to many of the other states in the region, the Ottoman empire and the Venetian republic were both well positioned to expand. Both states were internally unified and relatively stable, and both had deeply rooted commercial interests in the region. Venetian merchants dominated the trade in spices and luxury goods in the Mamluk ports of the Levant, while the Ottomans had a large

Opposite: Eastern Mediterranean

share of the profitable grain trade in the region.[21] In the mid-fourteenth century, the Ottoman state expanded west from the Anatolian peninsula, conquering Gallipoli in 1354, Adrianople in 1361, Kosovo in 1389, and a crusading army at Nicopolis in 1396.[22] But at the same time that Venice came to terms with its greatest rival, Genoa, in the 1381 treaty of Turin, the Ottoman state faced a Mongol invasion on its eastern frontier. Timur Lenk's Mongol armies inflicted a crushing defeat on the Ottomans at the battle of Ankara in 1402, where the sultan Bayazid was captured. Bayazid died in captivity the following year, leading to a decade of confusion over the Ottoman succession that did not end until Mehmed I took the throne in 1413.[23] This brief interregnum did not change the essential pattern of power politics in the region, but it did mean that for the first decade of the fifteenth century, Venice was without a serious rival in the eastern Mediterranean.

Venice took full advantage of this moment to create and maintain a flexible and durable empire, expanding along the Dalmatian coast and into the Aegean Sea as well as into its hinterland on the Italian mainland. In the forty years between 1380 and 1420, Venice more than doubled its territory and population. Venice extended its rule to Corfu and the mainland city of Butrinto in 1386; Argos, Nauplion, and Andros in 1388; Tinos, Mykonos, and Negroponte in 1390; Durazzo in 1392; Alessio in 1393; Scutari and Drivasto in 1396; Lepanto and Patras in 1407; Zara, Ossero, Arbe, Cherso, and Nona in 1409; Sebenico in 1412; Zonchio in 1417; and Spalato, Traù, Curzola, Brazza, Lesina, Pago, and Cattaro in 1420. Venice also ruled Athens for a brief period, from 1394 to 1402, and Thessalonica equally briefly, from 1423 to 1430. Venice extended its mainland dominions dramatically during the same period: Vicenza, Feltre, and Belluno in 1404, Rovigo, Verona, and Padova in 1405, Udine in 1420, Brescia in 1426, and Bergamo in 1428. By the late fifteenth century, Venetian territory stretched from central Italy to the Peloponnesus and beyond, to the islands of Crete and Cyprus, a distance of 29,694 square miles.[24]

Venice's fifteenth-century expansion was motivated by concern for both its profit and its honor. The Senate in 1441 stated that "our agenda in the maritime parts considers our state and the conservation of our city and commerce," suggesting that by the mid-fifteenth century, the defense of Venetian security and prosperity was tied into the maintenance of its maritime domains.[25] The economic motivations for Venetian empire were clear in its administrative priorities: throughout the empire, both local finances and large-scale economic decisions were in the hands of Venetians, either the Venetian rector or Venetian councils in the metropole. The Venetians imposed a system of standard weights and measures in their territories, controlled the currency, and carefully regulated local markets to the advantage of Venetian merchants.[26] In the case of key commodities, such as wheat or salt, Venice demanded that local producers sell only to the city at a fixed rate.[27] Venice also drew on the human resources of its subject cities, demanding that its territories provide sailors for its fleet or workers for its fortifications. Perhaps most importantly, the ports of the Adriatic and Aegean were safe harbors and staging grounds for Venice's semiannual galley convoys headed to and from the markets of the eastern Mediterranean. In the fifteenth century, the increasingly aggressive and powerful Ottoman state in the east and the fall of the buffer states in the Balkans made it necessary for Venice to control and defend these ports to ensure continued access. In these competitive circumstances, the small, independent lordships on the Dalmatian coast and Peloponnesus had less and less space in which to maneuver, and for them, submission to Venice was an option that offered a defense against the Ottomans. Venice, for its part, had no desire to see Ottoman power established on the shores of the Adriatic, just as it wanted to avoid any Genoese presence in its waters.

Unlike the thirteenth-century expansion, where the stroke of a pen gave Venice rights over a large portion of the eastern Mediterranean, the fifteenth-century expansion came in pieces. Venice used a combination of diplomacy, military action, inheritance, purchase, and voluntary submission to acquire its maritime empire, and each location that entered the Venetian empire did so with a different and particular set of factors behind its submission. The renewed period of Venetian expansion began with the Venetian takeover of Corfu, in 1386, where Venice used the opportunity provided by the death of Carlo of Durazzo to dispatch its fleet and convince the Corfiote assembly to submit to Venice. Venice then moved to consolidate its control over areas of the Peloponnesus and the Cycladic islands where it had previously exercised a loose hegemony; the example of Argos in 1388 is a case in point, where Venice convinced Maria d'Enghien to sell her rights over the city. In 1392, Venice inherited Durazzo, on the Albanian coast, from Giorgio Thopia, and Giorgio II Balsha (Balšić) Strazimir soon followed this lead, ceding the towns of Scutari and Drivasto in 1396. Venice purchased the city of Zara and the surrounding coastline from Ladislas of Naples in 1409 and besieged Sebenico into submission in 1412. During this expansion, the city of Cattaro had asked to submit itself to Venice six times; Venice finally accepted the city in 1420, at the same time it took Traù, Curzola, Brazza, Lesina, and Pago. In all of these cases, Venice used circumstance and opportunity to its advantage, actively maneuvering to build its regional empire piece by piece.

Greek Gateways: Corfu, Argos, and Nauplion

In the case of the 1386 takeover of Corfu, Venice had been aiming to dominate the gateway to the Adriatic for a number of years before the circumstances were favorable.[28] When Carlo III of Anjou-Naples, the island's ruler, died in 1386, some Corfiotes swore allegiance to Carlo's young son Ladislas, while others turned to Francesco da Carrara of Padova, who sent Giacomo degli Scrovegni and some Genoese troops to occupy the town's fortress. Venice acted quickly and dispatched Giovanni Miani with two galleys to the island. Miani addressed the community of Corfu, represented by an assembly of the Corfiote elite, promising them that Venice would honor their traditional rights and privileges.[29] The Corfiotes apparently agreed, and in May the flag of San Marco was raised over the city. After Venetian troops expelled Scrovegni and the Genoese, representatives from Corfu negotiated a treaty of submission to Venice, and in January of the following year Venice approved the customs and statutes of the island, affirming the landholders' traditional privileges, their rights to hold office on the island, and the continued existence of their communal council.

Even before Carlo III's death, Venice was concerned with the Corfiote elite's attitude toward possible Venetian rule of the island. As early as 1348, the Venetian Senate expressed an interest in the island, commenting that "it would be very useful for our affairs, in case we should be at odds with the king of Hungary, to have in our custody the territory and castle of Corfu."[30] In 1382, during negotiations for purchasing Corfu from Carlo of Durazzo, the Venetian Senate heard a number of proposals for acquiring the island, considering carefully the intelligence that at least a part of the nobility there were in favor of submitting themselves to Venice.[31] The Venetians did not leave the Corfiote nobility's continued favor to chance; in a "campaign of propaganda," the Venetian Senate instructed its consul on the island, Giovanni Panemsaco, to "assure these nobles and good men of Corfu in the way that to you seems best that they should remain constant and strong, and sustain them so that this thing can finish at the desired end."[32] By the time of Miani's address to the Corfiote assembly, Venice had already won a number of adherents among Corfu's elite. Venice's takeover, while it might have been aided by these local supporters, did not rest entirely on their approval; the Venetian fleet, military action against the Genoese, and a 1402 payment to Ladislas of Naples all played important roles as well.

The acquisition of Argos and Nauplion, which followed that of Corfu in 1388, was a case where a personal, dynastic connection to the Venetian state was transformed into a more formal and regularized one. Maria d'Enghien inherited

Argos and Nauplion from her father Guy in 1377; on his death, her guardians placed the castles of Argos and Nauplion under Venetian protection.[33] Strengthening the Venetian connection, Maria married the Venetian noble Pietro Corner, creating a dynastic link between Argos, Nauplion, and Venice. Corner died in 1388, and after his death, Venice persuaded Maria to cede her rights to the cities in return for 500 ducats a year. The Venetian chronicler Antonio Morosini's narrative of the sale emphasizes the danger from other powers in the region, specifically the Ottomans; he commented that the cities "were in obvious danger, because it was suspected that they would fall into the hands of the Turks or the Greeks, to the evident disadvantage of the aforesaid lady Maria to whom they legally belonged."[34] But before Venice could take possession of the cities, the despot of the Morea Theodore Palaiologos seized both cities after Corner's death in 1388.[35] Perazzo Malipiero, *provveditore* of Nauplion, took that city in 1389, but Theodore refused to relinquish Argos until 1394.

The acquisition of Argos and Nauplion via inheritance was similar to several other acquisitions in the 1390s. The death of Giorgio III Ghisi, hereditary lord of a third of Negroponte and the Aegean islands of Tinos and Mykonos, with no heirs, left the way open for the Venetian republic to assume more direct power over these protectorates. Ghisi was convinced to entail these territories to the Venetian republic in his will, and on his death in 1390, Venice assumed direct control of the three islands. Venice also regularized its rule on Negroponte in 1390. Since 1204, the Venetian *bailo* in the capital city of Chalkis had had a great deal of influence on Negroponte as a result of his role as an arbiter of disputes between the lords and residents of the island, but by 1390, Venice's "patient tenacity" paid off, and it became the sole and sovereign ruler of the island.[36] In all of these cases, the increasingly sharp competition for territory and superiority in the eastern Mediterranean left less room for local autonomy, pressuring Venice to formalize ties in its informal umbrella of alliances. And while Venetian military strength and its presence as a significant power in the area played a role in winning territory, the legalization of that acquisition rested on dynastic politics and inheritance.

An Albanian Foothold: Durazzo

Venice's strategy relied on inheritance, military pressure, and the idea of protection against foreign threats in the acquisition of Durazzo. In the fourteenth century, Durazzo was ruled by the Thopias, Albanian lords who were tributaries of the Serbian king.[37] Throughout the fourteenth century, Serbia acted as a buffer zone between Durazzo and the expanding Ottoman presence in the Balkans, but in the late 1380s and 1390s, Ottoman troops raided Serbian territory aggressively, inflicting heavy damage at the famous 1389 battle of Kosovo. By 1392 all of the Serbian kingdom was under Ottoman suzerainty, and there were Ottoman incursions into Durazzo's territory in 1391. Durazzo's lord, Carlo Thopia, was ill and unable to organize the city's defense. Venice, seeing the danger of an Ottoman foothold in the lower Adriatic and an opportunity for its own expansion, moved quickly. In 1388–89, Venice signed a treaty with Thopia providing for the city's defense, dispatched the Venetian fleet, repaired and garrisoned the fortress, and assured the city's grain supply.[38]

Venice also sent Giovanni Capello, the vice-captain of the Gulf, to take over the city's sea-tower, charging him with the delicate mission of assessing the local situation and encouraging the local inhabitants to pledge their loyalty to Venice. When Capello advised the Senate that Thopia's health was failing, it instructed him to convince the local elites, or barons, that Venice was only interested in conserving Durazzo and the good of the Christian faith as a whole; in order to make this argument more compelling, Capello was authorized to offer the barons stipends of as much as 500 ducats each.[39] At the end of 1389, Carlo Thopia died and Durazzo passed to his equally sickly son Giorgio, who died in 1392.[40] When Venetian *provveditori* proclaimed Venice's lordship to the citizens of Durazzo in November of that year, physical control of key elements of the city were already in Venetian hands. As was the case in Corfu, Venice did not want to rely simply on a treaty to assure its control but acted to control public perceptions as well as negotiating for formal transfer; throughout, a strong Venetian military presence stood behind the rhetoric of Venice's role as a disinterested and liberty-loving protector.

The Venetian establishment of power in Durazzo provides an example of the acquisition of territory through a combination of inheritance and voluntary submission, with a good deal of Venetian campaigning and gradual assumption of the city's military apparatus and protection before the formal takeover. A number of other cities in the southern part of the Adriatic coast entered the Venetian empire in a similar way. Giorgio II Balsha (Balšić) Strazimir, lord of Scutari and Drivasto, ceded both towns to Venice in 1396.[41] According to Morosini, Venice extended its dominion to both Durazzo and Scutari "because the Turks were at that time very powerful, and they feared that these places would come into their hands."[42] This sentiment was echoed by the Venetian Senate, which took into account "the great prejudice and injury which would occur in our undertakings if the city of Durazzo fell into the hands of the Turks."[43] From the Venetian perspective, these acquisitions via inheritance or "voluntary" cessation allowed the state to justify its expansion; when the Ottoman sultan, for instance, protested the Venetian takeover of territories in Albania and Greece, the Senate asserted that the new territories had been "legitimately acquired from legitimate lords."[44] As Ottoman power increased in the region, these local lords had fewer and fewer viable methods to maintain independent rule over their lands. From their perspective, a negotiated transfer of power to the Venetian republic was a more attractive option than an Ottoman invasion, and Venice deliberately presented itself as a reasonable alternative.

Dalmatian Doorways: Zara and Beyond

The idea of communal independence and negotiation and diplomacy with outside powers both played important roles in the 1409 Venetian reacquisition of the city of Zara, a key to controlling the upper Adriatic.[45] Throughout the 1390s and early decades of the fifteenth century, Venice had followed the struggle between rival claimants to the Hungarian throne—Ladislas of Naples and Sigismund of Luxembourg—but remained neutral in the face of numerous requests for alliances and assistance from the combatants. Ladislas's fortunes were at their peak after Sigismund and his crusading army suffered a crushing defeat at Nicopolis in 1396; the city of Zara, after a failed attempt to submit to Venetian authority, submitted to Ladislas's representatives in 1402. Venice had occasion to reconsider its position two years later, when Genoese galleys entered the Adriatic. Upon hearing of the Genoese penetration, and perhaps thinking of the disastrous Hungarian-Genoese alliance during the war of Chioggia, the Venetian Senate discussed the matter at length, "considering above all how important for our state it is that the regions of Dalmatia are favorable and not contrary [to us]."[46] Further arousing Venetian suspicions of Hungarian ambitions, Sigismund in 1404 pressed Venice for the tribute owed him under the 1358 treaty. The fear of the Genoese using Dalmatia as they had during the war of Chioggia, combined with Sigismund's newly aggressive stance on his right to tribute, made Venice much more amenable to the offers of sale and submission extended by the Dalmatian communes.

In 1408 Ladislas, whose fortunes in Hungary were rapidly waning, made his first offer to sell his claim to Dalmatia to the Venetians, asking 300,000 florins.[47] Ladislas had never been able to command much support from local nobilities, and as Sigismund and his barons recovered from their crushing defeat at Nicopolis, Ladislas's position became more tenuous. As the discussion over Ladislas's offer dragged on, the cities of Nona, Sebenico, and Traù rebelled against Ladislas's rule, causing the Venetians to lower the offering price to 100,000 florins.[48] Ladislas finally agreed, and the treaty ceding to the republic his remaining territories of Zara, Pago, Aurana, and the castle of Novegrad as well as all his claims over the rest of Dalmatia was signed in the Venetian church of San Silvestro on July 9, 1409.

Venetian diplomacy and cash had secured the republic a renewed claim on its former Dalmatian territories, but the concept of communal autonomy remained a strong one in the Dalmatian towns, particularly in Zara. The Zarentines were not happy they had been sold, and when the news of the sale reached the city, the Zarentines rose up against Ladislas's Neapolitan representatives, shutting them up in the citadel. According to Venetian accounts, the citizens then "raised the standard of San Marco, and . . . all the inhabitants of Zara shouted: long live San Marco!"[49] When the Venetian fleet arrived at the city on July 31, they found the Zarentines ready to submit to Venice as an independent commune, and the *provveditori* sent from Venice had to convince the citizens that they "would enter our dominion well and agreeably in such a manner that they would have all the honors and conveniences that they deserved." A core group of Zarentine nobles swore an oath of loyalty to Venice on behalf of the city as a whole; these nobles soon benefited from their close association with the Venetian rulers, while a group of pro-Hungarian nobles fled the city or were exiled to Venice.[50] To further convince the Zarentines they were not being treated as chattels to be bought and sold at will, the Venetian doge, Michele Steno, extended Venetian citizenship *de intus* to all Zarentine citizens.[51] A delegation of Zarentines traveled to Venice in August and September of 1409, when the Senate approved the city's statutes and privileges and the Zarentines swore their loyalty to Venice. As was the case on Corfu, the Venetian state offered the Zarentine elite privileges in return for allegiance, although it is important to note that these concessions were granted after Venice's physical control of the territory had been established.

The insistence of the pro-Venetian factions in Zara and Corfu on submitting to Venice as independent, autonomous agents bore marked similarities to practices in the towns of the Venetian *terraferma*. When the mainland cities came under Venetian rule, representatives from Padova and Vicenza claimed to have freely submitted to Venetian rule, although the free and spontaneous nature of that submission was often a dubious claim at best.[52] The idea of a free and voluntary submission to Venice was an attractive one to both Venice and the subject community, because it made Venetian rule look benign and its governance benevolent, an image the Venetian state had a clear interest in promoting. It also gave Venice an important ideological justification for expansion, enabling the

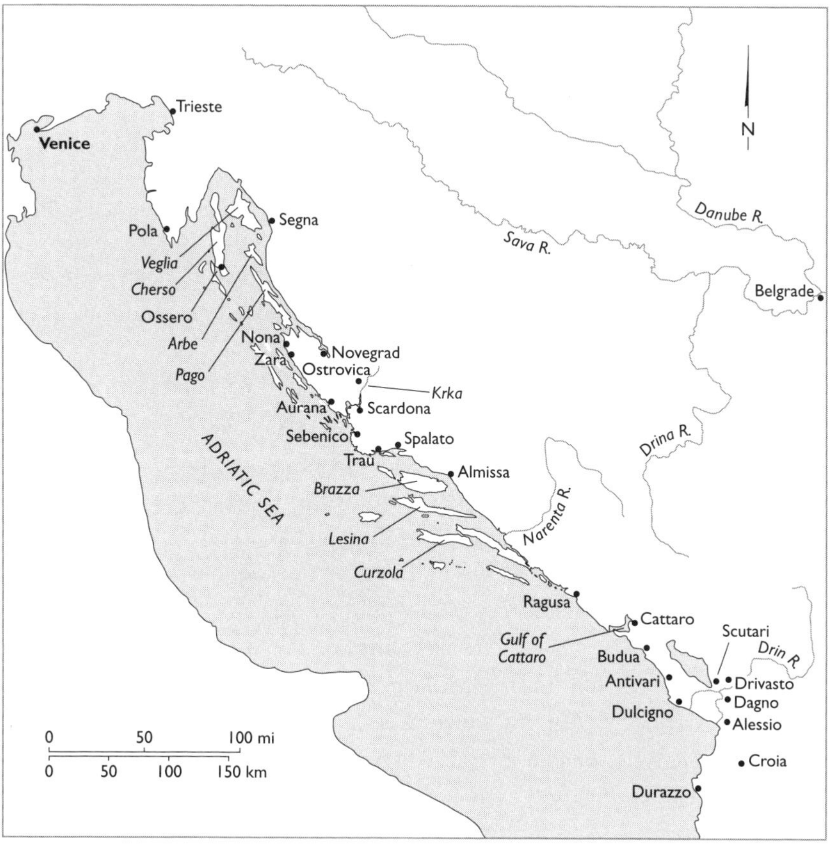

Dalmatian coastline

city to refute charges of expansionism by claiming that its subjects had invited its rule. On the other side, the idea of a free and voluntary submission, followed by a contractual negotiation over privileges, was an attractive idea to subject communities because it erased any memories of past opposition and made the city seem like an independent and autonomous entity. This could be a powerful motivation, as seen in the example of Zara, where the populace imprisoned Ladislas's representatives so the commune itself could submit to Venice and not be sold.

Zara proved to be the key to the rest of the Dalmatian coast. Immediately after Zara's submission, envoys from Nona, Arbe, Pago, Cherso, and Ossero all met the Venetian fleet and submitted.[53] Venice met little immediate resistance from Sigismund, whose hold on the Hungarian throne was by then uncontested, although he did encourage the Dalmatian towns to reject Venetian rule. As a result of these conflicting claims to sovereignty, the control that any central power exercised in Dalmatia was limited when the Venetians arrived in 1409, and pro-Hungarian and pro-Venetian factions battled in many of the towns.[54] Venice intervened to tip the balance in its own favor, while the pro-Hungarian factions were hampered by the fact that there was no material aid forthcoming from Hungary. When pro-Venetian persuasion failed, the Venetian fleet intervened. In Sebenico, the popular faction dominated and in 1412 expelled the pro-Venetian nobility, who occupied the two towers at the entrance to the harbor. The exiled nobles then asked for Venetian help, and the Venetian fleet then besieged the city and forced it to submit to Venetian rule.[55]

After the forcible conquest of Sebenico, Sigismund declared war on Venice, but the two parties signed a five-year armistice in 1413 to allow for the Council of Constance. When hostilities between Sigismund and Venice resumed in 1418, the islands of Curzola, Brazza, and Lesina submitted to Venetian rule in the face of the Venetian fleet.[56] The same fleet, led by the Venetian naval commander Pietro Loredan, met with some resistance in Traù and Spalato, but as had happened before, the pro-Hungarian forces were without external support and the pro-Venetian forces carried the day. Venice confirmed the privileges and customs of Spalato and Traù in July 1420, Curzola in September, Brazza in October, and Lesina in March 1421.[57] Cattaro, which in addition to being on the front lines of the Ottoman advance had been besieged several times by Albanian and Bosnian lords, had been petitioning to submit to Venice for decades, resorting to increasingly desperate appeals. Venice, equally politely, refused Cattaro's offers of submission five times, even when in 1414, the Cattaran envoys declared that they "awaited the arrival of Venice with the eagerness of the ancient patriarchs who in Limbo awaited the descent of Christ."[58] Despite the Cattaran skill at presenting Venice with arguments crafted to flatter the republic's carefully cultivated self-image, Venice did not accept Cattaro under its protection until 1420. Claims of voluntary communal submission in Corfu and Zara were tempered by the diplomatic and financial transactions that surrounded those cities' surrender; in the case of Cattaro, it seems that the commune did welcome Venetian rule.

The example of Cattaro demonstrates the complicated calculus of diplomatic, commercial, and strategic calculations that went into Venetian decisions to expand. In the cases of Corfu and Zara, at least a part of the community welcomed Venetian rule, and Venice in turn saw these territories as beneficial to their own interests. Both Corfu and Zara were essential to maritime control in the Adriatic, but even in these clear-cut cases, Venice waited to take over Corfu until it could do so "peacefully and quietly," and refused Zara's offer of submission in 1401, waiting until 1409, when the diplomatic and strategic situation was in its favor. In 1394, Venice refused a request from the community of Malvasia (Monemvasia) to enter Venetian protection after Theodore of Mistra surrendered the city to the sultan; the city also refused to accept Scutari from Giorgio II Balsha (Balšić) Strazimir until it was no longer in the hands of the Ottomans, and after sending a delegation to Valona to assess the revenues and defensive possibilities, refused to occupy that city as well.[59] On the other hand, Venice actively campaigned to obtain cities like Sebenico, Traù, and Durazzo, encouraging pro-Venetian factions and using its military to force submission when necessary. The Venetians wanted an Adriatic empire, but at the least possible cost.

Neither the Hungarians nor the Serbians were happy with Venice's expansion in Dalmatia.[60] The Serbian king was particularly opposed to Cattaro being in Venetian hands, because of the city's inland location, overlooking the strategic Gulf of Cattaro. Venetian troops defeated the Serbians in battle outside Scutari in 1422, and Serbia and Venice signed a treaty confirming Venetian control over Scutari, Dulcigno, and Cattaro in 1423. The Venetians also faced resistance from clan leaders in the mountains that surrounded Cattaro, in particular the Paštrovići, a family with extensive property in the region. In 1423, Venice offered to respect the clan's customary privileges in return for its defense of the region in Venice's name, and the clan leaders agreed.[61] The Venetians also needed to negotiate the terms of their new expansion with the Ottomans and in 1419 signed a treaty with the sultan Mehmed confirming their possession of many of their overseas possessions and agreeing to pay 300 ducats a year in tribute for Lepanto, Scutari, Alessio, and Drivasto.[62] The final negotiation confirming Venetian supremacy in Dalmatia was the 1437 treaty with Sigismund, who recognized Venice's control of the coastal cities in return for a payment of 10,000 ducats.[63]

Negotiating Submission: Communities and Their *Capitoli*

Venetian expansion was facilitated by the acquiescence or active alliance of segments of the Dalmatian population. As the emissaries from Cattaro emphasized, many of the smaller powers in the region saw an increasingly sharp choice between submission to the Venetians or to the Ottomans in the fifteenth century. The Dalmatian and Albanian towns had seen both Venetian and Hungarian overlordship in practice; Ottoman rule, in contrast, was an unknown quantity. Additionally, many of the Dalmatians shared bonds of religion with the Venetians while the rhetoric of crusade divided them from the Muslim Ottomans. Furthermore, as was the case on the Venetian mainland, many of the Dalmatian towns had limited participation in their communal councils and ruling bodies to a restricted oligarchy, giving the elites a shared culture and practice of power.[64] This did not mean that all members of the Dalmatian nobilities were in favor of Venetian rule; some remained loyal to the Hungarian king, and Venetian rectors sent a number of promonarchists to Venice in the early years of Venetian rule.[65]

Another reason Venice appeared as the best choice to some—in particular local elites—was its practice of negotiating with the communes and approving local statutes and privileges, although Venice reserved the right to change or adjust specific aspects of the statutes if they came into conflict with Venetian interests or honor.[66] The procedure of negotiating with subject communities over their statutes and privileges was a fairly regular one. Soon after Venetian troops entered the city, the communal assembly or representatives of the populace would send a list of demands, called *capitoli,* to Venice. The Senate would then review the requests and respond point by point, accepting, rejecting, or equivocating on each request. These requests and the Venetian responses were then codified into a solemn document, alternately called *capitoli, privilegia, concessiones, pacta,* or *deditio.* The Venetian reasoning for this practice was articulated in a 1394 Senate deliberation over a request from Capodistria that the city be ruled by its own orders and statutes. The Senate concluded that "[considering] how difficult it is to rule a city and change everything, [including] the statutes and orders on which it was founded, to please our loyal subjects in order that they have cause to persevere in their good disposition, we order our rector to . . . rule this city in civil and criminal matters after the form and order of their [the Capodistrian] statutes."[67] Communal statutes functioned as a locus of civic political identity for many communities, and by allowing their preservation and continued use, Venice eliminated one motivation for opposing its rule.[68]

In many cases, the first step in establishing Venetian administration was to determine what those local statutes and customs were. Even before Venice had physical control of Argos and Nauplion, the Senate instructed its *provveditore,* Perazzo Malipiero, to keep an account of local customs.[69] His successor, Vittore Morosini, was instructed to procure a precise edition of the statutes and send them to Venice to be corrected, but in 1396, Venice responded to a request from the bishop of Argos over his rights with regard to his peasants by saying, "We have no information on these laws and customs," indicating that Venice did not yet have a complete edition of the statutes.[70] In the case of Durazzo, Venice confirmed the city's statutes in August 1392, but the statutes themselves had been hidden, apparently in fear of the Thopias, and it was not until several months later that they were rediscovered in the library of the Franciscan monastery. At that point, Venice ordered a referendum among the "good men" of Durazzo to see if they wanted to be ruled by the statutes of Venice or these newly discovered statutes. In October of 1401 Durazzo submitted some of these statutes for approval to the Venetian Senate, and the Senate, waiting for the *bailo* and captain of Durazzo to authenticate them, repeated its acceptance of the statutory norms of 1392. Finally, in 1423, the Venetian Senate approved the ancient "privileges and customs."[71]

Venice did not unilaterally accept all communal statutes; as happened in Durazzo, the statutes had to be sent to Venice for review and acceptance, and the Senate carefully avoided limiting Venetian flexibility to govern as it saw fit. In 1397, representatives from Drivasto requested "that their ancient statutes be observed," and the Senate responded equivocally, stating that the rector there should adhere to local custom "when he sees it as just and reasonable," and that with time the inhabitants of Drivasto should "clearly see and feel the good fruits of our regimen, and will remain well-contented and not have any cause to quarrel."[72] Venice also refused to approve what it defined as "innovations" in communal statutes. Sebenico, Traù, and Spalato had updated their statutes under Hungarian rule to their own benefit and wanted Venice to approve these statutes. The Venetian Senate responded that the city would have all of the "liberties, honors, and conditions" it had held under Venetian rule previously but refused to approve any reforms introduced by the Hungarian kings. In Spalato, the commune also requested that Venice confirm the statutes from the time of the king of Hungary, but the *Signoria* responded that the Hungarian concessions made reference to a mode of election that was not in keeping with the "honor of the dominion."[73] The *Signoria* assured the commune that the elections would be "at the pleasure of the nobles of this city" but as Cozzi points out, this was a somewhat vague answer, as what might please the Spalatine nobility was left deliberately undefined. The *capitoli* provided both a point of negotiation between center and periphery and a flexible tool of governance, but later in the fifteenth century, as Venetian dominance was more firmly established and as the Ottoman border grew closer, the autonomy of the communes was gradually limited.[74]

Expansion's Intermission: Thessalonica and War in the Balkans

The Venetian acquisition of Thessalonica in 1423 marked the end of Venice's great age of expansion on its maritime frontiers. In 1423, the city was under siege by the

Ottoman army, and the population, despairing of Byzantine help, was divided between those who wished to hand the city to the Ottomans and those who looked to Venice for protection.[75] The city's ruler, the despot Andronicus, sent a delegation to the Venetian regime in Negroponte offering the city to Venice; the *bailo* there, Daniele Loredan, forwarded the request to Venice, and the Senate accepted it, after some deliberation. Venice followed its regular pattern of confirming the city's statutes and privileges, but the citizens had little time to enjoy them, as the Ottomans took the city seven years later. After the 1430 peace treaty with the Ottomans, Venetian trading interests in the eastern Mediterranean remained strong, but their ambitions toward further political expansion were curbed.

In the period of fragile peace that followed, the Ottomans continued to extend their control over the Balkans. The Venetians countered by taking the city of Antivari in the spring of 1433, but in general Venice avoided direct conflict, preferring to encourage its allies to anti-Ottoman action.[76] One of these sometime allies was John (Gjon) Castriot, an Albanian chief who held his territory through negotiating with both the Ottomans and the Venetians throughout the early part of the fifteenth century, receiving concessions from both sides. His son, Giorgio, better known as Skanderbeg, received honorary Venetian citizenship in 1438; in 1443, he seized the fortress of Croia (Kroja) and began an Albanian rebellion against the Ottomans.[77] Historians have disagreed on whether Venice was merely indifferent to Castriot's fight against the Ottomans or if the city actively attempted to thwart Castriot to avoid a united Albania; in any case, open war broke out between Castriot and Venice in 1447 over the city of Dagno (Danj).[78] In 1448, Castriot defeated both the Venetian forces, at the battle of Drin, and the Ottomans, at the battle of Oranik. Venice, seeing its Albanian cities of Durazzo and Scutari in danger, opened peace negotiations, and in October of 1448 agreed to pay Castriot an annual pension of 1,400 ducats a year and trade concessions in return for the city of Dagno. Castriot/Skanderbeg continued fighting the Ottomans until his death in 1468, at times with Venetian support and at times in a state of undeclared war.

Farther east, the Ottoman advances into the Balkans in the 1430s and 1440s drew the noose ever tighter around Constantinople.[79] Successive Byzantine emperors pleaded with the West to send help, but to no avail. Hoping for military help from the West, the Greek Orthodox delegation to the Council of Florence agreed to the Union of Churches in 1439.[80] The action was divisive among the Greek Orthodox populations both inside and outside the Byzantine empire. Neither Byzantine appeals nor agreements to church union were able to stave off the

Ottoman sultan Mehmed II's armies, which took the city of Constantinople in 1453. The fall of Constantinople and the resulting flood of Byzantine refugees set off a number of tremors in the Venetian empire. Waves of Greek Orthodox refugees flooded the *stato da mar* as well as the city of Venice itself, bringing with them the legacy of Byzantine intellectual and religious culture.[81] On Crete, these refugees contributed to the discontent with Venetian rule and played a large part in the conspiracy of Sifi Vlastos, a failed attempt to rebel discovered by Venetian authorities in 1453–54 and again in 1461–62.[82]

The Ottoman capture of Constantinople sparked renewed calls to crusade across the Latin Christian world. Venice's willingness to provide troops, money, or ships to the effort was lukewarm at best, but Venetian writers found a rich source of justification for Venice's overseas empire in the ideology of crusade. Venetian authors had long legitimated the city's naval dominance by pointing to its fight against pirates, and in Paolo Morosini's (1406–1482) treatise "Defense of the Venetians to the Princes of Europe against Her Detractors," pirates quickly became barbarians and Turks, buttressing Venetian claims to a long and glorious crusading history. "If it were not for the Venetian state," Morosini asserted, "the people [of Dalmatia, Albania, Greece, and Thessaly] would be Turkish," and went on to state that it was because of Venice's ongoing war against barbarians and pirates that the Adriatic was called the "Venetian Gulf."[83]

Ironically, just as Morosini and others were giving the Venetian empire a more definitive ideological shape, Ottoman forces were chipping away at the empire's physical manifestation. During the 1463–1479 war, Ottoman attacks reached deep into the Venetian sphere of influence, striking Scutari in 1472 and 1474 and reaching Friuli in 1477–78. Ottoman troops conquered Argos, the Albanian cities of Scutari and Alessio, and most seriously, the island of Negroponte.[84] In early 1470, the Ottoman fleet besieged the city of Chalkis, and by July of that year the island was in Ottoman hands. When the news reached Venice, the Milanese ambassador posted to the city reported that "all Venice was taken by dismay: the inhabitants, half dead from fear, said that the loss of all of the possessions of the mainland would have been a smaller blow."[85] The Venetian diarist Domenico Malipiero said that the news "threw everyone into a grand terror, and all doubted that continuing the Turk's victories, the state would be lost. Now, the greatness of Venice would be lowered, and our pride would be extinct."[86] In the formal peace of 1479 that ended the long, drawn-out conflict with the Ottomans, Venice renounced all rights over Negroponte, Argos, and Scutari and agreed to pay 10,000 ducats a year so that Venetian merchants could continue to trade in the Ottoman empire.

Venice's Second Wave of Expansion: Cyprus and the *Terraferma*

These losses brought the Venetian-Ottoman frontier to the edge of Venetian territory in the Balkans. The empire was not entirely on the defensive, however; as a counterweight to the loss of Negroponte, Venice acquired the rich and strategically important island of Cyprus, as well as the smaller territories of Veglia (Krk), Malvasia (Monemvasia), and Zante (Zakynthos). Venice also pushed its influence farther onto the Italian mainland, moving out from Cervia (1463) toward the city-state of Ferrara (1481) and Rovereto (1487). When seen in the context of Venice's mainland expansion in the 1480s, the acquisition of Cyprus thus fits into a "second wave" of imperial growth in the late sixteenth century.

While Venice did not formally assume control of Cyprus until 1489, the republic had considerable influence over the island's financial, military, and political life beginning in 1473, with the death of James II, the last Lusignan king.[87] As in many other cases, Venice had begun its campaign to consolidate its influence and control on Cyprus much earlier. In 1447, Venice had to assure Genoa that it was not thinking of conquering Cyprus, and over the course of the fifteenth century Venetian families, above all the Corner, but also the Michiel, Pisani, and da Lezze, gained a great deal of influence over Cyprus's economy.[88] The first step to formalizing Venetian influence on Cyprus came in 1468, when King James II signed a pact bringing the island under Venetian protection and married Caterina Corner, who was named a "daughter of the Republic." James died on July 6, 1473, leaving Caterina pregnant with the future heir to the kingdom, James III. Immediately upon hearing the news of James's death, Pietro Davila, the military commander of Cyprus, sent an escort for the Venetian *bailo*, Nicolò Pasqualigo, and presented him with the standard of the island, symbolically investing him with power over both the island and the queen. By August of that same year, Pietro Mocenigo arrived with the Venetian fleet to protect both the queen and Venetian interests, and he left six galleys stationed in the Famagustan harbor. The Venetian galleys and Venetian *provveditori* acted to support Caterina's, and therefore Venice's, claim to the throne against the archbishop of Cyprus and the Catalan party on the island.[89]

Even before the infant king James III died in 1474, the Venetian Senate acted to assure Venetian control of the island's fortresses, gates, towers, and walls, sending a hundred crossbowmen. Venice continued to send *bailii* to the island, as it had since the early fourteenth century, but beginning in 1474, elected counselors and from 1479 treasurers as well. The first two counselors, Francesco Minio and Alvise Gabriele, were directed to act in concert with Caterina "so that everything may appear to proceed from her," this giving at least the cursory impression that Venice was not angling to add the island to its empire but was acting in its adopted daughter's interests. Whatever appearance these counselors and their successors might have given, they went far beyond an advisory capacity—they had control of the island's finances and its military, were paid out of the Cypriot treasury, and had limited judicial functions as well. The counselors were so aggressive in promoting Venetian interests that in 1479 the Senate had to warn them not to arrive at judicial decisions without consulting their colleagues and, furthermore, their orders were not intended to allow them to reside in the queen's apartments.[90]

Caterina and her father, Marco Corner, complained vociferously to the Senate over the role of these Venetian counselors in the island's administration, but to no avail.[91] With financial, military, and judicial control of the island firmly in Venetian hands, Venice began to openly discuss formally acquiring the island and raising the flag of San Marco. From 1477 to 1479, the Senate considered colonizing Cyprus, first with Venetian noble families and second with refugees from Scutari, taken by the Ottomans in 1479, but both efforts failed.[92] By 1487, an envoy to Constantinople was instructed to inform the Ottomans "we have dominion there," and in 1488 Caterina reluctantly returned to Venice at the behest of her adopted parent. In February of 1489 the standard of San Marco was raised over Cyprus, although the formal ceremony of submission did not come until June 20. The Cypriots sent a delegation to present the island's *capitoli* and to ask for the conservation of their laws and privileges, including the right to have their appeals heard in Cyprus, not Venice, and the Cyprian *capitoli* were confirmed in August 1489.[93]

From Expansion to Defense: The Sixteenth Century

Cyprus was the last significant jewel Venice added to its imperial crown. Venice suffered a series of abrupt reversals of fortune beginning in the 1490s. News of the Portuguese circumnavigation of Africa filtered back to the city and the disruption of the spice markets of Alexandria called Venetian commercial supremacy into question, while the 1499–1503 war with the Ottomans challenged the city's naval preeminence in the eastern Mediterranean.[94] By the conclusion of this third war with the Ottomans, Venice had lost Coron, Modon, Lepanto, and Durazzo, although it did take the Ionian island of Cefalonia in 1500. A few years later, Venetians faced the combined papal, French, and imperial armies on their western frontier. These powers, angered by Venice's expansion onto the Italian mainland, banded together in the League of Cambrai in 1508, and by 1509 Venice had lost all of its territories on the mainland. Venice recovered its mainland domains within a decade, but the rest of the sixteenth century was an extended defensive action on its maritime frontier. Venice lost Malvasia, Mykonos, and Nauplion in the fourth war with the Ottomans (1537–1540) but managed to hold on to Corfu despite a devastating siege. The joint Spanish and Venetian victory over the Ottoman fleet at Lepanto in 1571 kept the *stato da mar* from being swept away completely, although the Ottomans did take Cyprus in 1570.

Venice ruled Crete until 1669 and its territories in Dalmatia and the Ionian islands until the fall of the republic in 1797. Every year, the Venetian doge rowed out to San Nicolò to renew the city's vows to the sea, but in the face of other contenders, the tranquility and ease of the marriage was gone. Malipiero narrated a 1499 exchange between a Venetian ambassador and an Ottoman pasha that symbolized the new, more troubled union between Venice and its empire. The pasha supposedly told a Venetian emissary, "Until now, you have been married to the sea. For the future, that is for us, who are more powerful by sea than you."[95] The ambassador was then forced to explain, one imagines rather reluctantly, that the ceremony referred only to a certain part of the sea, the Gulf of Venice.

Throughout these periods of expansion, development, and defensiveness, imperial strategies and policies were decided in the halls and councils of the Venetian state. Ambassadors and consuls negotiated with foreign rulers: drafting trade agreements, negotiating for peace, and declaring war. Within the Venetian empire itself, these long-term strategies and international conflicts encountered the day-to-day politics of imperial rule, and it was the men elected to serve as territorial governors who stood at this intersection of state policy and quotidian rule. Venetian councils determined the state's approach to religious difference, to economic development, and to military preparedness; Venetian governors negotiated with Greek Orthodox and Jewish residents of the *stato da mar*, oversaw the sale and shipment of wheat, wine, cheese, and other commodities, chased smugglers, and organized local militias and defense works. The success or failure of imperial policy in practice depended on the ability of these officials, mediators between center and periphery, to advance Venetian interests during their term of office. Venetian councils chose the patricians who filled these crucial posts, and how they did so is the subject of the next chapter.

TWO

Administrators of Empire

In 1486, the Great Council prefaced its deliberations on the method of electing administrators in Crete, Cyprus, and Constantinople by stating, "The islands of Crete and Cyprus are of such importance to our state in the Levant . . . Because of their location and importance, [it is best] to provide for every necessity in all respects, and as always [we should] send to their government and regimens our gentlemen of such reputation and authority that all of the inhabitants subject to them will remain content under the shadow and dominion of Our Serenity."[1] The Venetian state here made a clear connection between the quality of the men elected to serve abroad and the contentment of the subjects under their rule. Satisfied subjects, the prologue implied, would lead to a peaceful empire, thus preserving Venetian rule in the city's most valued maritime possessions. The prologue also points to the tension at the heart of Venetian electoral politics. Officially, almost any patrician was eligible for election to these posts: the Great Council often claimed that "our forbearers intended that all [patricians] should have an equal share in the government."[2] Electioneering, soliciting votes, or putting oneself forward were all outlawed; ideally, patricians would put aside any sense of personal interest when they stepped into the Great Council hall. On the other hand, the prologue indicates that some offices, in particular important posts on Crete and Cyprus, should only go to patricians of "authority and reputation," undercutting the stated idea of equality.

Venice's electoral politics as a whole were suffused with tensions between equality and exclusivity, virtue and vice, ideal and reality. The ideal elected official—a man dedicated to increasing Venetian honor and profit both at home and abroad—was a constituent part of the much discussed myth of Venice, which held that Venetian greatness was founded at least in part on the virtues of the Venetian nobles, who richly deserved their dominant role in the republic.[3] As Queller, Ruggerio, Finlay, Gullino, and others have documented, in reality the Venetian patriciate was no more or less virtuous than any other group—some obeyed the law while others flouted it, some sacrificed greatly in the service of the state while others manipulated the system to their own advantage.[4] One can find the same range of motivations among officials in the maritime and territorial states; individual patricians might see a candidacy for office as an unwanted duty, as a financial opportunity, as a way to enhance personal or familial status, or as a stepping stone to higher office in more exclusive Venetian councils. But as the authors of the 1486 prologue cited above acknowledged, not all candidates for office were capable of advancing the state's goal to maintain order, profit, and Venetian honor in its imperial domains.

Individual desires for important or lucrative offices and the state's interest in sending capable representatives to distant territories were negotiated in the Great Council, the site of the majority of elections to maritime offices.[5] Finlay, Romano, and Raines have all illuminated the degree to which *broglio*—the lively exchange of gossip, solicitation of votes, status seeking, and favor trading—spilled from the piazza into the council hall.[6] Strategies for obtaining a particular office began with the nominating committee. Candidates for each office were put forth by nominating committees composed of nine men, and nominating oneself was frowned upon, so candidates first tried to get friends and relatives onto the appropriate committee. The hopeful candidate then called in favors, lobbied his supporters, and tried to accumulate enough votes to win an election or avoid election to an undesired post. Despite electoral policies that were on the surface egalitarian, and without ever formally articulating the principles of the system, Venetian electoral politics were responsive to the desires of families and individuals for particular offices as well as to the qualities of any particular candidate.

Maritime Offices: Number and Organization

Maritime positions played a significant role in this search for offices simply because of numbers. The *Rulers of Venice* databank, which contains the first nine election registers from the *Segretario alle Voci*, now allows much more detailed and precise analysis of the distribution of offices and of political power within the Venetian state.[7] While the nature of the election registers themselves do not allow definitive answers to the questions of how many offices there were at any given time in Venice or precisely how many patricians served in those offices, the databank does allow us to approach those questions with more precision than was previously possible. Mozzato's analysis of the databank has concluded that over the course of the fifteenth century, there were more than 600 positions available in the Venetian government, of which 140 were within the city of Venice it-

TABLE 2.1

Offices outside Venice, 1349–1540

Date	Maritime	Mainland	Total
1349–1353	104	12	116
1362–1367	75	14	89
1383–1387	77	3	80
1400	71	16	87
1437	109	61	170
1493	138	113	251
1540	117	78	195

Sources: The figures for 1349–1387 are based on *SegV* registers 1–3; those for 1400–1540 are taken from Zannini, 438, 459–63. There is a fifty-year gap (1387–1437) in the *SegV* election records, making later fourteenth- and early fifteenth-century numbers difficult to determine precisely.

self (*de intus*) and 400 were external to the city (*de extra*), including governors, military officials, ambassadors, and captains of galleys.[8] Narrowing the field to positions directly concerned with maritime territorial administration—excluding ambassadors, military commanders elected only during wartime, and galley captains as well as *terraferma* administrators—there were between 71 and 138 administrative offices available on a regular basis in the period between 1349 and 1540 in the maritime state, as table 2.1 details.

The most obvious reason for the fluctuating number of positions available outside of Venice was change in the territorial state itself. The 1358 loss of Dalmatia, for instance, corresponds with the drop in maritime offices available in the second half of the fourteenth century, while the number of Venetian-held territories and the number of positions regularly available both expanded over the course of the fifteenth century. It was not only maritime offices that grew in number over this period—Zannini has estimated that the total number of offices in Venetian government grew by 30 percent, and there was also a gradual rise in the number of patricians eligible for and interested in holding office.[9] A number of patricians were dependent on these offices for their livelihood, and the intensity of competition for them increased greatly during the fifteenth century, in part because many of the more important offices continued to be filled by more experienced and prominent politicians.[10] This is the case for maritime offices as well: more experienced and prominent patricians held the most important offices in the maritime state, while lesser positions went to a much wider circle of candidates.

The most significant offices in the maritime state were the governors and captains of Zara, Corfu, Crete, and Cyprus, all regional capitals with some control over nearby towns and countryside.[11] The men who held these positions acted as the primary Venetian administrators in a region as well as in an individual city; the offices brought large salaries and correspondingly heavy diplomatic, administrative, and judicial responsibilities. In each of these regional capitals, the governor (count, *bailo,* duke, or lieutenant) was joined by a captain responsible for military matters; the positions of captain on Crete and Corfu evolved gradually, while captains were regularly elected from the beginning of Venetian dominion in Zara and Cyprus.[12] In theory, the governor was responsible for civil matters like judicial and financial administration, while the captain saw to military preparedness and public order. In practice, governors' and captains' jurisdictions frequently overlapped, meaning that the positions of governor and captain were relatively equal in salary, honors, and responsibilities.[13] These key posts could serve as stepping stones to positions of authority in the inner councils of Venetian government; they were filled with men who were politically experienced, in officeholding in general and often in maritime administration in particular.

The governors in the second tier of maritime offices—those in Cattaro, Coron and Modon, Durazzo, Negroponte, Nauplion, Sebenico, Scutari, Spalato, and Traù—still had heavy responsibilities, but headed smaller regimes of two or three other Venetian officials.[14] The governors in all of these locations combined the duties of rector and captain, administering justice as well as overseeing territories' military preparations. These governors were assisted militarily by a castellan, a captain of the town, or at times both; the castellan could take on the function of treasurer as well. Many of these territories had dependencies, so the *bailo* of Negroponte was responsible for Fitilei, Tinos, and Mykonos; the castellan of Coron and Modon was responsible for Sapientza and, briefly, for Athens; and the *bailo* of Durazzo was responsible for Alessio.[15]

The smallest regimes, consisting of one, or at the most two, Venetian officials, comprised a third tier of maritime offices. In locales such as Brazza, Dulcigno, Egina, or Malvasia, the Senate sent only one Venetian rector every two years; he would be accompanied by his entourage of retainers but was otherwise alone.[16] These less important offices had smaller salaries and a more constricted area of responsibility and they were filled by a rotating cadre of less experienced patricians. Subordinate offices in larger regimes—jobs as counselors, castellans, treasurers, or captains of the town—also tended to be filled by patricians with less political experience. These positions heading small regimes and acting as subordinate officials in larger regimes were the least prestigious, and the least remunerative, in the maritime state.

Patricians and Politics: Contests over the Distribution of Offices

It was this last group of offices that were the focus of the Venetian state's attempts to provide offices for needy patricians. There was certainly a growing awareness of the plight of impoverished nobles in the fifteenth century and numerous attempts to ameliorate their condition by awarding them offices and positions both inside and outside of Venice.[17] Venetian councils, however, did not view their entire government as fodder for the trough of public entitlement. The prologue to a 1392 Great Council decision increasing the salaries of some offices states, "Some of our *minor* offices, to which are usually elected our impoverished nobles," suggesting there were a restricted and well-defined number of positions set aside for purposes of the nobles' welfare.[18]

In the first decades of the fifteenth century, the number of offices available in the expanding territorial state grew, but prestigious and lucrative governorships went to a restricted circle of experienced patricians who rotated from post to post in the newly formed regimes of the territorial state. Clearly, Venetian councils were not prepared to hand sensitive and important positions in newly conquered territories over to just any patrician; instead, the same men were elected repeatedly to different offices, creating a core group of specialists in what might be called regime stabilization across mainland and maritime empire. Egidio Morosini, for instance, spent the last fifteen years of his life outside of Venice, heading regimes in Corfu (1403), Verona (1407), Padova (1409), Verona again (1410), Zara (1412), Padova again (1414), and Crete (1417), where he died in office.[19] Another such specialist was Marino di Luca Caravello, who served as castellan in Coron and Modon (1396); *bailo* of Corfu (1399); captain of the Gulf (1402); *podestà* of Capodistria (1403); captain of the Gulf a second time (1405), when he led the capture of Dulcigno, Antivari, and Budua; *podestà* of Padova (1406), and captain of Padova (1409).[20] Men like Morosini, Caravello, or Pietro di Giacomo Arimondo, who was captain in Rovigo (1395), *podestà* of Capodistria (1398), captain-general of the Gulf (1399), *podestà* of Treviso (1404), captain of Verona (1405), captain of Padova (1407), captain of Zara (1409), and captain of Crete (1414) formed the most visible part of this group of specialists in establishing regimes, but they were certainly unusual in the number of offices they held.[21] Men who held three or four offices were more typical, such as Marino Loredan, who served twice in Vicenza (1412, 1421) and twice in Treviso (1413, 1419); Antonio dalle Boccole, castellan of Coron (1408), count of Sebenico (1413), *podestà* of Verona (1418), and count of Cattaro (1420); or Vito da Canal, who was captain of Verona (1422), captain of Zara (1431) and captain of Crete (1435).[22]

This pattern of repeat officeholding, while small from a statistical point of view, loomed large in contemporary Venetian consciousness. There were periodic complaints in the Great Council against the monopolization of high office by the few, indicating a growing tension over the distribution of offices outside Venice. In 1408 the Great Council, referring to the tradition that offices should be shared equally among patricians, ruled that officials had to wait a year before being reelected to another post, and in August 1410 the ducal counselors introduced a motion to the Great Council restricting repeat officeholding, saying that it was only just that offices should be shared equally between eligible nobles.[23] The council imposed a four-year moratorium on officeholding for those who had served as count or captain of Padova, Verona, or Zara, a prohibition that was promptly ignored—Zaccaria Trevisan, count of Zara in 1410, was elected captain of Padova for the second time in 1412, and Egidio Morosini was elected to all three positions between 1410 and 1414.

It was in this context that Antonio Contarini, who had served as *provveditore* in Zara at the time of its submission to Venice, proposed that the Zarentine nobles be allowed to hold office outside of Zara. In September of 1411, the *Signoria* received reports that some of the Zarentine nobility were "not content with our dominion" and were soliciting help from the king of Hungary in overturning Venetian rule.[24] Twenty-nine prominent Zarentine families were sent to Venice because of doubts about their loyalty, and Contarini's proposal aimed to address this Zarentine discontent. Contarini argued that the Zarentines' hatred of Venetian rule came from their loss of the offices and honors they had enjoyed previously and which "under our dominion have stopped." He proposed that ten Zarentine nobles be absorbed into Venice's mainland administration and that another eighteen be allowed to rule in Venetian Istria and elsewhere in Dalmatia. The proposal was rejected; in an atmosphere of conflict over Venetian patricians' access to territorial offices, there was little support for the idea of broadening the pool of candidates beyond the patriciate itself.

The struggle over access to office continued through the 1420s and 1430s, not coincidentally the period of what Chojnacki has termed the *Second Serrata*, a legislative campaign that more tightly defined and regulated membership in the Venetian patriciate.[25] The Great Council in 1414 and again in 1430 revised procedures governing young men's entry into the patriciate, increasing state scrutiny over candidates' qualifications and emphasizing patrilineal descent.[26] At the same time the Venetian state was attempting to control membership in its councils, and thus the number of claimants for office, the Great Council repeatedly enacted legislation that established periods of *contumacia* for officeholders—in other words, officeholders were required to remain out of office for a period of time equal to their term in office. This legislation was intended to spread offices more widely among the patriciate, and measures were enacted in 1418, 1428, 1432, 1443, and 1450.[27] Both the legislation of the *Second Serrata,* which restricted eligibility for office, and the legislation on *contumacia,* which tried to make offices more widely available, show that the growing Venetian state was struggling with how best to include its patriciate in the governance of the new empire. The problem for the Venetian state was that while it had a clearly expressed principle that all patricians should share the offices and benefits of the state equally among themselves, the logic of imperial preservation demanded that more important posts be awarded to officials capable of governing in Venice's name.

The Midcentury Militarization of Maritime Administration

The constellation of offices in the Venetian maritime state shifted regularly, in response to local military and administrative needs as well as to electoral pressures in Venetian councils. Thiriet, looking at the thirteenth and fourteenth centuries, described maritime offices as "subject to a rigorous administrative uniformity," modeled on Venice's doge and six counselors.[28] As the Venetian empire expanded exponentially in the late fourteenth and fifteenth centuries, little trace of uniformity or regularity remained. The lack of standardization can be seen in the titles given the various officials, usually created by adopting whatever title was in local usage at the moment of the Venetian acquisition. The chief Venetian authority on Crete was thus a duke, on Corfu a *bailo,* in Zara a count, in Coron and Modon a castellan, and in Cyprus a lieutenant. (See appendix A.) The administrators were referred to collectively in Venetian documents as rectors (*rettori*) or as governors (*governatori*). Instead of enforcing rigorous policies of consistency, Venetian administration adapted to the particular circumstances of time and place, although this flexibility did not mean that the administration was without central direction.

This flexibility meant that when tension over officeholding mounted, as it did in the middle of the fifteenth century, the Venetian state was able to address concerns over the monopolization of territorial offices by adding positions to its maritime administration. In 1442, the Great Council created twelve new castellanships and twelve new maritime offices, all of which were specifically reserved for impoverished nobles.[29] (See appendix A.) Four more maritime offices were created in 1444, and in 1448, 1450, and 1454 the council tried to end the practice of awarding castellanies by *grazia,* a special privilege that circumvented the normal electoral process, and to shorten the castellans' term of office, again referring to the principle of sharing offices equally among the patriciate.[30] The creation of special positions for impoverished or less experienced office-seekers served to underline the unspoken restriction on the higher offices of the maritime state, which continued to go almost exclusively to experienced men of great "reputation and authority."[31]

Competition for lower offices was driven by patricians looking to begin a career in political, financial, or judicial administration as well as those who wanted positions for their salary. Girolamo di Pietro Diedo, for instance, held a castellanship in Corfu (1438), another in Aurana (1444), and served as a counselor in Corfu (1451) and in Canea (1455). (See appendix B.) He finished his career by holding some of the most important offices in Venice's territorial administration: count of Zara (1473), captain of Vicenza (1478), and captain of Bergamo (1481). Iacopo di Secondo Miani was treasurer in Crete (1441), counselor in Coron (1450), count in Dulcigno (1456), and rector in Rettimo (1467) before ending his career as *podestà* in Verona (1485). This pattern of service in the lower posts of the maritime empire was most likely undertaken for experience and for personal or familial advantage rather than out of financial hardship or necessity. Pietro di Ranieri Vitturi made a career out of service in the less prestigious posts: castellan at Cerigo (1451) and at Novegrad (1453), rector of Tinos and Mykonos (1468), *provveditore* at Croia (1474), *podestà* (1483) and then castellan (1493) of Nauplion, and rector of Rettimo (1497). Vitturi might have needed the salaries of these posts; he also gained a great deal of experience in maritime administration during his career.

By adding new positions or revising the duties of available positions, Venetian councils attempted to contain, if not to end, the tension over the patriciate's growing desire for office on the one hand and the state's need for authoritative and experienced governors in sensitive posts on the other. The Venetian patriciate as a whole, however, did not rush to fill these newly created maritime posts; the competition for office remained centered on prestigious, lucrative, or at least convenient positions. The position of treasurer of Nauplion, created in 1442, was filled for the first time in 1463. The position of salt official at Scutari was filled only six times between 1444 and 1479. The four counselor positions in Rettimo and Canea, created in 1442, were also difficult to staff. Only five candidates were elected to counselorships in Rettimo during the first twenty years of the position's existence, and one out of every three counselors in Canea refused the post or did not serve the full term during this period. Queller has pointed to this "apparent contradiction between the pursuit of public office and the rejection of it," concluding that the reasons behind an individual patrician's acceptance or refusal of an office lay with his own circumstances as well as the characteristics of the position.[32] The difficulty in filling minor posts in the maritime state indicates that these offices were neither desirable to individual patricians nor essential to the functioning of the empire, as they frequently went unfilled, at least by candidates elected in Venice.

In part, the patriciate's reluctance to take these newly created positions stemmed from the increasing dangers on the Ottoman frontier. In the wake of Constantinople's 1453 fall to the Ottomans, the Venetian government's attention increasingly turned to the defense of its maritime empire. In 1455, the *Dieci* considered a proposal that would have added four more offices to Venetian administration in the *stato da mar.* The council, however, rejected the idea of sending Venetian castellans to Avalona, Antivari, and Alessio; it did approve the institution of a captain of Corfu, but this position was filled only three times before 1490.[33] The same does not hold true for the nine new castellanies which Venetian councils began to fill beginning in the 1460s. Castellans began to be sent regularly to Antivari in 1486, Drivasto in 1465, Lepanto in 1465, Lesina in 1495, Nauplion in 1452, the city of Sebenico in 1442 and the Torre Grande of Sebenico in 1466, Spalato in 1470, and to Traù in 1443. These castles, and their commanders, formed Venice's defensive bulwark in Dalmatia, Albania, and continental Greece against the Ottoman advance in the Balkans.[34] As relations with the Ottoman empire deteriorated in the late fifteenth century, these castellans could be called on at any moment to defend Venetian territory and were responsible for maintaining the defenses of their territories in a state of constant readiness.

In addition to castellanies, the election of *provveditori*—temporary military and administrative officials—became an increasingly important part of Venice's defensive preparations in its maritime territories. The *provveditore* had supreme military and administrative powers in a territory and was supposed to work in concert with the regularly elected governor and captain, if there was one. *Provveditori* were initially sent to maritime territories at the moment of their entry into empire. For instance, Michele Contarini served as a *provveditore* on Corfu (1386), in Argos (1390), and in Durazzo (1392), all at the moment of Venetian acquisition.[35] Saracino Dandolo went from *provveditore* in Corfu (1386) to *bailo* of Negroponte (1387), where Venice was in the process of formalizing its rule over the island; he then served as captain of the Gulf (1392) and followed Contarini as *provveditore* of Argos (1394).[36] The *provveditore* in these situations played a crucial role, because the Venetian commander on the spot was responsible for negotiating the terms of surrender and setting the tone of Venetian administration. After the initial period of adjustment, *provveditori* continued to be elected sporadically in the case of a short-term threat, such as an uprising or attack.[37] As Venice's borders became increasingly militarized over the course of the later fifteenth and sixteenth centuries, *provveditori* were sent on an increasingly regular basis to maritime territories. In some locales, as in Crete, Zara, and Corfu, the *provveditore* became a permanent fixture in the already existing regime, while in other locales, such as Lesina, Nauplion, Modon, and Coron, the regularly elected rector received the title and powers of *provveditore.*

Career Patterns in Maritime Offices

Individual careers as well as larger patterns in officeholding reveal the tension between restricted access to important posts and the principle of spreading offices as widely as possible through the patriciate. A sample survey of the *Segretario alle Voce* registers 4 (1438–1457) and 6 (1465–1502) shows 56 percent of positions were filled by onetime officeholders, 25 percent of positions were filled by twotime officeholders, and 11 percent of positions were filled by threetime officeholders.[38] This pattern echoes the way patricians served on the mainland; Del Torre has shown that of all the officers who served in the *terraferma* from 1506 to 1540, only one-third ever returned to hold a second position in the territorial administration.[39] While the majority of officeholders in the maritime state held office outside of Venice only once, there were thirty-three individuals in the sample who held four, five, or six maritime offices during the period. The great majority of these individuals held at least one of the eight most important maritime offices, meaning that the men who served as governors and as captains in Zara, Corfu, Crete, and Cyprus were all experienced politicians.

By the time they took the reins of one of these regimes, most of these patricians had significant terms of service in both Venetian councils and in external magistracies. A survey of the 164 men who served in the 180 positions as rectors and captains in the four most important regimes between 1450 and 1500 reveals that 90 percent of the positions were filled by men with some type of prior political experience, and 60 percent were filled by men with experience in a regime outside of Venice, either in the maritime or *terraferma* domains.[40] Lorenzo di Lorenzo Loredan, Count of Zara (1450), arrived in the post having served in Traù (1448), Chioggia (1446), Cyprus (1441), and Murano (1438), as well as several terms as a senator. Bartolommeo di Marco Minio was count of Spalato (1453), counselor of Corfu (1462), and *podestà* of Nauplion (1479); he then served as captain of Cyprus (1497) and as captain of Crete (1500).[41] Paolo Antonio di Iacopo Miani followed his term as *bailo* of Corfu (1497) with a term as a ducal counselor;

he then served as captain on Cyprus (1503), duke of Crete (1510), and as lieutenant on Cyprus (1514); he returned to Venice to take a seat on the *Dieci.* Cosma di Paolo Pasqualigo was lieutenant on Cyprus (1499) and duke of Crete (1503); previously, he had been a captain of the Barbary galleys, a member of the *Dieci,* a Patron of the Arsenal, a *governor delle entrate,* and had served as captain in Famagusta (1493). Francesco Bembo arrived on Crete as duke (1413) having served as *bailo* on Negroponte twice (1401, 1406), in Verona (1409), and in Padova twice (1400, 1411).[42] Giovanni Pisani's experience took him to Verona twice (1438, 1440), Zara (1439), and Padova (1441); he also served on the *Quarantia,* the Senate, and as a ducal elector before being elected as duke of Crete (1476). Marco di Andrea Barbo was elected to serve in all four regimes, as *bailo* of Corfu (1472), count of Zara (1479), captain of Cyprus (1499), and duke of Crete (1500).

There was no discernable difference in the careers between those who served as captains and those who served as rectors; in fact, many officeholders moved from positions as captain to governor and vice versa. Bartolomeo di Matteo Vitturi was first captain (1483), then count (1493) in Zara. Andrea di Leone Venier was captain on Crete (1494) and then lieutenant in Cyprus (1497). Pantaleone Barbo was *provveditore* in Crete during the San Tito rebellion (1363), twice *bailo* of Negroponte (1366, 1379), the first Venetian *bailo* in Corfu (1389), captain in Crete (1389), and then duke (1395); Tomà Duodo first came to Crete as a judge (1407), then returned as captain (1438) and as duke (1443); Fantin Viaro served as the duke of Crete first (1427), then returned as captain (1443).[43] Gabriele Emo had served as a Venetian ambassador in Verona, Udine, and Ferrara, *bailo* in Negroponte, and as a field commander against the Veronese when he became captain of Crete (1406).[44] The ability to move from one office to another was possible because there was significant overlap in the duties and responsibilities of the two jobs, so experience as a captain would be useful in a term as governor and vice versa.

Among those who held more than one maritime post, there were several paths in maritime administration. Some returned to the same territory repeatedly, holding different positions each time; here, the usual pattern was to serve first in a less important office and return in a position of more authority, suggesting that the early positions acted as a training ground for more important positions. Nicolò di Antonio Loredan served as treasurer and castellan of Arbe (1465) and returned years later as count (1481), and Francesco di Andrea Bembo served as treasurer in Pago (1470) and quickly returned as count (1474). Giovanni Natale di Tomà Salamon was first treasurer (1488) and then captain (1516) in Zara.[45] Francesco di Andrea Contarini was first castellan and treasurer in Antivari (1496) and then count

(1516). Andrea di Andrea Venier began as treasurer and castellan (1441) in Scutari and returned as count (1453). Alvise di Simone Darmer was captain and *provveditore* (1502) and then *bailo* (1512) in Corfu, and Andrea di Giovanni da Canal was castellan in Corfu (1498) and returned as counselor (1516).[46] Giulio di Giovanni Bollani served in Crete as an officer of the night (1454) and returned as a counselor of Candia (1488), Zaccaria di Zanotto Calbo served as a counselor of Candia (1463) and then as rector of Canea (1473).[47] Marco Antonio di Alvise Contarini served as treasurer in Nauplion (1485) and returned as rector and *provveditore* (1504), Pietro di Francesco Ferro began as treasurer (1463) and returned as castellan (1487), and Marco di Nicolò Pizzamano also began as treasurer (1496) and returned as rector (1501). There were also a few individuals who returned to the same office twice.[48] The larger regimes, with multiple positions filled by Venetian patricians, thus had a flow of men familiar with the territory.

A second strategy of maritime specialization was to serve in multiple locations across the empire, gaining a wide range of experience in different places and different types of offices. Andrea di Maffeo Capello had experience in Beirut, Trebizond, and Constantinople before serving as *bailo* of Cyprus (1421) and as *bailo* of Negroponte (1427).[49] Francesco di Marco Cicogna served as the castellan of Cattaro (1466) and returned as count (1497); in between, he was *podestà* in Malvasia (1477) and Lepanto (1493) and captain in Famagusta (1483). His son, Marco di Francesco Cicogna, also served in the *stato da mar,* acting as castellan in Famagusta (1505) and *podestà* in Capodistria (1514). Antonio di Marco Zancani served as treasurer and captain of the town in Coron (1466); castellan and treasurer in Scutari (1472); rector of Sitia (1480); counselor of Crete (1494); castellan, captain, and *provveditore* of Modon (1499); and *provveditore* of Zakynthos (1521). Bernardo di Marco Barbarigo, who served as *bailo* of Corfu (1505) and as captain of Crete (1510), was known for his particular expertise in financial reform and tax administration, useful at a time when Venice was at war on the mainland and needed as much revenue as possible.[50]

Maritime Offices and Family Ties

Venetian councils awarded offices to individuals; Venetian political life, on the other hand, was a family business.[51] Venetian patrician families used maritime officeholding as a strategy to benefit from the maritime empire, combining officeholding with commercial, marital, and property interests abroad for the benefit of the family as a whole. Lane, Hocquet, and Doumerc, among others, have shown that the state's economic policies were frequently dictated by the interests of the merchant patriciate, combining a sense of public good with private interests.[52] The annual auction of the Venetian fleet was one of the most visible manifestations of the patriciate's dominance in economic and in political life. Shares in the Venetian fleet were auctioned off annually to societies of investors, and each galley then took the name of its principal investor for the year as it traveled to Beirut, Flanders, or Alexandria. The men elected as galley patrons and captains were vetted and approved by the Senate. Doumerc and Stöckly have demonstrated that there was a core of patrons and captains who invested repeatedly in the same galley routes; the Capello, Da Canal, and Bembo, among others, specialized in the routes to Cyprus, to Flanders, or to Barbary.[53] Furthermore, Doumerc and Judde de Larivière have shown that the investors and patrons of the galleys were often connected through marriage or kinship and that these ties grew stronger and the group more restrictive as the fifteenth century progressed.[54]

Historians have recently begun to look at maritime officeholding as another manifestation of the Venetian patriciate's mix of public and private interests, showing that the deliberate strategy of holding multiple offices in particular locales was a much more frequent aspect of Venetian political life than has been previously realized. Mueller's study of a branch of the Giustinian family has shown that in the 1440s some family members had a "virtual monopoly" on the castellanship in Corfu at the same time that others operated a small commercial enterprise on the island.[55] Mueller has also demonstrated the way commerce, marriage, and inheritance combined with officeholding to create a network of Giustinian connections and property that stretched throughout the Greek islands, including Negroponte, Chios, and Serifo.[56] Schmitt's work on family networks in Albania has demonstrated a similar phenomenon; he details how the Zorzi and the Contarini, among others, at times dominated the province's political offices while engaged in trade and commerce.[57]

When looking at officeholding throughout the Venetian maritime state, it is clear that this type of specialization was not exceptional—rather, it was a regular and enduring feature of Venetian political life. Certain families specialized in maritime officeholding, either in particular locales or in the maritime state as a whole. The significance of this specialization is not that certain families had a "lock" on maritime officeholding: as stated earlier, the majority of officeholders in the *stato da mar* held office there only once, meaning that most patrician houses participated at least once in the governance of the maritime state. Rather, by returning family members to the same locations repeatedly, the clan as a whole developed more permanent connections with residents of the territory. Close relatives from the Bondumier, Bollani, Calbo, Cocco, Donà, Loredan, Nani,

Sagredo, Tagliapietra, and Vallaresso all served in the same or nearby positions in the maritime state. These officeholders could draw on the collective wisdom and connections accumulated by fathers, brothers, uncles, and cousins who had previously served in the territory, allowing them to better penetrate the local networks of affiliation.

Maritime officeholding seemed to be a rite of passage in some families, with sons following the path of their fathers' maritime careers.[58] The Nani "dal Sesamo" family followed this pattern.[59] Iacopo di Giovanni Nani served as *podestà* of Dulcigno (1441) and as *podestà* of Nauplion (1455); his son Giovanni followed in his footsteps, serving as *podestà* of Nauplion (1490) and count of Cattaro (1494). Iacopo's first cousin, Francesco di Andrea Nani, was a treasurer in Candia (1453) and a rector in Rettimo (1461). Francesco's sons Michele, Girolamo, and Antonio all held positions on the island as well: Girolamo as treasurer in Candia (1485), Michele as counselor in Canea (1494) and as treasurer in Candia (1507), and Antonio as counselor in Canea (1497) and in Rettimo (1511). The phenomenon of sons following in the footsteps of their father's careers was not limited to the Nani family. Matteo di Marco Donà was rector of Canea (1421), *bailo* of Negroponte (1432), and duke of Crete (1437); his son, Bernardo, was also rector of Canea (1455) and duke of Crete (1466).[60] Pietro Cocco was rector of Rettimo (1435); he was followed shortly thereafter by his sons: Domenico was a judge on the island (1445), and Girolamo was a counselor in Canea (1446) and in Rettimo (1460). In the first half of the fifteenth century, Zanotto Calbo served on the Senate, as a ducal counselor, and as a ducal elector; he also was count of Scutari and captain of Zara (1435).[61] He had four politically active sons who held significant posts in the maritime state: Francesco, count of Budua (1445); Alvise, count of Lesina (1440) and Arbe (1455); Leonardo, count of Dulcigno (1446), *bailo* of Negroponte (1461), and count of Zara (1470); and Zaccaria, counselor of Crete (1467), rector of Canea (1473), and castellan of Coron (1479).

Some families created more extended networks in the maritime state through officeholding, with cousins and brothers overlapping in terms of service. The career paths of two branches of the Sagredo family intertwined in the fifteenth century.[62] Albano di Giovanni of the San Trinità branch of the clan held a number of maritime offices, as did his son, Alvise. (See appendix B.) Another of Albano's sons, Francesco, trailed in his father's footsteps in two locations: Albano (I) was *bailo* of Negroponte (1434) and Francesco was elected captain of the town (1444); Albano (I) was rector of Canea (1433), where Francesco was elected counselor (1447). In 1463, Francesco became gravely ill while serving as count of Lesina and was replaced by his son, Albano (II).[63] Albano (I) and Francesco both used

Lorenzo di Gerardo, from a separate branch of the Sagredo, as a guarantor (*plezius*), suggesting that the two branches remained connected by more than a shared surname. In the later part of the fifteenth and early sixteenth century, Lorenzo di Gerardo's descendants held four offices in Zara: Isidor di Gerardo as castellan of the citadel (1468); his uncle, Marco di Lorenzo, also as castellan of the citadel (1473); Isidor's brother and Marco's nephew Iacopo as castellan (1479); Pietro di Alvise, from the San Trinità branch, as count (1500); and Iacopo and Isidor's nephew Girolamo as treasurer (1508).

But were the Sagredo doing anything remarkable by holding four offices in the same place over the course of almost a half-century? In other words, were the Sagredo simply holding an average number of offices for their clan's size and importance? In order to tentatively answer this question, it is useful to view the Sagredo's Zarentine offices in the context of all the officials Venice sent to the city. From 1460 to 1510, the *Segretario alle Voci* records 158 posts filled in Zara (count, captain, treasurer, castellan, castellan of the citadel). Individuals from 67 of the 147 politically active patrician houses were elected to these 158 positions.[64] Therefore, offices in Zara were neither dominated by a restricted number of patricians nor were they spread evenly throughout the entire patriciate. Of the sixty-seven families who filled the offices, twenty-six houses sent one person, eighteen houses sent two members, nine sent three members, eight houses (including the Sagredo) sent four members, five houses sent five members, and one house, the Barbaro, sent six members.

Neither the Sagredo nor the largest and most influential Venetian houses dominated Zarentine offices; however, the number of offices the Sagredo did hold was disproportionately large, given the size and importance of the family relative to the rest of the patriciate. The Contarini, Morosini, Marcello, and Venier, families that both Sanudo and Barbaro counted as the largest and most prominent in Venice, each sent five members. (See table 2.2.) Offices were not, however, distributed strictly on the basis of family size and prominence. The Da Canal, while only half the size of the Marcello or Venier, also sent five members; the Donà, as large as the Marcello or Venier, were not represented at all. Turning to the families that sent four members to Zara during this period, it becomes clear that the Sagredo clan was significantly smaller than the other families in this group: the Bondumier, Diedo, Loredan, Michiel, Da Molin, Moro, and Trevisan all had more than twenty members, while the Sagredo only had twelve. It seems, then, that four Sagredo officeholders in Zara over fifty years was not the simple outcome of family size but instead resulted from a deliberate electoral strategy.

The pattern of certain families sending disproportional numbers of officials

TABLE 2.2
Office holding in Zara, Corfu, and Crete, 1460–1510

Cognomen	Family size, Sanudo	No. of Family nuclei in Barbaro 1450	No. of Family nuclei in Barbaro 1500	Chojnacki rank	No. of offices held in Zara	No. of offices held in Corfu	No. of offices held in Crete
Contarini	172	97	107	1	5	4	11
Morosini	102	58	53	2	5	4	3
Malipiero	81	28	38	41	3	4	6
Marcello	77	25	29	19	5	2	6
Venier	69	45	41	3	5	1	7
Donà	67	30	29	26	—	1	6
Michiel	67	31	35	12	4	1	5 (7 seats)
Loredan	52	27	28	6	4	3	3
Molin Da	50	18	32	15	4	4	8
Trevisan	50	18	23	13	4	1	4
Barbaro	38	12	18	24	6	—	3
Diedo	35	12	14	28	4	3	2
Canal, Da	34	19	31	—	5	4	5
Moro	34	13	15	—	4 (5 seats)	2	4
Bondumier	23	6	13	—	4 (5 seats)	2	4
Sagredo	12	7	5	—	4	1	—

Sources: ROV; Sanudo, *Diarii,* XLV: 569–72; Gullino, "Patriziato," 399–401; Chojnacki, "Formazione," 666 (Table 2-D).

to certain locations in the *stato da mar* also appears in the officeholding patterns in two other regional capitals, Corfu and Crete. On Corfu there were 138 offices filled between 1460 and 1510 (*bailo,* treasurer, captain, captain of the town, castellan, counselors). Seventy-three patrician houses sent members to fill these 138 offices, slightly more than half of all patrician houses. Of the seventy-three families who filled the offices, forty-three houses sent one person, thirteen houses sent two members, six sent three members, five houses sent four members, four houses sent five members, and one house, the Priuli, sent six members. On Crete during the same period, there were 332 offices filled (duke, counselors, captain, treasurer, judges, and officers of the night in Candia, rector and counselors in Rettimo, rector and counselors in Canea, rector in Sitia). Of the 104 families who filled the offices, thirty-three houses sent one person, eighteen houses sent two people, nineteen houses sent three members, twelve houses sent four members, ten houses sent five members, six houses sent six members, and six houses sent seven or more members. As in the Zarentine case, Cretan and Corfiote offices were not spread evenly through the entire patriciate, but neither were they the exclusive province of an elite few. Larger and more important families sent the most members overall, but some smaller families stood out for the disproportional number of offices they held, relative to their size and importance.

Families could specialize in a particular location or spread themselves throughout the maritime state. The Bollani developed a geographic specialty in Crete, returning to positions in the island's government repeatedly. Candiano served as a judge (1386) and his son, Matteo, returned several times to the island as well as to surrounding territories as rector of Tinos and Mykonos (1431), counselor of Crete (1438), rector of Rettimo (1443), and castellan of Coron (1447). Two of Matteo's sons also held positions on Crete, Candiano as captain (1466) and Nicolò as rector of Sitia (1443), at the same time his father was serving as rector in Rettimo.[65] A possible motive for the Bollani interest in Crete was the presence of a separate branch of the clan as noble feudatories on the island. The Boldù family also returned to Crete repeatedly: Andrea di Francesco Boldù went in 1439 as a treasurer; his brothers Castellano and Pietro followed him in 1441 to posts as a judge in Candia and a rector in Sitia, respectively; a fourth brother, Filippo, was also a rector in Sitia (1477), and a fifth brother, Nicolò, served as counselor in Candia in 1463, at the same time that his nephew, Francesco di Pietro, was in the city as an officer of the night.

The two branches of the Diedo family resident in the San Domenico and Santi Apostoli parishes in Venice offer an excellent example of the way maritime officeholding created a mesh of connections in a single family. It is certainly not coincidental that the Diedo appear prominently in the lists of galley captains as well as among the ranks of maritime officeholders.[66] Giovanni di Giacomo Diedo served as count of Drivasto (1408) and captain of the Beirut galleys (1414), and his brother, Bertuccio, was *bailo* in Trebizond (1408) and count of Scutari (1412).[67] (See appendix B.) In the next generation, Giovanni's sons Antonio and Domenico both served as galley captains in the Adriatic several times as well as holding significant maritime administrative posts, Antonio in Corfu (1434), Antivari (1443), and Crete (1448), and Domenico as rector of Rettimo (1453) and captain of Crete (1459). Three of Giovanni and Bertuccio's nephews also had maritime careers: Girolamo, castellan of Corfu (1438), castellan of Aurana (1444), counselor of Corfu (1451), counselor of Canea (1455), and count of Zara (1472); Iacopo, *podestà* of Nauplion (1462); and Marco, *bailo* of Durazzo (1445) and *provveditore* of Alessio (1461). Of this generation of cousins, Antonio, Marco, Francesco, and Simone all had sons and grandsons who continued the tradition of maritime officeholding. The Santi Apostoli branch of the family had a strong tradition of maritime officeholding as well: Bernardo di Vittore Diedo was count of Spalato (1438), and after his return, his nephew Alvise di Marco was elected count of Traù (1448) and later count of Zara (1462); and his son Nicolò served as count of Scutari (1451). Continuing the maritime connection, Nicolò married Orsa di Giovanni Mantiner from Modon, and their son, Pietro, served in Cyprus during the

Venetian takeover (1471, 1475).[68] This pattern of officeholding suggests that the family deliberately pursued maritime offices across generations.

The Diedo were a medium-sized clan, but the case of the Baffo family, much smaller and less politically prominent than the Diedo, again illustrates that the tactic of specialization was not strictly related to the size of the family. Andrea di Donado Baffo served as counselor in Crete (1445); his son Donado was counselor in Canea (1471); in 1487–88 his son Antonio was castellan in Famagusta while Donado was *podestà* in Antivari. In 1494, Antonio went to Crete as counselor; the following year, his brother Donado returned to Albania as *bailo* of Durazzo (1495). Another branch of the Baffo family also sent a number of members to maritime offices and contracted marriages with residents of the maritime state. Alvise di Lorenzo Baffo was *podestà* in Nauplion (1443) and castellan in Coron (1444); his son Maffeo began his maritime career as counselor in Canea (1452) and went on to serve in Coron (1473), Lepanto (1480), and Zara (1489). During Alvise's stint in Nauplion and Coron, his son Renuzzio married a woman from Modon (1443) and was later counselor in Nauplion (1450), and Alvise's daughter married Bartolomeo di Fergio Contarini from Coron in 1449.[69] These multiple and overlapping terms of service in the maritime state created expertise in maritime administration not only for individuals but families. These recurring connections also offered the opportunity to forge more permanent ties with residents of the *stato da mar* and with local elites.

Individual and family specialization in maritime offices brought benefits both to the Venetian state and to the individuals and families involved. The Venetian state was able to rely on officeholders' local expertise, administrative skills, and institutional knowledge of the territories where they served. Individuals and families, by returning repeatedly to the same territories, were able to build up networks of association and connection as well as local knowledge. In many cases, these officials expanded their institutional and administrative knowledge with personal, extra-institutional connections formed through marriage with local elites, property ownership, and commercial relationships. These individual associations were a double-edged sword for Venice's administration of its empire. They increased Venice's imperial reach while at the same time conflicting with the Venetian ideal of a nonpartisan and impartial territorial governor. Tension over individuals' and families' connections to places in the maritime state persisted within its growing administrative apparatus in the fifteenth century. These pressures played out in ritual and public space as well as through development of marital and property-owning connections, the subject of the next chapter.

THREE

Public Office and Patrician Family Strategies

Venice's vision of imperial governance very much resembled a large collection of city-states, each governed in Venice's name by a disinterested and temporary *podestà*. The state attempted to legislate distance between officials and subjects: all Venetian officials were forbidden to engage in commerce while in office, and commissions regularly included rules against eating with locals, except during a wedding; accepting gifts from locals; and—especially in the Cretan case—against marrying while in office.[1] All of these proscriptions were intended to ensure that the rector's role as a representative of the Venetian state was not complicated by his personal interests. This approach, however, was ill suited to Venice's sprawling maritime state, where the Venetian official was likely to be separated from those he ruled by language or religion, factors which complicated his already difficult task. Furthermore, the Venetian state in this period simply was not able to enforce many of the rules it promulgated, and there remained a constant tension between the state's attempts to make officeholding an impersonal public service and the exigencies of rule, which demanded that rectors make compromises and come into close contact with subjects. In order both to rule effectively and to benefit personally from officeholding, many rectors constructed networks of marital, commercial, and familial connections with the cities and subjects of the maritime state.

Each official received a commission detailing his responsibilities and regulating his conduct on taking office. In all of these documents, the official was ordered to "protect our honor," a combination that in theory struck a balance between communal statutes and Venetian flexibility, allowing the rector to take a wide range of actions as long as they did not harm the Venetian republic. Rectors were intended to represent Venetian strength, serenity, and justice while at the same time not angering those over whom they ruled. Several prominent politicians delivered orations at the beginning of the fifteenth century that articulated these expectations. Zaccaria Trevisan, a prominent early humanist as well as an experienced rector, delivered an oration to an audience of Padova citizens at the end of his term as captain of the city in March 1407. The address, directed to his successor Pietro Arimondo, praised Arimondo's typical virtues of humanity, clemency, and fortitude but added that in his previous government positions, Arimondo "had not induced scornful contempt, jealousy, or avarice in the people that you led, but were useful to many."[2] In his *Oration* to the politician and humanist Lodovico Foscarini, who held positions in Ravenna, Feltre, Friuli, Modon, Verona, and Padova, Benedetto Bursa praised Foscarini's learning, prudence, and judgment as to what would be acceptable to the citizens. Bursa states, "Your orders, though they were not incorporated among the city's written laws, yet so pleased the citizens, so they did take root in their souls, that even without official promulgation they shall endure forever in the mouths of men."[3] These versions of the ideal rector focused on results rather than an abstract ideal, on citizens' contentment or acquiescence rather than their moral improvement. The mark of a truly successful governor was his ability not to anger or upset the subjects he ruled—not to cause hatred, jealousy, or greed that would upset the peace of the Venetian state.

This ideal was extremely difficult to put into practice. Rectors were often hampered by scant local knowledge and a lack of money and troops, making it difficult to rule effectively.[4] Terms of office lasted no more than two years, certainly not enough time to appreciate the complexities of the local situation and to determine how the local populace was likely to react to decisions. In addition, many rectors were dependent on the local treasury for part or all of their salary, giving the locality some financial control over governors' actions.[5] Furthermore, rectors were hemmed in by a set of centralizing regulations and appellate practices that ensured that theirs was never the last word. Rectors were regularly forbidden from revoking or revising a judicial sentence of their own or of their predecessors; instead, subjects unhappy with a decision could appeal to Venice.[6] Rectors' commissions forbade them from using the power of their office to grant special favors, or *grazie,* to raise local officials' salaries or to give away state funds or property without permission from Venetian councils.[7] Venetian policy walked a fine line between reserving power to itself, protecting its representatives' prerogatives, and keeping its subjects contented; individual Venetian rectors were charged with determining the location of that line.

The multiplicity of pressures and interests brought to bear on officials in the Venetian maritime state was not unusual. Chittolini has described the difficult and often contradictory position in which governors found themselves in the Sforza domains, required on the one hand to assure that the duke's authority was respected and on the other hand to ensure that local autonomies and power structures were not disturbed.[8] Chambers and Dean point out that in Mantua, "for most practical purposes (arresting criminals and bandits, halting smuggling) officials needed the collaboration of the locality, while remaining dependent also on the locality for their salary. Without collaboration, an official could not penetrate the 'thick, solid network of solidarity and connivance that united the members of a community.'"[9] Chittolini, Chambers, and Dean all argue that overzealous, inflexible, or overly cautious officials disrupted the carefully balanced order of the state, while truly effective officials respected and worked through local power structures, connecting themselves to local elites through marriages or godparent relations, and creating positive evaluations of their rule through banquets and carefully timed acts of justice.[10] The particularity of Venetian politics was its deeply collective nature; although Venetian territorial governors faced similar pressures as those in the Mantuan and Milanese countryside, the Venetian state resisted officials' attempts to act on their individual interests or to form associations and connections with local subjects.

Ritual and Public Space

One area of tension between individual and public conceptions of officeholding was in the realm of ritual and public space. Officially, the Venetian state was careful to subordinate the person of the rector as well as its subjects to symbolic representations of the collective republic or the distant Venetian doge. Trevisan's 1407 oration and admonitions to his successor mentioned earlier took place at one of the key ritual moments that showcased the individual rector as a representative of the Venetian state—the entry of one rector and exit of another. After 1425, the Venetian Senate strictly prohibited the practice of ingoing and outgoing rectors meeting at the gate of the city and making speeches, as Trevisan and Arimondo had.[11] In 1458, the *Dieci* reiterated the prohibition, saying rectors should neither speak themselves nor allow subjects to assemble and to offer speeches praising incoming or outgoing officials.[12] Clearly, the Senate preferred that silent Venetian splendor take the place of individual articulations of ruling principles: the outgoing rector was only to say, "I consign to you this regimen," and the incumbent was only to say, "I accept." This impersonal exchange of formulaic expressions was to take place as part of a ceremonial reenactment of the subject city's submission to Venetian rule.[13]

While the new governor was to embody Venetian rule in these rituals, he was to do so strictly as a representative of the Venetian doge and republic. In 1420, the captain-general of the Venetian fleet and naval hero Pietro Loredan accepted Cattaro's submission to Venetian rule, a moment subsequently inscribed in the Cattaran statutes.[14] Loredan led a procession that wound through the city streets and finished before the cathedral of St. Triphon, raising the standard of San Marco in the town's piazza and in the city's castle. Loredan, together with the main body of the Cattaran citizens, then celebrated a solemn mass in the cathedral over the relics of St. Triphon, at which a number of Cattaran nobles swore an oath of loyalty to the Venetian doge and his successors, "which the magnificent Lord Captain accepted in the name of the Illustrious Doge." The mass praised the Venetian state and Venetian doge as well as Loredan himself, sanctifying Cattaro's submission and symbolically involving the city's saints in the professions of loyalty that bound Cattaro to Venice. The ceremony thus gave the Venetian official a central place while also reminding all involved that the official's primary role was as a representative of the Venetian doge and of Venice itself.

Venice tried to define the public spaces where these processions were held with collective symbols, not with individual monuments. Georgopoulou and Calabi have described the "Venetianization" of town centers in the *stato da mar:* Venetian authorities recreated churches and piazzas dedicated to San Marco, remaking the central public spaces in the image of Venice as a strategy of dominance and providing visual evidence of a city's membership in the wider Venetian state.[15] The lion of San Marco, not a portrait of any individual Venetian ruler, flew on the standard raised over the city and was emblazoned on fortifications, public buildings, and at the principal city gates.[16] A Venetian official's residence while in office was part of this public space. The governor's residence was typically located at the center of the town, almost always near the city's *loggia,* where much of the community's political and judicial business was transacted; if there were subordinate officials, they lived separately, often in the town's castle or fortifications.[17] A number of public functions and magistracies were based in the rector's palace; in Candia, Zara, Traù, and Curzola, for instance, local councils met in the rector's palace, and often the judicial magistracies were housed in or near the governor's residence as well, enclosing both governor and governed within Venetian space.[18]

Since the governor's residence was primarily a public space, Venetian councils tried to ensure that the building did not become a monument to any individual rector's presence or initiative. These palaces and residences were publicly owned and closely controlled, and rectors were not authorized to build or repair their palaces without permission from the Senate.[19] Many commissions contain the specific provision that the rector should not decorate any public buildings with his own coat of arms, or that he should do so only in paint, not in stone.[20] Presumably, this legislation was intended to ensure that the lions of San Marco had no competitors, but it was markedly ineffective. Even today many palaces, *loggie,* and fortifications boast prominent coats of arms, inscriptions, and plaques celebrating the rectors who lived in them or oversaw their construction; sixteenth-century fortifications regularly had inscriptions and coats of arms commemorating the Venetian officials who oversaw their construction.[21] In one example out of many, the Calbo family twice commemorated its presence in Sebenico by placing its coat of arms above the city gate, marking first Antonio Calbo's rule (1486–1489) and, a century later, Giovanni Calbo's term as count of Sebenico.[22] On Corfu, the state inquisitors ordered the removal of all statutes and inscriptions to Venetian officials, but to no avail.[23]

Both rituals and the built environment placed the Venetian rector at the center of an ideological complex designed to glorify Venice and the Venetian state; the difficult and delicate role the rector was meant to play was to accomplish this without glorifying himself personally. The Senate resisted public orations and coats of arms as elements that publicly transformed the rector from an impersonal representative of the Venetian state to an individual, with individual and familial interests. To further separate Venetian rectors from personal ties, the Senate tried to ban family members from accompanying territorial officials, although this proscription, like many others, proved extremely hard to enforce. In the thirteenth and fourteenth centuries, the commissions of the governors of Crete specified that the officials were not to bring their wives or children; there was a failed attempt to revoke this legislation in 1318, but the frequency of exceptions to the rule demonstrate that the prohibition was only enforced in theory, not in practice.[24]

By the fifteenth century, the Senate contented itself with asserting that rectors were responsible for the misdeeds of their family members, that the children as well as the parents were not to participate in commerce, and that the rector was not to award local offices to his relatives.[25] The ban on wearing mourning clothes for relatives while in office persisted through the sixteenth century, suggesting that, while the Venetian state had not been able to ban the physical presence of relatives, it still insisted on limiting their ritual presence.[26] Venetian councils also legislated that near relatives could not hold positions in the same regime at the same time, nor could close agnates vote for one another, although the former stipulation was not always respected.[27] Finally, commissions regulated the amount a governor could spend on public festivals and charitable giving on Christmas and Easter, limiting his ability to create a personal reputation for generosity or to waste the state's resources.

Marriage, Kinship, and Property

Venetian officials abroad regularly contravened both the letter and the spirit of the clauses in their commissions requiring them to act as disinterested supervisors of local affairs. Rectors decorated public spaces with their family heraldry, brought their families, sponsored processions, and gave orations on their entry to and exit from office. While Venetian policy continued to legislate against the conflation of public office and private interests, in practice many officeholders had individual or family ties to the territory or to the local elites, particularly Latin Christian elites. Recent scholarship has identified a mesh of interests, particularly property holding, that tied the Venetian patriciate to its *terraferma* domains, but, with the exception of Schmitt's studies on Albania and Mueller's work on Corfu and the Giustinian family, there has been very little work on similar connections between the Venetian patriciate and the maritime domains.[28] Initial findings suggest that the Venetian patriciate, and in particular Venetian officeholders, did have an array of kinship and economic ties to the maritime domains. This mix of public and private could be detrimental to Venetian administration as a whole, as seen in the prosecutions for corruption discussed in chapter 6, but they could also stabilize a regime, providing informal contacts and solutions to the difficulties of rule.

No matter whether a family sent two or twenty members to administrative posts in the maritime state, the connection made through officeholding was by necessity temporary. One of the primary strategies for transforming this short-term link into a more permanent bond was marriage, and some patrician families did use their members' terms of service abroad as opportunities to establish lasting links with local elites.[29] Marriages between Venetian patrician and elite families in subject territories offered benefits to both sides. Non-Venetians were not subject to the same dowry restrictions as applied to Venetian citizens; therefore, these marriages were often extremely lucrative for the Venetian families involved.[30] Brides from subject populations brought cash and landed estates as dowries to their Venetian husbands as well as connections into local society. For the elites who married sons or daughters into the Venetian patriciate, the marriage could serve as a gateway to the benefits and privileges distributed by the Venetian state, since "marriage into the nobility opened both direct and indirect avenues to the centers of power in Venetian society."[31]

One marriage demonstrating this mesh of family alliances and foreign policy is that of Zorzi Cernovich (Crnojević) of Montenegro and Isabetta Erizzo, most recently recounted by Wright.[32] Cernovich ruled northern Albania from 1490 to

1496, when he was expelled by the Ottomans and fled to Venice. By the time of his marriage to Isabetta Erizzo, in 1490, both her father and brother had spent time in the region as Venetian officeholders. Isabetta's father, Antonio, had a maritime career that included a stint as *provveditore* at Dagno (1464–1467), next to the Cernovich lands, and Isabetta's brother Paolo was count of nearby Cattaro (1489–1491) when the marriage took place.[33] The marriage between a Venetian patrician daughter and Balkan lord not only united two families, it also allied the Venetian state with the ruler of a threatened frontier, benefiting state interests as well as family strategies.

It is difficult to place cases like the Cernovich-Erizzo union into a broader framework, because there are very few sources that offer a perspective on the overall incidence of Venetian marriage to subjects within the empire. Two sources that allow an initial survey of the phenomenon are Marc'Antonio Barbaro's *Libro de Nozze Patrizie* and the *Avogaria di Comun*'s *Cronaca Matrimoni.*[34] While Barbaro's *Nozze* registers, like his *Arbori* of patrician genealogies, do not offer reliable data for the thirteenth or first part of the fourteenth century, his work becomes much more exact for later centuries, offering a useful entry point into patrician marriage patterns of the fifteenth century. Both Barbaro's *Nozze* and the *Avogaria di Comun*'s records, compiled as part of the Venetian state's new attention to descent in the fifteenth century, do have a distinct bias toward recording the marriages of Venetian patrician sons, not daughters, because the children of women who married outside the Venetian patriciate were not eligible for entry into the Great Council. The *Nozze* and the *Cronaca* registers therefore include the names of Venetian patrician daughters and non-Venetians only irregularly, but their focus on male patricians permits a preliminary assessment of the extent to which Venetian patricians married individuals from within the maritime empire.

Between 1390 and 1540, these two sources recorded over five hundred marriages between Venetian patricians in which at least one partner was identified as a resident of the maritime state. Well over half of these marriages were between Venetians and the Veneto-Cretan patriciate—cases in which both partners had Venetian surnames and one or both of the marriage partners were identified as "da Candia." Venetian patricians identified as being from Arbe, Corfu, Coron, Cyprus, Durazzo, Modon, Negroponte, Sebenico, Zante, and Zara also married other Venetian patricians. Removing these interpatriciate marriages from the sample leaves over two hundred cases in which the *Nozze* and the *Cronaca* record Venetian patrician marriages with subjects of the maritime state who were not among the Venetian patriciate. As with the phenomenon of repeat officeholding, the significance of these marriages lies not with their numerical weight but with their effect on Venice's imperial administration. By opening avenues into local society for Venetian patricians and into Venetian society for local elites, these marriages created lasting bonds between center and periphery that helped to stabilize Venetian rule abroad.[35]

In Dalmatia, members of the Arimondo, Badoer, Balbi, Baseggio, Bon, Caravello, Condulmier, Contarini, Da Canal, Da Mosto, Da Molin, Da Ponte, Dandolo, Diedo, Erizzo, Ferro, Foscari, Garzoni, Gradenico, Lambardo, Marcello, Michiel, Morosini, Pasqualigo, Tagliapietra, Tiepolo, and Venier families married individuals from Dalmatian towns. Out of the fifty-three marriages recorded in the sample, fourteen were with Zarentines, twelve with Sebenicans, seven each with residents of Spalato and Arbe, three with residents of Lesina, and between one and two with residents of Brazza, Cherso, Nona, and Traù. In Zara, the Venetians overwhelmingly married into the pro-Venetian segment of the Zarentine nobility, making alliances with members of the Matafari, Begna, Grisogono, and Sopa families.

The marriage alliances between the Venier clan and the Begna and Matafari of Zara led to exchanges of property and influence as well as the creation of familial ties. In 1419, Nicolò Venier's son, Tommaso, the grandson of Doge Antonio Venier, married Chiara Matafari of Zara, daughter of the Zarentine noble Guido Matafari; her dowry included two villages surrounding the castles of Zemonico and Novegrad.[36] The Venier-Matafari marriage was most probably agreed upon during the groom's father, Nicolò di Antonio Venier's, term of office as captain of Zara (1416–1418). The Matafari were among the wealthiest and most influential patricians in Zara: between 1382 and 1409, seven Matafari served as the city's count and two—Nicolò and Pietro—held the archiepiscopal seat.[37] In 1397, Sigismund of Hungary had confiscated the brothers Guido, Lodovico, and Pietro Matafari's property and exiled them from the city; Pietro died in exile, but Guido and Lodovico returned as partisans of Ladislas of Naples in 1403 and received title to Curzola, Lesina, and Brazza in return for their loyalty.[38] When Venice took control of Zara, Guido Matafari was among the city's representatives to Venice, and in 1410 the Senate confirmed his ownership of Novegrad in fief.[39] Guido also acted as the republic's representative to the Bosnian noble Sandalj in negotiations over the castle of Ostrovicia.[40] Another Venier from a distant branch of the family, Francesco di Santo, married the daughter of the richest man in Zara, Simone Begna, in 1435.[41] The Venier thus received property and political influence on a local level, while the Matafari and Begna received access to Venetian society through their patrician in-laws, received favors and privileges from the Venetian state, and saw children and grandchildren enter the Venetian patriciate.[42]

The Arimondo clan, much smaller than the Venier, also combined officeholding and marriage to establish a network of formal and informal affiliations with subject territories. Pietro di Giacomo Arimondo, the incoming captain of Padova so fulsomely praised by Zaccaria Trevisan in 1407, went on to serve as captain of Zara (1409) at the moment of its entry into the Venetian empire.[43] When he arrived, he had a connection to the Zarentine noble family of the Grisogono through marriage. Like the Matafari, the Grisogono had been exiled from Zara during Sigismund of Hungary's ascendancy.[44] While out of Zara, the Grisogono in 1400 arranged a match between Prospera, daughter of Zuanne Grisogono of Zara, and Nicolò di Lorenzo Arimondo, a distant cousin of Pietro di Giacomo's. (See appendix B.)

The affective tie between Arimondo cousins was continually reaffirmed in the next generation: Nicolò and Prospera had three sons who were registered in Venice's *Balla d'Oro,* and Pietro di Fantino's son, Ambrogio, stood as surety for Nicolò and Prospera's son Cristoforo when he was presented to the *Balla d'Oro* in 1437.[45] Nicolò's cousin, Prosdecimo di Donato Arimondo, served as surety for Nicolò and Prospera's son Girolamo in the *Balla d'Oro,* and Prosdecimo's brother Marino served as surety for Nicolò and Prospera's son Giorgio. The connection between the Arimondo family and Dalmatia continued throughout the century, with members of the Arimondo family holding offices in Traù, Cherso and Ossero, Sebenico, Arbe, and Spalato.[46] Nicolò Arimondo himself served as count of Pago (1423), and his son Cristoforo served as castellan of Aurana (1447).[47] Both the Grisogono and the Arimondo benefited from the connection—the grandchildren of the Grisogono entered the Venetian Great Council, providing a conduit of influence for their maternal relations, and the Arimondo obtained an entrée into Zarentine society, one the family took advantage of in later years with its officeholding.

The Arimondo clan's involvement in the maritime state was not limited to Dalmatia. Nicolò's two uncles, Pietro and Donato di Fantino Arimondo, both held positions in the Adriatic in the first decades of the fifteenth century. Pietro di Fantino was *bailo* of Durazzo (1407) and Donato di Fantino was count of Scutari (1409), ambassador to Albania (1412), rector of Canea (1415), *bailo* of Corfu (1419), and *bailo* of Negroponte (1424). Either during or after his term of office in Corfu, Donato acquired property on the island; one of Donato's sons, Antonio, was a member of the Great Council of Corfu and in 1443 was elected as one of the council's ambassadors to the Venetian Senate.[48] In 1449, Antonio's heirs Fantino, Donato, and Francesco sold the property to Giorgio Tomasin of Corfu.[49] Donato di Antonio also married into one of the island's leading baronial families, the San Ippolito.[50] Here, officeholding was followed by both property ownership and marriage, creating a long-term Arimondo presence on Corfu.

Donato Arimondo was one of a number of Venetian patrician families that married Corfiotes: members of the Baffo, Baseggio, Bollani, Bondumier, Capello, Da Canal, Contarini, Coppo, Da Ponte, Da Renier, Da Molin, Donà, Erizzo, Gritti, Loredan, Malipiero, Michiel, Morosini, Orio, Pasqualigo, Pizzamano, Querini, Salamon, Tiepolo, Trevisan, Viaro, Zancani, and Zorzi made similar alliances. As was the case in Zara, these marriages were overwhelmingly with members of the Corfiote Latin elite like the San Ippolito: Venetians married into the Altavilla, Avrami, De Gothis, De Luxera, Midei, Morello, Roditi, Padovan, Petretin, and Tomasin families. The Angevin period on the island had left Corfu's elite divided between Greek and Latin, and the distinction persisted into the Venetian era, with the council regularly electing both Greek and Latin judges and syndics.[51] The Altavilla, De Gothis, Petretin, and San Ippolito families, all among the island's Latin elite, each contracted numerous marriages with the Venetian patriciate during the fifteenth century. Several of these marriages between Venetian and Corfiote elites can be correlated with Venetian patricians' terms of office on Corfu. Vito di Pietro Salamon was Captain of Corfu (1490) and his son Pietro married the daughter of Antonio Rodatti of Corfu (1518).[52] Pellegrino di Pietro da Canal was a counselor in Corfu (1512); while there, he married a daughter of Manoli Avrami da Corfu, and the Da Canal appear in Corfiote councils from 1524.[53]

The *Assises of Romanie*, the legal code in force on the island, allowed female succession to the island's fiefs, which meant that the marriages between Venetian patrician men and Corfiote heiresses resulted in a significant number of Corfiote properties passing into Venetian hands.[54] The phenomenon was so pronounced that the Corfiote historian Antonio Marmora claimed that "the majority of the fiefs in Corfu passed to Venetian lords, who inherited them through the dowries of their wives or only daughters of families that became extinct."[55] Six of the fourteen holders of the island's twenty-four baronies in 1515 were Venetian, and all of these six were either sons or husbands of Corfiote women: Andrea Bragadin, Michele Tron, Pietro Malipiero, Girolamo Malipiero, Giovanni Battista Erizzo, and Fantin Viaro. Corfiote council membership lists from the fifteenth and early sixteenth century also demonstrate that a number of individuals with Venetian patrician surnames had won a place in Corfiote political society.[56]

The history of the De Gothis family shows the way officeholding, marriage, and property ownership could combine to Venetian benefit. The De Gothis family married three daughters to Venetian patricians during the first century of Venetian rule. In 1434, Altadonna di Guglielmo de Gothis married Pietro di Marino Pasqualigo; when he died, she remarried into another Venetian patrician family, the Da Renier.[57] Altadonna had a brother, Arsenio, but within a generation this property had left De Gothis hands as well, when Arsenio's daughter, Fiordelisse, married Giorgio di Luca Viaro, castellan of Corfu (1472), during his term of office, and the property passed to the couple's youngest son Fantin Viaro.[58] Another De Gothis, Diana di Cola, married Stefano Capello in 1424.[59] The couple had a daughter, Ludovica, who also married a Venetian patrician, Girolamo Bragadin, assuring that her portion of the property remained in Venetian hands. A third De Gothis woman, a daughter of Nicolò, married Antonio Malipiero in 1466, joining the De Gothis property she brought with her to the existing Malipiero holdings on the island.[60] Antonio Malipiero's brother Vido had married a Corfiote woman in 1442 and was listed as a Corfiote baron in 1453 and in 1476.[61] In the next generation, both Vido and Antonio had sons who remained connected to the island—Vido's son Arsenio in 1482 married the daughter of Nicolò Moro of Corfu, and Antonio's son Girolamo inherited the barony.[62]

The De Gothis and Capello family fortunes were also intertwined in this period. The Santa Maria Mater Domini branch of the Capello family's involvement in Corfiote society during the Venetian period can be traced to Giovanni Capello's term as *bailo* of Corfu (1410), which presaged the three generations of the family's involvement in Corfiote society that formed the background for Stefano's marriage to Diana de Gothis. (See appendix B.) Giovanni's son Stefano "da Corfu," most likely settled on Corfu at least semipermanently. Both Stefano's son, Marino, and his nephew, Stefano di Marino, married daughters of Corfiote barons: as mentioned above, Stefano married Diana de Gothis, and Marino married Maria from the San Ippolito family.[63] Marino and Maria's son Giovanni's marriages clearly reflect a deliberate strategy to consolidate Venetian property on Corfu. In 1469, Giovanni married his cousin Stefana di Nicolò Capello, also from Corfu. After her death, Giovanni married the daughter of Valerio da Mosto, and then turned to the Malipiero of Corfu for his third wife, marrying the baron Vito Malipiero's daughter in 1477. Together, these marriages bound the Capello, Malipiero, and De Gothis into a dense network of marital and property connections on Corfu.

The marriages of the Corfiote San Ippolito family, which like the De Gothis dated to the Angevin period, show how the Venetian state could benefit from the marital connections of its members. The San Ippolito family, one of the most important on the island, married four daughters into the Venetian patriciate over the first century of Venetian rule, allying with the Zancani in 1424, the Capello in 1433, the Arimondo in 1451, and the Loredan in 1455; they also contracted a marriage with a Loredan daughter in 1457.[64] These alliances with the Loredan came in the wake of Giovanni di Daniele Loredan's term as *bailo* of Corfu (1447–1449), and the Loredan–San Ippolito marriages constituted a double bond between the families, as Giovanni's son Francesco married Marsilio San Ippolito's daughter and Giovanni's daughter married Adam San Ippolito. Adam San Ippolito was not only among the island's largest landowners, he had commanded a Venetian company of harquebusiers in Patras in 1418 and was praised for his defense of Corfu during Genoese attacks in 1432.[65] In 1449, the Venetian Senate sent him to negotiate with the captain of Santa Maura for the island's surrender: the mission was not successful, but the Senate praised his action. Precisely at the time that Marsilio and Adam San Ippolito were contracting their alliances with the Loredan, the Venetian Senate ordered the *bailo* of Corfu to use the influence of Adam San Ippolito to assist in driving the Aragonese forces away from the Albanian coast.[66] The Venetian state thus benefited because San Ippolito was enmeshed in a web of marital relations that aligned his family interests with Venetian ones.

As on Corfu, the Cypriot elite was a mix of Latin and Greek individuals, a situation created by the Crusades and inherited by Venice.[67] On Cyprus, members of the Badoer, Barbarigo, Balbi, Belegno, Bembo, Bragadin, Calbo, Condulmier, Corner, Da Molin, Da Mosto, Da Pesaro, Donà, Duodo, Marcello, Morosini, Orio, Pasqualigo, and Querini married Cypriots. Arbel has shown the intersection between officeholding, marriage, and property ownership that bound certain elements of the Greek nobility to the Venetian regime on Cyprus.[68] The Da Pesaro family, for instance, held a number of offices in the early years of the Venetian regime on the island as well as forming multiple marriage ties with the Cypriot Synglitico family. Andrea di Bartolommeo da Pesaro was a counselor (1516) and in 1520 his son, Bartolommeo, married Apolonia Synglitico; Girolamo di Luca da Pesaro was lieutenant (1491) and in 1502 his son, Andrea, married one of Apolonia's cousins; in 1522 a second of Apolonia's cousins married Bartolommeo di Luca da Pesaro, who had been counselor (1497). Another of Cyprus's first administrators, Cosma di Paolo Pasqualigo, captain (1493) and lieutenant (1500) married his son, Agostino, to a Cypriot woman, and Cosma di Agostino married a daughter of the Cypriot noble Zacco Constefano in 1541.[69] These marriages brought the Cypriot families access to local offices and benefits on Cyprus as well as offering access to Venetian society and economy. The alliances offered economic and administrative benefits to the Venetian patriciate as well, in the form of landed property and commercial opportunities.

Marriage, Property, and Patrician Legitimacy on Crete

The same pattern of officeholding, intermarriage, and property ownership can be seen on Crete but was complicated by the existence of the Veneto-Cretan nobility on the island. Families might send some members to administrative posts while other members engaged in commerce in the same territory, as Schmitt documents for Albania, but as he points out, these moments did not result in the formation of a Veneto-Albanian elite analogous to the Veneto-Cretan nobility.[70] Furthermore, the Venetian state's increasingly restrictive policies on membership in the patriciate at the beginning of the fifteenth century were casting doubt on many Veneto-Cretans' claims to patrician status. In the thirteenth century, when many of the original colonists went to Crete, the Venetian patriciate had not yet undergone its closing, or *Serrata*, but by the fifteenth century, there was growing pressure on the Veneto-Cretans to document and prove their claims to patrician status. In this context, the marriages between Veneto-Cretan patricians and officials from Venice were exchanges not only of property and influence but of connections and legitimacy. These Veneto-Cretans regularly married into Venetian families as a strategy allowing them to keep one foot firmly in Venice and the other in Crete. The situation on Crete was further complicated by the Venetian state's desire to police ethnic and religious boundaries between Latin and Greek on the island. There were policies discouraging or forbidding marriage between Greek and Latin, but like many of Venice's regulations they were markedly ineffective, and there was significant intermarriage and mixing between the island's Greek and Latin populations despite the prohibition.[71] Among the island's Greek-Cretan elite, the Calergi family, and to a lesser degree the Ialina family, stand out for the number of marriages contracted with Latins.

In many cases, the rectors sent from Venice created the initial connection between the Veneto-Cretan and Venetian patriciates, and marriages intertwined with terms of office. Francesco Cocco was rector of Rettimo (1397) and a counselor in Candia (1422); his son, Nicolò, married Zanetina Vizzamano, from the Cretan branch of the Vizzamano family, in 1433. Nicolò then went on to hold positions as rector of Canea (1467) and captain of Crete (1472), two of his sons married women from Cretan families, and Giacomo was a counselor of Canea (1472) at the same time his father was captain.[72] In another example, Nicolò di Pantaleone Ghezzo was rector of Sitia (1450) at the same time his brother, Antonio, served as an officer of the night (1449) and then as a judge (1453) in Candia and as castellan of Cerigo (1454). Their sister, Maria, married the Veneto-Cretan feudatory Pietro Zorzi. When it came time to register Maria and Pietro's son, Gratiano Zorzi, in the *Balla d'Oro* in Venice, it was his maternal grandfather Pantaleone who presented him, and his maternal uncle Nicolò who testified on his behalf.[73] Marriage ties and officeholding on Crete worked together to build lineage and patronage bonds, providing residents of Crete with an entry into Venetian political society and offering officeholders from Venice connections on which they could draw when governing the island.

As the above examples suggest, registrations in the *Balla d'Oro*, or *barbarella*, an annual lottery allowing young patricians to enter the Great Council before the age of twenty-five, were an important part of affirming these connections. Candidates in the *Balla d'Oro* needed sponsors to testify to their legitimacy and to their nobility, and blood and marital kinship relationships were asserted at this pivotal moment in a young patrician's political life.[74] Not only fathers, but mothers, paternal and maternal uncles, in-laws, and cousins took their places as guarantors or as sponsors, giving the young man a place in the dense network of interrelations that lay between Venetian patrician families. When the *Balla d'Oro* candidate was from a family resident abroad, entrants often turned to their Venetian cousins to present them to the *Balla d'Oro* and to smooth their way into Venetian political life. For instance, Marco Polani, rector of Canea (1437), presented his relative Zuanne Polani, resident of Canea, to the *Balla d'Oro* in 1436.[75] The practice was particularly common among Veneto-Cretan nobles, and when examined together with Veneto-Cretan marriage practices, it reveals a strong web of connections between different branches of the same family, connections formed and reinforced through officeholding as well as marriage.

The Tron family's network of marital and property relationships in Corfu and in Crete intersected and overlapped with the political involvement of its members during the course of the fifteenth century, involving the Tron in multiple aspects of the Venetian system that tied colonial elites to the center. In Venice, two separate branches of the Tron distinguished themselves in maritime officeholding and in politics in general in the late fourteenth and early fifteenth century: Donato di Marco Tron served as duke of Crete (1383) and *bailo* of Negroponte (1386) as well as holding a number of important ambassadorships. Donato's sons and grandsons also held multiple maritime offices. Among his grandsons was the future doge Nicolò Tron (1471–1473), who made a fortune as a merchant based in Rhodes before entering political life.[76] Michele di Nicolò Tron, a distant cousin of the future doge, returned to the maritime state multiple times, serving as counselor on Crete (1452), count of Scutari (1460), and *bailo* in Corfu (1465). During his term of office on Corfu, his son, Ettore, married into the Corfiote baronial family of the De Luxera (1465); Ettore's son Michele inherited the barony and the family was involved in Corfiote political life through the sixteenth century.[77] Ettore's brother Benedetto was a counselor on Corfu (1475), while his brothers Priamo and Andrea each served on Crete, Priamo as duke (1498) and Andrea as rector of Rettimo (1480) and of Canea (1493). As indicated by Nicolò's 1471 accession to the ducal seat, the Venetian Tron held a wide range of important offices within the city of Venice itself, counting among their number *avogadori di comun,* senators, *capisestieri,* ducal counselors and electors, and three procurators of San Marco.

Sometime during the fourteenth century, a branch of the Tron family established itself on Crete, purchasing at least one fief on the island.[78] The Cretan branch of the Tron had occasion to be grateful for the political prominence of their Venetian cousins during the early fifteenth century as the legislation of the *Second Serrata* placed increasing pressure on colonial elites to prove their claims to Venetian nobility.[79] The Veneto-Cretans of Crete who wished to document their membership in the Venetian patriciate had traditionally pointed to their descent from the original Venetian settlers of the island in the thirteenth century. By the early fifteenth century, the legal requirements for membership in the Venetian patriciate became more stringently focused on patrilineal descent, meaning that many of the Veneto-Cretans who claimed patrician status were in danger of being excluded from the patriciate because their fathers and grandfathers had not been documented as members of the Great Council in Venice. Beginning in the 1360s and increasing through the 1420s, 1430s, and 1440s, over one hundred Veneto-Cretans petitioned the *avogadori di comun* for recognition and documentation of their patrician status.[80] When the Veneto-Cretan registrants in the *Balla d'Oro* lottery are considered as part of this movement, the phenomenon of Veneto-Cretans seeking to document their membership in the Venetian patriciate becomes even more pronounced.

The Tron of Candia seemed ready to find themselves on the losing end of this process, as events suggested they lacked the documentation needed to convince the *Avogaria* of their ancestors' presence in the Venetian patriciate.[81] Donato di Bartolomeo Tron of Candia was almost excluded from the patriciate in 1402 because the *avogadori* claimed he had not proved that his grandfather Nicolò of Candia had been a member of Venice's Great Council; it took three very close votes in the *Dieci* before he squeaked into the patriciate.[82] Donato's son Michele of Crete also had a difficult time proving his membership in the patriciate in

1431.[83] In 1397, Donato's cousin Michelotto di Pasquale had unanimously been accepted as a legitimate patrician. While the two men shared a grandfather, Michelotto's brother, Nicolò, in 1398 married Fantina di Antonio Orio, and Nicolò and Fantina reaffirmed their family's connection to Venice over the next decades, marrying a son and two daughters into patrician families in Venice.[84] Their son, Michele, was introduced to the *Balla d'Oro* in 1422 by Leonardo Caravello, who was later duke of Crete (1429).[85] In the same year, the *Collegio* found a judicial sentence against Michele Tron of Candia to be "against compassion and fairness" and overturned it.[86] When it was time for residents of Candia Michele and Nicolò Tron and their cousin Apachele to enter the *Balla d'Oro,* all three turned to connections in Venice for sponsorship. Antonio, son of the island's former duke Luca Tron (1438), sponsored Michele and Nicolò in the 1450s.[87] Apachele called on Nicolò Duodo, who had served in Crete as a judge (1443) and as a treasurer (1451), to present him to the *Balla d'Oro* in 1457.[88] The Veneto-Cretan branch of the Tron thus drew on family ties as well as connections made through officeholding to affirm their continuing membership in the Venetian patriciate.

The brothers Luca and Paolo di Donato Tron's experience in office on Crete and their family connections intertwined with their political experience in councils and assignments in the city itself. Luca arrived on Crete in 1439 already connected to Cretan society through marriage, as his son Eustachio (Stae) had married Antonio Contarini of Candia's daughter in 1434.[89] Luca had also encountered several Cretan families before arriving on the island through his position as an *avogador di comun,* approving the registration of noble sons from the Cretan branches of the Barozzi, Matono, Zancaruolo, and Lulin clans.[90] After his return from Crete, Luca again served as an *avogador,* and approved the registration of noble sons from the Cretan branches of the Marino, Salamon, Corner, and Querini clans, in this case with the possibility of personal familiarity with the family.[91] Luca was also a ducal counselor several times after his return to Venice, and proposed acts benefiting specific residents of Crete. He spoke in the *Collegio* in 1442 in favor of Marco Bevardo and Giorgio Scordili of Candia, who were appealing a ruling on Giorgio's will, and supported Giorgio Darnistin's application for a *grazia* in the Great Council.[92] As an *avogador,* he presented a case in the *Quarantia* that exonerated Zuanne Tutu, an ex-scribe of Pediada, of any misconduct in his office.[93] When Stefano of Arbe's debt for port taxes in Candia was lowered from 80 to 20 *hyperperi,* the record notes that the *grazia* had first been granted by Luca Tron, the former duke of Candia.[94] Luca also supported a petition for debt relief from Giorgio Capello of Candia and Giorgio Abramo's request to lessen the back rent owed on a property he had leased.[95]

Luca's brother Paolo served on the commission sent to the island to settle feudatories' outstanding debts (1420) and returned to Crete as captain (1429).[96] On his return, he played the role of local expert for the Venetian state. In 1454, in the wake of an uprising planned by a group of Greek nobles led by Sifi Vlastos, the *Dieci* convened a special committee to examine the problem, and Paolo Tron was among those elected.[97] In fact, the commission was comprised of a number of former officials on Crete, including the former duke Bernardo Balbi (1450), two former captains, Bernardo Bragadin (1450) and Nicolò Bon (1448), and Marco Venier, twotime rector in Sitia (1423, 1427) and treasurer in Candia (1444). These men brought direct personal knowledge of local conditions to the government's deliberations, enabling the *Dieci* to craft a response appropriate to the situation.

Despite legislation against local involvement and the short terms of offices abroad, Venetian maritime governors built up multiple layers of connection to places and people of the maritime state through individual and family repeat officeholding, marriage, and property ties as well as economic endeavors. Those connections continued after an official left office on an informal and on an official level. Most rectors held an ex officio seat on the Senate upon returning to Venice and were expected to make proposals regarding the territory in which they had just served.[98] An ex-governor could also act as an advocate in Venetian councils for individual subjects from the maritime state, guiding requests for *grazie* and special favors through the right channels or sponsoring a particular piece of legislation, and acting as a mediator between center and periphery, as we will see in chapters 4 and 5. But behind the principle of a purely public office affirmed by Venetian legislation lay a seething mass of the demands, obligations, and connections that accompanied each official to his post.

The informal, personal connections that bound Venetian individuals and families to residents of the *stato da mar* smoothed the workings of the Venetian state's more impersonal institutions such as the judicial system and the application process for favors and privileges. While this type of collaboration between individual governors and subjects solved or facilitated some of the problems of Venetian imperial administration, it created a whole new set of difficulties. A well-connected governor advanced the interests of those tied to him, but many subjects experienced the connections between rector and local elites as damaging to their own interests. The citizens of Cattaro, for instance, in 1441 complained that Venice had given the count too much authority; according to Cozzi, "the community was convinced that only Venetian authority would be able to help them to dissolve the suffocating collusions between Venetian rectors and the most powerful elites."[99] The Venetian state, the officeholder's family and colleagues, and both elite and common subjects all had distinct agendas and desires that were only sometimes compatible with one another and with the rector's official duties. The conflicts that arose were resolved on an individual level, through the continuous litigation inherent in the Venetian judicial system, and on a collective level, through the communal embassies and appeals. A rector thus needed to walk a very fine line between serving his own, his subjects', and the state's interests: when he misjudged the location of that line, he was prosecuted for corruption or incompetence, as we will see in chapter 6.

FOUR

Imperial Justice

One of the primary sites of negotiation and contestation between Venetian institutions, territorial officials, and subjects was the Venetian judicial system. As was the case in many other early modern empires, law was a primary tool for the assertion of imperial power abroad. In the Venetian context, the idea of justice was the centerpiece of Venetian self-presentation as a good republic and the administration of justice was a carefully protected imperial prerogative in both the maritime and mainland states.[1] The rector's important role in providing justice was emphasized in his official commission, in advice literature, and in civic ritual.[2] Ideally, the administration of justice would enhance the prestige of the Venetian state, building its reputation as a resolver of disputes and as a guarantor of social stability. The problem, particularly for Venetian officials sent out to put this lofty ideal into practice, was how to reconcile the multitude of different interests and claims in local communities while at the same time protecting Venetian imperial authority and prerogatives.

The nature of Venetian justice itself was complex, with overlapping jurisdictions and rotating bodies of courts with constantly changing personnel. In the maritime and mainland states, the system was further complicated by local statutes and customary law, special privileges and feudal jurisdictions, the participation of local judges in the process, and widely varying rights of appeal. This jurisdictional complexity was what made the complicated and fragile system work. Rather than providing definitive solutions to local disputes, the Venetian judicial system gave both elite and, to a lesser extent, common residents the opportunity to pursue their claims and articulate their grievances in a space controlled by Venetian interests. Venetian justice—formal judicial proceedings combined with the possibility of multiple appeals—formed a kind of ongoing negotiation with subject communities. The parties involved in this negotiation were certainly not equal, as the Venetian state retained the final word, but many subjects were able to exploit the jurisdictional complexity of the Venetian judicial system and to employ strategies of what Muir has termed "continuous litigation," or the use of the legal system as venue for mediation between governors and governed.[3] Venetian officials played a key role in the operation of this system, both on a local and an appellate level.

An excellent example of how this process of judicial negotiation worked in practice comes from Crete. In 1393, during the regime of the duke Marino Storlado, there was a public auction of lands in the west of the island, in the district of Canea. Marco Corner, a member of the Veneto-Cretan elite, purchased a plot of land from Jacobine Calergi, the widow of Giovanni Calergi, a member of the Greek-Cretan elite.[4] After the auction, Pietro Mudazzo, another Veneto-Cretan patrician, challenged the sale, claiming that his brother Zanachi and his son were in fact the heirs to a portion of the Calergi property that had been sold and that therefore Jacobine had no right to sell Corner the land. The case was heard by the ducal court on Crete, composed of the duke and his two counselors. The fragmentary records do not record the decision, but the case must have been decided in favor of Calergi's sale, as the case was then appealed to the *auditori di sentenze,* an appeals court in Venice that heard civil cases. The judge in this instance, Daniele Bragadin, supported Mudazzo's claim on the land and invalidated the sale. Marco Corner then appealed the case to the *Avogaria di Comun,* a separate appeals court in Venice whose jurisdiction overlapped the *auditori*'s. The judge in this case reversed Bragadin's judgment, saying that the *auditori* had not given Corner an opportunity to defend his interests.

In addition to demonstrating the way determined litigants could exploit the multiple Venetian appeals courts and magistracies, this example suggests the existence of a judicial network that drew different interests into the system—Venetian state officials sent abroad to rule in the name of the republic, local landowners, and the judges and magistracies that heard appeals in Venice. This judicial network existed through all of the Venetian territories, but the thickness of the network varied from place to place and was thickest on Crete, as can be seen in the size of the Venetian judicial system on the island, the number of judges elected in Venice, and the number of appeals to Venice from Crete. Venetian officials and judges played a central role in all stages of the process. Many of the judges in appeals cases had themselves served as officials in the maritime state, or would go on to do so later in their careers, creating another layer of density within the judicial network and a further node of connection between center and periphery.

The differences in local judicial systems stemmed from the different circumstances under which territories had been incorporated into the Venetian state. Thiriet's view that Venetian law did not allow for local influence has been modified by Jacoby and Cozzi, who have pointed to the divisions and differences between territories that came under Venetian rule immediately after the Fourth Crusade and those that entered the Venetian state later, after having developed local feudalized institutions or strong communal statutes.[5] In addition to the differences in legal administration from town to town, different ethnic and religious groups also had access to their own laws and customs.[6] This balance between local statutes, Venetian law, and individual status all had to be sorted out by the Venetian rector in his role as judge.

Local Judicial Customs and Practices

Crete, Modon, and Coron—under Venetian rule from the thirteenth century on—did not have written *capitoli* formally acknowledging a body of statutes and privileges as was the case in the mainland states, Corfu, Dalmatia, and Albania. Nevertheless, customary legal practice and Byzantine legal traditions did find a place in these judicial systems. In the cities of Coron and Modon, the castellans used Venetian law, while the *Assises of Romanie* were applied outside of the towns.[7] On Crete, a judge's oath of office stipulated that he should first consult Venetian statutory law and then precedent. If both these sources were silent, he should judge "by approved use and custom," and finally, he should proceed according to his best judgment.[8] In practice, judges on Crete did rely on both Venetian statutes and customary law. Santschi has found numerous references to Venetian statutes in commercial disputes, while in cases of semifree and unfree personal status judges turned to customary law.[9] Maltezou has demonstrated that numerous decisions on land use were based on Byzantine customs and traditions; like Cozzi, Maltezou also points to the difficulty inherent in disentangling mingled Byzantine and Venetian traditions.[10] Jacoby has argued for continuity in civil law, showing that Venice adopted many Byzantine fiscal practices which necessitated the use of Byzantine legal traditions.[11] By the fifteenth century, Venetian magistracies had acknowledged the application of customary laws in certain circumstances in Crete. In a 1421 decision, the Venetian *Signoria* ruled that a sentence was invalid because it was "against all truth and fairness . . . and against the statutes, laws and customs of Venice and of the island of Crete," a clear recognition of local legal traditions.[12]

The connections binding Crete and Venice were deeper and longer-lived than in most other places in the *stato da mar;* evidence of the density of these ties can be seen in the extent of the Venetian judicial system on the island. Because Venice had replaced the Greek nobility during the thirteenth century conquest with its own colonists and continued to exclude most, although not all, Greek Cretans from governing councils, much of the judicial system was staffed by patricians elected in Venice or by Veneto-Cretan patricians elected by local councils.[13] Canea, Rettimo, and Candia each had their own *giudici di petizion, di proprio,* and *di prosopo,* as well as officers of the night and officers of the peace.[14] These bodies were composed of one or two judges from Venice and as many as six locally elected judges. Before 1490, official Venetian policy mandated that judges and officers of the night should be elected in Venice and sent to Crete for short periods; however, Venetian election records show that in practice this did not happen.[15] On average, only two judges were sent from Venice annually, meaning that the other positions remained vacant or, more likely, were filled on Crete, as a 1390 case from the ducal court indicates. In a dispute between Francesco Michiel, a judge *di petizion,* and Zuanne Grioni, a judge *di proprio,* both residents of Crete, Duke Domenico Bon declared that Michiel would serve until the arrival of two judges from Venice and Grioni should succeed him.[16] If only one judge came, the second post would go to Grioni. The conditions of this sentence specified that even in the case that there was a delay in the arrival of the judge from Venice Grioni would begin serving in the post, suggesting that the late or nonarrival of Venetian judges was a frequent enough occurrence to plan for and that Veneto-Cretans filled the vacant posts. There is also a hint that in certain circumstances, a council of feudatories joined the ducal court.[17] As happened in other localities within the Venetian empire, Venetian-elected officials administered justice alongside local judges; the difference in Crete was that many of these locally elected judges were also Venetian, at least in origin.

Corfu, Negroponte, and the territories of the Peloponnesus and Aegean islands passed through a period of feudal Latin rule before they came under Venetian rule in the fourteenth century, and local law, codified in the *Assises of Romanie,* continued to be applied after the Venetian acquisition.[18] Jacoby's magisterial study *La Féodalité en Grèce médiévale: Les Assises de Romanie,* traces the development and application of this legal code before and after the Venetian acquisition, demonstrating the way that Venetian policy respected local customs while reserving criminal jurisdiction to itself. In Negroponte, Venice used its judicial prerogatives to gain control over more and more of the island: through mediating disputes between the *terciers*—the feudal lords of the island—the Venetian *bailo* in the capital city of Chalkis became the supreme judicial authority on the island.[19] Venice formally acquired Negroponte in 1390, and the commissions of *bailii* sent to the island after 1393 stated that the *bailii* were to decide "according to custom"; where custom was lacking, they were to use their conscience or the most correct customs of "usus Imperii Romaniae" that they could find.[20] The Venetian *bailo* and his counselors were assisted in their judicial duties by first three, and then two, locally elected judges, but despite this local involvement, the lack of a definitive redaction of the *Assises of Romanie* evidently led to some tension. The community of Negroponte in 1412 and again in 1416 requested that the Venetian governors there rule according to local statutes and customs, and in 1421 Venice repeated the order to its judges to apply local laws and customs.[21] At that point, Venice also ordered that the governor of the island convene a council of twelve inhabitants who were to collect "the customs of the Empire of Romania as correctly as possible" and send that collection to Venice for approval, which it did in 1451.[22]

In the case of Corfu, Venice's acceptance of local legal traditions was explicit at the outset of Venetian rule: the *capitoli* guaranteed the barons' seigniorial rights over their fiefs and *villani* as well as stating that the Corfiotes could continue to live under "the good and time honored customs which they have had."[23] As was the case in the mainland cities, the Corfiote *capitoli* balanced acceptance of local legal customs with Venetian law, giving Venetian rectors the right to judge both civil and criminal cases using Venetian law and reserved for Venice the right to modify local traditions.[24] Locally elected judges joined the *bailo* and his counselors in judicial deliberations; these judges, who were able to judge civil cases below a certain monetary value, were elected annually in the Corfiote Great Council.[25]

When Venice acquired Cyprus a century later, it followed a similar pattern and allowed local legal customs to continue. Even before Venice's formal assumption of sovereignty in 1489, the counselors and captains sent to advise Caterina Corner from 1474 acted as judges as well as advisers, and their commissions directed them to dispense both criminal and civil justice using "the statutes and customs of that city."[26] Unusually, there was no mention of Venetian law or the *arbitrum* of Venetian judges in the commissions of Venetian magistrates on the island even after the queen's abdication. On Cyprus, the law code in use was the *Assises* of Jerusalem, dating back to the Frankish period on the island. By 1531 the Venetian government had realized the need for a copy of this legal code in Italian instead of French. Doge Andrea Gritti ordered the Venetian regime on Cyprus to have the *Assises* translated into Italian, and the result was printed in Venice in 1535.

The tradition of autonomous or semiautonomous communal government, expressed through communal statutes, was deeply rooted in the cities of the Dalmatian coast. Venice acknowledged the continued existence and application of these statutes in its pacts of submission with these communes, although the balance between Venetian and communal law differed from town to town.[27] In Zara, the Venetian count was to judge civil cases in concert with four Zarentine judges, "considering God, justice and our honor, the good of the Venetian state and the community of Zara."[28] In criminal cases, the count had to consult his local counselors, but cases were judged "considering God, justice and our [Venetian] honor," omitting the good of the Zarentine commune, and in serious cases, like arson, theft, or piracy, the count could rule without consulting his local counselors. In contrast, on Pago, a small island without Zara's strong negotiating position, the Venetian count judged even civil cases only "considering God, law, and the justice and honor of our state," and the two counselors from Pago were excluded from even hearing criminal cases.[29] Most of the towns on the eastern Adriatic littoral fell somewhere in between these two extremes, with three or four judges elected in local councils who could hear civil cases in concert with the Venetian rector and who had a consultative role in criminal cases.[30]

On paper, the balance of judicial authority was heavily weighted in favor of the Venetian rector. Dalmatian communal statutes were heavily based on Roman and Byzantine law, unlike Venetian law; Venice, in contrast to most other Italian states, was not dependent on Roman precedents.[31] Venetians were proud of their own legal traditions as providing more flexibility and as more able to accommodate changing circumstances and traditions, and Venetian rectors were not required to have any specialized legal training nor any particular knowledge of local statutes and customs, relying instead on *arbitrum,* or individual judgment.[32] But with the flexibility of *arbitrum* came the expectation that the rector would exercise it without offending the subject populations, a difficult task for an official with no knowledge of local politics or of local law. While officials did not necessarily have any knowledge of local statutes, during their term in office it was often their responsibility to ensure that the Venetian government did not contravene these statutes.[33] Particularly in Dalmatia and Corfu, rectors' ability to use *arbitrum* to resolve judicial cases was sometimes undercut by instructions not to innovate; the count of Curzola, for instance, was "not to innovate in any way."[34] This reliance on local statutes left officials "hostage to the advice of local lawyers who mediated between Venice and the provincial oligarchs."[35]

The more the Venetian rector was bound by custom and statute, the larger a role the local judges could play, although their influence became a point of contention in many Dalmatian communes. These judges were typically nobles, and popular factions frequently turned to the Venetian state to limit the nobles' power. In Zara in 1410, after an energetic protest from the citizen council, noble judges were excluded from hearing criminal cases against citizens.[36] The Zarentine *popolo* also requested, and received, translators and the right to choose their own defense attorneys. From one perspective at least, it seemed that the Zarentines were less concerned about Venetian encroachment on local tradition than they were interested in using the Venetian state as a tool in their ongoing factional struggle. Overall, while the specific balance of power between local statute and the *arbitrum* of the Venetian judge varied from place to place, the principle of Venice's right to exercise its judicial prerogative when it chose remained strong.

Rural Justice

In much of the empire, Venetian justice was a primarily urban phenomenon. Outside of the cities, local lords and castellans had varying areas of judicial competence and autonomy, forming an alternate judicial network that only sometimes intersected with Venetian institutions. In Negroponte, Corfu, and the Peloponnesus, the *Assises de Romanie* provided for the judicial competency of lords and landowners in their own districts.[37] In Dalmatia and Albania, where the lords outside of the cities were on the frontier of Venetian empire and had traditionally had a great deal of independence, local judicial competence was negotiated through statutes and individual treaties with Venice. For instance, the treaty between the Paštrovići family of northern Albania (Zeta) and Venice granted them the right to "govern and administer civil and criminal justice, using their ancient customs and traditions" in their own territory.[38]

On Crete, the island's sixteen castellans were the main Venetian authority in rural areas, responsible for military and financial matters as well as minor criminal and civil cases originating in their district.[39] The men who served in these offices were a mix of patricians sent from Venice for short periods and Veneto-Cretans. Because many castellans were themselves local landowners, justice in the castellans' courts was often characterized by a negotiation between a variety of local interests. A pair of cases from the district outside Candia highlights the manner in which different groups and individuals used the Venetian court system as an arena in their contest for local power and influence. Renier Dandolo, a Veneto-Cretan noble resident in the district of Pediada, outside of Candia, in 1491 brought a case against another resident of Pediada, Manusso Casanello, in order to reclaim the 500 *hyperperi* Dandolo claimed Casanello owed him.[40] During the duration of the case, the castellan of Pediada, Francesco Trevisan, confiscated property from Casanello as a guarantee but failed to return it after the case's conclusion. Casanello had to return to the ducal court in Candia, which ordered Trevisan to return to Casanello his "things and animals." Renier Dandolo was doubtless familiar with Casanello's situation; only two years earlier, a group of villagers from nearby *casale* Pala had asked Dandolo to intervene with the ducal court in Candia in order to reclaim their property, like Casanello's sequestered by the castellan during a lawsuit.[41] The villagers of Pala had successfully brought a lawsuit against the local Veneto-Cretan feudatories Girolamo Mattio and Marco Venier in the ducal court but needed to turn to another local noble, Renier Dandolo, to secure the return of their property. Dandolo's role in the two different cases also highlights the transitory and overlapping nature of judicial alliances: in the first case, the castellan confiscated Casanello's property because of his debt to Dandolo, while in the second case, Dandolo acted as an advocate for the villagers of Pala against the castellan of Temene. The network of associations between local landholders, officeholders, and magistrates was dense, but the interests of each party could shift from case to case.

Local courts provided a space for subjects to air their grievances and negotiate their disputes in a space controlled by Venetian interests; the vast majority of judicial matters in the Venetian empire occurred on this level, but the records of these local courts have in large part disappeared. The exception to this documentary loss is on Crete, where the records of the ducal court in Candia have been preserved in the *Memoriali* and in the *Sentenze;* one can also see the workings of local justice in the series *Ducali e Lettere.*[42] These records provide a unique view into the workings of Venetian justice on a local level, although for purposes of comparison it is important to remember that the judicial network on Crete was denser and Venetian rule longer-lived there than in other parts of the *stato da mar.* Viggiano's analysis of the workings of the ducal court has demonstrated that the island's elites used the court to assert social status and to protect their property rights, a process he calls the "institutionalization of conflict."[43]

In a 1399 case, Donato Serigo sued his neighbor, Andrea Corner, for destroying a public road that had run through Corner's village of Cheramuci.[44] In a similar case over property rights which took place almost a century later, the Veneto-Cretan nobles Zuanne Corner and Vincenzo Querini had constructed mills on a waterway passing near their estates, when their neighbor Andrea Querini blocked them, causing the water to back up.[45] Corner and Querini appealed to the ducal court, which ordered Francesco Trevisan, the castellan in the district, to go to Andrea's estate and forbid him to interfere with the mills on pain of a 500 *hyperperi* fine, and to let the water flow in its natural bed according to "communal custom." Feudatories also turned to the ducal court to adjudicate their interfamilial disputes; for instance, Antonio and Nicolò Abramo turned to the ducal court to decide what proportion of tax each was responsible for on their inherited property.[46] These types of cases made the ducal court an important resource for the island's property-owning elite.

Feudatories and tenants also turned to the ducal court to mediate in cases where villagers' claims of communal privilege or traditional rights of access clashed with local elites' assertion of their property rights. In 1450, two feudatories in Pediada, Francesco Mazzamano and Pietro de Mezzo, complained vociferously about villagers allowing their pigs free rein on their estates.[47] After a voluminous correspondence with the duke's court on the customary rights of the villagers in this situation, the castellan of Pediada warned the villagers to keep their pigs penned, giving the two feudatories permission to kill any foraging pigs they might find on their land. In another conflict over communal rights versus private ownership, the freemen (*franchi*) of *casale* Pirigotisse appealed to the ducal court against Michele Marin's usurpation of communal property—he and a companion had occupied some communal lands and then demanded payment from the freemen for access.[48] The court, defending the villagers' property rights, ruled that Marin either buy the land or not charge for its use. In some cases, the ducal court acted to defend villagers from the impositions of their local lords. Duke Nicolò Lion overturned a sentence of the castellan of Bonifacio against the widow Çali Varucha, whose mill, cow, and other things had been impounded to cover a debt of her late husband, saying that he did not intend that poor widows be treated this way.[49] He instructed the castellan to return Çali's things and to make sure she "did not have further occasion to return before us." The ducal court did not always rule in favor of the villagers, but its existence provided an option for mediation between villagers and landowners.

One significant obstacle to appeals from villagers was the feudatories' substantial rights over the dependant peasants who resided on their fiefs. The feudatories used the ducal court to assert their privileges, and these could also be used to discourage peasant lawsuits. In 1450, Constanzo Macarulo successfully petitioned the ducal court in Candia for permission to evict the majority of the residents in his village of Elia because of their "bad lifestyle."[50] The same Constanzo also complained about his peasants' pigs, which were foraging freely, and claimed that he had the right to kill the pigs.[51] In another case from 1450, Paolo Dandolo of Castle Temene insisted that his peasants needed to obtain his permission before marrying, and he prosecuted Giorgio Casanello of *casale* Chiparissi and his daughter for her unauthorized marriage to a man from another village.[52] In these instances, the Venetian judicial system ultimately failed to provide any redress for the peasants, and for every case that was recorded, there were many more instances of injustice which did not reach Venetian courts for fear of reprisals.

Resistance from lesser magistrates and the cost of justice were also obstacles to appeals. Castellans in particular acted to assert their own exclusive jurisdiction in cases from their districts, sometimes going to extreme lengths to keep cases from the ducal court. One castellan of Pediada, Paolo Dandolo, took a single case and divided it into three parts, each worth under 10 *hyperperi*, so that the case would fall within his jurisdiction.[53] In some appeals, the original judge took steps to defend his decision, presenting evidence or traveling to Candia to argue before the court; when Giovanni Pizzamano, castellan of Pediada, learned that three of his sentences had been appealed to the ducal court, he wrote to the duke hoping to secure the opportunity to defend his sentences.[54] In 1471, ambassadors to the Venetian Senate explained that rectors of Canea, Rettimo, and Sitia who wanted to avoid their sentences' appeal sometimes "condemned people to prison for three days or more, and [thus the case] is judged as a criminal matter, and the appeal is avoided."[55] A second obstacle to appeal, particularly for impoverished rural communities, was the cost of justice: as Thiriet observed, Venetian justice did not come cheaply.[56] But despite the obstacles, the ducal court on Crete did exist as a resource for some individual peasants or village communities.

Justice on Appeal

Venetian officials abroad acted within the confines of local justice and were sometimes enmeshed with local interests. Subjects could go beyond the rector's local court and bring their cases to central Venetian magistracies, thus circumventing or reversing a rector's judgment. Rarely, cases from the maritime state could be heard in Venice in the first instance, but usually cases reached Venetian magistracies through the appeals process.[57] This appeals process provided an essential link in the system of judicial mediation linking center and periphery in the Venetian empire; scholars of the mainland state have focused on Venetian justice as an important link between governors and governed, and Cozzi has identified the appellate process as a "nodal point" and as one of Venice's most carefully protected imperial prerogatives in the maritime state as well.[58] In Venice, there were two primary bodies that heard appeals from subject territories: the *Avogaria di Comun*, generally responsible for criminal prosecutions, and the *auditori nuovi di sentenze*, responsible for civil litigation.[59] Most commonly, appeals were heard in the courts of the *Quarantia*, either the civil or criminal branch, but rarely, cases were referred to the Minor Council or to a Venetian court such as the *giudici di forestieri* or the *giudici di petizion*.[60] Also, while the *Dieci* were not institutionally an appeals court, they reserved the right to intervene in cases when they saw fit, opening another avenue for appeal.[61] Throughout the system, appeals were a locus for mediation in a three-pronged negotiation between Venetian central magistracies, Venetian officials, and subjects.

Cases could spend decades making their way through this appeals system, with judgments going first one way, then the other. In 1461, the *Quarantia* issued a ruling in favor of Giovanni Condopietro of Negroponte, in a case where the original judgment had been rendered in 1422.[62] Another case, dealing with the dowry of Frangula, wife of Domenico Venier, was heard first by *giudici di proprio* in Crete and then by the ducal court in Candia in 1402. The case then proceeded to the *auditori di sentenze* in Venice and finally, in 1421, was brought by the *avogadori di comun* to the Minor Council, where Frangula received a favorable judgment.[63] In 1490, the *avogadori* presented the *Quarantia* with a case that had originated over twenty years earlier.[64] Alvise Baffo, count of Sebenico (1463), had auctioned off a village originally belonging to Antonio Vrancić, with all of its rights and goods, to Antonio Luzić, to cover Vrancić's debt to the communal treasury. Vrancić appealed Baffo's confiscation and sale, and in 1484 the *auditori nuovi* revoked the sale, restoring the property to Vrancić. In 1490, the *avogadori* brought the case to the *Quarantia*, arguing that the sale had been legal by virtue of a 1446 Senate decision and that the property should be returned to Luzić's heirs. The *Quarantia* was at first unanimously undecided, and even after six rounds of voting, the *avogadori*'s case failed to gain the necessary votes.

Cases that dragged on for over thirty years or that went through three appeals were certainly exceptions, but for those with the social status and resources to pursue multiple appeals, the Venetian system offered nearly limitless opportunities to continue litigation. In the fifteenth century, a struggle over jurisdiction and preeminence between the *Avogaria* and the *auditori nuovi* affected the way appeals from the maritime state were handled, and when cases were prosecuted by first one, then another magistracy, it opened more possibilities for litigants to find a favorable prosecutor and court.[65] The jurisdictional boundaries between the *auditori* and the *Avogaria* seemed clear in theory—civil matters to the *auditori* and criminal to the *Avogaria*—but the practical distinction between the two bodies was not as evident. In the first half of the fifteenth century, the *avogadori* overturned a number of sentences issued by the *auditori nuovi* in an attempt to expand their jurisdiction. By the second half of the fifteenth century, Venetian councils had begun to rein in the *Avogaria*'s attempt to expand its jurisdiction: in 1468, the Great Council repromulgated the capitulary that barred the *Avogaria* from hearing civil cases, and in 1474 the council forbade the *Avogaria*'s attempts to make its own rulings inappellable.[66] Venetian magistracies also began to reject the *avogadori*'s prosecutions of cases previously heard by the *auditori nuovi.* In 1473, the *avogador* Francesco di Delfino Venier tried to overturn the *auditor* Alvise di Giovanni da Mosto's sentence against Michele Calonito of Canea; after three very close votes in the *Quarantia,* Venier's proposal failed.[67] In addition to this shift in power between the *avogadori* and the *auditori,* the *Dieci* also began to hear cases in the last quarter of the fifteenth century, although on a much more discretionary basis.[68] These struggles between judicial bodies in Venice played out to the benefit of litigants, who were offered multiple and competing venues for appeal.

The overall frequency of appeal to each magistracy is extremely difficult to determine, as the records of the *Avogaria di Comun* are much more complete for the fifteenth century than are those of the *auditori nuovi.* The correspondence of the duke of Crete and the *Ducali e Terminazioni* registers from Zara both suggest that appeals to the *auditori nuovi* were numerous, perhaps because of their jurisdiction over inheritance and land disputes.[69] What does emerge from the records is, that among appeals that reached Venice from the maritime state, there were a preponderance of cases from Crete, almost three times as many appeals as exist from other locations.[70] This can be at least partially explained by the comparatively large population of Venetian and Veneto-Cretan elites on the island, who were accustomed to Venetian law, who wanted to have their case heard by Venetian officials, and who had the resources to pursue their appeals in the central magistracies. Additionally, the Venetian administration on Crete had more direct control over the local judiciary, bringing cases more firmly within the orbit of the Venetian appellate system.

While Venetian magistracies were reluctant to turn authoritative judicial powers over to territorial governors by limiting subjects' rights of appeal, the same magistracies were also reluctant to be overwhelmed with appeals from the periphery. There was thus an ongoing tension in Venetian policies governing rights of appeal, which shifted between trying to limit appeals to the center and affirming the system's ability to offer Venetian justice to all subjects. The appeals process offered a flexible and subtle way for Venice to regulate its system—to regularize the administration of justice and to correct or overturn decisions of rectors that had demonstrated bad judgment or had engendered community resistance. Furthermore, encouraging appeals from its subject territories could unify its judicial administration and bolster Venetian authority against communal privileges and autonomies, so it was not in Venetian interest to limit appeals too strictly or rigidly.

Accordingly, the legislation that governed appeals from the maritime state walked a thin line. In 1395, the Great Council affirmed subjects' right to appeal to Venice, forbidding a rector from returning to the same location within a certain period, because subjects might fear retaliation if they appealed his sentences.[71] In 1407 and again in 1411, the Great Council reaffirmed subjects' right to appeal the sentences of their rectors, and in 1437 the Senate decided to reimburse the expenses of all subjects who came to Venice to petition or complain.[72] On the other hand, in 1403 the *Dieci* remanded a case the regime on Crete had referred to them, stating that "it was not correct to send such a case to Venice" and that the duke and the regime had "ample power to regulate these affairs," and in 1436 a chief of the *Quarantia,* Bernardo di Giovanni Marcello, complained about the ever-growing numbers of appeals from "certain doctors and foreign advocates."[73] In 1477, the Great Council set a limit on cases from Crete, stating that in view of the distance and difficulty of the trip to Venice, the *auditori nuovi* should bring between six and twelve appeals from the island every six months.[74] In 1507, the Senate, again recognizing the distance and expense of appeals, raised the minimum monetary value of cases heard in Venice from 100 to 200 ducats.[75]

Venetian magistracies also tried to protect Venetian justice while limiting appeals to the center by creating a regional system of appeal. In the later fifteenth and sixteenth centuries, regimes in Zara, Sebenico, Corfu, and Candia took on the function of regional appellate courts, part of a larger process of regional consolidation and centralization. On Crete, the ducal court in Candia heard appeals from the smaller courts in Canea, Rettimo, and Sitia, as well as appeals from the island of Cerigo.[76] All pending legislation in Negroponte was also transferred to the ducal court in Candia after the island fell to the Ottomans in 1470.[77] In Albania and Dalmatia, appeals went to Scutari, Sebenico, Cattaro, or Zara, depending on the value of the case. For example, from Antivari, Nona, or Dulcigno, a case worth under 100 *hyperperi* would be appealed to Scutari or Cattaro, one between 100 *hyperperi* and 100 ducats would go to Zara, and a case worth more than 100 ducats would be appealed directly to Venice.[78] The multiplicity of options offered the possibility of continuing appeals in different venues for determined litigants.

Opportunities and Obstacles to Appeals

The system's formal regulations of appeal could often be circumvented by *grazie,* or permissions to appeal regardless of jurisdiction or other inhibiting circumstances. Inhabitants of the *stato da mar* regularly received *grazie* enabling them to bring their appeals to Venetian courts; while the records of these awards are fragmentary, it is possible to see that these *grazie* were used in a wide variety of circumstances. Some *grazia* awards allow an appeal to a specific Venetian magistracy: Nicolò Langadoti of Candia received permission to bring his case before the *auditori vecchi,* and Marino Mischo of Traù, Marino of Dulcigno, Nicolò Sumariupa, Domenico of Sebenico, and Michele Silvestro of Traù all received permission to appeal to the *auditori nuovi.*[79] Some subjects from Dalmatia received the right to have local statutory law applied to their appeals. Giovanni de Palasio, archdeacon of Cattaro, was allowed to appeal to the Cattaran council under the customs and usages of Cattaro, and Pietro Umaro of Zara received permission to appeal his son's conviction to the count of Zara using that city's statutes and customs.[80] Some of the *grazie* specifically granted permission to appeal despite some obstacle, most frequently the death or absence of the Venetian rector of the territory. Catizia of Zara, Stefano Capito and Reynoldo de Gothis of Corfu, Giorgio Dandolo of Crete, Giovanni de Ventura of Coron, Leonardo Venier of Negroponte, and Guglielmo de Pagiano of Scutari all received permission to appeal, despite the absence or death of the Venetian rector in the case.[81] All of these *grazia* awards speak to the possibility for appellants to circumvent obstacles to appeal using the *grazia* process.

From subjects' perspectives, continuous litigation in Venetian courts could be an opportunity as well as a burden. Some subjects preferred to bring their cases directly to Venetian courts, bypassing local courts and feudal lords' jurisdictions.[82] Of course, this system was primarily accessible to the elite; thus, conflicts over property and inheritance between the maritime state's wealthiest inhabitants often ended up before Venetian courts. The struggle between Andrea and Nicolò Matono over Pietro Matono's estate on Crete and the dispute between the sons and heirs of Antonio Luzić of Sebenico and his creditor, Antonio Vrancić, both were heard in Venetian courts.[83] Many of these cases reveal complicated family networks of alliance and assistance in bringing appeals, as happened in the 1403 adjudication of Andrea Dandolo of Crete's will. Roberto and Pietro Morosini, who were not brothers, appeared before the court as representatives for the absent Vittore Morosini, himself a representative of Andrea's widow Maria and Marchesina, respectively mother and wife of Andrea's son Zuanne Dandolo.[84] The other claimant was Zanachi Dandolo, son of Vitalis and Maria, acting on behalf of his wife, Isabelle, who also had a claim on Andrea's estate. Regina, daughter of Francesco Barozzi and wife of Matteo Calergi, came to Venice with her representative, Antonio Zancaruolo, who had sold Regina's fief of Calosithea, to defend their actions in this sale.[85] The *auditori nuovi* also overturned a judgment made in Zara against Pria, wife of Francesco de Petrachiso of Spalato, over some property claimed by Simone Philippo de Rosa.[86]

A much smaller number of appeals reached Venice from peasants or nonelites. While it was certainly easier for elites to access the Venetian court system, the ideal of Venetian justice was that it was available to all. This attention to common as well as noble subjects gave rise to charges from subject elites that Venetian rectors were favoring peasants.[87] A case from Negroponte demonstrates both the way Venetian justice could provide redress against local landholders and how difficult it was for nonelites to pursue such cases. In 1415, after an eighteen-year court battle, Pietro and Angelo Andiocho of Negroponte were declared not to be *villani* of the Ghisi family. According to the case record, the Andiocho appeal was part of a larger conflict over free and unfree labor, where many Greeks on Negroponte were struggling to preserve their free status and many Latin landowners were trying to enforce claims of servitude. The ancestors of Pietro Andiocho had been granted their liberty, a privilege recorded in a 1312 letter to then-*bailo* of Negroponte Nicolò Venier. In 1397, Giovanni Alberto, then *bailo* of Negroponte, ruled that Pietro Andiocho was in fact a *villanus* of the Ghisi family. Pietro died in prison, insisting that he was not a *villanus* of the Ghisi, and his son Angelo continued the legal battle, until in 1415 the *Quarantia* in Venice issued a ruling in his favor.[88] So while Venetian justice was available to nonelites, positive outcomes could be long in coming.

Even when groups of peasants were able to introduce their claims in the Venetian legal system, elites' power and connections often proved more persuasive, as in a 1465 case from Crete in which Jacopo Agamno and a group of peasants obtained a sentence against the feudatory Nicolò Grimani "in his absence."[89] Grimani was later able to appeal the case to the *auditori nuovi* in Venice and have the sentence reversed in his favor. Kostas Lambrinós has located an extraordinary case from the late sixteenth century in which the complaints of the villagers of Melidoni, near Rettimo, against the impositions of their local lords Francesco and Marco de Mezzo, reached the *Dieci* in Venice.[90] One of the witnesses in the case, Manoli Dafnomili, was assassinated by Francesco de Mezzo's bastard son Pietro, illustrating the powerful pressures feudatories could bring against peasants who tried to complain about poor treatment.

Communities as well as individuals could use the judicial system as a way of entering into negotiation with the Venetian state. Communal councils sent embassies to the Senate and offered formal petitions and protests, but appeals from whole communities also appear in the judicial record, providing yet more evidence of the strong link between the administration of justice and governance. In some cases, communes turned to the Venetian judicial system to mediate disputes among themselves. For instance, in 1487 and again in 1493, Zara and Pago brought their dispute over the rights and regulations on the sale of salt to the *Avogaria.*[91] Communes also used the judicial system to protest actions of their Venetian rectors. In 1460, the *avogadori* brought an appeal before the Minor Council from the nobility of Arbe, who charged that a recent ducal letter was against the privileges and concessions granted to the community of Arbe; as a result of the lawsuit, the proclamation was revoked.[92] In this way, the Venetian judicial system became an arena in which the Dalmatian communes could defend their statutes. Some Venetian rectors took care to understand these statutes and refer to them in their decisions, as Matteo Badoer did in a 1427 case in Cattaro.[93] When rectors did not, communities could bring judicial appeals against them, as the community of Pago did in 1424, when it accused its rector, Nicolò Arimondo, of selling communal lands to private individuals.[94]

Overruling the Rectors

Subjects in the Venetian maritime state used the judicial system to further their own interests; Venetian rectors and the Venetian state used it as a tool of administration, mediation, and power. The appeal of a Venetian rector's decision became a place where the Venetian state could set limits on rectors' power and regulate their administrative practices. Venetian courts often canceled or revoked a sentence because the official had stepped outside his authority or gone beyond "what he could do," indicating where the limits of rectors' power lay in practice.[95] Appeals were also a locus of struggles between local officials over jurisdiction and authority, and through its appeals magistracies, the Venetian state was able to regulate these conflicts to a degree. In 1476, the *Quarantia* overturned the duke of Crete Andrea Lion's 1463 sentence against the Greek priest Emmanuele Voluopulo, ruling that the court in Candia did not have jurisdiction and that the case should have been heard in the court of Rettimo.[96] Venice was, however, willing to make exceptions in cases it viewed as serious. In 1485, the *Quarantia* heard an appeal of the regime in Candia's sentence against Leonardo Dolfin. The ducal court had declared Dolfin a murderer and apostate and permanently banished him from the island for killing Antonio Manchrino, a secretary for the judges *di proprio.*[97] Ruling that the regime in Candia could not usually hear this type of case, the *Quarantia* nonetheless allowed the sentence to stand, thus allowing the regime to dispense justice while not setting a precedent. A similar ruling came out of a land dispute in Coron in 1347. In this case, the castellan, Giovanni Gradenigo, issued a sentence that the litigant, Giovanni Ambello, claimed had overstepped the castellan's authority and was ignorant of previous promises he and his brothers had made regarding this property. The Senate replied that despite the terms of his commission, Gradenigo could hear this case and issue a judgment.[98]

Conflict between Venetian officials was not limited to struggles over jurisdiction. Rectors with judicial powers sometimes used their authority in struggles against other officials, something that Venice tried to control through judicial appeals as well as through legislation and detailed commissions. The rector of Canea, Marco Loredan, attempted a prosecution of Domenico Venier, a wheat official in Canea, after examining his accounts and discovering fraud.[99] Loredan was unable to successfully punish Venier, and Venier's eventual privation of the office was effected by the *Avogaria di Comun*. Loredan also attempted to fire Emmanuel Grasso, a scribe of the judges *di proprio*, who had been absent from his post, but had his sentence overturned because Grasso argued he had been absent because he was quarreling with Francesco Querini and was frightened to appear, an excuse which the *avogadori* found sufficient.[100] The castellan of Coron, Dardi Foscarini, in 1442 removed Pietro Orido from his position as the scribe of the castle there, which the *avogadori* charged he had no right to do.[101] In Capodistria, the former rector Stefano Pisani brought charges against the treasurer Andrea Grisono for the mismanagement of the city's treasury, but the *Quarantia* in Venice decided that Grisono had made an honest error.[102] In 1414, Roberto de Ariglia, a cavalry officer in Scutari, appealed to the *avogadori* because he had been removed from office, and the *avogadori* agreed to review the case, saying that Roberto had the highest possible honor and a good reputation.[103]

The appeals process also checked the judicial excesses of Venetian officials when they were aimed at subjects as well as other officials. When a particular judge engaged in judicial misconduct, he himself was prosecuted in Venetian courts. One Cretan judge, Marco Minotto, was convicted of conspiring to produce false testimony and fraudulently condemning Marco Venier.[104] This situation, however, was the exception—much more common were instances where judges were not acting out of malice, but where nonetheless ignorance or incompetence or personality conspired to produce an unacceptable decision or series of decisions. In these cases, it was sometimes easier for the Venetian state to overturn a single decision rather than begin a full-scale investigation into poor governance. Some rectors, for instance, had an unusually high number of decisions overturned. Pietro Mudazzo, rector of Rettimo in the late 1420s, had six cases appealed to the *avogadori*, and all were overturned; some can be attributed to an ignorance of the law and some to deliberate overstepping of bounds.[105] In 1409, the *avogadori* asked the regime of Durazzo to suspend a sentence against a woman from Durazzo, Chiara, widow of Giovanni de Regio, who had registered a complaint against the city's former rector, Pietro Arimondo, for certain excesses committed against herself and her late husband.[106] Governors who consistently issued unjust or incorrect sentences, were a liability to the Venetian administration, and the appeals process allowed Venice to control the effects of the poor administration of justice on a local level.

Venetian magistracies tended to overturn or adjust sentences they judged as too harsh for the crime, or in instances where it seemed the judge was using his discretion to revenge slights to himself. In 1490, Duke Marino di Francesco Garzoni condemned Nicolò Tagliapietra, treasurer of the officers of the night on Crete, to loss of his office and one month in prison because of some harmful words of his, which the *Quarantia* ruled was too severe a punishment and revoked.[107] Similarly, Marco Morosini, rector of Rettimo, condemned brothers Nichiforo and Michele Erota to 25 *hyperperi* and six months in jail, because while he was out inspecting forts, the boys had broken into the palace and played with his seal. Finding this sentence too harsh for what they viewed as a boyish prank, the *avogadori* revoked the sentence.[108] When Antonio Bonamigo of Canea wrote some "shameful and dishonest words" about Pietro Diedo, rector of Canea and was put in prison, the *avogadori* released him.[109] In 1422, captain of Crete Giacomo Gussoni's sentence against Michele Tron was found to be "against clemency and fairness" and overturned.[110] Venetian magistracies could also adjust penalties, as happened in a 1470 case from Zara in which Evangelista Aurifice was banned from all of Dalmatia for the murder of Giovanni Didroli.[111] The *Quarantia* ruled that his crime was not premeditated and adjusted his sentence accordingly, so that Evangelista was not banned from all of Dalmatia, just from Zara. These interventions acted to limit rectors' absolute authority, or to correct the effects of poor justice.

A number of appeals turned on questions of testimony, improper procedure, or judicial negligence. Antonio Belvedere of Corfu successfully appealed the 1492 sentence he had received in the Venetian *bailo*'s court, and Marino of Arbe successfully appealed his condemnation in 1489; both cases turned on the lack of proof, or "bad information."[112] Sentences could also be challenged if the Venetian rector ignored or misunderstood local customs and statutes. In one of few appeals from Cyprus, Vittore Marcello, archbishop of Livosia, brought a case to Venice in which his condemnation was canceled because the regime of Cyprus had been "disobedient and negligent to our customs for the rectors of Cyprus, which for the dignity of our dominion should not be tolerated."[113] Rectors' lack of attention to communal statutes and local norms also provided a basis to overturn a sentence. In 1451, the Minor Council canceled the Venetian count Antonio di Nicolò Marcello's sentence of 25 lire against Giovanni Griuicić of Lesina because "the condemnation was against the form of Lesina's statutes, by which one cannot be condemned for more than ten lire."[114] At the same time, the Minor Council revoked two of Marcello's other sentences, because he had overstepped his commission and gone "beyond what he could do."

Patrician Officeholding and Maritime Justice

At all levels of the Venetian judicial system, the officials involved in prosecuting and adjudicating cases held significant influence over the process. Castellans and local lords acted as judges in minor cases as well as investigators and executors of judicial sentences for the urban courts; some forwarded their opinions along with case information. While the *grazia* system made it difficult for rectors to permanently block the appeal of a truly determined litigant, rectors could call on both personal influence or their control over evidence and paperwork pertaining to the case, either obstructing or easing the passage of an appeal. Typically, when the *auditori nuovi* or the *avogadori di comun* decided to hear an appeal from the *stato da mar,* they wrote to the rector where the case had originated and requested that he forward the official documents of the case.[115] Some officials took a personal interest in seeing their sentences validated in Venice. When the duke of Crete, Egidio Morosini, learned that Antonio Pasqualigo was appealing one of Morosini's decisions to the *auditori,* Morosini explained that his court had ruled against Pasqualigo and in favor of the representative of Antonio's father, Lorenzo, and that furthermore, after hearing the evidence, the *auditori* would arrive at the same conclusion.[116] In 1526, the duke of Crete refused to send the necessary paperwork in Andrea di Zuanne Dandolo's appeal, explaining that in his opinion the case was not appellable.[117]

Appeals from the maritime state, of course, were not heard in a vacuum. The men who served as *avogadori, auditori nuovi,* on the courts of the *Quarantia,* and in the Minor Council were tied into the same network of personal and family connections that the rectors of the maritime state were. Many *avogadori* or *auditori* served as rectors in the maritime state either before or after their term as magistrates, and for many Venetian officials, service on judicial magistracies in Venice was interwoven with time in magistracies abroad. In the fifteenth century, *avogadori* were typically older and more experienced than *auditori* or judges on the *Quarantia,* so the overlap between men who held the most important positions in regimes abroad and the *avogadori* is particularly pronounced.[118] Some began their careers in Venetian judicial magistracies and then went abroad, as was the case for Nicolò di Bartolomeo da Canal, who served on the *Quarantia* (1438, 1442) as a *giudice del procurator* (1443), and then as count of Pago (1445).[119] Nicolò di Alvise Foscarini served as an *auditor vecchio* (1475), then as an *avogador* (1489) before his captaincies in Cyprus (1491), Crete (1494), and Verona (1497).[120] Others served in overseas administrations first and returned to Venice to hold positions on judicial magistracies. Leonardo Caravello, for instance, headed regimes in Treviso (1425), Verona (1427), and Crete (1429) before holding a post as *avogador* (1434).

Most common were those who moved back and forth between judicial positions and overseas administration, being elected to increasingly important positions over the course of their careers. Nicolò di Francesco Cocco served as an *auditor nuovo* (1454) and on the *Quarantia* (1443), as rector of Canea (1467) and captain of Crete (1472) and then of Bergamo (1478) before being elected to the *Avogaria* (1482).[121] Candiano di Matteo Bollani began his career in Venetian magistracies, serving on the *Quarantia* (1441), the *giudici di petizion* (1443), the *auditori vecchi* (1446), and the *auditori nuovi* (1451).[122] After a stint in the Senate (1454), he then went abroad as captain of Crete (1466), returned to the *Avogaria* (1469), and then went to the *terraferma,* serving as captain in both Brescia (1471) and Verona (1474), punctuated by a second term as *avogador* (1472). Marco Lippomano squeezed a term as *avogador* (1438) between stints in regimes in Zara (1427), Verona (1432), Crete (1435), and Padova (1439); Luca Tron, Fantin Viaro, and Delfino Venier followed a similar pattern.[123] The time between offices varied: some passed directly from one post to another, while others had periods of five or ten years between magistracy and regime. For instance, Alvise di Marco Querini was castellan of Modon (1470), count of Scutari (1475), *avogador* (1482), and captain of Crete (1485). Baldassarre di Paolo Trevisan alternated terms in the *Avogaria* (1488, 1495) with positions on Cyprus (captain 1489, 1501). Zaccaria di Ettore Bembo served as *bailo* of Corfu (1430), *avogador* (1440), and then as captain of Crete (1447).[124]

Even within this pattern of service abroad and in Venetian magistracies, the overlap between the duke and captain of Crete and the *avogadori* stands out. Of the 147 men elected as duke or captain of Crete from 1380 to 1500, 37 (25 percent) were also elected to the *Avogaria* in the same period. Some, such as Andrea Donà, Giovanni di Luca Morosini, Domenico di Francesco Bollani, or Domenico Bon, were first *avogadori* and then part of the regime on Crete; others, such as Tomà Duodo, or Pietro di Maffeo Emo returned from Crete to the *Avogaria.*[125] Still others, such as Bernardo di Pietro Bembo, alternated service on Crete with terms in the *Avogaria*—Bembo was elected first *avogador* (1486), then duke of Crete (1490), and *avogador* again (1494). These careers indicate that service on the *Avogaria* and in high-level positions on Crete were perceived as complementary; the strong pattern of service in both positions speaks to the particular density of the judicial network between Venice and Crete. In contrast, very few of the men elected as counts of Zara or Sebenico or as *bailo* of Corfu were also elected to the *Avogaria,* highlighting the concordance between the regime in Crete and the *Avogaria.*

The effects of this overlap can be seen in the connections between high officials and *avogadori* involved in the appeals process. *Avogadori* pursuing appeals from the maritime state might have their own sentences as rectors brought before the same court at a different time. For instance, Antonio Diedo served as the duke of Crete from 1447 to 1449 and after his return had three of his sentences challenged and overturned by the *avogador* Nicolò Bernardo.[126] In 1454, Diedo was elected to the *Avogaria,* and the two men together prosecuted a case originating in Crete.[127] As an *avogador,* Diedo himself then prosecuted several cases originating on Crete, cases for which he was likely aware of the circumstances and perhaps the personalities involved because of his experience and family connections on the island.[128] Continuing the circle of association, one of the cases Diedo had ruled on as duke of Crete was prosecuted—and successfully overturned—in 1455 by his colleague in the *Avogaria* Matteo Vitturi.[129] In another example, Andrea Mocenigo served as an *avogador* in 1435 and then was elected duke of Crete in 1441.[130] After his return to the city, the appeal of one of his sentences of banishment was prosecuted by Luca Tron, himself a former duke of Crete.[131] The *Quarantia* were evidently deeply divided between these two experienced public servants' viewpoints, and there were five very close votes before Mocenigo's sentence was overturned. This movement from magistrate to rector and back again meant that while the institutional interests of the imperial administration and the courts of the metropolis might have remained separate, the personal interests of the men who ran the system were often enmeshed.

The overlapping magistracies of the Venetian judicial system and the circulation of patricians through offices in the *stato da mar* and magistracies in Venice created ample possibilities for negotiation. The use of *grazie,* special pardons or favors, was another avenue for negotiation. *Grazie* that canceled or adjusted judicial sentences intersected with the formal judicial system, although sometimes the boundary between the continuing litigation of the appellate process and the intervention of *grazie* was unclear. *Grazie* that commuted or canceled sentences offered a wide variety of reasons for doing so. For instance, Zuanne Argiro of Castelnuovo successfully appealed to Venice for a release from his prison sentence on the basis of his extreme poverty, as did Zuanne Gavala; the Greek priest Georgios Papadopuli, who had been condemned to a 100 *hyperperi* fine and six months of prison and who, for "fear of jail wandered the world," received a *grazia* canceling his sentence.[132] Zorzi Filippi of Brazza, who had been banned from the island on the basis of "certain denunciations," had his sentence lifted by *grazia*, and Nicolò Zorzi of Lesina was absolved of his fine of 50 lire.[133]

As in the practice of formal appeals, Venetian rectors played an important role in the promotion of judicial *grazie*. Stefano, goldsmith of Sebenico, had his request supported by Marc'Antonio Erizzo, count of Zara (1428) and Paolo Vallaresso, formerly *provveditore* in Dalmatia.[134] Iacopo di Paolo Donà, count of Sebenico, supported the request of Maria, the widow of Michele Petrinić of Sebenico, in her complaint against Giovanni Cumenarchi.[135] In other cases, it seems the *grazia* was intended to evade the Venetian rector. Guglielmo de Pagiano, an inhabitant of Scutari, had received a fine from the Venetian count Giovanni Boldù, (1434), and he received permission to appeal to the *auditori nuovi* even in Giovanni's absence.[136] The daughter of Luca Bovinić of Brazza was granted permission to appeal the sentence of the ex-count Nicolò Zancani (1427) to the *auditori nuovi*, even though he had died and thus could not defend his original ruling; Nicolai Plati of Argos, an inhabitant of Negroponte, and Leonardo Venier of Negroponte received similar permissions.[137]

The judicial system played a significant role in tying the disparate parts of the maritime state together. It offered multiple venues in which a Venetian administrator could assert his authority—at times acting as an advocate, at other times acting as an obstacle—both institutionally and extra-institutionally. Both the judicial system and the *grazia* system were characterized by a combination of individual influence exercised within institutional parameters. Subjects could benefit from this influence or contest it within the confines of the same system. Subjects pursued their appeals and manipulated the multiple venues within the judicial system in a way that demonstrated a high degree of familiarity with the politics of justice in Venice. The same thing can be said about subjects' pursuit of the special favors, pardons, and privileges dispensed through the Venetian *grazia* system, which is the subject of the next chapter.

FIVE

Negotiating Empire

Maritime officials were crucial mediators between central institutions and peripheral regions. Their role extended from family networks to economic exchanges to the heart of Venice's system of political patronage. In Venetian terminology, a whole range of special favors, permissions, pardons, remissions of debt, and awards of privileges and offices were referred to collectively as *grazie* (*gratie*). The Venetian state, like many other Italian city-states of the time, relied on this type of informal political patronage to facilitate the workings of its more formal institutions. In recent years, scholars have come to see patron-client relationships as an essential part of the operation of the Renaissance state, and the distribution of offices, benefits, and favors as something that "lubricated" the workings of political institutions.[1] For Molho, patronage operated "in the interstices of the state, offering members of various groups, orders, associations or geographical entities access to rewards, offices, prizes, protection, fiscal advantage, judicial clemency, and the like."[2] Historians of Florence in particular have examined the dense network of friendships, alliances, and reciprocal obligations between individuals created by the distribution of these favors.[3] These interlocking and overlapping connections tied members of neighborhoods together, defined political factions within Florence itself, and stretched out into Florence's territorial domains, offering benefits to individuals from subject cities as well as to Florentines.[4]

The Venetian system of granting *grazie* to individual petitioners fulfilled a similar function in Venetian politics, offering different individuals and groups within the Venetian state access to rewards, favors, and advancement. The unusual aspect of political patronage in Venice was the collective, state-centered nature of the process. By the fourteenth century, a petition for a *grazia* was first presented to the doge and his counselors, second to the *Signoria* (the doge, the Minor Council, the chiefs of the *Quarantia*), third to the *Quarantia*, and finally to the Great Council, where it needed two-thirds approval.[5] By the fifteenth century, *grazie* were also granted by the Senate, and in rare cases by the *Dieci* as well, although the majority continued to pass through the Great Council and the *Quarantia.* This procedure guaranteed that private requests for preferment or privilege had to pass through more public forums. Despite this intensively public vetting process for personal requests, the Venetian *grazia* system has left only fragmentary documentary traces, meaning that "the actual operation of the patronage system is obscure."[6]

A request from 1516 offers an example of the way current and former territorial governors were involved in the *grazia* approval process. When the Venetian Senate considered a request from Marino Loredan and his wife Cateruzza, a couple from Rettimo, to build a kitchen onto their home, three former Venetian officials of Rettimo offered testimony supporting the petitioners' request.[7] Zaccaria di Marco Priuli, rector of Rettimo (1509–1511), stated that while the space for the kitchen had been granted by his successor, he supported the request; Priuli's successor, Filippo di Pietro Salamon (1512–1514), also encouraged the Senate to approve the grant, saying that he had seen the building and that it was a useful construction. One of Priuli's counselors in Rettimo, Alvise di Lunardo Barbaro (1508–1510), also testified that he had seen the building and that it was "an ornament to the suburb and useful to the [city's] treasury." Ultimately, the Senate granted the permission; the interesting aspect of this case, however, is not the fate of the Loredan kitchen but the continuing involvement of former officials in the affairs of the territory they had administered after their term of office was over and they returned to Venice. The case of the Loredan kitchen was not unique; *grazia* requests granted to subjects of the maritime state regularly included the Venetian governor's or ex- governor's support for the proposal.[8]

These requests for privileges and special favors also show that ex-officials remained in contact with the residents and subjects of empire, creating webs of connections between officials and residents. Girolamo di Mosé Venier's correspondence with Spalatines after he left office offers a rare glimpse into the way these informal, personal contacts were maintained. Venier had lent money to Luca di Balistarius, and received regular payments on the debt through 1498.[9] Venier used Girolamo Cambio, a Spalatine citizen and member of a Florentine banking family, as his agent—Cambio collected money on Venier's behalf, managed the house Venier bought or leased in the city, and sold an ox and some wheat from property Venier owned nearby.[10] Two other Spalatines, Giovanni Arneri and Antonio Xagrovich, also collected money and acted on Venier's behalf in the city.[11] These financial ties between ruler and ruled were only one of a wide range of extra-institutional transactions that could occur between Venetian patrician officials and imperial subjects.

Given the complexity of the approval process for *grazie,* it is highly likely that individual patricians acted as patrons and steered requests through the halls of the ducal palace. And as Venier's letters suggest, governors and former governors offered an important node of access into that system for imperial subjects. The *grazia* records, however, allow only a glimmer of the exercise of this personal influence.[12] The registers that record *grazie* contain entries that are typically so brief as to be almost cryptic, usually giving only the recipient's name, the nature of what he received, and the date the request was approved in the Senate, ducal council, and Great Council. In addition, many of the original registers have been lost; for the fifteenth century, only eight registers remain, many fragmentary and badly damaged, and the series ends completely in 1445.[13] There are *grazie* recorded in the Senate deliberations that fill in some of the gaps for the second half of the fifteenth century, but without the full series it is very difficult to determine how the system as a whole changed over the course of the century.

However imperfectly, these records do show that *grazie* were a particularly important tool of governance for Venice's maritime state, where access to formal institutions such as legislative or judicial councils was often complicated by distance or expense. *Grazie* provided an alternate avenue for negotiation between center and periphery, and even a casual scan of the records reveal that favors to residents of the *stato da mar* played a significant part in the system of governance. In 1409, one in four favors registered, or 30 out of 134, went to residents of the *stato da mar.*[14] In 1424, out of 256 *grazie* registered, 43 went to residents of the *stato da mar,* or roughly one in six.[15] In 1432, one in five favors registered involved residents of the *stato da mar;* in 1439, one in four; and in 1441, 39 out of 231 total favors went to residents of the *stato da mar.*[16] The few hints of personal influence that remain visible in these records are instances where former Venetian officials testified on the supplicants' behalf, presenting *grazie* that were then confirmed by Venetian councils or offering advice to those councils on granting favors to particular individuals.

Rewarding Residents

Since Venetian maritime officials played a central role in the procurement of *grazie* for residents of the *stato da mar,* it should come as no surprise that a number of *grazie* were awarded to the same local elites who were affiliated with the Venetian patriciate through marriage. In Zara, for instance, the Begna, Matafari, and Grisogono families all received a number of *grazie* from the Venetian state, both in the period immediately after the Venetian acquisition and in later centuries as well.[17] In Corfu, members of the De Gothis, Altavilla, and San Ippolito families, all allied with Venetian patrician families, received a number of privileges and benefits from the Venetian state.[18] There is slender but suggestive evidence that some of these local elites used their influence and ability to procure favors in Venetian councils to build patronage networks of their own. In 1472, an entry in the *Ducali e Terminazioni* registers in Zara reported that Antonio Grisogono wished Criutarno Carich to receive the judgeship in the town surrounding the castle of Novegrad.[19] The Venetian state approved the request. No documents spell out what role Grisogono played in influencing Venetian officials to grant Carich the desired post, but his name's inclusion in the final record suggests that his recommendation had been important. This case offers rare testimony of the way private patrons other than Venetian rectors could affect state systems of influence.

Grazia awards to local elites with personal or family ties to Venetian patricians were only one part of a much larger system actively supported by the Venetian state. Venetian councils regularly granted *grazie* to subjects as a reward—or an inducement—for loyalty to Venice. Many of these awards came in the decades immediately following the imposition of Venetian rule, suggesting that the Venetian state used *grazie* as a way of rewarding those who had helped in the acquisition as well as a way of diffusing resistance. For instance, in 1412 the Senate awarded Luca di Stantio Cosicich (Kosičić) 300 ducats annually in return for his work bringing districts in Dalmatia "under our shadow."[20] In 1420, citing the fact "that all the captains, rectors, and nobles who were party to his work report wonderfully on his actions," the Senate gave Tomà Jurich (Jurić) of Sebenico a similar award.[21] Nicolò Zurastevich (Djurašević) of Cattaro received permission to reside in Cattaro permanently and 8 *hyperperi* a month in return for bringing the village of Zernovich under Venetian rule.[22] Antonio de Petropizolis, the Venetian consul in Durazzo before its entry into the empire, was rewarded for his help in acquiring the city with the position of officer of the night and an annual salary of 100 ducats.[23] On the recommendation of the Venetian *provveditori* Michele Contarini and Paolo Querini, six soldiers in Durazzo also received pensions because of their loyalty during the transition.[24] Similarly, the *provveditori* of Zara, Leonardo Mocenigo and Fantino Michiel, in 1412 recommended that Antonio Margariti of Pago receive 24 ducats annually because of his prompt and loyal actions on behalf of Venice on the island of Arbe.[25] The policy of rewarding loyalists was a centralized one, but Venetian rectors on the ground played an important role in recommending who should receive these *grazia* awards.

In addition to rewarding individuals because of their aid in acquiring new territories, Venetian councils made a number of awards to powerful and influential elites in their territories. These benefits and privileges were not connected to any specific action but rather to a more general sense of loyalty, suggesting that the Venetian state was attempting to neutralize possible sources of dissent. Venice offered elites in Dalmatia, Albania, and Cyprus yearly stipends, tax concessions, and local offices. In Zara, the Detrico family patriarch, Simone, received a number of state favors for himself and for his sons, including a stipend of 100 ducats a year, a position in the Zarentine treasury, and permission to import horses.[26] These *grazia* awards to elites were similar to other Venetian policies that encouraged loyalty and identification with the Venetian state among non-Venetians, such as granting citizenship to influential foreign lords as a strategy of alliance.[27] Mueller has shown that Venice also used its financial markets to bind investors' interests to its own. The Balkan lords Gregorio Curiacovich and Sandalj Hranić, for instance, invested in Venice's Grain Office, giving them a motive for supporting Venetian interests.[28] All of these methods, including *grazia* awards, were attempts to make sure that these elites had an interest in the success or failure of the Venetian state.

Grazia awards were not limited to elites; soldiers and impoverished residents of the *stato da mar* also received subventions, pensions, and local offices.[29] These subventions could take the form of an annual pension, such as the 2 ducats a month for the term of her life received by Chiriachia Zotta, the mother of Zuan Raphael of Zonchio.[30] Venice also frequently awarded posts as scribes and chancellors using *grazie*, as well as a number of military offices in Venetian fortresses and among Venetian troops stationed along the frontiers of the *stato da mar*.[31] A number of these posts were granted to "buoni servitori," soldiers or sailors who had already proved their worth and loyalty. In 1444, for instance, the *bailo* of Corfu Zaccaria Bembo requested that Corfiote resident Constantino Chachuri's faithful service in the Venetian fleet be rewarded; Chachuri received a post in the castle of Corfu for life.[32] These types of rewards reached beyond elites to offer assistance to others in the Venetian empire, although as in the case of the benefits of the judicial system, the majority of *grazia* awards went to elites and those with the resources to pursue their own interests in the Venetian system.

Residents of Crete were the most frequent recipients of special favors in the maritime empire, receiving well over half of the total number of *grazie* recorded for the *stato da mar*. Since the Veneto-Cretan elite was closely tied to the Venetian patriciate through relationships of marriage or business partnerships, it had more access to the necessary connections to introduce a petition into the labyrinth of the Venetian councils and ensure that it received a favorable hearing.[33]

In 1436, Nicolò and Filippo Querini of Candia appeared before the Great Council in Venice and complained that they had been waiting over a year to receive an answer to their petition for a *grazia*.[34] Not only did the Querini receive their desired *grazia*, but the Great Council ruled that, in the future, votes on *grazie* should be recorded in writing.

The Cretan branch of the Querini's ability to mobilize support within the Venetian government without the mediation of a current or former Venetian official speaks to the more direct route many Veneto-Cretan patricians had to the halls of government. While Veneto-Cretan patricians received many of the *grazie* granted to residents of Crete, nonpatrician and non-Latin Cretans also received benefits and privileges from the Venetian state. Among the Greek-Cretan nobility, the Calergi clan was perhaps the most closely connected to the Venetian state and the Venetian patriciate and accordingly received a number of *grazie* in the fourteenth and fifteenth centuries a clear benefit of its continued loyalty to Venice.[35] In 1442 and again in 1450, the Venetian state aided another of these Greek Cretan nobles with ties to the Venetian patriciate, Antonio Ialina, with his debts to Jewish creditors, both because he had suffered business setbacks, losing all his goods in Constantinople, and because he had a reputation as "a noble man of the sea and a patron of ships, and his daughters married into the Cretan nobility."[36] While it was rare, Jews also received *grazie*. Jacoby has located an instance from the early fourteenth century where the regimen on Crete awarded the office of *missetarius* to a Jew, Šabbetay, although this eventually brought the opprobrium of a local inquisitor; Ottaviano Bonavuta and Hismaelis, both Jews, also received *grazie* in 1434.[37]

Responding to Rebellion

From the perspective of the Venetian state, the benefit of granting this type of *grazia* was the creation of a sense of loyalty and gratitude among subjects. This was particularly desirable during times of crisis, when the Venetian state needed as many loyalists as possible. Venetian councils regularly used *grazia* awards during and after moments of tension or rebellion in the maritime state to reward those who remained loyal and helped Venetian forces during the crisis. The *grazia* awards were combined with Venetian use of force to respond to revolts and unrest. This practice can be seen at work in the aftermath of the San Tito rebellion on Crete (1363–1365). A 1364 deliberation in the *Collegio* specifically connected awards and privileges with loyalty to the Venetian state; one proposal commented that "there are many poor Greek nobles, to our damage . . . It would be good and useful for our purposes to reduce the said banned [nobles] to seriousness and loyalty with a full remission of debt."[38] After Venetian troops had put down the rebellion, the Senate rewarded several individuals for their loyalty to Venice during the conflict: Niccolò Sanguinario of Rettimo in 1367, Micheletto Rosso of Candia in 1368, and Marco Betto in 1388.[39] The Senate also declared in 1376 that *villani* on Crete who had demonstrated particular loyalty to Venice should be granted their freedom.[40] Rewards like these did not only recompense those who had risked life or property for Venetian interests but offered an implicit promise of benefits to those faced with a similar choice in the future.

Venetian councils also rewarded loyalty in the aftermath of a rebellion in the northern Albanian territories of Scutari and Drivasto (1399–1402). Giorgio II Balsha (Balšić) Strazimir had ceded the territories to Venice in 1396 rather than see them lost to the Ottomans, but while Venice taxed the local population in the first years of its rule, it did not strengthen the region's defenses with the revenues.[41] In 1399, there were several outbreaks of violence against Venetian rule—crowds sacked parts of Scutari, and while Venetian troops retained control in the cities, the surrounding countryside was not under Venetian control. Venetian troops restored order in 1402 and Venetian *provveditori* began confiscating property from those who had rebelled and rewarding those who had been loyal. There was some tension over the way this policy was implemented, and in 1404 the Senate heard complaints that the *provveditori* were taking the goods of subjects without good reason and they were also giving away the goods of the commune to the detriment of Venetian rule.[42] In the aftermath of the unrest, Lorenzo Soranzo, count of Scutari (1406–1408) rewarded loyal Scutarians with *grazie*, and when his awards were ratified in Venice on his return, the Senate stated that it was "to the evident good and convenience of our commune to capture the goodwill of certain lords and nobles of Albania, and to keep them in love and goodwill of our dominion."[43] At the same time, the *provveditori* Roberto Morosini and Iacopo de Rippa continued to sort loyalists from traitors and to reward one group with the property of the other, and Albanians continued to protest these decisions before Venetian magistracies.[44] By 1416, the confiscations, appeals, and privileges had created some confusion over landowning, and Venice created a commission of three nobles to survey the province of Scutari and to record the various concessions that had been made.[45]

By following its military response to rebellions with rewards to those who remained loyal to Venetian rule in times of crisis, the Venetian state established a pattern that lasted through the turbulent years of the later fifteenth century. While it is difficult to see the overall patterns of change in the system because the *grazia* registers end in 1445, it is clear that Venetian councils continued to follow a policy of offering stipends, offices, and other benefits to loyalists. This continued practice of using material rewards to encourage subjects' loyalty can be seen at work during and after the conspiracy of Sifi Vlastos on Crete, revealed to Venetian officials in 1453–54 and again in 1460–1462. As M. I. Manoussacas, who discovered and published the core Venetian documents on the conspiracy, has demonstrated in his monograph *The Conspiracy of Sifi Vlastos (1453–1454) and the New Conspiratorial Movement of 1460–1462,* the primary motivation behind the planned rebellion was religious.[46] The conspiracy took its name from its supposed leader Sifi Vlastos, a member of a noble Greek family of Rettimo, who conceived a plot to arrest and "cut to pieces the rectors and the nobility of the city" and then to name a relative of the just-deposed Byzantine emperor king of the island.

The conspiracy failed because it was betrayed to Venice by a Greek priest, Iannis Lima, and a Jewish merchant, Davide Maurogonato. Lima heard of the conspiracy and traveled to Venice, where he met Maurogonato, who came from Crete.[47] The two revealed the conspiracy to the *Dieci* in Venice and Maurogonato returned to Crete, where he informed the regimen of Candia of the plot and its leaders. The subsequent investigation then interrogated Vlastos and his wife and daughter to find the coconspirators. All the conspirators were not caught, and in 1460 an unknown person threw a pack of letters at Zuanne Miliseno's house which revealed that the conspiracy remained active.[48] Miliseno, a Greek noble like Vlastos, turned the incriminating letters over to the Venetian administration and in retaliation Iannis Gavala murdered him in his sleep a week later. Miliseno's letters denounced Pietro Zancaropoulo, the *protopapas* of Rettimo, as "neither a Catholic Christian nor loyal to our dominion," and the Venetian administration eventually sent him into house arrest in Belluno.[49] Venice also arrested several other Greeks, including the priest Iannis Argyropolus, Manoli Lima, and Costas Chavalarci and expelled all the Greek priests and monks arriving on the island from the Morea.[50]

The conspiracy reveals the Greek Cretans' strong resentment of Venetian religious policies toward the Greek Orthodox Church. Venice controlled the island's religious hierarchy, closely monitoring the ordination of priests and appointing state-sanctioned officials, the *protopapas* and *protopsaltes,* to administer the Cretan church.[51] The Union of Churches between the Greek Orthodox and Latin branches of Christianity, proclaimed by the Council of Florence/Ferrara in 1439, and Venice's promotion of the union exacerbated the long-standing religious tensions in Cretan society. The patriarch in Constantinople had accepted the union as the price of Western military aid against the Ottomans, but the majority of the Orthodox faithful had rejected it. As a result, the Greek Orthodox clergy was divided between Unionist priests—those who continued to follow Orthodox rites and liturgy but recognized the authority of the Roman see—and anti-Unionists, those who continued to give allegiance to the patriarch of Constantinople. Venice tried to promote the union among the island's clergy by offering stipends to Unionist clergy, but only a handful of priests accepted the offer. Immediately before the conspiracy was discovered, the Venetian state imposed a pro-union candidate as *protopapas.* The Venetian sources described the rejected candidate Zaninus as young and disloyal, saying he was "not only schismatic but incites every heresy," and in 1452 replaced him with Marco Paulopolus, who was "a promoter of the Union and aged, literate, and loyal to our state."[52] While an older man, loyal to the Venetian state and kindly disposed toward church union, was the best choice from the perspective of the Venetian state, he certainly would not have satisfied the Orthodox community, particularly those anti-Unionists newly arrived from Constantinople who took an uncompromising view of the defense of the Orthodox faith and the need to defend Byzantium against Latin encroachment.[53]

In addition to the religious issue, Venice's financial demands and the actions of the Venetian officials on the spot contributed to the atmosphere of general discontent with and resentment of Venetian rule. The Venetian state had stepped up its fiscal demands on Crete to pay for defenses against the Ottomans, specifically targeting the Greek clergy for a contribution. Doge Foscari wrote that he did not doubt that the Greek clerics would bring their offering with anything but joy "for the good and universal use of the Christian community," but this was perhaps an overly optimistic view of their reaction.[54] In Rettimo, where the conspiracy was centered, there was considerable civic discord and confusion in the spring of 1453. Bernardo Manolesso, the captain of the town, was concerned with fighting a lawsuit designed to deprive him of his office and was unable to control the situation when factional violence broke out.[55] "Grave discords and divisions sprang up between the principal citizens of our city of Rettimo, both [sides] proceeding around the city armed, exchanging words and fighting with arms." The rector of Rettimo attempted to contain the violence by imposing harsh fines on insults and brawling, but this did not deter the citizens, who "came into the square displaying their weapons and fighting, in the presence of the rectors and counselors, without any fear of the regimen or the fine imposed on them."[56] Although the description of events in the document passes over the specifics of this conflict in silence, it does create an image of a turbulent, divided city in which Venetian authority was tenuous and often ignored completely, and it was in this context that Vlastos and his followers planned their uprising.

The people involved in this conspiracy and its betrayal illustrate the divided loyalties which existed in the island's religious and ethnic groups: Vlastos, Miliseno, and Gavala were all members of the Greek noble *archondopouloi* clans, but Vlastos and Gavala turned against the Venetian state, while Miliseno revealed the conspiracy to Venetian authorities. Similarly, Pietro Zancaropoulo and Iannis Lima were both Greek priests, but one plotted against the Venetian state while the other was instrumental in revealing the conspiracy. Davide Maurogonato, a Jewish merchant, also chose to demonstrate his loyalty to the Venetian state. Both Lima and Maurogonato were rewarded for revealing the conspiracy to the Venetian state.[57] Maurogonato received some personal privileges, including the right to carry arms, but he also used his status as a proven Venetian loyalist to negotiate for an improved position for the Jewish community as a whole in Cretan society. He requested and received the right for the Jewish community to return to Castro Bonifacio and Castelnuovo, from where they had been expelled years earlier, and renounced any personal financial reward in return for a general exemption from taxes and duties for the Jewish community as a whole. Iannis Lima's assertion of political loyalty to Venice won him fuller participation in the political life of the island and a position in the island's clerical hierarchy; Venice awarded him the position of *protopapas* of Candia and a yearly subsidy of 1,000 *hyperperi* as well as full Cretan citizenship for himself and his descendants.[58]

The Venetian policy of offering rewards and *grazie* in return for demonstrations of loyalty also enabled them to recruit as a spy Georgios Gavala, a member of the same clan as the conspirator Iannis.[59] In 1470, a peasant of Crete petitioned the *Dieci* for a reward in return for his loyalty during the Vlastos rebellion; he wanted freedom from his legal status as a *villanus* and permission to live in Venice with his wife and son.[60] The Venetian practice of rewarding loyalty had some influence on these choices, demonstrating the way in which the Venetian system of patronage interacted with other networks of patronage, identity, and loyalty on the island.

In addition to offering personal benefits to loyalists, Venice also attempted to turn conspirators against each other by offering up to six absolutions to those who turned in their compatriots, either alive or dead.[61] This type of offer was becoming standard in Venetian domains, but it was employed on Crete specifically in the context of the Vlastos conspiracy. Almost everyone on Crete had one or more friends or relatives under a sentence of banishment, so the initiative appealed to a wide range of people, and a number of the conspiracy's alleged leaders were captured by other citizens. Zuanne Calergi, a noble from Rettimo, turned over two leaders, the priests Manoussos Herculeos and Leondachi Turlinos, and Zuanne Chavalarci was absolved from exile for capturing Vlastos himself.[62] Andrea de Grecis turned in the priest Paulo Caliva in Canea and asked that Antonio Aplada and the Venetian noble Francesco Gradenigo, who had been condemned for the murder of the *villanus* Georgios Calvi, be released from their sentence of exile, and they were.[63] De Grecis also asked for Manoli de Pilotis's release from his sentence for theft, but the regime in Candia refused to grant this request for absolution. Zuanne da Molin turned in Giorgio Calergi and asked that his relative Zaccaria Trevisan be absolved.[64] It is impossible to know, of course, if these men who were turned over to the Venetian state were actually guilty of conspiracy or if they were involved in some private feud with their captors. In any case, residents of Crete complained about the practice in 1455, and the offer was rescinded.[65]

Debt Relief

Venetian councils often explicitly granted offices or financial relief via *grazia* as a reward for loyalty to the Venetian state, pulling Venetian subjects into a network of interest and affiliation that connected them to the state. The *grazia* system was also a large part of the way Venetian rule functioned in its territories abroad, providing yet another avenue for negotiation between center and periphery. Subjects used the *grazia* system to solicit pardons, tax exemptions, and offices and benefits, favors that the Venetian government granted in order to increase subjects' loyalty to the Venetian state. But while this state-centered patronage system provided a powerful tool of negotiation and of governance, it also undercut the formal and institutional arrangements, particularly with regard to local treasuries and local offices. Both Venetian officials and local communities launched periodic complaints against the use of *grazie*, arguing that their use violated custom, tradition, and established privilege. The Venetian government's policy in response to complaints over *grazie* was one of outward flexibility and accommodation, and a less obvious insistence on its own right of nomination and election to key posts within local administrations. In the conflicts over *grazie*, communal delegations played an important role, demonstrating that the Venetian government continued to negotiate with subject territories well after the *capitoli* and pacts of dedication were signed.

One of the most common types of *grazie* granted to residents of the *stato da mar* were cancellations or lessening of a debt burden.[66] Some debts were remitted because of poverty or difficult circumstances, as when the state lessened Filippo Pizansano's debt to the Cretan treasury of 3,000 *hyperperi* because he had eight children and was in prison, or lowered Micheletto Baffo's debts "considering his poverty."[67] Other awards mention the recipient's loyalty as well as difficult circumstances. When Tomà and Nicolò Missich of Sebenico received debt relief via *grazia*, the Venetian count in Sebenico attested that they had suffered many calamities and misfortunes, and pointed out that their father, Giovanni, had been a devoted and deserving citizen.[68] While these types of *grazia* awards could create goodwill toward the Venetian state and alleviate concerns about residents fleeing Venetian domains because of their debt burdens, they also undercut the revenues of local treasuries.[69] There was persistent legislative concern from Venetian councils that Venetian rectors were supporting *grazie* for debt relief too liberally. In 1427, commenting that debtors easily obtained safe-conducts, or extensions on the time of repayment, "to the great damage of our commune," a ducal letter ordered the count of Zara to ensure that subjects repaid their debts to the commune of Zara.[70]

Many of these *grazie* that lessened or canceled debts pertained to subjects' financial obligations to the state, but the Venetian council also granted *grazie* in cases of indebtedness to private individuals. In the first part of the fifteenth century, delegations from the Veneto-Cretan feudatories and the Jewish community on Crete petitioned the Venetian Senate in turn over the practice of granting *grazie* for debt relief. Many of the island's elite, Venetian patrician families such as the Zen and Pasqualigo as well as non-noble feudatories like the Cavalario and Baffo, had been forced into bankruptcy or had to sell their fiefs because of their debts.[71] A former Venetian governor of Crete, Luca Contarini, in 1386 proposed to the Venetian Senate that the Cretan treasury should take every possible measure to collect from debtors immediately; however, those who could not pay should receive *grazie*.[72] The Senate responded by offering general temporary amnesties and establishing commissions to oversee debt cases in 1388, 1400, and in 1411.[73] These acts apparently covered both the feudatories' obligations to the public treasury and to private lenders, as in November 1415, a delegation from the Jews of Crete complained to the Senate that many of the debtors had received a total remission of their debts.[74] In response, the Senate allowed harsher measures against debtors and those suspected of hiding assets, at the same time ordering the communal treasury on Crete to force debtors to pay what they owed. In the spring of 1416, the feudatories sent a delegation to the Senate protesting that these harsher measures meant that they were again in danger of losing their land because of the numerous debt prosecutions pending in court.[75] The Senate, by a margin of only one vote, approved a suspension of all debt trials against the feudatories until their representatives presented their case in Venice.[76]

Venetian policy in this situation swung from one solution to another, responding to the concerns of the most recent delegation to visit. In 1416, the Senate imposed a solution that aimed to satisfy both parties: debtors were given from five to twenty years to repay their debts at fixed interest rates, depending on the severity of their financial crisis.[77] Venice also mandated a commission of nobles from Crete to oversee the individual agreements between debtors and creditors. The regime in Candia, however, could not find three nobles on Crete to serve on the commission who did not themselves owe money, and the Senate had to send three nobles from Venice to form an impartial commission. Even then, a group of Jewish creditors complained that there were debtors on the council charged with making accords, and the *avogadori* overturned these settlements.[78]

Secondly, the commission had a difficult time applying the Senate's formula for debt resolution in practice and requested further instructions on how to negotiate the required debt agreements.[79] By 1418, when the two-year general amnesty for debtors was over, only 138 cases had been resolved out of a registered 1,970—less than one-tenth of the outstanding cases.[80] The commission was renewed for another two years, and in 1420, the Senate sent a special commission of three *provveditori* to examine the "nature and origin" of the feudatories' private debts, whether owed to Jews or Christians, and named two syndics specially charged with examining cases of outstanding debts to the state.[81] When the special *provveditori* arrived, they were determined to finally resolve the outstanding debts, but their efficient and forceful settlements stirred up a great deal of resentment among the Cretans, who protested that they were being forced into agreements and that their debt was increasing because they had to travel to Candia and meet with the special commission.[82] The Senate annulled the forced contracts and ordered the *provveditori* to travel around the island to meet with the debtors, strictly instructing the regime in Crete to negotiate agreements between creditors and debtors. In order to address what the Venetian state perceived as the problem of Jewish land ownership, the Senate also forbade Jewish creditors to accept land as guarantee for a loan.[83]

While the barrage of delegations from Crete over debt remission eventually slowed, the tension over the difficulties financial *grazie* caused continued. Debtors continued to receive debt remissions in Venetian councils to the detriment of local treasuries. In 1442, creditors in Rettimo complained to the Senate that it was impossible for them to collect what they were owed, and in 1465, there were complaints that creditors had resorted to physically attacking their debtors to recover their money.[84] In 1451, the Senate issued a proclamation that there would be no more cancellation of debt in Venice without first consulting the rectors of the territory concerned.[85] In 1454, the Venetian government again circulated a sweeping order throughout the maritime state, ordering that "communal debtors should not receive *grazie,* nor should rectors grant such *grazie.*"[86] Despite this announcement, the practice of awarding *grazie* for debt in Venice continued. For example in 1459, the Senate approved *grazie* for Marco Diedo, Manoli Calotari, and Giorgio da Porto of Crete, all debtors of the communal treasury.[87] The Venetian state's responses to repetitive complaints over *grazie,* like the endless appeals seen in Venetian courts, refused to give a final and definitive answer. Instead, the Venetian government acted as a mediator, allowing all parties to continue to press their claims with at least a hope of future success.

Local Offices: Privileges and Protest

Venetian councils used *grazie* to award local offices and benefices, or eligibility to hold such offices, to individuals in the maritime state. At times, the offices were granted because of individual merit; in other cases, they were granted on the basis of family loyalty. But when the Venetian Senate granted an office via *grazia* to an individual or family to create a sense of loyalty or to reward specific actions, it removed control of that office from local councils. Communal councils throughout the maritime state were charged with the responsibility of electing counselors or judges to assist in the administration of justice and military officers such as galley commanders (*sopracomiti*) as well as city functionaries: notaries, tax officials, supervisors of public health, doctors, surgeons, and schoolmasters.[88] In regional capitals the councils also elected territorial officials: Corfiote citizens were elected as castellans or governors in Butrinto, Saiate, Lepanto, and Parga; Spalatines were elected as governors in Poglizza. These offices, while certainly minor when compared with the authority and resources of Venetian magistracies, constituted an important source of power, income, and status for local elites, who regularly protested when Venetian awards of these offices via *grazia* took control of these offices.

Because *grazie* were sometimes awarded on the basis of family loyalty, they could become a kind of family property. Izzoli de Tarviso received a position as an infantry commander in Zara because of his father's loyalty, and Pietro Avonal's judgeship in Lamari, on Crete, passed to his brother after his death.[89] In 1469, Luca Pavilovich asked to be confirmed as the judge of the village of Ceaschiane in the district of Zara, pointing to the "many good opinions of the probity and loyalty" of his father, Giorgio, and to the fact that his mother and many other relations continued to reside there. The Venetian state approved his request, commenting that such an appointment would follow "a natural sequence and our customs."[90] Dimitri di Modon received both a pension and several local offices, one of which passed to his sons on his death.[91] Pietro de Ca' de la Stupa, an inhabitant of Corfu, was granted permission to be elected to local office despite his status as a communal debtor because of his family's long history of service in Venetian armies.[92]

Given this understanding of benefices and privileges awarded on the basis of family loyalty, it was a short step to allowing benefits and offices to be inherited. In Arbe, Cresci de Maura had received a post in the salt office for ten years; when he died in the seventh year of his term, the former counts of Arbe advised that his son, Marino, be able to complete the remaining three years of his father's term.[93] In 1442, a number of former governors of Modon and Coron testified to the excellent and faithful service rendered to the chancellery in Modon by Giovanni Aurelio of Negroponte for over forty years and recommended that one of his sons receive the post in gratitude for the father's service.[94] There was some tension over this practice of making local offices and benefices a family affair, probably for fear that *grazie* were going to slip out of Venetian control. In 1453 a ducal letter to the count of Zara instructed him that when one of the fiefs in and around Aurana (Vrana) became vacant, it was not to devolve automatically to the fiefholder's heirs but had to return to the city's rector, who was forbidden from conceding the fiefs via *grazie* and instead should investigate what was best for the Venetian state.[95]

Allowing local offices to become family property through *grazia* awards benefited individual subjects of the *stato da mar,* but it undercut the regular methods of appointment to local office, guaranteed by tradition and by law. Local protests over the use of *grazie* were frequently articulated in terms of eligibility for office, using the claims of local custom and tradition to insist that offices were reserved for residents or citizens. While the dynamics of special privilege and general protest were nuanced by different concerns in the Dalmatian communes and in the Greek territories, residents from across Venice's empire periodically sent communal delegations to request that Venice curtail the use of *grazie* to award local offices. In the face of this pressure from various interest groups, Venice pursued a dual and delicately balanced policy—making frequent declarations that only proper electoral procedures should be followed and making equally frequent awards of office by *grazia.*

In the Greek territories, eligibility for office and membership in communal councils was one of the ways of defining ethnic identity. Coron, Modon, and Corfu all had systems dividing offices between Greek and Latin residents, and when Venice awarded these offices via *grazie* to outsiders, it disturbed the balance within the council itself.[96] In 1439, the inhabitants of Coron and Modon complained that the seven castles of the district were being awarded for life, meaning that fewer inhabitants could participate in them.[97] In a rare instance of subtle protest against the system of dividing local offices between Greek and Latin, representatives from the community of Nauplion presented themselves to the Senate in 1445 and asked for a number of local offices to be eliminated, claiming that the offices were useless and a burden on the local treasury.[98] The Senate complied, but several months later, the *podestà* of Nauplion wrote to the Senate denouncing the representatives as false. The false representatives were Greek, he said, and all the offices eliminated had been for Latins. The Senate reinstated the offices, but this incident demonstrates that despite practices dividing local offices, there remained tension between Greeks and Latins as well as between Venetians and locals.

The cycle of privilege and protest can be seen clearly on Crete, where over the course of the fourteenth and fifteenth centuries, Venetian councils issued multiple stern warnings to the regime in Crete declaring that offices should only go to eligible citizens and specifically forbidding the practice of granting *grazie* for these offices, but the same Venetian councils continued to grant offices by *grazia* on Crete.[99] A particularly sharp conflict over the practice emerged in the mid-fifteenth century. *Grazie* granted in Venice undercut the ability of the Venetian regime on Crete as well as local councils to fill local offices, and following a 1449 feudatory delegation to the Venetian Senate complaining about *grazie* granted "against our concessions and laws," Venetian officials on Crete began to enforce prohibitions against them.[100] Venetian officials revoked four appointments in the early 1450s: Marco Grioni's captaincy of the city of Candia, Marco Matono's command of the castle at Castelnuovo, Bernardo Manolesso's captaincy in Rettimo, and Nicolò Avonal's appointment as judge of Lamari.[101] The men complained to Venice, and in all four cases the *Collegio* in Venice rejected the protests and affirmed the supreme authority of the Venetian councils in these matters. The Senate was willing to pass legislation in favor of representatives' requests but refused to limit its own authority or flexibility when it came to the enforcement of these laws.

In 1455, the *Dieci* in Venice took up the matter, instituting reforms addressing complaints that offices were given on the basis of "friendship or patronage, not out of need or equality," and at the same time, the feudatories in Candia sent a second delegation to the Senate.[102] The representative, Antonio de Mezzo, claimed that ill-intentioned people were circumventing election on a regional level by traveling to Venice from Crete and soliciting offices there, a practice which led to inept and corrupt candidates holding office, and he asked the Senate to impose severe penalties to end the practice.[103] The Senate mandated a fine of 300 ducats for anyone who came to Venice to seek office on Crete, but neither this fine nor the *Dieci*'s general initiative acted as a deterrent—or their effect was only temporary—because in 1487 Marco Corner came from Rettimo with an almost identical complaint. Corner asked the Senate to intervene in the distribution of castellanies and captaincies in the district and assure that the posts were only given to nobles and feudatories as specified in 1449.[104] His complaint highlighted the tension over eligibility for office and the ways *grazia* awards disturbed local agreements over inclusion in political life. In response to the 1487 delegation, the Senate raised the fine for petitions to 500 ducats, but the problem continued, with new complaints in 1490, 1499, 1501, and 1502, again demonstrating the *Signoria*'s commitment to the flexibility represented by *grazie.*[105]

On Corfu, the debates over eligibility for local offices, civic identity, and inclusion in communal councils were shaped by the *capitoli,* or communal privileges Venice had approved when Corfu entered the Venetian state. The *capitoli* gave elective powers over local offices to Corfu's municipal councils, and Corfiote delegations to Venice repeatedly referred to these *capitoli* when framing their petitions.[106] In 1406, communal representatives requested that the Venetian *bailo* only award communal offices for one year. In 1408, the Senate wrote to the regime in Corfu asserting that the offices of the *comestabelaria,* castellan of Porto Ferro, castellan of Sant'Angelo, and the salt official were an exception to the original *capitoli* and that since they remained under Venetian control the *bailo* should fill them.[107] By 1413, the Corfiotes had succeeded in regaining control over the posts of commander and the castellan of Porto Ferro.[108] The Senate agreed that the offices were "under the jurisdiction of the city of Corfu," but reserved the right to name the translator, and asserted that the *grazia* giving Pietro Capiza the castle of Parga should be respected. In 1422, another delegation from Corfu complained that Venice, "not remembering the first privilege conceded to its subjects," was giving local offices to non-Corfiotes via *grazie.*[109] The Senate responded that anyone holding office via *grazia* given more than six months from the date the *bailo* of Corfu received its order should lose the office and that any further *grazie* granted by Venetian rectors should not be observed.

The problem of eligibility and access to office remained a heated issue on the island throughout the fifteenth century, in particular with regard to inclusion in Corfu's civic council.[110] In 1440 a delegation returned with a very similar complaint, requesting a minimum ten-year residency on Corfu to be eligible for local office and protesting that "Albanians and Cefalonitans" were receiving offices.[111] The Senate agreed that local offices should not be given via *grazie*, but refused to agree to the proposed ten-year residency requirement. Senators argued that the *bailo* of Corfu, in order to increase population on the island, had the right to exempt immigrants from taxes and duties for five years. Once these immigrants began paying taxes, the Venetian Senate declared, they were eligible to participate in all the benefits and offices of the island. Corfiotes complained in 1478 that "strangers" were usurping offices that should be reserved to Corfiotes and in 1489 complained that the communal council responsible for electing local officials was crowded with "those who should not enter."[112] The 1489 delegation also protested commercial *grazie*—all wheat and grain was supposed to be brought only to the city, but "at different times this concession and *grazia* [to the island] has been interrupted," so that the city and the personnel of the Venetian fleet housed there had great difficulty in procuring enough to eat. The representatives wanted to forbid all *grazie* exempting individuals from the obligation to bring wheat to the city. The Senate responded mildly to both complaints, reiterating that the rectors and the admiral of the Venetian fleet should follow the stated policies and concessions granted to the island. The Senate also defended Corfiote privileges from other subject territories. In 1511, a delegation from the territory of Parga, governed by an official elected in Corfu, complained to Venice that Corfu had been sending inexperienced governors, "of a vile condition," who paid more attention to their own commercial affairs than to the good of those they governed. The Pargians wanted an official elected directly in Venice.[113] Venice responded that it had conceded the right to elect a governor to the Corfiotes and it was unwilling to infringe on these rights.

Residents of Negroponte were similarly concerned that local offices should not be given to outsiders. In the wake of a 1418 delegation to Venice, the Senate informed the regime of Negroponte that certain offices on Negroponte had been given to "foreign people," which caused "maximal disturbance and displeasure in the community of Negroponte."[114] The letter instructed the *bailo* to award offices on Negroponte only to "our citizens and loyal subjects of Negroponte." In 1426, representatives from the island complained that castles on the island were not being properly maintained and were therefore making the island more vulnerable to Ottoman attack; they requested that the castles be given to good men and that the positions be salaried.[115] In this case, it was not the method of appointment that was at issue, but the result. The representatives made no direct reference to the practice of *grazia,* but the Senate responded that after the term of Antonio Giustinian's *grazia* had ended, it would no longer award castles or captaincies on the island in this way.

In Albania, struggles centered not around communal offices but around the positions of village chief and village *proniarie,* a position that brought financial and juridical control over the village. As was the case with municipal offices, the Venetian state often granted these positions as rewards for loyalty, and it encountered the same problems of conflicting interests and complaints. For instance, when Vlado Kalodjurdjević (Vladi Calogerzi) of Scutari went to Venice in November 1447 to demand a reward for his merits, the Senate gave him the title of chief and *proniarie* of the village Obliqua (Oblik).[116] The Venetian rector of Scutari protested this appointment because the treasury of Scutari was thus deprived of considerable revenues, and the Venetian Senate in March 1448 rescinded the award, then reawarded the village to Kalodjurdjević in December of that year. Kalodjurdjević had little time to benefit from his privilege, as in 1449 the armies of Vlk Branković and Skanderbeg set the territory aflame, and by June of 1449 the territory was again in the hands of Scutari's treasury. This case demonstrates the number of different groups invested in these appointments—local elites, Venetian rectors and treasuries, and the villagers themselves, who actively participated in the Venetian system of petition and privilege, using it as a venue for struggles over power and control on a local level.

When Venetian rectors in Albania also attempted to grant village chiefdoms or *pronie* to local elites, they often met considerable resistance from the villagers themselves, who relied on assertions of ancient privilege and tradition in their complaints to Venice. Božić has argued that villagers preferred to be led by a chief rather than by a *proniarie,* who had more judicial and financial control. Accordingly, the villages of Sigeci and Chacharichi each sent representatives to Venice and received concessions that they should be free from *proniarii;* instead, they would be led by chiefs.[117] In Dulcigno, the community resisted the Venetian rector's attempts to assert his control over territory and villages surrounding the city, demanding in a 1426 delegation to Venice that it not install any *proniarie* in its territory.[118] Similarly, in Antivari, the Venetian rector was not permitted to assign revenues outside of the city but only to mediate in patricians' and plebeians' disputes over who got what revenues.

Village chiefs and local elites also used the Venetian system to strengthen their own positions. Božić has reconstructed the interesting case of one such Albanian village, the site of a drawn-out power struggle between Albanian elites, the Venetian Senate, and the villagers themselves.[119] After the Venetian takeover, the village chief of Balladrini (Balldrêni), Alexius Began, used the Venetian Senate to have himself named *proniarie* of the village, an action that provoked a delegation of twelve villagers, led by the local priest, to travel to Venice and complain. The delegation explained that the Venetian count of Scutari had exiled their previous *proniarie*, Nicola Ducagin (Dukagjin), because of his rapacious attitude toward the villagers and their property. In 1438 the Venetian Senate forbade rectors in Scutari to give Balladrini a *proniarie* without the express permission of the Senate. Ten years later, however, after the village rebelled against Venetian rule during the Skanderbeg conflict, Alexius Began's sons promised to regain control of the territory for Venice and were named *proniarii* of Balladrini in return.

Communal Delegations

In all of these instances of dispute and complaint, the communal delegation played an important role in Venetian subjects' ability to interact collectively with the Venetian state and to make their demands heard in the imperial capital. These delegations, while usually recorded in the Senate records, were one avenue for negotiation with imperial subjects. In 1407, a list of demands from a Corfiote delegation was recorded in the *Grazia* registers, and both Venetian legislators and representatives referred to the privileges granted a whole community as "*grazie*."[120] These archival and linguistic overlaps seem to indicate that from a Venetian perspective, communal delegations were similar in nature to individual petitions for special favors—both added flexibility to the Venetian system of governance, opening up an important avenue of communication in what amounted to a three-pronged negotiation between rectors, Venetian government, and subjects. Together with the administration of justice and the system of state patronage, communal delegations created a strong network of connections between Venice and its territories.

Both territories that entered Venetian control through a formal act of submission and those that had been conquered outright or purchased sent representatives on a regular basis to the Venetian Senate. From 1400 to 1450, for instance, Arbe sent five delegations, Corfu four, Crete two, Drivasto six, Durazzo seven, Negroponte five, Pago eight, Scutari four, Sebenico six, Traù one, and Zara four.[121] Clearly, these delegations formed an important part of the relationship between the Venetian government and its subject territories. Valentini notes that for the Albanian cases, communities like Drivasto or Cattaro that had petitioned to come under Venetian rule sent more delegations than places which had been sold or conquered, like Scutari.[122] For territories that had communal statutes or privileges, *capitoli,* these acted as a focus for disputes, both between Venetian officials and the community, and between different segments of the community itself; in practice, the *capitoli* were a living document, subject to constant revision and reform, enacted through a process of petition. The Venetian responses to these delegations came to be written into statutes and to act as a further source of local law.[123]

These communal delegations moved much of the decision-making process out of the hands of local rectors, who sometimes resisted the end run around their own authority by obstructing the meetings of local councils or the elections of representatives. The Senate also at times tried to limit the amount of time spent listening to petitions from its subjects. In 1435, the Senate voted to allow the *Collegio* to respond to the requests of the delegations, given that there were requests from Negroponte, Pago, Spalato, and Traù "that were not of great importance" and made a similar decision the following year when faced with delegations from Tinos, Mykonos, Arbe, and Sebenico.[124] In 1492, the *Dieci* objected to the growing size of the delegations, something the *Dieci* judged to be "against the honor of our *dominio*" and henceforth limited delegations to no more than four representatives.[125] Despite this occasional resistance, the delegations remained an important link between center and periphery.

The constant negotiation inherent in Venice's dialogue with the representatives meant that Venetian imperial policy was in fact very responsive to interest groups, and those who could afford to sponsor a trip to the capital were more likely to have their concerns heard and to have their interests shape policy. Because these continuing delegations to the Venetian capital did mean a larger share in policymaking and power, there were bitter intercommunal struggles over who had the rights to send orators in the delegations. The deep divisions between nobles and commoners in many of the Dalmatian towns manifested themselves in these contests for control over delegations, and while many of the orators positioned themselves as the protectors of communal practices and traditions for the *università,* or whole body of citizens, at times there were multiple delegations from different factions in the same city.[126] The Venetian Senate used the disagreements between these delegations as a way to mediate local conflicts and to strengthen its own power on a local level.

Venice could not always rely on the ties of a shared religion or common culture to encourage collaboration; *grazie* acted as both inducement and reward to subjects who chose to participate in the Venetian system of administration. The Venetian administration remained only one player in webs of local alliances, and often not an authoritative one. Some rectors used their influence to procure *grazie* for their allies, while other rectors saw *grazie* from the Venetian state as challenges to their own power. In one instance, the *Signoria* in Venice gave Girolamo Rasćović of Zara permission to carry arms within the city, even at night; when the count of Zara, Leonardo Calbo, tried to prohibit Rasćović from carrying arms to preserve public order in Zara, he received an angry letter from Venice, stating that he had caused "some complaint that we order one thing and you order another."[127] Furthermore, special favors and rewards could only go so far to reconcile subjects to the fact of Venetian domination. In order to function properly, the Venetian rectors had to maintain a delicate balance between rewarding particular subjects and relying on institutional arrangements. When a Venetian governor was unable to maintain that balance, or when he angered subjects through excessive demands or corrupt behavior, he disturbed the fragile equilibrium of the administrative arrangements between local and central authority. In order to avoid this, the Venetian state attempted to control its rectors through prosecutions for misconduct in office, which is the subject of the next chapter.

SIX

Syndics, Prosecutions, and Scandal

The Venetian state, like many others in the late medieval and early modern period, legislated furiously against the conflation of public and private interest; at the same time, many governors were only able to accomplish their public duties within a web of personal and informal connections that both benefited the governors and their families and stabilized the Venetian state. "The line between effectiveness—in judicial and financial terms—and corruption was thus a fine one."[1] Donald Queller has meticulously detailed the instances where individual Venetian patricians crossed that line, showing that patricians frequently embezzled, cheated, took bribes, and schemed either to gain office or to avoid it, notwithstanding the civic myth that described the patriciate's selfless devotion to the republic.[2] But as many of Queller's critics have noted, the problem is not simply that there was a gap between ideology and practice in Venetian politics. The central fact remains that, even though Venetian officeholders regularly did not live up to their own ideals, the Venetian state as a whole governed effectively and with a great deal of stability. In fact, much of what Queller defined as corruption could actually be described as adherence "to the alternative social norms of private influence and network building."[3] For Chittolini, the interweaving of private and public interests strengthened Italian city-states' government and institutions, and he views supposed "corruption" through this lens, stating that "those scorned practices of misgovernment . . . might be better understood and judged in historical terms as elements of cohesion and consolidation of the state."[4]

Venice's maritime state certainly fits this model: rectors' extra-institutional connections facilitated the functioning of often unwieldy institutions. The problem then becomes how to explain the numerous prosecutions for bad government and official malfeasance in Venetian courts, and the answer lies in the sources of resistance to Venetian rectors' informal networks of influence. The Venetian state was wary of its governors developing local power bases that could work against central institutions, and residents of the maritime state looked to the

Venetian state to cut through the webs of collaboration that tied Venetian rectors to powerful local elites. These different interests in limiting rectors' power can be seen in the prosecutions against rectors accused of malfeasance or improper behavior. The most common charges in these prosecutions were that the rector had acted against "God, justice, and the honor of our dominion," reflecting the state's concern for its reputation and institutions, or that the rector had caused "scandal and murmuring" among subjects, reflecting residents' resistance to rectors' attempts to benefit themselves and their associates.[5]

The cases illustrate that the process of controlling and inspecting officials' actions was itself deeply embedded in the same network of relationships, ongoing appeals, and personal interests that characterized other realms of Venice's imperial administration. One example of the personal nature of these prosecutions is that of Girolamo di Mosé Venier. In the summer of 1486, the syndic of the Levant, Andrea da Pesaro, was traveling between the cities of the Dalmatian coast and the Ionian islands, investigating Venetian regimes and collecting complaints from Venetian subjects. During his tour, he received a complaint about Venier, count of Spalato at the time. The exact charges against Venier are not recorded, but Venier's correspondence demonstrates that the controversy centered on Venier's collusion with some of his local associates to reelect the town's doctor to a second term.[6] Da Pesaro clearly felt the situation was serious enough to require immediate action, and he offered the Senate enough evidence of the "murmuring and indignation of that city and subjects" that Venier had caused, and "the confusion and crisis of our things," that on August 11, the Senate voted to order Venier to return to Venice immediately. At the same time, the council elected Fantino di Agostino Coppo as vice-count of Spalato and sent him to take Venier's place. Da Pesaro ordered Coppo to suspend payment of Girolamo's salary and to sequester his goods pending the outcome of the trial. Venier traveled back to Venice and organized his defense, hiring two advocates, Michele Pensaben and Bernardino Grasso, to argue on his behalf before the *Avogaria di Comun*.[7] In October of 1486, Venier's advocates defended him before the Senate. In Sanudo's account of the matter, there is a strong sense of personal animosity in the trial: according to him Da Pesaro "remained undone, and was roundly outwitted" by Venier and his advocates.[8] After the Senate voted not to proceed against him, Venier then returned to Spalato and had resumed his duties as count by the spring of 1487, where he remained until his successor, Pietro di Lorenzo Foscarini, arrived in April 1488.

After his narrow escape, Venier did not slink away in shame or try to put the incident behind him. Rather, he immediately began an extended campaign to receive his full salary from the treasury of Spalato. According to the terms of his commission and his own accounts, Venier was to receive 600 ducats from the treasury of Spalato, in return for serving thirty-two months.[9] Evidently, part of this sum had been used to pay Fantino Coppo, and among Venier's papers is a list of justifications for why he should receive the balance of his salary. Venier argued that he had not left Spalato for his own reasons but had returned to Venice at the request of the *Signoria;* furthermore, he reasoned, since he had been found not guilty and returned to his office, it would be just not only to pay him his salary but to reimburse him for his expenses for the trial and the voyage to Venice. Venier justified his request with reference to the law, writing, "The law contained in the commission of the count of Spalato intends that the rectors do not lose salary when they come [to Venice] for the affairs of the *Signoria* and I have not come for anything else."[10] He also justified his request by referring to similar cases where officials had been obliged to leave their posts yet had received their full salaries. Finally, Venier reasoned, because of his service in this office, he was not able to hold another office or regiment for at least fourteen months.

Syndics and Rectors in the Judicial Arena

As Venier and Da Pesaro's actions show, prosecutions did not take place with an impersonal state weighting an individual's actions against a rigid legal standard. The prosecutions were both public and personal in nature. When an official was prosecuted for his behavior in office, the charges against him were read in Venetian councils and the evidence debated in the Senate or the *Quarantia,* thus becoming a matter for discussion among the politically active patriciate as a whole and perhaps serving a didactic function for future officials. The prosecutions also indicate that the line between acceptable and unacceptable behavior in office was extremely flexible, depending on the dynamics of trials in Venice as well as local custom and practice. Trials over rectors' behavior in office, like Venier's, were where the actual line between acceptable and illicit behavior was worked out.

Bernardo di Iacopo da Canal's prosecution for embezzling money from the fortifications of Antivari during his term as *podestà* there (1496–1498) demonstrates the sometimes complicated road from accusation to conviction. The first mention of Da Canal's trial came in October of 1499, when the syndics Bernardino Loredan and Nicolò Dolfin proposed to the Senate that, because of the "malli portamenti fatti," Da Canal should be put in prison to await his trial; presumably, they feared he would flee Venice to avoid the charges.[11] He was placed in the Nuovissima prison, but by December the *Collegio* had released him. In

February of 1500 the syndics presented some accusations against Da Canal in the Senate, but apparently no action was taken until June 29 of the same year, when the syndics again petitioned the Senate to retain Da Canal, at which point the Canal family appeared before the council, protesting it was not ready to defend Bernardo and its advocates were not prepared. On July 14, Loredan presented the syndics' case against Da Canal to the Senate. Da Canal strongly disputed the charges; the discussion of the case extended over two days. On July 17, Da Canal's advocates made such a scene that they were expelled from the council; the case seems to have remained in limbo after this point, as in September the ducal counselor Antonio Tron proposed that the Senate expedite Da Canal's case.[12] The Senate took up the matter again on September 19: Da Canal's advocate, Rigo Antonio de Gothis, spoke at length in his defense, and on September 22 the syndic Nicolò Dolfin responded. Then the trial closed with Iacomo da Canal, Bernardo's son, making a passionate speech asking for justice for his father.

The Senate was deeply divided over the case, and found Da Canal guilty by a margin of only one vote.[13] The ducal counselors and syndics then presented four possible punishments: all included restitution of the money and a fine but differed in the prison sentence and length of time Da Canal would be banned from office. Finally, Domenico Bollani's proposal was accepted. Da Canal was sentenced to spend a year in prison, remaining there until he could pay back the money he had stolen; he was also banned from holding any offices for four years and had to give the syndics 100 ducats as a fine. The sentence specifically included the provision that Da Canal could not receive any *grazie* lessening the sentence, but by March of 1501, Da Canal had apparently had at least part of the sentence suspended, as the orators from Antivari complained that his reimbursement to their treasury had been stopped.[14] In August of 1501, Bernardo's son Iacopo was elected commander of the castle at Lesina, and Bernardo apparently accompanied him to the island. In 1502, his son reported that Bernardo had died; he had been strangled by a woman as he was attempting to rape her and thrown out of the castle window.[15] Da Canal's extended trial illustrates, among other things, the burden placed on the syndics to pursue prosecutions against officeholders—when Da Canal was finally convicted, the 100–ducat fine went to the syndics personally, presumably as payment for their work on the case. It also shows the often hidden machinations, delaying tactics, and difficulties involved in prosecuting officials for their behavior in office.

Cases against rectors arrived at trial through a combination of denunciations and investigation. The institution of syndication was by no means limited to Venetian administration, but one particularity of the Venetian practice of syndication was its mobile nature—rather than a centralized process, the syndics of the Levant traveled to the various locales of the *stato da mar.* Venice sent syndics to their maritime domains from at least the early fourteenth century, and in 1396 the Senate ruled that, from that point on, there should be four syndics of the Levant elected every four years.[16] Election records suggest that the average interval between syndics' elections was closer to five or six years, but inspectors were sent regularly through the century. The surviving documentation of these journeys, however, is slim. In general, the results of syndics' investigations were recorded only if a denunciation reached the state of prosecution before a Venetian magistracy. Even then, the cases rarely offer hints as to where the accusation originated, nor do they contain a complete record of all officials accused of corruption or malfeasance; they only offer a picture of the most serious and scandalous cases, those in which investigation resulted in a formal prosecution.

When syndics were sent out on tours of inspection, they were instructed to publicly proclaim upon arriving in a city that they were ready to listen to anyone with a grievance against a Venetian official.[17] The syndic must have heard many complaints at this stage that he did not act on, introducing an early sorting among the various complaints.[18] A syndic would then investigate the accusation, collect evidence and witness statements, and then present the matter to the *avogadori di comun* in Venice. The charges were brought to trial either by the *avogadori* or by the syndics themselves.[19] In some cases, syndics were sent to investigate particular matters, as when the syndics Antonio Gradenigo and Lorenzo Honoradi were instructed to give special attention to the treasury in Crete, because of suspicions about fraud there.[20] In another case, the Senate dispatched investigators to Crete to inquire into the activities of the former ducal counselors Zaccaria Vitturi and Andrea Malipiero.[21]

The fact that Girolamo Venier was recalled from office to Venice to respond to a syndic's accusations was unusual but not unprecedented. The *Dieci* had recalled Francesco Priuli from his office as castellan of Modon in 1406.[22] In 1445, the *Dieci* dispatched Benedetto da Lezze on a secret mission to remove Andrea Donà from his post as duke of Crete, ordering Da Lezze to sail directly to Candia without stopping in order to avoid forewarning Donà of his arrival.[23] Once there, Da Lezze was to ask Donà to come to the ship to receive a message; when Donà arrived on board, he was to be clapped in irons immediately. Only then could Da Lezze inform the captain-general and counselors in Candia of Donà's arrest. Donà, who had served as *podestà* of Padova before going to Crete, was accused of financial fraud in his administration of that *terraferma* city and of plotting with Francesco Sforza. He was also Doge Francesco Foscari's son-in-law, and his involvement with Sforza had come to light during an investigation of Foscari's son Jacopo. In another instance from 1458, the Senate wrote to the castellan of Modon, Alvise Contarini, that they had heard reports of his counselor Bartolomeo Erizzo's "astonishing audacity," and if Erizzo did not immediately stop using the state's money as his own and abusing the soldiers stationed there, he would be severely punished.[24] In the majority of cases, however, officials who faced prosecution for their behavior in office did so after their time in office was over.

Communal Delegations and Complaints against Rectors

In addition to waiting for a syndic to appear locally, subjects themselves could come and complain to Venice directly about their rectors, often via communal delegations. In 1449, orators from Antivari appeared in the Senate; among their nine queries and protests was one dedicated to the conduct of Iacopo di Vittore Dolfin, recently *podestà* of Antivari (1446–1448).[25] The Antivarians, whose city had only come under Venetian rule a short time previously (1443), began by praising the governance of a number of the other recent Venetian rectors sent to the city, declaring themselves much comforted by the rule of Marco di Leonardo Priuli, castellan of nearby Scutari (1439–1441), who had taken responsibility for Antivari during the conflict with Skanderbeg, and Andrea di Donato Corner (1444), the first Venetian *podestà* sent to Antivari after Venice's formal acquisition of the city. Corner died soon after taking office, and Andrea di Andrea Venier, who had just finished a term as castellan in Scutari (1441–1443) took his place.[26]

Venier was replaced by Dolfin, whom the Antivarian orators described as the opposite of his predecessors; they stated that "one could well compare him to Nero." According to the orators, the community of Antivari had already complained about Dolfin to a syndic, a *provveditore,* and to the *avogadori di comun,* illustrating their detailed knowledge of how to use the Venetian system to denounce a rector who offended them. Dolfin's main offense was to have treated a number of Antivarian citizens with suspicion and to have exiled some as traitors, charges that the Antivarians denied. The orators went on to state that Pietro di Nicolò Arimondo, Dolfin's successor, had consoled the citizens with his "justice, reason, and humanity," and praised him for putting down rebellion against Venice in the countryside between Antivari and Cattaro. The orators requested that Venice send Marco Priuli or Andrea Venier in Arimondo's place. The Senate did not respond to the Antivarians' request for particular rectors but instead stated somewhat vaguely that it was certainly the Venetian state's intention to send good and just rectors. The Senate also declared that Dolfin would be punished as he deserved.

It was, however, not Iacopo but Girolamo di Vittore Dolfin, who was prosecuted and found guilty for his behavior in the nearby territory of Budua, where he had been rector from 1446 to 1448.[27] Girolamo, like Iacopo, had caused a great deal of "scandal and murmuring" among Venetian subjects. The first of the five charges against Girolamo detailed an incident in which Giorgio Clibarius, a citizen of Budua who supplied Dolfin's household with bread, brought some burnt or otherwise unsatisfactory bread, which caused Dolfin to "explode in rage," assaulting Giorgio and knocking out two teeth. Dolfin then kept the unfortunate baker in prison for four days, causing great scandal and comment in the city. In another incident, Dolfin deeply offended the Zetan (northern Albanian) noble Zanovich family by charging three Zanovich who were in Budua on business with horse theft. Dolfin had the three nobles imprisoned and beaten without bringing any formal charge or trial against them, with the result that the Buduans could not travel to Zeta and vice versa, something which caused great inconvenience for the Buduans. Dolfin also unjustly imprisoned many Buduan citizens and required bribes for their release, extorted merchandise from foreign boats driven to Budua by storm, and imprisoned and then exiled a local priest, "to the maximum prejudice of the people's spirits." Despite the specificity of the charges, the *Quarantia* in Venice were divided over Dolfin's guilt, and in the end he was convicted by only one vote, fined 100 lire, and banned from holding future offices in Budua or in Albania.

The thread that runs through many of these prosecutions is the idea that the officials' actions had caused "scandal and murmuring" in the cities where they ruled. Since the system was based on denunciations and complaints, either to a syndic or to a Venetian council, it follows that the crimes most likely to be prosecuted were those that angered subjects. Knapton, looking at Alvise Querini's 1477 conviction for his actions as rector of Rovereto, on the Venetian *terraferma*, suggests that the line between good and bad governance lay not where it was drawn by legislators but was instead based on custom and practice.[28] Querini had been convicted of selling justice, imposing fines without trial, and other types of extortions. All of these things were illegal; the real problem was not in the commission of a technically "illegal" act but in the fact that Querini had gone too far, crossing the invisible and unwritten line of customary practice and engendering complaints against him in Venetian courts.

Venetian subjects most frequently complained about extortions, monetary as well as material. The 1461 protest of the inhabitants of Traù to the syndics Antonio di Delfino Venier and Giulio di Girolamo Contarini is exemplary in this regard. The residents complained that a new practice had been introduced that all the cultivators of the district had to carry straw to the rector's palace to supply both the rector's household and his stables. The residents indignantly informed the syndics that "we have never been, nor will we ever be, men who carry straw to horses."[29] Officially, rectors were forbidden to take goods from their subjects or to demand goods or services as a function of their position. This stricture was part of many commissions, and in fact was so important to Corfiote residents it was included in Corfu's 1386 submission to Venice.[30] When rectors did demand goods and services—either as a bribe to facilitate some official action or as a traditional privilege of the position—subjects used their communal delegations to protest. In 1415, the Senate heard complaints that the castellans in western Crete had been abusing their powers for a number of years, imposing huge fines and requiring extra labor from the inhabitants, eventually forcing a number of indebted residents from their land.[31] In 1439, representatives of the peasants of Modon protested that they should not have to provide straw for six horses, as the castellan only had four horses. Furthermore, they complained, the rector was not empowered to force the peasants to join him on the hunt. At the very least, the peasants petitioned, he should ask for the services of either the peasants or their animals, but not both at the same time.[32] When a rector demanded too much, he crossed the boundaries of custom and raised the ire of the inhabitants.

Subjects also complained when rectors appropriated property, either for their own or communal needs. Marco Dandolo, rector of Rettimo (1390–1392), took advantage of his control of communal property in the most egregious way, forcing people to sell or donate their houses to him and constructing in their place a palace for himself, using state timber and the labor local peasants owed to the commune. He also embezzled money from the grain tax revenues, used material from the castle of Rettimo's tower to construct a turret on his own house, and diverted the communal water supply for his own convenience.[33] Bernardo Nani, rector of Lepanto (1465–1467), was also prosecuted for appropriating the goods of the residents and the house of a man named Hector Sayfu.[34] A number of rectors used their judicial function to demand goods and services or to extort goods from residents. Luca Contarini, rector of Rettimo (1383–1386) and then rector of Canea (1386–1388), was condemned in 1389 for his "regime of infamy," during which he used his powers as judge for his own benefit, falsely imprisoning a citizen without cause and failing to dispense justice properly but instead causing many offenses by his "shameful, insulting, and dishonest" public statements.[35]

Nicolò di Andrea Foscolo, *bailo* of Corfu (1417–1419), was prosecuted for holding the goods of a deceased merchant despite the claims of the merchant's son and sisters.[36] Antonio Diedo, duke of Crete (1447–1449), took some possessions of the Grimani against the form of their father's will.[37] In 1491, the *Dieci* proceeded against Andrea di Zaccaria Giustinian, count of Lesina (1489–1491), who had been bribed not to prosecute two brothers for monetary fraud.[38]

The denunciations themselves could easily become tools in contests between governor and governed. Antonio di Benedetto da Lezze (1477) was the last Venetian count of Scutari and was the Venetian representative who surrendered the city to the Ottomans in March 1479.[39] On his return to Venice in April of 1479, Da Lezze was knighted for his service to the state. The following month, Da Lezze appeared before the *Collegio* and accused several Scutarian citizens of disloyalty. The *Dieci* then interrogated these citizens, who proclaimed their innocence and in turn denounced Da Lezze, claiming that he had falsely informed the *Signoria* that Scutari could not possibly hold out against the Ottoman siege when in fact there were supplies for at least four months. The *Dieci* investigated the matter, forming a special committee (*Zonta*) to question Da Lezze under torture. Da Lezze eventually confessed and was sentenced to one year in prison, banned from further officeholding, exiled to Capodistria for ten years, and fined 500 ducats. He also had to return the golden vest and prize money he had received from the state.

In rare instances, there is evidence that denunciations against former officials were part of ongoing personal disputes. As seen in chapter 5, it was a regular function of an official's position to use his office to influence Venetian councils and to bring requests to them on behalf of individuals. Records rarely explain what it was these officials received in return, but occasionally it becomes clear that there was a certain quid pro quo. In 1420, the *avogadori* heard an appeal from Silvestro Floranite of Canea.[40] Michele Trevisan, former rector of Canea (1419), had declared Silvestro eligible for the chancellery in Canea and all other offices in Canea, something he was not empowered to do. This favor apparently had a cost, because one of Trevisan's associates, Emmanuel Argyropolus, then brought a great quantity of salt to Silvestro's house to be stored there, presumably as part of some commercial transaction Trevisan was trying to hide. Silvestro, however, refused to allow him to do so. Trevisan then prosecuted Silvestro for selling salt in small and large quantities and fined him for doing so. The Minor Council canceled Trevisan's sentence against Silvestro; the significance of the case is that it reveals the favor trading that could go wrong and end up in prosecution.

Not every denunciation resulted in a conviction, nor did a conviction necessarily mean the end of an official's career.[41] Gabriele di Benedetto Emo, who was *bailo* of Negroponte (1391–1394), is a case in point. Emo and both of his counselors, Antonio Michiel and Eustacchio Cocco, were prosecuted for actions that "brought disgrace onto the regime." Unusually, Domenico Polani, a Venetian patrician resident on Negroponte, was also prosecuted for his "shameful and disgraceful words" against Emo and for "sowing discord between [Emo] and his counselors, against the honor of the dominion and to the infamy and shame of the regime."[42] Polani had to pay a fine of 200 lire, while Emo had to pay a fine of 200 ducats and was excluded from offices for five years. After his sentence was served, he went on to serve in some of the most important posts in the empire: he was a ducal elector (1400), captain in Vicenza (1405), captain in Crete (1406), captain in Padova (1409), and captain in Verona (1411).

Maritime Dynasties and State Prosecutions

One of the most common offenses for which officials were prosecuted were extortions and outright theft from communal treasuries or private individuals—financially benefiting from the office, an offense often described in Venetian records as "putting one's hand in the commune's money." In 1359, a regular series of penalties were introduced for officials and governors who were convicted of theft from communal coffers. Penalties included restitution of the amount taken, fines, and exclusion from office for a specific period or permanently.[43] Queller has interpreted the frequency of these offenses as evidence of the way Venetian patricians failed to live up to their own ideals, but when seen against the background of Venice's imperial expansion and the specialization of some families in particular locales, the matter is slightly more complicated. In the first decades of the fifteenth century, at the beginning of Venice's imperial expansion, there were a series of elaborate prosecutions for embezzlement and theft against maritime officials. Many of the individuals prosecuted were part of families with strong economic interests in the region, and taken together the cases suggest that the Venetian state was using the prosecutions to demarcate the degree to which officials could mix public and private interests in their exercise of office.

One instance is the 1417 prosecution of Matteo di Bertuccio Gradenigo, *bailo* of Durazzo (1412–1414).[44] The prosecutors presented six charges against Gradenigo, all centering around his appropriation of public and private property for his own ends. During his term in office, Durazzo was under threat of attack from Turkish forces; in anticipation of a siege, the city had been provisioned with a large quantity of grain, stored in houses throughout the city. Gradenigo sent two of his servants to requisition the wheat from the citizens to distribute among the *stipendarii*, an action which caused much complaint among the Durazzan citizens, who were left without supplies themselves. He also took and sold the horses of the *armigeros* at triple their value, underpaid the *stipendarii*, and had an agent of his sell a boatload of wheat in Ragusa. The latter action both contravened Gradenigo's commission, which forbade him from participating in commerce, and flouted the Venetian control of the grain trade, which constrained its subjects to sell wheat only in Venice or in other Venetian territories. The prosecutors charged that Gradenigo's actions had caused a great deal of "scandal and murmuring" among the citizens of Durazzo; Gradenigo was found guilty, condemned to six months in the lower prisons, fined 1,000 lire, and banned perpetually from all offices in Albania.

At first, the prosecution against Gradenigo appears to be a case in which a rector attempted to use his term of office to personally profit as much as possible, angered the population, and was caught. Matteo Gradenigo, however, was just one of many Gradenigo with interests and connections to Venetian Albania.[45] Matteo's first cousin Maffeo di Marco Gradenigo was one of the first Venetian counts in Scutari (1397), and Iacopo di Marco from a separate branch of the Gradenigo had been instrumental in the Venetian acquisition of the province in the 1390s, serving as *provveditore* in Albania (1396).[46] In the next generation, Iacopo's son Francesco (1450) and Maffeo's son Girolamo (1442) were both *bailii* of Durazzo. Giovanni Gradenigo, the bastard son of a patrician, served as the castellan of Durazzo between 1415 and 1430 despite being denounced by Domenico Bondumier as ineligible because of his parentage.[47] Schmitt has found that Giovanni Gradenigo was a merchant in Scutari during the same period, 1418–1429, indicating the intertwined political and economic interests that tied the family to Albania. Pasquale di Maffeo Gradenigo combined mercantile and political interests in the province for over forty years, and was elected *bailo* of Durazzo (1440) and *bailo* of Antivari (1460). When Matteo's prosecution for his actions as *bailo* of Durazzo is viewed in the context of his family's political and commercial interests in Albania, it seems that the case was an attempt to set limits on the Gradenigo family's combination of public and private benefit in their officeholding.

The prosecutions of Pietro di Vittore Diedo demonstrate the complicated and often indecisive route these prosecutions could take. Diedo was part of a family with extensive maritime connections, and he himself served as a counselor in Candia (1408), as rector of Canea (1413), and as *podestà* of Nauplion (1418).[48] (See appendix B). After his term in Canea, Diedo's judicial rulings came into question. In July of 1416, the *Collegio*, on the recommendation of the *avogadori*, overturned two of Diedo's sentences, including his conviction of the chancellor of Canea, Antonio Bonamigo, for some "ugly and dishonest words against the honor of the said Pietro."[49] By 1417, the *Signoria* in Venice had launched a full-scale investigation into Diedo's activities in Crete, and in May of 1417 the regime in Crete sent an *avogador,* Antonio Premarin, to Venice with a dossier assembled on Diedo's actions "against honor, justice, and the form of his commission."[50] This investigation, however, did not result in a prosecution or conviction, and in 1418 Diedo was elected as *podestà* of Nauplion. Unhappy subjects and complaints of corruption again followed in Diedo's wake as he returned to Venice. In 1421, the *protopapas* of Nauplion, Nicola Pigassi, appeared before the *avogadori* protesting that Diedo had unjustly removed him from office.[51] The syndics who visited Diedo's regime in Nauplion presented some charges against him, but in July 1422 the Senate voted that the syndics had been too severe and canceled two of their sentences, including one against Diedo for adultery and fornication.[52] Four months later, an evidently divided Senate reconsidered and voted by a margin of three votes to prosecute Diedo, based on four separate charges.[53] Diedo was sentenced to six months in the lower prisons, banned from holding any future offices in Nauplion, fined 500 lire, and ordered to give back Helena Damiano her dowry, of which Diedo and her husband had unjustly deprived her.[54]

Like the Gradenigo and the Diedo, the Loredan family was involved in the maritime state through both commerce and politics in the first part of the fifteenth century, and several Loredan officeholders were prosecuted for malfeasance.[55] Pointing to the increasingly frequent Venetian practice of using the judicial system as a venue for pursuing "vendettas," Romano has identified the ongoing feud between the Foscari and the Loredan factions in Venice as a part of what animated at least one of these convictions.[56] In Albania, Giuliano Loredan was elected *podestà* of Drivasto (1415) and vice-*bailo* of Durazzo (1425); he was also active as a merchant during this time.[57] Giorgio Loredan was elected *bailo* of Durazzo (1410), and Ferigo di Alvise was elected to the same post in 1435.[58] Andrea di Gaspare Loredan, *podestà* of Drivasto (1406), was prosecuted in 1410 because "not respecting God, justice, nor the honor of our dominion, he had recklessly presumed to put his hand in the money and goods of our commune," stealing over 2,000 lire during his time in office.[59] Loredan had then fled Drivasto rather than face charges in Venice, and he was deprived—in absentia—of all offices for life and banned from the Great Council itself for five years. Andrea di Gaspare's conviction came about fifteen years after Iacopo Loredan had been prosecuted for his actions in both Crete and Corfu.[60] Iacopo faced four charges that he had acted "against the honor of our dominion, against his oath and the form of his commission, and to the reproach and shame of his office," and the Senate eventually voted to ban him in perpetuity from offices in the treasury of Corfu and for two years from all external offices and levied a fine of 500 lire.

Daniele di Fantin Loredan, from a different branch of the Loredan clan, held multiple offices in Venice's maritime empire and was prosecuted multiple times for his actions in office. He was elected the Venetian consul in the Black Sea trading post of Tana in 1409, and when he returned to Venice in 1413 he faced a twelve-point prosecution for his behavior in office.[61] According to the *avogadori di comun,* he had continued as a merchant throughout his term as consul, sending merchandise on Venetian ships with agents as well as trading on his own behalf. He did not maintain the horses, servants, or household specified in his commission. He also refused to give back large quantities of money, silver, and merchandise that Venetian merchants had deposited with his office. Daniele instead forced them to accept letters of exchange he had written himself, although these letters were not accepted in Venice. When some merchants came through Tana with slave women that pleased him, Daniele invited them to his house, claiming that he wished to buy some servants. Once the women were in his home, he had sex with them but did not buy them, a "devious trick" that brought shame to the Venetian state he was representing.[62] By a large margin, the Venetian Senate found him guilty and fined him 200 ducats in addition to ordering him to restitute what he had taken from the merchants' deposits.

Soon after this conviction, Loredan appeared before the *avogadori* again, this time for beginning an altercation with one Guglielmo Roucho at the *giudici dell'esaminador*'s office. For his insulting words and actions, Loredan was fined 50 lire. These prosecutions and convictions did not keep Loredan from being elected to a second post in the Venetian empire—in 1422, he was elected *bailo* of Negroponte. While the detailed records of the charges brought against Loredan do not survive in this case, he was prosecuted in 1433 on twenty-six separate counts, in which he acted "against God and justice and to the perpetual infamy of the regime."[63] Loredan was sentenced to a year in prison, fined 400 ducats, and ordered to return slaves that he had evidently taken and to repair the monastery of San Francesco, which he had evidently damaged. He was also banned for five years from holding any office outside of Venice and banned perpetually from returning to the regime of Negroponte. Even this was not the end of Loredan's political life, although it was the last time he was elected to an office outside of Venice: in 1438, he was elected to a term in the Senate.

The Querini family was another maritime dynasty which had one of its members prosecuted for his behavior in office during the early fifteenth century. The clan as a whole combined semi-independent lordship over the Aegean islands of Amorgos and Stampalia with officeholding in directly ruled Venetian territories and economic interests in and around the maritime state.[64] Not surprisingly, the Querini held a large number of offices on Crete, Coron, Modon, and Negroponte in the late fourteenth and early fifteenth century, and their network of officeholding encompassed Dalmatia and Albania as well. In 1416, one of these Querini, Paolo di Marino, returned to Venice from his position as count of Scutari to face a host of accusations of financial misdealings, extortions, and embezzlements. Querini had created a scandal in the city when, using his authority as a Venetian official, he imprisoned a man named Medono Armano until Armano agreed to dissolve his daughter's marriage, at which point Querini himself began a sexual relationship with the woman. The record of the prosecution states that this was done "to the maximum shame and infamy of our state and to the vituperation, shame and infamy of his own regime." Querini subsequently conceded Armano the exclusive right to sell wine in small amounts in the public market, contravening the long-standing custom in Scutari. Querini also attempted to mollify Medono by confiscating the wine of a poor woman, Chiarana Fornaria, and giving it to him, "to the great muttering of the loyal subjects of our state and all this [was] done to the shame of the said regime."[65]

In a separate incident, Querini commanded a married woman to appear in his court, and upon seeing her, used some unrecorded tactic to compel her to return to the castle repeatedly, at night, where both he and his relative Hieronimo Querini had sex with her. On one occasion, this occurred while the citizens of Scutari were assembled outside, waiting for Querini to emerge and to pronounce judicial sentences, an occurrence which not surprisingly caused considerable "murmuring and scandal" among the citizens of Scutari. Querini was ultimately sentenced to six months in the lower prisons and perpetually banned from holding offices not only in Scutari but in all of Albania, fined 500 lire, and forced to make monetary reparations to both Chiarana Fornaria and Medono Armano.

In the same year, possibly the same Paolo Querini was involved in a protest against the judgments of the syndics of the Levant, which originated on Crete. Five former rectors of Rettimo—Pietro Nani (1393), Paolo Querini (1398), Antonio dalle Boccole (1405), Michele Duodo (1407), Marco Polani (1409)—and counselor of Crete Nicolò Marcello (1409) had been habitually demanding meat from local butchers without payment.[66] The syndics Nicolò Erizzo, Jacopo Michiel, and Francesco de Garzoni had brought the case to the *ufficiali alle rason* and fined each rector 17 ducats, but the former officials appealed, arguing that the *ufficiali alle rason* did not have jurisdiction in the case. One of the litigants in this trial,

Pietro Nani, had already been prosecuted and punished for his behavior while rector of Canea. The Nani clan were feudators of long standing on the island, and Pietro had served multiple times on Crete: as officer of the night (1383), as counselor in Candia (1386), and as rector of Rettimo (1393), and then as rector of Canea.[67] In 1402, the *avogadori* brought eleven charges against Nani.[68] They accused him of commandeering territories surrounding the castle of Bicornia, which commanded the coast to the east of the city, and property on the outskirts of Canea itself, ruining the fortifications and damaging the land. As a judge, he had refused to expedite the restitution of dowries to the widows of plague victims; instead, he had "illegally and dishonestly extorted" a percentage of their dowries from them. Nani's wife had obtained many of these same widows' long-term leases on arable land "with little money and many promises." Nani had also taken hides from the tannery and objects in silver and gold from local merchants and had ordered the city's inhabitants to work on his palace. Finally, when he had received a gift of meat from a local butcher, not only had he accepted it, but then resold it, scandalizing the populace at large. He was found guilty, had to pay a 600 *lire di piccoli* fine and was perpetually banned from the island of Crete.

In the 1430s and 1440s, there were a series of scandals involving officials from maritime families in Crete and Negroponte. The first was a prosecution against Andrea di Maffeo Capello, *bailo* of Negroponte (1427–1429). Before going to Negroponte, Capello had been *bailo* of Trebizond (1417), *bailo* of Cyprus (1421), and captain of the Alexandria galleys.[69] In 1433, the syndics Nicolò Memmo and Pietro Bembo presented thirty-three separate charges against him, including his theft of 800 ducats from the communal treasury.[70] Capello was sentenced to a year in prison, fined 300 ducats, and perpetually excluded from all territorial governorships. Five years later, the *avogadori* presented a second case against a former official from Negroponte, Antonio di Andrea Giustinian. Mueller has detailed the extensive connections this branch of the Giustinian family had with the maritime empire, including lordships in the Cyclades and in Negroponte.[71] Antonio di Andrea was a merchant in Albania, where he was accused of plotting with the Turks and banned from Durazzo and Albania in 1427. Giustinian was then elected as counselor of Negroponte in 1434, and in 1438 the *avogadori* brought four charges against him, all centering around his sexual exploitation of local women.[72] He was sentenced to four months in a lower prison, fined 400 lire, and perpetually forbidden from holding office in Negroponte or returning to Negroponte at all for five years.

The prosecutions against Giustinian and Capello were limited to their individual actions on Negroponte. In the case of a Cretan corruption scandal beginning in the 1430s, multiple members of the Sagredo family were implicated. As discussed in chapter 2, the Sagredo held an unusually high number of maritime offices; the family also were Veneto-Cretan feudators of long standing and owned land on the island.[73] In the 1430s and 1440s, the cousins Albano di Giovanni and Lorenzo di Gerardo both held offices on Crete, Albano as rector of Canea (1433–1436) and Lorenzo as a judge (1439–40) and as an officer of the night (1443–44); both were prosecuted for their actions in office, although only Lorenzo was convicted. (See appendix B.) Albano's son, Francesco, also served on the island, as a counselor in Canea (1447), and he was also prosecuted and convicted for his actions in office.

Albano Sagredo, rector of Canea (1433–1436), was prosecuted but not convicted in a widespread scandal uncovered by the syndics of the Levant Pietro Bembo and Nicolò Memmo in 1432. The prosecutions arising from the syndic's investigation stretched back over fifteen years, revealing what had clearly been a long-term scheme to subvert the workings of the judicial system. Two successive rectors of Rettimo, Pietro di Luca Mudazzo (1426–1431) and Pietro Darmer (1432), were accused and convicted of accepting bribes, selling offices, and offering favorable judicial sentences to the highest bidders.[74] The counselors of Crete, Lorenzo Davanzago (1415–1417) and Domenico Bembo (1424–1426), were also convicted. Secondo da Pesaro was fined 796 ducats, condemned to two years in prison, and perpetually banned from all of the offices and benefits of the *Signoria*. A decade later, Albano's cousin Lorenzo di Gerardo Sagredo confessed to having stolen 883 *hyperperi* from the commune as a judge and 2,770 *hyperperi* as an officer of the night on Crete.[75] He had to return the money as well as pay a fine, and he was permanently banned from offices as a judge or officer of the night on Crete and, for five years, all offices.

At approximately the same time that Lorenzo was being tried for embezzlement, his nephew Francesco di Albano Sagredo was elected as counselor in Canea (1447) and then Rettimo (1448). While in office, he "fell in love" with Zania, the wife of Pietro Zane, a Venetian feudator in Rettimo.[76] He gave orders that Zania meet him to consult over certain business of her husband's, a meeting that apparently took place near her house, because Sagredo then entered the house and attempted to rape her. Zania called to her husband upstairs, who came down, grabbed Francesco, and began to beat him. Pietro and Zania Zane then denounced Sagredo to the rector of Rettimo Marino da Molin and to the *Signoria* in Venice, which sent the captain of Crete, Nicolò Bono, to investigate the matter in the place of an *avogador*.[77] When the trial came before the Senate, Sagredo was convicted, losing his office on Crete and receiving a fine of 100 ducats and a five-year ban on holding further offices on the island. This proscription did not end Sagredo's connection with the island, as his daughter married into the Veneto-Cretan patriciate shortly after her father's term in office, contracting an alliance with Marco Manolesso di Pietro of Candia in 1450.[78] Neither did the conviction end Sagredo's career: in 1464, he was count in Lesina, and when he returned from this posting, he faced a second prosecution for bad governance, in 1468.[79]

Judging the Judges

The syndics were the state agents responsible for investigating and prosecuting many of the above instances of corruption, but the syndics themselves were not immune from prosecution. Several syndics brought accusations against maritime officials only to find themselves embroiled in counteraccusations and appeals brought by the rectors they had been sent to investigate.[80] The syndic Tomà Minotto was prosecuted in 1376 for engaging in commerce while on his tour of inspection.[81] Giovanni Orio, a syndic in 1407, was punished because when he was in Modon, he "wished to fornicate" and searched out an inhabitant, Margarita Palmerie, and had sex with Maria, her adopted daughter.[82] After two close votes in the *Quarantia,* Orio was fined 100 lire. While there is no record of who denounced these two syndics, it is not impossible that the rectors in the territories they visited had reported their behavior.

A number of other syndics had their accusations and judgments appealed to other Venetian magistracies. Syndics were charged with investigating public, not private, activities, and many of these appeals turned on the division between the two realms. In 1414, a whole series of syndics' convictions against private persons in Crete were turned over to local authorities, and in 1415, the *avogadori* brought a case to the *Quarantia* overturning syndic Jacopo Michiel's fine against the former rector of Canea Pietro Civrano, contending that this case was "purely a civil matter, and should not be considered by the syndics but by the *auditori di sentenze.*"[83] In 1438, Giovanni Moro proposed that syndics be banned from investigating officials' private conduct, particularly "fornication and adultery"; the measure was a popular one and passed with ninety-eight in favor and six against.[84] The Venetian model of continuous litigation was deeply embedded in its practices of empire, and not even centralizing institutions of the state like the syndics were immune.

Cases in which syndics attempted to decide cases dealing with private individuals were appealed, almost always successfully. The syndics Giovanni Cocco and Michele Surian had fined the Jews of Rettimo, who appealed the judgment in

1403 and won.[85] In another appeal against the same syndics, nine Veneto-Cretan nobles who held locally elected offices appealed the fine levied against them, arguing that they had not been properly tried.[86] Mordecai, a Jew of Negroponte, successfully appealed Andrea Ghisi's condemnation in 1415, arguing that Ghisi had exceeded his commission by condemning a private person.[87] Matteo di Napoli of Negroponte appealed against Ghisi and his colleague Nicolò Erizzo's fine of 500 *hyperperi* as well.[88] Matteo was a state treasurer in Negroponte, and the syndics had condemned him for the way he had handled an auction, so Matteo could claim neither status as a private individual nor that his actions had been private. He did win the appeal on the grounds that the syndics' judgment had been contrary to a Senate decision of May 29, 1402. The *Quarantia* reversed the syndics' judgment against Bono di Stamati and Giorgio Azalini of Coron in 1456 because the syndics had gone beyond what they should do by involving themselves in the matter.[89] Three days later, the *Quarantia* sustained another appeal against the same syndics, this from the castellan of Coron Tomà Michiel, who had been fined for his poor financial government.[90] In 1467, the *Quarantia* voided the syndics' judgment against Giovanni Calasati of Canea, stating that the syndics' duties included prosecuting officials and rectors, not private individuals.[91]

Syndics were, of course, deeply embedded in the same network of personal connections and alliances of which the officeholders they investigated were a part. Syndics' career patterns took them from inspectors to officeholders to Venetian magistracies, meaning that a man who was in charge of inspecting a regime one year could be running the same administration a decade later, or vice versa. Nicolò Foscolo, for instance, was first a syndic (1404) and then *bailo* of Corfu (1417); after his return, he was convicted for financial misdeeds in office. Both Luca di Donato Tron (1408, 1414) and his brother Paolo (1420) were syndics in the maritime state, and both went on to hold official posts in Traù, Crete, and Zara. Lorenzo Soranzo was a syndic in the Levant (1396) then count of Scutari (1404). Nicolò di Antonio Memmo was first a syndic (1431) and then captain of Zara (1446). Antonio di Delfino Venier was a syndic in Dalmatia (1460) and then returned as count (1466). The office of syndic also overlapped with family patterns of officeholding. Bartolomeo Nani was a syndic and *provveditore* in the Levant in 1396, during the same period when Pietro Nani was holding office in Crete. These overlapping terms as investigators and then governors undermined syndics' roles as impartial state agents, drawing them into the same networks of collaboration and accommodation the state and some residents protested against.

The syndics were not immune from accusations of corruption or of using their office to pursue private agendas. In 1441, Marco Bevardo of Candia charged the syndic Biagio Venier with acting out of personal animosity toward himself and his family and using his position as a syndic to "ruin and destroy this Marco and his house . . . to the fourth generation."[92] Specifically, Venier had attempted to expel Ca' Bevardo from the Great Council on Crete by questioning the former duke of Crete Francesco Foscari's 1413 ruling that Marco's ancestor Bernardo di Giorgio Bevardo was a legitimate feudatory and council member. According to Marco Bevardo, it was because of Venier's hostility that he had been expelled from the Cretan council. The *Quarantia* in Venice fined Venier 100 lire and ordered him to remove himself from all future cases involving Bevardo; the council also restored Bevardo to his status as a legitimate member of the Cretan nobility.

Only a few years later, another Veneto-Cretan feudator brought similar charges against the syndic Antonio Gradenigo. Filippo Querini of Candia complained to the *avogadori di comun* in 1449 that Gradenigo had "proceeded fraudulently and maliciously, to his own shame and the impediment of the office of syndic." The *avogador* assigned to the case, Nicolò Bernardo, investigated the charge and concluded that it was not Gradenigo but Querini who was bringing false accusations. Bernardo recommended that the *Quarantia* dismiss the charges against Gradenigo, but after two rounds of voting the *Quarantia* decided to proceed with the charges against Gradenigo. The following year, the Senate heard the case against Gradenigo, in which he was charged with deliberately trying to ruin Filippo Querini by "advancing hateful and injurious words against him and threatening to destroy him" as well as bringing Querini to Venice and holding him there for a year, although he had no charges to bring against Querini. The prosecutors in the case proposed that Gradenigo pay Querini 120 ducats to reimburse him for his travel expenses. The Senate voted negatively on this proposal, although by a very close margin, meaning that Gradenigo did not have to pay anything to Querini.[93]

One of the most egregious examples of a syndic using his authority for personal benefit comes from the syndics Andrea Ghisi and Nicolò di Stefano Erizzo's 1413 tour of inspection on Negroponte. The first appeal against Erizzo's actions while in office came from Tomà Bernardo, a notary on Negroponte.[94] Erizzo had charged Tomà with disobeying his orders, an accusation that gave rise to an exchange of insults between Erizzo, Bernardo, and Ghisi. Erizzo had then fined Tomà 500 lire, but the *Quarantia* in Venice found that since Erizzo had been involved in the original fight, he was not competent to judge the case arising from it. Erizzo faced a much more serious accusation the following year. The *avogadori* presented evidence that Erizzo had threatened Andrea de Thachis, a former notary on Negroponte, with arrest and torture, compelling him to leave the island. Erizzo then expelled Andrea's wife and children from his house, which Erizzo took possession of himself, together with all of Andrea's goods and servants. Erizzo installed a slave woman as the mistress of the house "to show the maximum contempt for the wife of the said Andrea." Erizzo then auctioned off Andrea's goods and servants in the public marketplace of Negroponte, purchasing for himself or via agents some goods and a slave girl at prices far below what they were worth. One of the slave women, who had been bought by Giovanni Lippomano on Erizzo's behalf, escaped and fled the island. Erizzo, using his position as syndic, detained and tortured some of the *stipendarii* to discover where she had gone, keeping them in prison for over two months. Finally, as Erizzo was returning to Venice, he discovered that Andrea de Thachis was making his own way to the city to complain about the extortion he had suffered. Erizzo caught up with Andrea on Corfu and caused him to be detained there for months.

Andrea eventually reached Venice and presented his evidence to the *avogadori,* who brought the case to the *Quarantia.* This magistracy was evidently not totally convinced by the evidence, as the first two rounds of voting were inconclusive.[95] A third vote found Erizzo guilty and ruled that he had to return Andrea's slaves and repay him for his lost goods, as well as reimburse him for his expenses in bringing the case. Erizzo was also forbidden to serve as a syndic again, nor could he or Andrea Ghisi involve themselves in any matter touching on Andrea de Thachis. Unusually, the *avogadori* reserved the right to proceed against Andrea Ghisi at a later date, something they then did in April of 1416.[96] Ghisi and Erizzo were each ordered to pay Andrea de Thachis 50 gold ducats, and Erizzo was ordered to pay 27 *hyperperi* of Negroponte as rent for the time he had lived in De Thachis's house. These cases show the possible difficulties of obtaining conviction against officials who were prosecuted, and the relatively light punishments for those who were convicted.

Taken together, prosecutions against officials demonstrate the negative side of the private influence and interests that permeated Venice's imperial administration. An official could use his local knowledge to rule more effectively or to offer sage advice to Venetian councils; the same official could use that same local knowledge to extort goods and services from subjects or to pursue a personal vendetta. The Venetian system provided venues for subjects to complain when officeholders exceeded the bounds of custom or took aim at a particular individual. Venetian magistracies could redress the balance disturbed by its officials through its appeals courts and responses to communal delegations. Syndics could also bring prosecutions against officials who caused outrage among subjects, but they themselves could cause as many difficulties as they solved for subjects. But even when they were prosecuted in Venice for their actions in office, these officials left a bitter cocktail of resentment and grievances in their wake. This official misconduct placed a strain on Venice's already fragile state structures. When war and economic difficulties were added into the mix, as was the case in the early sixteenth century, the sinews of empire could easily snap.

SEVEN

Fault Lines of Empire

The problem of official corruption, misbehavior, and patrician arrogance weighed heavily on Venetian minds at the turn of the sixteenth century. A series of crises had shaken Venetian patrician confidence in the excellence of their government, the inviolability of their city, and the security of their state. When news of the Portuguese discovery of a route to the Indies and the resulting disruption of Venetian markets in the Levant reached the city, the banker and diarist Girolamo Priuli forecast that the tidings meant the ruin of Venice.[1] Almost simultaneously, a disastrous third war with the Ottomans from 1499 to 1503 confirmed what many had feared, that the Venetian fleet was no longer the dominant naval force in the eastern Mediterranean. To the west, Venice's expansion onto the Italian mainland had roused the pope, France, and the Holy Roman empire to join forces against the republic in the League of Cambrai. Venice's armies met the league's in battle outside the village of Agnadello in May of 1509, and the Venetian army was completely wiped out. In the wake of this disastrous battle, the cities of the Venetian *terraferma* one by one opened their gates to enemy forces. In order to explain these shocking events, a number of Venetian patricians turned to moral explanations, in particular pointing to the failings of the Venetian patricians who served as provincial administrators and officials. Priuli accused the Venetian mainland administrators of living in unseemly luxury, of neglecting their duty to dispense justice and instead accepting bribes and suppressing subjects' complaints and appeals.[2] Sanudo lamented that the loss of the *terraferma*—and more importantly its revenues—"was all caused by our bad government."[3]

Bad government, of course, was not limited to the mainland state. In the first decades of the sixteenth century, it combined with structural tensions and long-standing resentments to create waves of unrest in the *stato da mar* as well as the *terraferma*.[4] Scholars of the *terraferma* have pointed to the defection of the mainland nobilities in the face of French and imperial armies and outbreaks of popular violence like the Cruel Carnival of Udine as evidence of the hidden fissures and tensions of the Venetian rule that were revealed when the traditional Venetian mechanisms of negotiation and compromise were put under stress by war and economic difficulties.[5] There was a similar dynamic in the maritime state, and "scandal and murmuring" turned to violent protest in several locations, notably on the Dalmatian island of Lesina (Hvar) from 1510 to 1514 and in the western part of Crete from 1523 to 1529. Both cases have been the subject of detailed monographic studies: Gabelić's work on the revolt at Lesina, *Ustanak hvarskih pučana (1510–1514)* (The Rebellion of Hvar's Plebeians) and Papadia-Lala's analysis of the Cretan uprising, *Agrotikés tarachés kai exegérseis stē Venetokratoúmenē Krētē (1509–1528). E epanástasē tou Geōrgiou Gadanoléou-Lyssogiōrgē* (Agrarian Disturbances and Uprisings in Venetian Crete (1509–1528): The "Rebellion" of Georgios Gadanoleou-Lyssogiorges).[6] Together, the two cases demonstrate not only the way pressures from European-wide events made local structures extremely vulnerable but also highlight the differences in social structure and in the dynamics of the Venetian response in the maritime context.

A comparison of the Venetian response to the uprisings in Dalmatia and in Crete shows the limits of coercive power and the deeply rooted structures of appeal in Venice's empire. The Venetian state did use military force to repress the popular uprisings in both Lesina and in Crete, but the military solutions were nuanced by the same reliance on negotiation, appeal, and continuous litigation seen elsewhere in Venetian imperial administration. Venice sent its fleet to both Lesina and to Canea after hearing of the violence, and in both cases unruly mobs dispersed in the face of Venetian naval power only to reform after the fleet had moved on. The Venetian state then sent special military commanders—Sebastiano di Marino Giustinian to Lesina and Girolamo di Zorzi Corner to Crete—with instructions to punish the leaders of the rebellion. Both commanders were members of families with long traditions of maritime officeholding and investment, and Corner was connected to Cretan society by marriage. Giustinian and Corner confiscated rebel property, executed or exiled leaders of the rebellion, and issued judicial sentences punishing participants. The residents they had been sent to repress almost immediately responded by criticizing the commanders' actions and appealing their sentences in Venice. Venetian courts ultimately reversed many of Giustinian and Corner's rulings against the rebels, eloquent testimony to the persistence of the culture of appeal and negotiation in the Venetian system.

Disturbances in Dalmatia

Venice's territories in Dalmatia and Albania had suffered heavily from Turkish attacks during the third Ottoman-Venetian war (1499–1503), and the Ottoman pillaging of the countryside slowed but did not cease after the formal end of hostilities.[7] Ottoman aggression acted as a major destabilizing force in the area, both in terms of a persistent feeling of insecurity on the part of the residents and in very practical economic terms. In many cases the territory Venetian forces actually controlled had shrunk to within sight of the city walls; Venice's inability to protect the countryside led to decreased agricultural production, decreased tax revenue on that agricultural production, and hunger and scarcity in the cities.[8] The Dalmatian communes that had submitted to Venetian rule to gain a measure of protection against Ottoman forces were particularly frustrated at the failures of Venetian defenses, and delegations from the region repeatedly demanded newer fortifications, more troops, or more diplomacy from Venice, help that was not forthcoming.[9]

This constant pressure frayed social relations in many of the Dalmatian communities. In 1501, the count of Antivari, Pietro Tiepolo, reported that there were discords between the nobles and people in the city, in part because they were divided over how to respond to the "neighboring enemies."[10] Also in 1501, the count of Arbe, Alessandro di Alvise Contarini, wrote to the *Signoria* in Venice that there would be "great scandals" if 30 percent of the treasury was sent to Venice as had been ordered.[11] On Arbe in 1506, the Venetian rector Zaccaria Vallaresso blamed his difficulties in governing on the divisions between the nobles and *popolani* that made it "every day more difficult to proceed, this for some troublemakers and malevolent ones who work only to sow hatred between one part and the other."[12]

Any chance of increased defenses for the long Balkan border with the Ottomans disappeared after 1509, when all available military forces were engaged on the Italian mainland. The fiscal pressure of these years on the city of Venice was enormous.[13] While Venice's army size and military spending dramatically increased between 1509 and 1520, the vast majority of those expenditures went to the mainland, meaning that the maritime territories paid high taxes but saw few benefits in terms of defense. Treasuries in the maritime empire, where expenses outstripped revenues under normal circumstances, had been subsidized in some cases by the much richer cities of the mainland. After 1509, those subsidies disappeared, leaving the maritime cities to cover their rising costs of defense on their own. For the residents of Venetian Dalmatia, the attrition due to Ottoman raids combined with the high Venetian demands for taxes and soldiers to produce a situation with frightened and hungry residents, crumbling defenses, and empty treasuries. In the spring of 1510, the Ottomans mounted a series of raids, and the Venetian governor of Zara reported that "our poor subjects are disturbed and doubting, and this land has been badly devastated at the same time that they have given eighty men to the Loredan galley, and they always give to our galleys."[14]

The situation exacerbated a rarely articulated bitterness and resentment over Venetian rule in the Dalmatian coastal towns. There were, of course, Dalmatian nobles who made their fortunes through Venetian alliances, but others were loyal to Hungary or simply anti-Venetian. An exceptional moment that reveals the often hidden resistance to Venetian rule occurred in 1458, when the *Dieci* in Venice noticed that one of the Zarentine communal statutes, accepted and confirmed by Venice in 1409, was distinctly anti-Venetian. It likely dated to the 1358–1409 period of Hungarian rule, as it called for a solemn procession commemorating the day Zara left "the tyrannical service of Venice" and the release of a prisoner as a symbol of the Zarentine release from Venetian oppression. "To the disgrace of the Venetian dominion," this statute was discovered in the orders of the Zarentine council and in the commissions of the Zarentine judges, and it "represents their long-standing hatred against Venice and our *dominium* and recalls and introduces in young readers bad thoughts and ideas that are not appropriate." The *Dieci* canceled the statute immediately, ordering that the statute be rewritten so as not to offend Venetian honor. Adding insult to injury, it seemed that the offending statute had not simply been overlooked but had been "introduced within living memory and ignored by those who ruled Zara." While the Venetian empire was run partly on negotiation, the rhetoric of voluntary submission and compromise covered over a great deal of resentment and resistance.[15]

Local nobles in both the mainland and maritime cities often resented their loss of offices, privileges, and power to Venetian overlords. A group of Padovans in 1509 sent a delegation to the emperor in which they lamented their subjection to "3,000 Venetian tyrants."[16] Like the Padovans, factions within the Zarentine, Sebenican, and Spalatine nobilities hoped to find a greater degree of local autonomy under a more distant ruler and used the chaos of Cambrai to encourage a change of regime. At the outset of the war of Cambrai, the Venetian ambassador in Zagreb, Pietro Pasqualigo, reported that there were several conspirators attempting to convince the king to take back Dalmatia, assuring him that they had many relatives in the coastal cities who would help in the effort.[17] In 1510, the *Dieci* warned the governors of Zara to watch for contacts between certain Zarentine citizens and the king of Hungary. While Hungary was under some pressure to join the League of Cambrai, these attempts by disaffected Dalmatian nobles to convince him to join their cause ultimately failed.

All of these brewing tensions exploded in a tumult that swept through Friuli, Carinthia, Slovenia, and Dalmatia at the beginning of the war of Cambrai.[18] There were demonstrations of discontent in many of the Venetian territories along the Dalmatian and Albanian coast, including Arbe, Cattaro, Veglia, Antivari, and Sebenico. In all of these cases, the immediate cause of the turmoil was the commoners' vociferous demands for entry into communal councils and the nobles' equally strident denials of such an entry.[19] This was not a new conflict; in 1435 and again in 1441, a delegation from Sebenico to the Venetian Senate had complained that the nobles of Sebenico were working their way around the custom of admitting one commoner to the council of nobles each year on the feast of St. Michael by regularly taking "bastards, sons of priests and dissolute men, old men with no sons and of the lowest condition" rather than opening their ranks to important and influential commoners in order to "keep the rest of the citizens underfoot."[20] More than three-quarters of a century later, in the uneasy atmosphere of wartime scarcity, the commoners of Sebenico were still complaining about the nobles' abuses. "Discords, sedition, and scandal" broke out between the two groups in December 1510 and delegations of both the noble and popular factions arrived in Venice in the spring of 1511.[21] That summer a group of commoners attacked and killed a Sebenican nobleman and sacked at least ten houses in the city; when the *Dieci* asked the Venetian count what steps he had taken, he replied that he had been unable to respond to these events or punish the guilty parties because he had so few soldiers.[22] The role of Venetian representatives in the turmoil differed from place to place. The count of Cattaro, Angelo Malipiero, was called to nearby Antivari to adjudicate the differences between noble and popular factions there, while there were processions in Arbe's piazza against the count there, Simone Orio.[23]

Urban Uprising: Popular Violence at Lesina

There were similar disturbances on the island of Lesina in late 1510 and 1511, but the factional violence there went beyond urban insurrection and turned into a four-year rebellion against the aristocratic—and Venetian—order. In February of 1510, popular leaders from both the town and country districts on Lesina swore an oath to destroy the nobility on the cathedral's cross, which then miraculously "wept with blood."[24] Then in May, a group of *popolani* attacked nobles in the town.

Different observers offered alternate explanations for the attack: according to Nicolò da Molin, the Venetian count of nearby Brazza, three popular instigators—Matteo Ivanić, Giacomo Blascović, and Zuan Sorella—had roused over two thousand armed men to attack the nobles of the city.[25] According to Sanudo, the count of Lesina, Antonio Lippomano, wrote to Venice confessing that he "was not without fault" in the events, although he did not provide details on how he contributed to the uprising.[26] The commander of the Venetian fleet, Girolamo Contarini, reported that the violence had been sparked by three young noblemen of Lesina, who "had committed some dishonesties against the women of the inhabitants there, which was the cause that incited them to arm themselves . . . saying that they no longer wished to be under the feet of these nobles nor have their houses shamed by the nobles in any way."[27] Whatever the initial spark, the mob had threatened to burn the nobles in their houses unless they agreed to allow commoners to enter the Great Council of Lesina and the right to be elected as communal officials. After obtaining this agreement, the rebels then sacked the houses of the nobles, many of whom fled to neighboring towns and islands.

When Contarini arrived in the port of Lesina with the Venetian fleet, he exhorted the people to lay down their arms and return to their houses, which they did. He then sent two representatives of each faction to present their demands in Venice; he also warned the *Signoria* that if the popular faction obtained access to the council, it would "give grounds for similar requests from the people of all the other cities of Dalmatia, from Albania to Istria, and it would be the cause of many discords."[28] At the same time that the Senate in Venice was considering the requests of both the noble and popular orators from Lesina, the state sent a syndic and *provveditore,* Giovanni Navagero, to the island to investigate the noble and popular complaints and to gather evidence.[29]

Navagero's mission was designed with the appearance of impartiality more than anything else: his private instructions included orders to immediately suspend the three regulations the popular faction had compelled the nobles and Venetian count to accept. More tellingly, Navagero's salary was to be paid by the Lesinan nobles, who had offered to give him 40 ducats a month without the obligation to give any account of his spending.[30] Navagero's mission did not deflect further violence; in the summer of 1511, the Venetian count in Lesina reported that the houses of thirteen nobles in nearby Lissa had been sacked and that he was on his way to investigate the matter.[31] At the same time, a group of Lesinan men prepared to send a new and more radical request to Venice, asking for the establishment of a Great Council of Lesina that was to be open to all (*tutto el popolo*), and that this council should then elect seventy to eighty members annually to a smaller council that would then act as a sort of Senate; the proposal would have effectively eliminated any meaningful distinction between nobles and commoners.[32]

Historians have interpreted the events at Lesina in a variety of ways. Croatian historians have pointed to the commercial dynamics of Dalmatian society in this period, seeing the social upheavals of the period as a result of an increasingly prosperous merchant and artisan class protesting its exclusion from politics.[33] Andro Gabelić, in his monograph on the rebellion, follows a Marxist line of interpretation in his emphasis on class struggle; he argues that the uprising in Lesina was not a spontaneous outbreak of violence but a planned campaign with defined goals that included all segments of the non-noble population, from wealthy urban citizens to peasants from the more rural areas.[34] Angelo Ventura saw the Dalmatian turmoil as broadly comparable to events in the subject cities of the *terraferma.*[35] For Ventura, the Dalmatian people's protests against the exclusivity of the councils of nobles, and Venice's eventual defense of the nobles, were further evidence for his thesis that Venetian territorial administration was committed to upholding an artificial aristocratic order. Ventura, however, has some difficulty fitting Venice's extremely slow response to the Dalmatian crisis into his scheme of aristocratic repression.

There is no denying that the Venetian state's response to the disturbance of the peace in Lesina and in the rest of Dalmatia was slow and halting. It was not until the radical proposal to restructure communal government along egalitarian lines was added to the open violence in Sebenico and the mounting threat of renewed violence in Lesina that the *Dieci* turned to a more military solution. Sebastiano di Marino Giustinian was elected as a *provveditore generale* with both military and judicial powers in the fall of 1511.[36] Giustinian was notorious as the *podestà* who had consigned Brescia to the French in 1509; not only had he surrendered the city, but he and his sons had escaped the city while the captain, Marco Dandolo, mounted an ultimately futile defense and ended in a French prison.[37] Giustinian was then sent as military governor to Istria, where he conducted a markedly unsuccessful defense of the province's northern border. In the fall of 1511, the Venetian Senate removed him from his command there and instead sent him as military governor to Dalmatia. But rather than rushing to the scene of the turmoil, Giustinian wintered in Capodistria, waiting for money and provisions.

Even when he left Capodistria in the spring of 1512, Giustinian did not hasten to the scene of the crisis in Lesina but spent much of the spring and early summer investigating the behavior of Venetian officials in Zara and nearby Veglia. His focus on official misconduct recalls Priuli's concern with bad government as a cause of popular discontent with Venetian rule. Giustinian investigated the *provveditore* of Veglia, Francesco di Michele Michiel, who was rumored to be involved in some scandal with the count of Zara, Lorenzo di Lorenzo Correr, and the captain there, Leonardo di Maffeo Michiel. Giustinian ultimately arrested four men and sent them to Venice, including the chancellor of the Zarentine administration.[38] Almost a full year after his election, Giustinian finally arrived in Sebenico, where he reported that he had arrested fourteen men, "leaders of the people and other seditious men"; two of them he had hung, and the rest, he said, he would punish as God inspired him.[39] It seems that even at this point, there were criticisms of Giustinian's methods and decisions, and Giustinian defended himself against these unknown critics in a letter addressed to his son that ended in Marino Sanudo's hands, declaring that he fully expected he would be criticized in the Senate on his return to Venice.[40]

While Giustinian continued his slow progress down the coast toward Lesina, the disturbances there continued. In May of 1512, the *Dieci* wrote that they had heard of new "discords, sedition, and scandal."[41] The Venetian count, Antonio Lippomano, appears to have approved an accord between the nobles and *popolani*, as in July of 1512 the *Dieci* reprimanded him, stating that "what you have done could not be more contrary to our intention" and ordering him to cancel the agreement.[42] While the *Dieci* invited the representatives from Lesina to come to Venice and present their demands, the council almost simultaneously wrote to Giustinian, explaining that it had no intention to "innovate" or to approve the *capitoli* proposed by the Lesinan people.[43] The Venetian state here relied on the tradition of negotiation between center and periphery to delay decisive action until its military forces arrived. When Giustinian and the fleet finally arrived in Lesina in the fall of 1512, he immediately condemned to death sixty-five men he declared to be the leaders of the revolt and confiscated the rebels' property. He also besieged the port of Vrboska, where a number of the rebels and their leader, Matteo Ivanić, were camped. Giustinian lost the engagement badly and had to flee. In September, Giustinian wrote to the *Signoria* that there had been a ceremony of peace in the cathedral and that the two leaders of the rebellion were willing to come to Venice under a safe-conduct; the *Dieci* responded by ordering Giustinian to proclaim that Matteo Ivanić and Giacomo Blascović and his father must present themselves within a month or they would be condemned in absentia.[44]

When Giustinian returned to Venice in November of 1512, he proudly trumpeted his own adept conduct of the war, but he faced considerable criticism for his actions in office. Venice's strategies of appeal to the center now worked against Giustinian, as representatives of both the noble and popular factions traveled to

Venice on Giustinian's heels, some to present their demands to the Venetian state, but many to denounce Giustinian himself.[45] When Giustinian made his report to the Senate, which according to Sanudo lasted over three hours, he said "many impertinent things to excuse himself for the fires he made in a village near Lesina."[46] On that Sunday, a group of Lesinans appeared on the stairs of the Great Council and shouted insults against Giustinian during the meeting. Their protests against Giustinian continued for the next two years. In 1513, a group of Lesinans appeared before the *Signoria* denouncing Giustinian for having condemned sixty-nine men without any cause.[47] The following year, in the summer of 1514, a Lesinan named Zorzi, in Venice to pursue a case against Giustinian, accosted him on the steps of the ducal palace and insulted him.[48] In the aftermath of the first attempt to put down the rebellion, Giustinian personally absorbed much of the Dalmatians' outrage while the Venetian state remained a venue of mediation and appeal for both sides.

Rather than fighting the Lesinans' appeals and charges against him, Giustinian doggedly pressed his cases against the Venetian governors of Dalmatia, in particular Zuan Francesco Miani, the former count of Sebenico.[49] Giustinian first tried to introduce his case against Miani in March of 1513 but was unsuccessful, as in the summer of 1514 he complained that every time he tried to introduce this matter of "great importance" to the Senate, it was sent to the *Quarantia*.[50] In September of 1514, Giustinian presented the *Quarantia* with an accusation against Miani that totaled over 130 pages; Miani countered with over one hundred pages of his own testimony and evidence.[51] Giustinian charged that Miani had had sex with a nun and another woman, both of whom he had "used in a bad way and against nature." Giustinian further charged that Miani had had a certain Zuan Barbier killed in order to cover up his crime.[52] Miani's advocates denied these charges, but Miani was found guilty and imprisoned. Miani's relatives then appealed to the *avogador* Pietro Contarini, claiming that all the evidence in the case had not been considered. On the following day, Contarini spoke on Miani's behalf in the council, saying that the council was being tricked and sending for Giustinian's chancellor in Capodistria to investigate some of the evidence that had been presented. Contarini's defense was ultimately unsuccessful; while Miani was not directly charged with contributing to the uprising against the Venetian state in Sebenico, it seems he shouldered at least some of the blame.

In contrast, the Lesinans' appeals against Giustinian were successful, and all of Giustinian's convictions and confiscations against the Lesinan rebels were overturned in Venetian courts. In December of 1514, there was a general amnesty for all except the eight leaders of the revolt.[53] The amnesty came after the last outbreak of overt revolt in Lesina, which occurred in the summer of 1514. Five nobles were killed on their own lands, and in August a group of protesters burst into the city and killed twenty-six nobles.[54] In response, the Venetian commander Vincenzo di Nicolò Capello was sent to deal with the "extremely evident danger to our state."[55] He arrived in Lesina in October, hanging twenty leaders of the rebellion from the yardarm of his galley and punishing or banishing others. On the orders of the *Dieci,* all other Lesinans were absolved; Giustinian's condemnations and confiscations were rescinded, and the popular faction's request to add a treasurer from the people in addition to one from the nobility was granted.[56] The count of Lesina, Vincenzo Donà, followed these instructions to the letter and apparently pardoned Matteo Ivanić and the other leaders of the revolt who were still at large. In November he received an angry letter from the *Dieci* reprimanding him for having pardoned everyone, including the eight heads of the rebellion, which had not been their intention.[57] The *Dieci* instructed Donà to put a price on Ivanić's head and to hang him immediately if he was captured. In December the *Dieci* confirmed to Donà that Giustinian's sentences were canceled and that he should return all the confiscated property to the rightful owners.[58] While Ivanić was never captured, the rebellion did end at this point; the Venetians sponsored a ceremony of peace between the nobles and *popolani* and allowed the corpses of the rebels to be removed from the city walls and returned to their families for burial.[59]

In the final assessment, the causes of the rebellion can be attributed largely to poverty, constant raids by the Ottomans, and persistent tensions over the nobles' privileged position in society. The Venetian administration's response, once these factors had caused social and economic tensions to explode into violence, was deeply conditioned by the process of continuous litigation and appeal to central magistracies, so that no solution imposed by commanders on the ground was final. Several of the officials, in particular Lippomano and Donà, were unwilling to take any sort of action without consulting with Venice, and when they approved concords or pardoned rebels they were reprimanded and ordered to revoke or cancel their orders. When officials did act on their own initiative, as Giustinian did in condemning sixty-five men, their decisions were then subject to appeal and criticism in Venice, making individual Venetian representatives and not the state itself the focus of controversy.

Background to a Crisis in Crete

The Ottoman banditry of the Balkans took the form of pirate raids on the naval frontier, but the economic and social effects of these depredations on Crete were similar to those seen in Dalmatia. Pirates were a constant fear along the island's coasts, and inhabitants would regularly flee at the sight of a sail on the horizon.[60] During the third Venetian-Turkish war (1463–1479), orators from Sitia asked that the district be exempted from taxes, saying that the area had been pillaged by Turkish pirate raids and that whole families were relocating to Candia in search of greater safety.[61] These raids disturbed both agriculture and commerce on the island, and were made worse by a series of earthquakes which disrupted island life and ruined thousands of houses, churches, and public buildings. The earthquake of May 1508 was particularly devastating; a Venetian official described it as "terrible, horrendous, and terrifying . . . it ruined the majority of the land, and that which remains standing is uninhabitable."[62] Other quakes followed in 1517, 1522, 1524, 1525, and 1531.[63] Large numbers of people fled Candia in panic after the 1508 earthquake, believing that the Turkish corsair Kemal-Reis would hear of the island's misfortune and take the opportunity to attack.[64] There were also several outbreaks of plague in this period, one in Canea in 1513 and another throughout the island in 1523–24, which coincided with an earthquake.[65] Sanudo reported that because of this earthquake many fled to cities, where they died of plague.[66]

In addition to piracy and natural disasters, the Cretan treasury felt the effects of the war of the League of Cambrai and Venice's loss of its mainland territories—and their subsidies for maritime treasuries—quite keenly. Venice had shifted many of these fiscal burdens to the treasury in Crete, despite strong protests from the island's administrators.[67] The economic pressures of war, attacks from Ottoman pirates, and frequent natural disasters created a volatile situation, particularly combined with the long-standing ethnic and religious resentments on the island. The situation was clearly ripe for unrest, particularly among the peasants, who were the most vulnerable due to the heavy taxes, fees, and obligatory labor services the state as well as landlords imposed on them. Already in 1508, the duke of Crete, Alvise Arimondo, described an unsettled countryside where "many peasants are always rising up, where before they had remained peaceful . . . and dedicated to the world of agriculture."[68]

The Venetian administrators on Crete in these years were also partially to blame for the rebellion. As was the case in many other peasant rebellions, the situation spiraled out of control in part because "the authorities lacked the political skill or will to defuse potentially dangerous situations."[69] In fact, the energies of a number of Venetian administrators on Crete in these years were almost entirely dedicated to internecine power struggles. In June 1497, the rector of Rettimo Gabriele Pizzamano's death led to open conflict in the streets between the replacement sent from Candia, Antonio Zancani, and Pizzamano's two counselors, Antonio Baffo and Bernardino Polani.[70] Baffo and Polani refused to recognize Zancani's authority, and Baffo declared himself vice-rector of the city, an act that "encouraged that land to sedition, so that part obeyed him and part obeyed Zancani." Adding to the general disorder, a servant of Polani's killed a servant of Zancani's during a brawl and was arrested by Zancani's forces. Polani and Baffo then helped this servant escape from Zancani's custody, and Polani hid the man in his own house. Zancani and his forces then attacked Polani's house, captured the murderous servant, and decapitated him. Rettimo was in a state of open warfare between the two government factions, and the situation was only settled when the captain of the island, Girolamo da Pesaro, rode with his troops to the city and forced its inhabitants to accept Zancani's authority. Polani and Baffo were arrested and sent to Venice, where they were tried and condemned by the *Dieci*.[71]

The fighting rectors of Rettimo were not an isolated case. In 1513, the rector of Canea, Michele di Antonio Memmo, was in such conflict with his counselors that Venice was forced to send a syndic to the city. A dispute between the rector of Rettimo, Francesco Barbarigo, and his counselors, lasted throughout 1525–26.[72] Duke Nicolò Zorzi admonished Barbarigo, saying, "You are surely aware that nothing can compromise the job of rector more than can discord, that when the factions among them fight, all the rest of the society is hurt." Zorzi here made a clear connection between the unity and concord of the Venetian administration and the peace of society in general. He instructed Barbarigo to act swiftly to punish any violent or armed quarrel, and he also highlighted the importance of continuity between administrations, going on to say, "keep in sight that which your predecessors have done in the assembly, and always cut off conflicts at the start so that they can live united without compromising anyone." Unfortunately, few of Venice's administrators on the island heeded Zorzi's advice.[73]

Rural Revolt in Western Crete

Some of the more egregious examples of Venetian officials' misconduct come from the mountainous district of Sfakia, southwest of Rettimo—not coincidentally, the epicenter of the rebellion in the 1520s. The Venetian *provveditore* of the region had outraged the inhabitants through his extortions and inept and partisan administration of justice, and in 1509 the Sfakians complained to the ducal regime in Candia.[74] The duke cautioned the *provveditore* against any future rulings made for his private benefit or out of his personal loyalties and ordered him to assemble the population of the area, including those whom he had insulted, and "with appropriate words placate them, and in the future govern them . . . with the dexterity, prudence, circumspection, and moderation which we look for in our rectors, so that our loyal people do not have any reason to complain of any bad administration of justice." This measure was apparently not effective, as by January of 1510 Arimondo had received fifty-three complaints from the peasants of the district and a request that he send syndics to adjudicate them.[75] Arimondo responded by again instructing the *provveditore* to reform his behavior, saying, "Don't give them any further cause to come and complain," but in 1512 there were new disturbances in the district.[76] The duke ordered the *provveditore* to proclaim a total ban on carrying arms in the district, with harsh penalties for anyone committing acts of violence.

In response to these outbreaks of violence, the regime in Candia dispatched the captain of Crete, Bernardo di Marco Barbarigo. Barbarigo, the son of the former doge, Marco, had served as *bailo* of Corfu (1505) before he was elected as captain on Crete. After his arrival in the spring of 1511, he marched through the western part of the island and confiscated a great deal of land and goods. As in the case of Giustinian's sentences and condemnations in Dalmatia, the residents of western Crete quickly petitioned against these sentences and confiscations. The Cretan delegation to Venice was led by two Veneto-Cretan feudatories, Fabricio Corner and Vincenzo Zorzi, and presented a petition in Venice arguing that Barbarigo had confiscated lands that their families had owned for more than three hundred years, and it was these sentences which had stirred up so much armed protest. Barbarigo defended himself, saying that he had earned over 60,000 ducats for Venice, but nonetheless the *Dieci* suspended the confiscations. Back on Crete, the regime in Candia chastised the *provveditore* of Sfakia for not enforcing the sentences of exile against the "murderers, assassins, and other malefactors" of the district. Describing "great confusion and the condition of the lands . . . [that] is a grave impediment to justice" there, the duke and his counselors renewed the sentences of exile and confiscation handed out earlier.[77]

Matters on Crete were thus in a delicate state; residents of western Crete had lived through decades of instability and violence caused by earthquakes, pirates, and plague as well as the infighting of Venetian officials. It was into this environment that Sebastiano di Marino Giustinian, the much reviled *provveditore* of the campaign in Dalmatia, was sent as Barbargio's replacement as captain of Crete. In fact, Giustinian had been elected captain of Verona but had volunteered to serve in Candia instead, where he would be in a position to help his relatives on Andros and in Constantinople.[78] There was some minor difficulty in his election to this post, as one of his relatives, Girolamo di Benedetto Giustinian, was serving as rector in Rettimo. Sanudo commented that "I have seen this law [against relatives serving together] observed, but here it was not followed." Giustinian arrived in the port of Candia in July to great fanfare and began to inspect the island's defenses and military preparedness. In the fall of 1520, Giustinian reported to the *Signoria* in Venice that there were some disturbances in the area around Canea and recommended that those responsible be punished, warning that "if the *villani* near Candia should imitate their actions, and the Turkish armada should come to the island, these *tristi* would deliver it to them."[79]

The disturbances and scattered incidents of violence in western Crete turned into open rebellion in 1523. The rector of Canea Benedetto di Marco Barbo's death in 1523 led to squabbles between his counselor and a replacement from Candia over who should fill his position, meaning that only one other official, the counselor of Canea, Girolamo Querini, was on the scene at the beginning of the popular protest, marked by a widespread refusal to pay taxes.[80] The revolt began outside the city of Canea, on the property of the Venetian landowner Lorenzo Massolo. In 1523, Massolo had requested the *Dieci*'s permission to sell his holdings, saying that the "the general hatred [the *villani*] have toward our family is such that it is not without grand danger of my life that I live there."[81] In a supporting letter, Querini blamed the peasants' hatred on Lorenzo's father, Pietro, saying that he had treated his *villani* so badly that what had been the three hundred richest and most obedient peasants on the island "were reduced to such desperation that there is no more remedy for it" except to allow Massolo to leave.[82]

The disturbances that had begun on the Massolo property in Chiaramea soon spread throughout the district of Canea, including the city itself. Querini reported that the peasants from Chiaramea "without fear or any respect came to the porte . . . to assassinate and kill people, with little honor for the *dominio* and [setting] the worst example for all the island."[83] By the time Domenico Trevisan, the captain-general of the Venetian fleet, arrived to quell the nascent uprising, the rebellion had grown to about six hundred *villani* protesting against the landowners of the district and refusing to pay their taxes or dues.[84] He ordered the protesters to return to their lands and pay their taxes, promising they would not be prosecuted for their behavior as long as they continued to "live quietly,"[85] and his orders, or the intimidating power of the Venetian fleet, induced the peasants to leave the city and give up their violent protests, at least temporarily.

Trevisan sharply criticized the administrators on Crete in his report to the *Dieci,* saying that the uprising had gotten out of hand because the island's officials had not acted decisively enough. He observed that, when faced with the disturbances on Massolo's property in Chiaramea and the refusal of the *villani* to pay their taxes, the administrators had been reluctant to use severe repressive measures because they feared that the upheaval would alert the Ottomans to the island's weakness and "make some strange thoughts come into [the sultan's] head."[86] The danger of Ottoman attack was of paramount concern to the Venetian officials on the island and efforts to improve defenses and fortifications absorbed much of their attention in these years, to the detriment of the already infuriated peasants. In 1525, the duke Nicolò Zorzi ordered peasants from the district of Milipotamo, located between Rettimo and Candia, to perform their labor services at the fortifications of Paleocastro, on the peninsula overlooking the Gulf of Candia.[87] The rector of Rettimo, Francesco Barbarigo, countermanded this order and sent all the peasants back to Milipotamo. When Zorzi heard that his order had been revoked, he wrote to Barbarigo, angrily ordering him to see that the peasants return to work at Paleocastro. Barbarigo responded that there were so many Ottoman ships around the island that it was too dangerous to order them to work on the coast, also pointing out that since Milipotamo was part of Rettimo's district, its peasants should perform their labor service there and not in the district of Candia. In response, Zorzi wrote that he had reasons for his order Barbarigo was not aware of and that the peasants should return to Paleocastro.[88] The situation was further destabilized by the deaths of Barbarigo and Donato Marcello, captain-general of the island, during their term of office and strife at Ierapetra, on the island's southern coast.[89]

In 1526, there was a new round of conflict centered in Santa Nichita, a Venetian castle in the district of Canea, again due to poor administrative practices and incompetent—in this case absent—officials. The castellan of Santa Nichita was missing when the regime in Candia received a series of complaints from the area's inhabitants, and the Duke and his counselors were obliged to write to Sfakia and Canea in an attempt to locate the man and force him to return to his post.[90] In the castellan's absence, the commander of the castle guard was in charge, and it was his soldiers who were responsible for the "insults" to the residents. Certain soldiers were favoring their relatives, and the regime in Candia instructed the commander that he could either fire the guilty soldiers and replace them himself or that the captain in Candia would send some replacements.[91] The commander was also administering justice in the castellan's absence, and to avoid future complaints of partiality or of laxity, the regime in Candia ordered him to limit his activities to the collection of evidence and to forward the cases to Candia for adjudication, so that criminals' prosecutions and punishments "will be an example to the others." As in the previous instances of violence and protest, Venetian officials responded with stopgap and ad hoc measures to end the immediate source of conflict. At the first sign of repression, many of the peasants would flee into their mountain strongholds, where they remained until the temporary measures of the local Venetian magistrates had faded. In 1523, during the Chiaramea disturbances, Querini complained that "because of their fortified places we can do nothing."[92]

Another official claimed in 1527 that in the more remote villages of Sfakia, Venetian officials wielded no authority at all and in fact had been afraid to visit these places for as long as fifteen years.[93] In a seventeenth-century chronicle loosely based on the peasant disturbances of the early sixteenth century, the Venetian chronicler Antonio Trevisan stated that the peasants' leader, Georgios Gadanoleou-Lyssogiorges, had set up an entirely separate government in the mountains, with himself as rector and his allies as captain, grand chancellor, and mayor.[94] Papadia-Lala's analysis makes clear that these events had only a loose connection with what would eventually become known as the Gadanoleou rebellion, the subject of Spiridon Zambelios's famous novel *Cretan Wedding*. Papadia-Lala has convincingly attributed the underlying cause of the revolt to the burden of the heavy taxes, fees, and obligatory labor services the state as well as landlords placed on the peasants, and similar peasant rebellions in other parts of Europe lend further support to this motivation for the movement.[95]

As in the first stages of the uprising at Lesina, the Venetian state was initially slow to respond to the violence. By the end of the 1520s, however, Venetian attention turned from the war of Cambrai to the constant upheaval in western Crete. In the spring of 1527, the *Dieci* ordered Girolamo di Giorgio Corner, captain-general of the island, to raise an army and attack the rebellious villages, telling him to do whatever it took to "securely eradicate them and have them cut to pieces," giving him permission "to have their villages destroyed and to confiscate their goods and to make every other harsh provision that seems to you will set an example and terrorize other rebels."[96] Even before his election as captain, Corner's marriage to the daughter of the Veneto-Cretan feudatory Marco di Antonio Mudazzo meant that he had significant connections to island society, connections that proved useful in his task as captain.[97] Corner's father-in-law, Marco Mudazzo, was married to a daughter of Matteo di Andrea Calergi, and when Corner left the city of Candia in the fall of 1527 with two hundred riflemen and three hundred infantry, he was accompanied by Andrea Calergi.[98] Corner's family connections were a double-edged sword: they offered him a network of local alliances on which he could draw for support, but they also posed the potential for conflicts of interest.

Corner's troops marched through the mountains for about two months, hunting and capturing suspected rebels, threatening the women and children who had been left behind in the villages, and confiscating or destroying rebel property. Corner finally exiled about 560 of the district's inhabitants, either sending them to Cyprus or condemning them to the galleys.[99] In what had become a familiar pattern, however, many of Corner's measures were protested, appealed, and overturned. Corner's replacement as captain-general, Alvise Benedetto, immediately suspended all of Corner's proclamations and legislation against the rebels upon his arrival in 1528. In July of 1528, the *Dieci* ordered the governors of Rettimo, Sitia, and Canea to enforce Corner's banishments, but the governors remained hesitant; there was also a collective appeal against Corner's decrees from the residents of Alicambo, a village in the west of Crete.[100] In November of the same year, Duke Iacopo di Donato Corner, from a distant branch of the Corner clan, wrote to the *Dieci* explaining that Girolamo Corner's violent repression of the peasants of Sfakia had not only failed to end the rebellion but in fact had caused more disturbances throughout the island. The Duke explained that while he had informed the reluctant regional rectors that Captain Corner's orders had come from the *Dieci* and thus must be obeyed, some of the island's officials remained reluctant to enforce Corner's decrees.

Corner's sentences of banishment did not turn out to be permanent either; a number of the six hundred men sent to Cyprus purchased passage on a Venetian ship and returned to the island the following year.[101] Predicting that with their return "there will be without doubt a lot of confusion," Corner requested public funds to chase down the returned *banditi,* but the island's government refused to authorize the necessary funds.[102] Corner faced this criticism of his actions by blaming the continuing disorder on Crete's other governors, saying if the regime had acted more harshly against the rebels they would have been too terrorized to return to the island.[103] Corner, who remained on the island after his term of duty was finished, sent a strong protest to the *Dieci,* arguing that his actions had been both within the realm of his commission and within his rights as captain-general.

While the general pattern of residents appealing the decisions of the Venetian commanders sent to repress them remains valid in the Cretan case, there are also several distinct differences between the Venetian response to events in Dalmatia and events in Crete that point to the larger structural distinctions between the two societies. Given Crete's long history of resistance to Venetian rule, the Venetian state was much quicker to label the Cretan peasants' actions as a rebellion than had been the case in Dalmatia; Venetian officials on Crete almost immediately began to refer to seditious men, disobedient evildoers, and rebels.[104] In Dalmatia, Venetian commentators had described the events as disturbances and scandals between nobles and the people, and interpreted them as anti-Venetian only by extent—that by disturbing the peace of the republic they were rebelling against the order Venice had pledged to provide. While the initial behavior in both cases was the same—peasants attacking noble landowners and demanding more reasonable economic terms—on Crete, the landowners in question were Venetian, while in Lesina they were Dalmatian, giving a specifically anti-Venetian flavor to Cretan protests against landowner exactions. Perhaps because of this difference in perception, the repression on Crete was much more violent and widespread. Giustinian initially condemned sixty-five men in Lesina, and Vincenzo Capello eventually executed twenty men. In comparison, Corner's march through western Crete was extremely violent, and he ended by banishing almost six hundred men to Cyprus.

Despite these differences, the basic structure of the Venetian response to the unrest in both Crete and Lesina was similar. In both cases, the republic sent a part of its fleet at the first sign of unrest—Girolamo Contarini went to Lesina and Domenico Trevisan went to Canea—but both of these commanders, pressed with threats on other fronts, only stayed briefly, ordering the protesters to lay down their arms and return to their homes. Which the protesters did, only to take up their arms again as soon as the Venetian fleet was over the horizon, demonstrating the effective limits of military intervention. In both cases, it was only after several years that Venetian forces made a more comprehensive effort to dig out dissent at the root, executing or exiling the leaders of the rebellion, as Sebastiano Giustinian did in Lesina and Girolamo Corner did on Crete, and even then these harsh responses were conditioned by subsequent appeals, compromise, and negotiation.

From one point of view, the Venetian response to these moments of crisis might be defined as slow, halfhearted, and ineffective. But seen from another perspective, the Venetian approach proved to be remarkably adept at moving conflict out of the streets and into its own magistracies. By 1514, at least some Lesinans were no longer locked in battle with one another but were focused on appealing Sebastiano Giustinian's actions in Venetian courts and on maligning him personally on the steps of the ducal palace. By 1528, a number of residents of western Crete had ended their uprising and refusal to pay taxes and were pursuing their grievances against Girolamo Corner in Venetian courts. Military campaigns rooted out the most pernicious sources of dissent, but a great deal of conflict was routed through the Venetian judicial system, which provided a second outlet for mediating conflict and restoring public order.

A Hollow Empire? Defending Dominion in the Sixteenth Century

By the third decade of the sixteenth century, the Venetian state had put the dramatic events of the war of Cambrai and the maritime rebellions behind it but had to confront a much deeper and more permanent change in its international position.[105] Venice's former rivals for power in the region—Genoa, Hungary, and the Byzantine empire—had given way to increasingly centralizing states that completely encircled Venetian territory. To the north, west, and south were the Hapsburg domains in the regions of Austria and Hungary, united under Charles V with the Iberian peninsula, the Kingdom of Naples, and Milan. To the east was the Ottoman empire, which under Selim I and Suleiman the Magnificent expanded to include the Balkans, much of Hungary, and the former Mamluk territories of Syria and Egypt. Venice's maritime domains were a thin sliver in between these two giants, and Venetian subjects and officials found themselves on the front lines of interaction. In addition, Venice's economic hegemony in the region was challenged as well; not by the Portuguese entry into the spice trade that Priuli had feared but by competitors from Northern Europe who increasingly entered Mediterranean markets in the sixteenth century. As a sign of the Venetian state's new and conflicting priorities, the state-sponsored merchant fleets ended in 1530, as the state's galleys were increasingly needed for defensive purposes.[106]

One telling incident as to Venice's new status on the international stage comes from Sebastiano Giustinian's long and varied career. In between his tours of duty in Lesina and in Crete, Giustinian was the ambassador to the English court. In 1516, Giustinian was confronted by two unnamed English lords, who sneeringly remarked, "These Venetians are fishermen."[107] Giustinian, according to himself, replied that such an assertion would not have been made by one who had been to Venice and seen the city, its Senate, and its nobility. Moreover, he said, the Christian faith had been founded by fishermen and that the Venetian fishermen had defended it against the infidel—a spirited response, but one that left Venice's future in such a defense in doubt.

It was, in fact, the Spanish and Austrian Hapsburgs who led Christian armies in the sixteenth century. The Hapsburg and Ottoman empires clashed to the north and to the south of Venetian domains, at Mohacs (1526), Vienna (1529), and

Tunis (1535). In 1537, Venice allied with Spain in a war against the Ottomans (1537–1540), but the city's changed role in the Mediterranean was signaled by the battle of Prevesa, off the coast of mainland Greece south of Corfu.[108] In September of 1538, the Venetian fleet tried to trap the Ottoman fleet against the coast, but at a crucial moment the commander of the imperial fleet, Andrea Doria, retreated, leaving the Venetians to face the Ottomans alone. The Ottoman fleet, led by the famous corsair Barbarossa, plundered the western part of Crete in 1538, after laying waste to Corfu. Prevesa and its aftermath were emblematic of the new Venetian position in the eastern Mediterranean: struggling to maintain its position in the region in the face of inconstant allies and powerful opponents.

As Venice accepted its new status as a secondary power in the region, its policies toward the maritime state shifted as well, concentrating on conciliation and defense. Between 1537 and 1571, the Venetian state spent astronomical sums on updating and reinforcing the defensive fortifications of its maritime cities.[109] In some ways, this new focus on defense responded to maritime residents' determined appeals for stronger protection, although the new fortifications served Venetian state interests as well. In 1542, Venice established the *provveditori alle fortezze* to oversee building of a defensive belt around its territories, and the *provveditore generale del regno di Candia* took on wider jurisdictions and responsibilities on Crete from the 1530s on. Throughout the Venetian empire, the Venetian state reorganized its treasuries and introduced fiscal reform and sent syndics and *provveditori* to streamline administration and raise funds for the defensive works. These fortifications created a military stalemate with the Ottomans. Venetian infantry could well defend fortified cities but were less effective in the countryside, while the cavalry forces used by the Ottomans in the Balkans dominated the countryside but were unable to take a fortified city without a significant army. This stalemate might have looked impressive, but one perceptive observer in the seventeenth century noted that the fortresses of Dalmatia and Albania "are all for the most part uninhabited and barren . . . and serve only to maintain the appearance of a great empire."[110]

Venetians at home and in Europe might have employed anti-Ottoman rhetoric to their own advantage, but on the frontier Venetian officials were strictly enjoined to avoid offending their Ottoman counterparts at all cost. The Venetian-Ottoman border was extremely porous, as the religious and political dividing lines crossed a society that was wound together economically and culturally. The job of mediating and controlling the varied interactions between Ottoman and Venetian subjects fell to the Venetian rector. In 1515, Francesco di Andrea Tagliapietra was sent as count to Sebenico with the following instructions: "As you have understood . . . it is our firm desire that [peace with the Ottomans] be maintained and not interrupted by any of our rectors or our subjects."[111] The same admonition, to live "quietly and in peace" with the neighboring Ottomans was repeated in Bernardo Balbi's 1530 instructions as count of Sebenico.[112] When Alvise Mudazzo returned from his term as count of Cattaro in 1530, he reported that as soon as he had entered office, he had sent presents to the Ottoman representatives "as is the custom, and with whom I exerted myself to co-exist well."[113] In 1543, when Stefano Tiepolo was elected captain-general of the Venetian fleet, the Venetian state told him that "the principal cause of your election has been for the preservation of our state and our desire and firm intention to keep the peace with the most serene Signor Turco."[114] In some ways, the Venetian empire's pragmatic approach to empire had expanded outward, encompassing its powerful neighbors as well as its subjects.

Offices in the Venetian Maritime State

Dates of Venetian domination	Place name	Region	Chief Venetian official	Subordinate Venetian officials with dates of election
1393–1478	Alessio (Lješ)	Albania	Provveditore	Camerlengo e Saliniere (1444–1475)
1405–1412, 1421–1423, 1443–1571	Antivari (Bar)	Albania	Podestà	Castellano (1486–1489) Castellano e Camerlengo (1496–)
1409–1797	Arbe (Rab)	Dalmatian island	Conte	Camerlengo e Castellano (1444–)
1388–1463	Argos	Greece	Provveditore e Capitano (1442 on)[a]	
1394–1402	Athens	Greece	Capitano	
1420–1540	Aurana (Vrana)	Dalmatia	Castellano (1442 on)[b]	
1420–1797	Brazza (Brać)	Dalmatian island	Conte	
1405–1412, 1442–1797	Budua (Budva)	Albania	Podestà	
1420–1797	Cattaro (Kotor)	Albania	Conte[c]	Camerlengo (1438–)[d] Castellano (1445–)
1500–1797	Cefalonia (Kefallonia)	Ionian island	Provveditore	Castellano
1363–1797	Cerigo (Cederico)	Greek island	Castellano[e]	
1409–1797	Cherso (Creš) and Ossero (Osor)	Dalmatian islands	Conte	
1204–1214 1386–1797	Corfu (Kerkyra)	Ionian island	Bailo	Capitano (1455–)[f] (2) Castellano (1386–) Camerlengo (1386–1440) Capitano del Borgo (1442–) (2) Consiglieri (1410–1423, 1442–)[g]

continued

Dates of Venetian domination	Place name	Region	Chief Venetian official	Subordinate Venetian officials with dates of election
1206–1500	Coron (Koroni, Corone)	Greece	Castellano[h]	(2) Consiglieri Capitano del Borgo e Camerlengo (1451–1500)[i] Capitano (1479–1500)
1211–1669	Crete (Candia)	Mediterranean island	Duca di Candia	Capitano (1367–) (2) Consiglieri di Candia (2) Camerlenghi (3) Signori di Notte[j] (c. 1340–1490) (3) Giudici (c.1340–1490) Rettore di Canea (Chania) (2) Consiglieri (1442–) Rettore di Rettimo (Rethimno, Rethymno) (2) Consiglieri (1442–)[k] Rettore Sitia (Setia)
1420–1797	Curzola (Korčula)	Dalmatian island	Conte	
1473/1489–1571	Cyprus	Mediterranean island	Luogotenente[l]	Capitano (1490–) (2) Consiglieri (1474–) (2) Camerlengo (1479–) Capitano del Salinario (1490–)
1444–1478	Dagno (Danj)	Albania	Provveditore	
1396–1423, 1444–1478	Drivasto (Drivast, Drishti)	Albania	Podestà	Castellano (1465–1478)
1405–1412, 1423–1571	Dulcigno (Ulcinj)	Albania	Conte e Capitano	
1392–1501	Durazzo (Dürres)[m]	Albania	Bailo	
1451–1537	Egina (Aegina)	Greek island	Rettore	
c. 1340–1470	Fitilei (Fitelos, Ptelion)	Greece	Rettore	
1407–1499	Lepanto (Navpaktos)	Greece	Rettore	Castellano e Camerlengo (1465–1499)[n]
1421–1797	Lesina (Hvar)	Dalmatian island	Conte	Castellano (1495–)
1464–1540	Malvasia (Monemvasia)	Greece	Podestà	
1206–1500	Modon (Modone)	Greece	Castellano	(2) Consiglieri Capitano del Borgo e Camerlengo (1442–1500)[o] Capitano (1479–1500)

Dates of Venetian domination	Place name	Region	Chief Venetian official	Subordinate Venetian officials with dates of election
1388–1540	Nauplion (Napoli di Romania)	Greece	Podestà e Capitano	Camerlengo (1463–)[p] (2) Consiglieri (1442–1450, 1519–) Castellano (1452–)[q] Castellano di Rocca (1508–)
1390–1470	Negroponte (Eubea, Evvia)	Greek island	Bailo[r]	(2) Consiglieri Capitano del Borgo (1442–)
1409–1797	Nona (Nin)[s]	Dalmatia	Conte	
1409–1797	Pago (Pag)	Dalmatian island	Conte	Camerlengo (1439–)
1453–1537	Schiato, Scopelo (Skyatos, Skopelos)	Greek islands	Rettore	
1453–1537	Schiro (Skyros)	Greek islands	Rettore	
1396–1479	Scutari (Skadar)	Albania	Conte e Capitano	Saliniere (1444–1472)[t] Castellano e Camerlengo (1409–1479)[u]
1412–1797	Sebenico (Šibenik)	Dalmatia	Conte	Castellano (1442–)[v] Camerlengo (1442–) Castellano della Torre Grande (1466–1470)
1420–1797	Spalato (Split)	Dalmatia	Conte	Castellano e Camerlengo (1470–)[w]
1423–1430	Thessalonica (Thessaloniki, Salonica)	Greece	Duke	Capitano (1423–1430)
1390–1715 (1537 Mykonos)	Tinos and Mykonos	Aegean islands	Rettore[x]	
1420–1797	Traù (Trogir)	Dalmatia	Conte	Castellano (1443–)
1480–1797	Veglia (Krk)	Dalmatian island	Provveditore	Castellano e Camerlengo (1483–)
1482–1797	Zante (Zakynthos, Zacinto)	Ionian island	Provveditore	
c. 1000–1358	Zara (Zadar)	Dalmatia	Conte	Capitano (1409–) Castellano (1409–)
1409–1797				Camerlengo (1427–) Castellano della Cittadella (1442–) Castellano di Novegrad (1453–)[y]

Note: The table includes all locations that were directly ruled by Venice between 1380 and 1540 and that had an official elected in a Venetian council as a governor. The table thus excludes places such as Almissa, Patras, Butrinto, and Parga, which were under Venetian protection but governed by officials elected on a local level. Unless otherwise noted, all the information in the table is taken from *The Rulers of Venice* databank, which ends in 1524. Positions without an ending date presumably continued to be elected after 1524.

continued

[a]Before 1442, Argos was administered jointly with Nauplion. After 1442, the rector of Argos was paid from the treasury of Nauplion, and judicial appeals were heard by the Venetian rector in Nauplion: *MC, Liber Ursa*, f. 142v–143r, 1442 June 15.

[b]Before 1442, Aurana was under the direct control of the count of Zara.

[c]After 1494, *SegV*, reg. 8, f. 85, lists the title as "Rettore e Provveditore."

[d]The treasurer appears in *SegV*, reg. 4, from its beginning in 1438; because of the missing register, it is difficult to state definitively whether treasurers were elected consistently from 1420 on. From 1466, the treasurer also had the title "capitano della citadella."

[e]After 1504, this position's title changed from castellan to "provveditore and capitano."

[f]The *Dieci* established the position in 1455, but it was only filled three times (1455, 1465, and 1469) before 1490.

[g]The counselors' positions were eliminated in 1423 and reinstated in 1442: Sathas, III: 347, 1423 April 30; Bacchion, 38. There was a proposal to replace the treasurer with two counselors in 1406, but it was rejected: Sathas, II: 158–60, 1406 Nov. 30; Thiriet, *RDS:* II, nos. 1236 and 1388.

[h]In the thirteenth and fourteenth centuries, the position of castellan was shared between two or sometimes three castellans who were responsible for both Coron and Modon; see Hodgetts, 45–95. Nicolò Vallaresso was evidently castellan of both cities in 1394; see *S Misti*, reg. 43, f. 43v, 1394 July 24, but before the election registers begin in 1437, the position evidently was divided into two, one castellan for Modon and one for Coron.

[i]A captain of the town for Coron was elected in 1451 and 1455, and, from 1465 on, a single official was elected who had the duties of both treasurer and captain of the town.

[j]The statutes originally called for four officers of the night and three judges to be elected in Venice, but the number of officers of the night was reduced to three in 1392; there were rarely that many actually elected in the later fourteenth and fifteenth centuries. The position was turned over to the Great Council of Candia to fill in 1490.

[k]The counselors of Canea and Rettimo received 250 ducats a year: *MC, Liber Ursa*, f. 142v–143r, 1442 June 15 and 23. In Rettimo, the position was established in 1442, but candidates were not regularly elected until after 1466.

[l]Venice elected a *bailo* of Cyprus until 1489, when Caterina Corner abdicated and the republic was the sole ruler of the island. At that point, the *bailo* was replaced by a lieutenant.

[m]The Senate mandated a treasurer be sent to Durazzo as well as a bailo in 1393: Valentini, "Stabilimenti," 868. No treasurer for Durazzo, however, appears in the *SegV* election registers, meaning that the position was likely eliminated before 1438.

[n]A castellan was elected in 1455.

[o]The captain of the town took on the responsibilities and title of treasurer in 1481.

[p]The position of treasurer was added by the Great Council in 1442, but no candidate appears in the election registers until 1463.

[q]In 1460, the Great Council voted to eliminate the position of castellan for five years due to expense: Thiriet, *DAV*, II: no. 1560. From 1473 through 1490, the same man was elected as castellan and as treasurer or the position of castellan went unfilled.

[r]The *bailo* of Negroponte was elected regularly from 1211 on; counselors were elected less regularly throughout the fourteenth century. The responsibility of the offices changed after 1390, when Venice took direct control of the island, but the positions and titles did not.

[s]DAZ, *Ducali e Terminazioni*, I, f. 6r, 1414 July 27, specifies that the count of Zara appoints and pays the salary of the count of Nona.

[t]The position was not filled regularly: candidates were elected in 1445, 1446, 1451, 1455, 1465, and 1472.

[u]Valentini, "Stabilimenti," 868, dates the institution of the treasurer's position to 1409.

[v]The position was filled irregularly until 1465.

[w]A castellan was elected in 1451. In 1453, there was an election for the position of treasurer, but it was refused by five different electees and the position was not filled again; Pederin, "Spalato," 329, shows that the position was instead filled by local nobles. In 1464 and again in 1465, there was an election for castellan, but it was not until 1470 that a castellan and treasurer was regularly elected in Venice.

[x]Rectors were not elected regularly until 1430.

[y]The position was filled irregularly; before 1453 the castellany was under the direct control of the count of Zara.

APPENDIX B

Genealogical Charts

The Sagredo, Santa Trinità *parish*

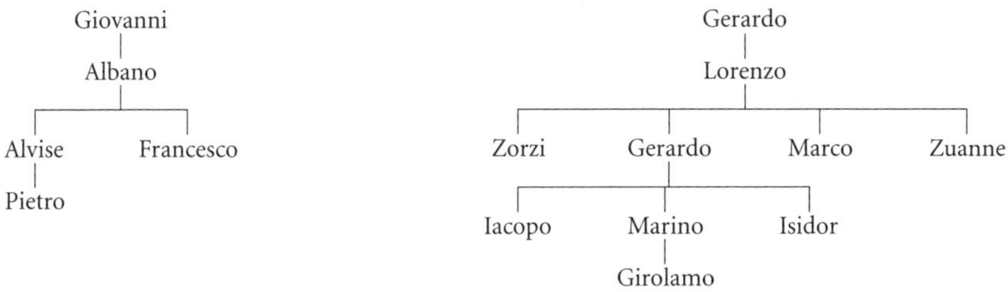

Sources: Rulers of Venice; Barbaro, *Arbori,* VI, f. 501–4.

The Arimondo

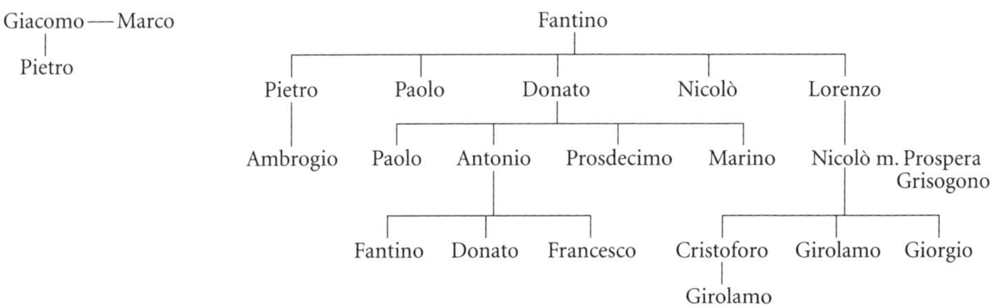

Sources: Girgensohn, *Kirche, Politik,* II: 599–604; Barbaro, *Nozze,* f. 8v–9v; *AvC, Cronaca,* reg. 107, f. 2r–v; *AvC, Balla d'Oro,* reg. 163, f. 13r; *PSM de Citra,* reg. 82, n. 6, f. 1r; HAC, *Enetikē Dioikēsis,* reg. 454, n. 2, f. 1r; HAC, *Enokratia,* n. 5, f. 271r.

The Capello Family, Santa Maria Mater Domini *parish*

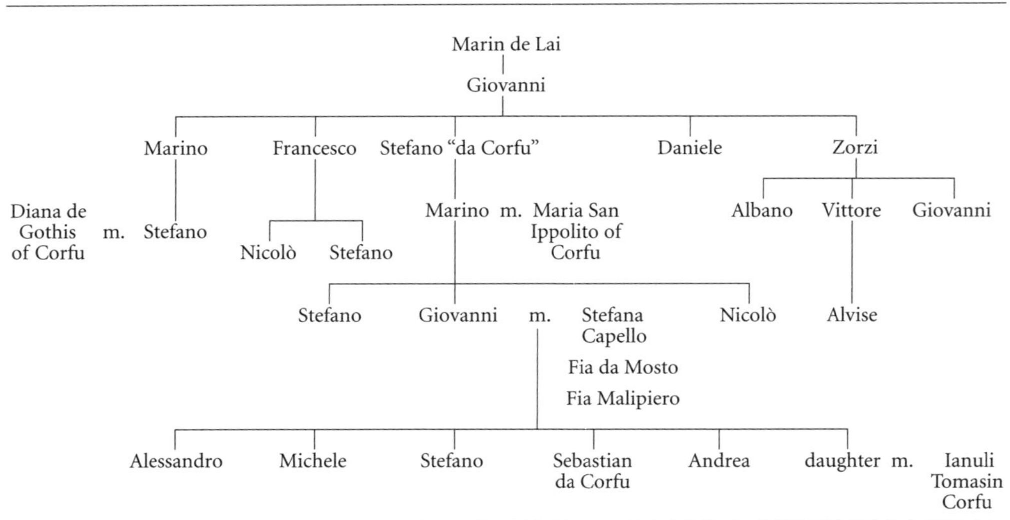

Sources: Barbaro, *Arbori,* II. f. 255 and 273; idem, *Nozze,* f. 99v; *AvC, Cronaca,* reg. 107, f. 77r–v; *Rulers of Venice.*

The Diedo Family

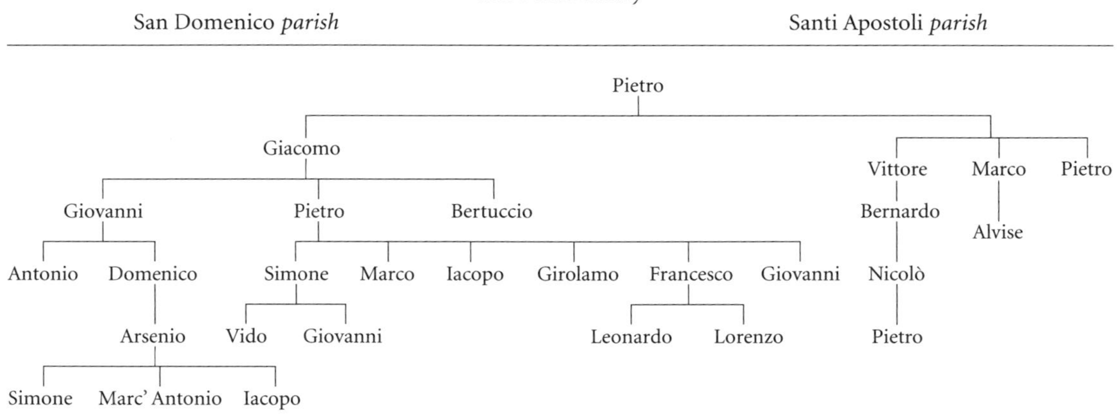

Sources: Rulers of Venice; Barbaro, *Arbori,* I. ff. 221, 216, 233; Rossi, *DBI* 39 (1991): 756–81.

NOTES

Abbreviations

AAV	Valentini, ed. *Acta Albaniae Veneta Saeculorum XIV et XV*
ADC	*Archivio di Duca di Candia*, ASV
AR	Jacoby, *La Féodalité en Grèce médiévale: Les* Assises de Romanie
ASV	Archivio di Stato di Venezia
AvC	*Avogaria di Comun*
b.	busta/buste
BL	British Library
BMV	Biblioteca Marciana di Venezia
BSR	Biblioteca del Senato, Rome
Capi X	*Capi di Dieci*
Commissiones	Ljubić, ed. *Commissiones et relationes venetae*
DAV	Thiriet, ed. *Délibérations des assemblées vénitiennes concernant la Romanie*
DAZ	Državni Arhiv Zadar (Historical Archives of Zadar)
DBI	*Dizionario Biografico Degli Italiani*
DI	Noiret, ed. *Documents inédits pour servir a l'histoire de la domination Vénitienne en Crète, 1385–1485*
DVL	Thomas and Predelli, eds. *Diplomatarium Veneto-Levantinum: Acta et Diplomata*
f.	folio
HAC	Historical Archives of Corfu
Listine	Ljubić, ed. *Listine o odnošajih izmedju Južnoga slaventsva*
MP	Chrysostomides, ed. *Monumenta Peloponnesiaca*
ProvvF	*Provveditori sopra Feudi*
PSM	*Procuratori di San Marco*
r.	recto
RDS	Thiriet, ed. *Régestes des délibérations du Sénat de Venise concernant la Romanie*
ROV	Kohl, Mozzato, and O'Connell, eds. *Rulers of Venice* (online database)
RV	Thiriet, *La Romanie Vénitienne au Moyen Age*

RVEM	Cozzi and Knapton, *La Repubblica di Venezia nell'età moderna*
Sathas	Sathas, ed. *Documents inédits relatifs à l'histoire de la Grèce au Moyen Age*
SegV	*Segretario alle Voci*
Urkunden	Tafel and Thomas, eds. *Urkunden fur Alteren Handels und Staatsgeschichte der Republik Venedig*
v.	verso
VP	Queller, *The Venetian Patriciate*

Introduction

1. The phrase "written on water" comes from Subrahmanyam, "Written on Water," 42–68. For useful definitions of early modern empires, see Pagden, *Lords,* 13; Doyle, 12–19, and Abernethy, 18–21.

2. Bushnell, 17; Radding, 162–95; Khoury; Tilly, 102–3; Barkey, 276; Perdue, 555–58; Goffman and Stroop.

3. Benton, "Legal Spaces," 700.

4. Helpful introductions to the vast literatures on each of these empires are Subrahmanyam, *Portuguese Empire;* Elliott, *Empires;* and Canny. For the effect of distance on imperial communication and policy, see Banks.

5. Elliott, "Europe."

6. Subrahmanyam, *Portuguese Empire,* 224–28; see also the essays in Burkholder, *Administrators of Empire.*

7. *S Mar,* reg. 12, f. 87v, 1486 Aug. 11.

8. Sanudo, *Vite dei Dogi,* II: 564.

9. Venier's relevant correspondence can be found in *PSM, Misti,* b. 3, nos. 1, 8, 9, 16–19. The Venier family tree is in Barbaro, *Arbori,* VII: f. 246–47.

10. *PSM, Misti,* b. 3, n. 1.

11. Lane, *Maritime Republic,* 42; idem, "Roots of Republicanism"; Grubb, "Four Decades," 50; Bullard et al. For a sharp critique of Lane's approach to Venetian political history, see Cochrane and Kirshner, 333–34.

12. The bibliography on Venetian commerce and its overseas economy is vast; Crouzet-Pavan, *Venice,* 84–96, offers an overview with bibliography, and other essential starting points are Luzzatto; Ashtor, *Levant Trade;* Jacoby's studies collected in *Recherches sur la Méditerraneé, Trade, Commodities and Shipping,* and *Byzantium, Latin Romania;* Arbel, *Trading Nations;* Mueller, *Venetian Money Market;* Costantini, *Repubblica nata sul mare;* Doumerc, "Dominio del mar."

13. Hocquet, *Sel et la fortune.*

14. Lane, *Maritime Republic,* 122–34; Doumerc, "Dominio del mar"; Stöckly.

15. Doumerc, "Crise structurelle"; Doumerc and Judde de Larivière, "Rôle du Patriciat"; Judde de Larivière.

16. Arbel, "Colonie," 964. Unless otherwise noted, all translations are mine.

17. Ashtor, "Venetian Supremacy," 52, concludes that while Venice was economically dominant in the Levantine trade, this supremacy did not translate into a "veiled

political hegemony," and Doumerc, "Tana," 261, points to the fact that Venetians distinguished between "luoghi di Levante" and "luoghi di la Signoria."

18. *PSM, Misti,* b. 3, nos. 1 and 3.

19. Pagden, *Peoples,* xxiv, makes this observation for a number of historical empires.

20. Brown, *Venice and Antiquity,* 77–81.

21. Benton, "Legal Spaces."

22. There is a strong argument for including Istria in a consideration of the *stato da mar.* Ultimately, it was excluded here for archival reasons, as some of the deliberations are in the series *S Terra.* For analyses of Istria's position between *terra* and *mar,* see Ivetić, *Oltremare;* Viggiano, "Note."

23. The essays in *Florentine Tuscany,* ed. Connell and Zorzi, provide an excellent introduction to this topic.

24. Chittolini's approach is spelled out concisely in his contribution to *Origins of the State;* see also idem, "Italian City-State"; Romano and Martin, "Reconsidering Venice," 12.

25. Romano and Martin, "Reconsidering Venice," 7–8.

26. Ventura, *Nobiltà;* for its reception, see Grubb, "Four Decades," 72–76; Romano and Martin, "Reconsidering Venice," 5–15; Knapton, "Nobiltà."

27. Viggiano, *Governanti.*

28. Grubb, *Firstborn;* Muir, *Mad Blood;* Law, "Verona"; Knapton, "Istituzioni centrali"; idem, "Tribunali veneziani." For further studies, see Knapton, "Nobiltà."

29. Papadia-Lala, *Thesmos,* includes an extensive bibliography; the discussions in Karapidakis, *Civis Fideles,* Arbel, "Urban Assemblies," and McKee, *Uncommon Dominion,* 31–56, are also useful.

30. Balard, *Romanie génoise;* and idem, "Amministrazione genovese."

31. Šimunković, "Politica Linguistica."

32. See, e.g., the two important volumes edited by Arbel, *Intercultural Contacts* and *Latins and Greeks.*

33. McKee, *Uncommon Dominion,* 109, 124; idem, "Greek Women"; idem, "Households."

34. Dursteler, 21.

35. Ivetić, "Storiografie," 126.

36. Braudel, *Mediterranean.*

37. Horden and Purcell; Horodowich, "New Venice," 6–10; De Vivo, 169; Romano and Martin, "Reconsidering Venice," 8; Balard, "Etat," 17–36.

38. See the essays of Papadia-Lala, Karapidakis, and Kitromilides in *Italia-Grecia.*

39. Paladini.

40. Ivetić, "Dalmazia e Slavi," 125–43. See also idem, "Storiografie," for an analysis of Italian and Croatian historiographical traditions and Pederin, "Mito di Venezia," for the nineteenth century in Croatian intellectual culture, especially for Ljubić's monumental contributions.

41. *Etat et colonisation; Coloniser au moyen âge; Partage du monde.* Armesto's *Before Columbus* and Verlinden's classic collection of articles *Beginnings* also point to the continuity of colonial practice between Mediterranean and Atlantic worlds.

42. McKee, *Uncommon Dominion.*

43. Queller, *VP,* 29–51.

44. Muir, "Was There Republicanism?" 137–67; Benton, *Law and Colonial Cultures.*

ONE · The Shape of Empire

1. Muir, *Civic Ritual,* 122; Crouzet-Pavan, *Venice,* 46–49.

2. Grubb, "Four Decades," 72–73.

3. Cessi, *Repubblica di Venezia,* 355–56. See also Dudan, *Dominio veneziano,* 49–55; and Praga, *Dalmatia,* 139.

4. Thiriet, *RV,* 105–6. More recently, Madden, 198, has questioned the initial Venetian commitment to conquering Crete, stating that Ziani and his counselors were initially reluctant to extend Venetian influence outside the Adriatic proper.

5. Borsari, *Dominio veneziano,* 9–25.

6. For accounts of this journey, see Lane, *Maritime Republic,* 24–27; Brunelli, 274; and Nicol, 43–44. For a detailed history of the early Venetian advance in the Adriatic, see Ducellier, "Adriatique," 141–99.

7. The literature on the Fourth Crusade and the Venetian part in it is vast. The best overviews are Nicol, 124–47; McNeal and Wolff, II: 153–86; Queller and Madden, 55–78. For studies of the interaction between Byzantium and the West after the Fourth Crusade, see Jacoby, "Encounter of Two Societies"; idem, "Byzantium to Latin Romania"; idem, "Etats latins en Romanie"; and idem, "Social Evolution in Latin Greece."

8. Thiriet, *RV,* 76–107; Ravegnani, "Romània veneziana," 183–91. The documents dividing the territories of the Byzantine empire are published in *DVL,* I: 444–52, and *Urkunden,* I: 452–501, and discussed in McNeal and Wolff, II: 182–84, Carile, "Partitio."

9. Madden, 173–94.

10. Nicol, 157; Borsari, "Veneziani delle colonie," 128; Lock, 147–49; Ravegnani, "Romània veneziana," 197–200; for studies of specific families, see Loenertz, *Ghisi;* idem, "Quelques îles grèques"; idem, "Querini"; and Thiriet, "A propos de la seigneurie."

11. For the rapid acquisitions and losses of territory in this period, see Rösch, 233–63; Jacoby, "Venezia d'oltremare," 263–99; Nicol, 158–61; Ravegnani, "Romània veneziana," 212–27; Ducellier, *Façade Maritime,* 136–51; Madden, 198–200.

12. The treaty with Boniface is published in *Urkunden,* I: 513–15; the best description of the circumstances surrounding its signing is found in Madden, 183–87. See also Ravegnani, "Conquista veneziana," 33–35; Borsari, *Dominio veneziano,* 11–25.

13. Gallina, "Affermarsi di un modello," 29–30; Cozzi, *RVEM,* I: 181–95; Thiriet, *RV,* 180–215. See Maltezou, "Historical," 17–47, for an overview of the island's history and Papadaki, "Storia di Creta," 71–82, for an analysis of the Greek historiography of the island.

14. McKee, *Uncommon Dominion,* 19–56; Jacoby, "Social Evolution"; idem, "Colonisation militare." Pietro Ziani's 1211 grant of land to the colonists, the *Concessio Insulae Cretensis,* is published in *Urkunden,* I: 129–36. The larger fiefs, *cavallerie,* were granted to knights, *milites;* and the smaller fiefs, *serventerie,* were allocated to foot-soldiers, *pedites.* Santschi, in *Notion de 'feudum,'* considers the system as at least par-

tially feudal, but Jacoby has convincingly refuted this argument; see his "Colonisation militaire" and "Encounter of Two Societies."

15. For other examples of fiefs granted directly by the Venetian state, one must look no further than the Zarentine hinterlands; see DAZ, *Ducali e Terminazioni*, I, f. 123r, no. 410, 1452 Oct. 4 and f. 125v–126r, no. 417, 1453 July 17, for grants of fiefs in Aurana (Vrana) and Novegrad. See Asdrachas, "Rendita feudale," for a discussion of feudal landholding in Corfu.

16. Maltezou, "Historical," 22–25; Borsari, *Dominio veneziano*, 27–66.

17. My account here follows that of Krekić, "Venezia e l'Adriatico," 58–56, Cozzi, *RVEM*, I: 4–5, and Praga, *Dalmatia*, 121–33. For a detailed account of Venice's overseas holdings in the fourteenth century, see Borsari, "Veneziani delle colonie," 127–58.

18. Thiriet, "Sui dissidi," 699–712; McKee, "Revolt of San Tito," 173–204; idem, *Uncommon Dominion*, 133–67.

19. Lane, *Maritime Republic*, 195–96; Crouzet-Pavan, *Venice*, 75–79; Mueller, "Effetti."

20. For detailed examinations of contests for power in the region, see Fine, 389–404 and 453–546; Praga, *Dalmatia*, 133–39; Krekić, "Venezia e l'Adriatico," 59–78; Cozzi, *RVEM*, I: 19–23; Setton, "Catalans and Florentines."

21. Ashtor, *Levant Trade*, 245–69; Brummett, 131–41.

22. Inalcik, 9–22; Dávid, 71–90.

23. Kastritsis offers a detailed summary of this period in Ottoman history.

24. Gallina, "Affermarsi di un modello," 18.

25. *S Mar*, reg. 1, f. 67v, 1441 Nov. 11, cited in Tenenti, "Senso dello stato," n. 6.

26. Gallina, "Affermarsi di un modello," 35; Thiriet, *RV*, 303–49; Cozzi, *RVEM*, I: 191–92; Valentini, "Stabilimenti," 242–44; Mueller, "Imperialismo monetario"; Stahl, *Venetian Tornesello*.

27. There is a wide literature on Venetian commerce in commodities in its maritime state; for an overview and further bibliography, see Cozzi, *RVEM*, I: 183–85; Knapton, *RVEM*, II: 326–96 and 536–40; Jacoby, "Changing Economic Patterns"; Thiriet, *RV*, 303–52; Lane, *Maritime Republic*, 56–65; Luzzatto, 133–214; Ashtor, "Venetian Supremacy." For examples of Venetian monopolies on salt and wheat, see Hocquet, *Sel et la fortune;* Gallina, *Società coloniale*.

28. Nicol, 322–25, gives a vivid account of Venetian maneuvering to obtain Corfu; see also Bacchion, 19–33; Arbel, "Colonie," 959–60; Thiriet, *RV*, 399–403; Ravegnani, "Conquista veneziana."

29. Thiriet, *RDS*, I: nos. 698, 703–4, 712, 720–21, 729–31, 733; Karapidakis, *Civis Fidelis*, 48–58; Bacchion, 28–31; Papadia-Lala, *Thesmos*, 275. The Corfiote petitions and Venetian response are published in *DVL*, II: 199–209.

30. Tenenti, "Politica veneziana," 311; see also Lunzi, 85.

31. Kohl, *Records*, no. 2799; more generally, nos. 2798–2800, and Lunzi, 86; Jacoby, *AR*, 258.

32. *Collegio, Secreti*, reg. 3, f. 6r, 1382 May 20, discussed in Nicol, 323.

33. Lock, 160; Jacoby, *AR*, 238; Thiriet, *RV*, 359; Fine, 430; Cessi, "Venezia e l'acquisto"; Topping, "Morea," 153–54; Setton, "Catalans and Florentines," 247–52.

34. Morosini, *Codex,* II: 191.

35. *S Secreta,* reg. E, f. 46v, 1388 Dec. 12, published in Chrysostomedes, *MP,* no. 45. The treaty of sale is published in *DVL,* II: 211–15.

36. Gallina, "Affermarsi di un modello," 26. Loenertz, *Ghisi,* 172–83; Jacoby, *AR,* 185–211, and idem, "Consolidation," 151–87. Tinos and Mykonos were placed under the jurisdiction of the *bailo* of Negroponte in 1391 but were later rented out or given in fief over the protests of the residents. On this point, see Jacoby, *AR,* 239–41.

37. My account here follows Valentini, "Stabilimenti," 202–6, and Ducellier, *Façade Maritime,* 490–509.

38. Kohl, *Records,* nos. 3079–82, 3100, 3125, 3152.

39. Ducellier, *Façade Maritime,* 496, from *S Misti,* reg. 40, f. 140r, 1388 Oct. 23.

40. Kohl, *Records,* nos. 3296–97 and 3348; Valentini, "Stabilimenti," 206; Ducellier, *Façade Maritime,* 500–501.

41. Strazimir offered the territory to Venice in 1394, but Venice did not accept until February 1396, when it was no longer occupied by the Ottomans: Kohl, *Records,* nos. 3463, 4310, and 4348; Valentini, "Stabilimenti," 207–10.

42. Morosini, *Codex,* II: 193; Fine, 420.

43. *S Misti,* reg. 40, f. 140r, cited in Valentini, "Stabilimenti," 204, n. 18.

44. Valentini, "Stabilimenti," 208.

45. My account here follows Krekić, "Venezia e l'Adriatico," 66–78. See also Fine, 488–91; Praga, *Dalmatia,* 145–47; and Pederin, "Venezianische Verwaltung," 100–103.

46. Krekić, "Venezia e l'Adriatico," 73–75; *Listine,* V: 26, 1403 Nov. 6.

47. *Listine,* V: 142–45. Benvenuti, *Zara,* 23–44, reconstructs the events of the Zarentine entry with a triumphalist flair; see also Praga, *Dalmatia,* 139–45.

48. Krekić, "Venezia e l'Adriatico," 79–82; the sale is found in *Listine,* V: 177–79, 181–99.

49. Praga, *Dalmatia,* 145; *Listine,* V: 210, 212–13.

50. *Listine,* VI: 12, discussed in Benvenuti, *Zara,* 24; Pederin, "Venezianische Verwaltung," 122.

51. *Listine,* VI: 11–12, 1409 Sept. 5; Mueller, "Aspects," 47–48.

52. See Grubb, *Firstborn,* 6–27; Law, "Verona," 11; Ventura, "Dominio," 172.

53. *Listine,* VI: 18 (Nona), 44–45 (Cherso and Ossero), 48–49 (Arbe), 99–101 (Pago).

54. See Raukar, *Zadar,* 301–6, for economic divisions between noble and nonnoble groups.

55. Pederin, "Šibenik," 816–17.

56. Fine, 490.

57. *Listine,* VIII: 25–29 (Spalato), 29–31 (Traù), 46–52 (Curzola), 54–56 (Brazza), 75–77 (Lesina).

58. Praga, *Dalmatia,* 147; *Listine,* VI: 152, 1414 June 5; for earlier appeals, see *Listine,* V: 62, 1405 Aug. 3; *Listine,* VI: 53–54, 1410 Feb. 7 and 140, 1411 Feb. 9.

59. *S Misti,* reg. 42, f. 155r, 1394 March 5, published in Chrysostomedes, *MP,* 135; for Valona, see Ducellier, *Façade Maritime,* 504–5.

60. Fine, 517–20.

61. Venice also offered citizenship to Giorgio Balsha, Radić Crnojević, Vlk Bran-

ković, and Sandalj Kosača; see Valentini, "Amministrazione," 844–49; Fine, 419. Asonitas, "Relations," 280, points out that in Albania, Venice regularly used grants of citizenship as a "method of obtaining political influence."

62. *DVL,* II: 318–19; Melville-Jones, 20.

63. *Listine,* IX: 103–5, 1437 July 29.

64. For the closing of the Dalmatian town nobilities: Fine, 342; Ventura, *Nobiltà,* 116–19; Krekić, "Developed Autonomy," 188–89, 196; Schmitt, "Monumento," 40–42; Mueller, "Aspects," 33–34; Budak, 187.

65. In 1411, twenty-nine noble families of Zara were sent to Venice, and in 1421 eight patricians and four citizens of Sebenico were sent to Venice: Gullino, "Frontiere," 21; Pederin, "Spalato," 328.

66. Cozzi, "Politica del diritto," 35–68; idem, *RVEM,* I: 251–54; Ortalli, "Curzola," 206; idem, "Entrar nel dominio," 52–54; Valentini, "Stabilimenti," 197; Jacoby, *AR;* Muir, "Sources of Civil Society," 397; Grubb, *Firstborn,* 8–13; Law, "Verona."

67. Kohl, *Records,* no. 3384.

68. Ortalli, "Curzola," 202; Schmitt, "Monumento," 46–47; Piergiovanni.

69. Kohl, *Records,* no. 3122, 1389 Feb. 18.

70. Kohl, *Records,* no. 3461, 1389 Aug. 16.

71. Kohl, *Records,* nos. 3298, 3575; Schmitt, "Monumento," 43–44, n. 97; Valentini, "Stabilimenti," 218–19. There was a similar confusion over Sebenico's privileges, see *Listine,* VII: 22, 1412 Nov. 21.

72. Kohl, *Records,* no. 3529, 1397 March 13.

73. Cozzi, "Politica del diritto," 65–66; *Listine,* VI: 289.

74. Schmitt, "Monumento," 44; Ortalli, "Curzola," 218; see also Pertusi, "Dulcigno"; Fine, 492–95; Budak, 193; Benvenuti, *Zara,* 198; Vilfan, 46–49.

75. Melville-Jones, 27–40; Gullino, "Frontiere," 32–38; Romano, *Likeness,* 57–59 and 85–86; Nicol, 367–70.

76. Fine, 530–92.

77. Skanderbeg's status as an Albanian national hero means that there is a wide historical literature devoted to him: for a review of the sources and much of the early literature, see Noli, 75–104; on Skanderbeg and Venice more generally, see Noli, 33–44 and 63–75; Schmitt, *Venezianische Albanien,* 295–314; Schmitt and Saint-Guillain, "Actes inédits."

78. Noli, 39–41, offers a summary of events leading up to the war and Venice's defeat; Schmitt, *Venezianische Albanien,* 299–306, offers a more detailed account.

79. The most detailed account of this gradual advance remains Setton, *Papacy,* II: 1–38 and 82–137.

80. On the council of Florence and its aftermath, see Setton, *Papacy,* II: 39–81; Gill; Hussey; Lock, 193–239.

81. There have been a number of studies on the impact of refugee Byzantine scholars on the West; excellent points of departure for this literature are Monfasani, *Byzantine Scholars in Renaissance Italy,* and Geanakoplos, *Greek Scholars in Venice.*

82. The major study of this conspiracy is Manoussacas, *Sēphē Vlastou;* see chapter 5 for further discussion.

83. Morosini, "Defensio venetorum," 215. For Morosini's work and career, see King, 132–40.

84. For studies of the war, see Lopez, "Principio della guerra"; Babinger; and for the actions leading up to the Ottoman attack and the siege of Negroponte itself, see Fincati.

85. Cozzi, *RVEM,* I: 58; for the Italian reception, see Meserve, "News from Negroponte."

86. Malipiero, II: 58–59.

87. For the Venetian takeover of Cyprus, see Magnante. Mas Latrie and Hill also provide detailed accounts of the island's history, although they have now been corrected on many points; see the essays of Benjamin Arbel, collected in *Cyprus, the Franks, and Venice.*

88. Iorga, III: 223, 3 Aug. 1447. See Jacoby, "Citoyens, sujets et protégés," for the populations affiliated with Venice before 1473; Cozzi, *RVEM,* I: 62; Arbel, "Greek Magnates"; idem, "Cypriot Nobility"; Richard, "Économie coloniale?" In 1426, the Venetian Angelo Michiel lent the Lusignan king 5,000 ducats in return for a franchise on the island's salt revenues: Imhaus, "Chypre," 24. For the Corner's economic ties to Cyprus before 1473, see Luzzatto, 178–79; Coureas, 112–16.

89. Mas Latrie, *Histoire,* III: 348–52; Hill, III: 660–742; Arbel, "Reign of Caterina Corner"; Richard, "Chypre du protectorat."

90. Mas Latrie, *Histoire,* III: 370–420; Mas Latrie, "Documents nouveaux," 497.

91. Mas Latrie, "Documents nouveaux," 456–63; Hill, III: 715–21.

92. Sanudo, *Vite dei Dogi,* I: 93, states that it was in fact Marco Corner, Caterina's father, who proposed the plan to colonize Cyprus "so it would be a Venetian colony like Crete," and that Corner's death derailed the plan. My thanks to Holly Hurlburt for this reference.

93. *S Mar,* reg. 12, f. 199r, 1489 Jan. 17.

94. See the essays of Tenenti, Lane, Gilbert, and Tucci in *Renaissance Venice.*

95. Malipiero, 195, cited in Tenenti, "Sense of Space," 26.

TWO · Administrators of Empire

1. *MC, Liber Stella,* reg. 24, f. 73r–v, 1486 May 28.

2. *MC, Liber Ursa,* f. 82v, 1428 Nov. 30.

3. Queller, *VP,* 3–28; on the myth more generally, see Muir, *Civic Ritual,* 13–61; Grubb, "Four Decades," 50–60; Romano and Martin, "Reconsidering Venice," 2–9.

4. Queller, *VP;* Ruggiero; Finlay, *Politics;* Gullino, "Patriziato."

5. The Senate had the right to nominate candidates, and rarely, to elect them. Candidates for a post were determined by a particular number of *mani,* or nominating committees, members of which were chosen by lot. Sanudo, *De Origine,* 72–75, lists the number of *mani* for each office; this number in many cases was increased from two to four in the electoral reform legislation of 1515. The Senate could then nominate its own candidate by scrutiny (*scrutino*), meaning that a post could have as few

as two or as many as seven candidates: Finlay, *Politics,* 59–60 and 90–91; Queller, *VP,* 85–112; Lane, *Maritime Republic,* 258–65.

6. Finlay, *Politics;* Romano, *Likeness;* Raines.

7. The *Rulers of Venice* database was in its final editing stages at the Renaissance Society of America as this volume went to press. It will be accompanied by several introductory essays, also available online, that will explain the scope and limitations of the Venetian electoral registers, the manner in which the data contained in the electoral registers is represented in the databank, and the pitfalls and potentials for interpreting the data.

8. Mozzato, 13–15.

9. Zannini, 437; for the growth in the patricians seated in the council, see Todesco, 119–64; Gullino, "Patriziato," 388–92.

10. Zannini, 420–25; Viggiano, *Governanti,* 67–68. For the value placed on age and experience in Venetian political culture, see Finlay, *Politics,* 124–41; idem, "Age and Politics"; Chojnacki, "Political Adulthood"; and Viggiano, "Aspetti politici," 473–505. Patterns of officeholding in Florence were comparable: see De Angelis, 167–68; Zorzi, "Giusdicenti e operatori," 520. Mozzato, 26–30, demonstrates that a restricted group of prominent nobles repeatedly held office in the Senate. Several scholars have used collective political biographies to identify typical career patterns and to trace the influence of certain groups of Venetian patricians: see Grendler, "Tre Savii"; idem, "Leaders"; Stahl, "Prosopography," 41–131; idem, "Office-holding"; Viggiano, *Governanti,* 51–146; Del Torre, 224–26; Girgensohn. Only Stöckly, 67–310, treats the maritime state directly, analyzing individual and family patterns in galley patronage and captaincies.

11. Chittolini, "Italian City-State," 598–99; Vilfan, 48. For Zara, see Praga, *Dalmatia,* 152; Benvenuti, *Zara,* 26; Pederin, "Venezianische Verwaltung," 151–54; for Corfu, Bacchion, 7–8; Jacoby, *AR,* 258–66; for Crete, Karapidakis, "Administration," 186–210 and 259–68; Papadaki, "Axiōmata," 99–136; for Cyprus, Mas Latrie, *Histoire,* III: 838–46; Grivaud, 192–94.

12. See Gasparēs, "Mētropolitikē," and *Listine,* VI: 24–25, 1409 Sept. 25, for examples of captains' commissions in Crete and in Zara, respectively.

13. The captain often sat with the governor as a judge and had primary jurisdiction over all soldiers in the territory. The captain was also responsible for all decisions regarding the territory's security but was usually instructed to make these decisions in concert with the governor. See *S Misti,* reg. 40, f. 115r, 1388 June 2, published in Noiret, *DI,* 19; *ADC,* b. 50, reg. 1, f. 269v–70r, 1390 Dec. 4; Ljubić, *Commissiones,* I: 16–21.

14. For Coron and Modon, see Hodgetts, 39–127; Jacoby, *AR,* 223–26. For Durazzo and Scutari, see Valentini, "Amministrazione"; idem, "Stabilimenti," 222. For Negroponte, see Jacoby, *AR,* 185–211; Major, 247–49. For Nauplion, see Wright, "Minio," 37–52; Jacoby, *AR,* 213–22. For Sebenico, see Pederin, "Šibenik," 818–20; for Spalato, Pederin, "Spalato," 324–28; for Traù, see Ljubić, *Commissiones,* I: 5.

15. Sathas, I: 140; Thiriet, *RV,* 184; Kohl, *Records,* no. 3427.

16. The rectors of Brazza, Budua, Cefalonia, Cerigo, Cherso and Ossero, Curzola,

Dulcigno, Egina, Fitilei, Malvasia, Nona, Schiati and Scopolo, Schiro, Tinos/Mykonos, and Zante were alone. For commissions of the count of Cherso and Ossero, see *Listine*, VI: 44, 1409 Dec. 13; for studies of specific locations, see Jutronić; Jacoby, *AR*, 237–52; Pertusi; Ortalli, "Curzola."

17. Queller, *VP*, 29–50.

18. *MC, Liber Leona*, f. 61v, 1392 Aug. 10: "aliquia officia nostra de minoribus in quibus eliguntur continue de nostris pauperibus nobilibus," italics mine.

19. Unless otherwise stated, all of the following information on elections is taken from the beta version *Rulers of Venice* database; the date in parentheses following the officeholder's name is the date of election to the office.

20. For Caravello's complete career, see Girgensohn, II: 647–63; he ended his life as a *procurator di San Marco* and was a competitor for the ducal seat in 1423: Romano, *Likeness*, 25–30.

21. Girgensohn, II: 599–604, reconstructs Arimondo's career in some detail.

22. For Da Canal, see Girgensohn, II: 630–31. Other examples of the pattern include Zaccaria Trevisan, who served in Padua (1405), Verona (1408), Zara (1410), Padova again (1412); Albano Badoer, duke of Crete (1399), *podestà* in Treviso (1405), *podestà* of Verona (1409); Francesco (Franzi) Foscari, rector in Feltre (1406), captain in Vicenza (1409), duke of Crete (1411), captain of Verona (1421), and governor in Friuli (1423); Rosso di Pietro Marin, castellan of Coron (1400); Roberto di Marco Morosini, ambassador and *bailo* to Cyprus (1399), *provveditore* in Padova (1404), *provveditore* in Albania (1408), and *bailo* of Corfu (1410). See Girgensohn, II: 608–19, 761–62, 920–31, and 983–97; Romano, *Likeness*, 13–17.

23. *MC, Liber Leona*, reg. 21, f. 180r and f. 198v–199r, 1408 Dec. 2 and 1410 Aug. 14.

24. *Listine*, VIII: 181–84; Cozzi, *RVEM*, I: 199, citing *S Secreta, Deliberazioni*, reg. 4, f. 192v–193r, 1411 Sept. 7; Gullino, "Frontiere," 21.

25. Chojnacki, "Social Identity"; and idem, "Nobility, Women."

26. *MC, Liber Leona*, reg. 21, f. 241v, 1414 March 18 and *MC, Liber Ursa*, reg. 22, f. 88r, 1430 March 5. Chojnacki, "Social Identity," 347, also points to laws of 1402 and 1404, which mandated the use of patronymics in electoral procedures, as emphasizing patrician lineage.

27. *MC, Liber Ursa*, reg. 22, f. 27v, f. 82v, f. 96v, 151v, and f. 178r; see also Queller, *VP*, 45–49.

28. Thiriet, *RV*, 190.

29. *MC, Liber Ursa*, f. 141r–43r, 1442 April 15, June 15 and 23, discussed in Queller, *VP*, 43. The new maritime offices were: rector of Argos, treasurers of Nauplion and Sebenico, counselors of Canea and Rettimo, commander of the citadel in Zara, and captains of the town in Corfu, Modon, and Negroponte.

30. *MC, Liber Ursa*, f. 157v, 1444 June 12. The offices were: treasurer of Cattaro, a treasurer and castellan in Arbe and in Alessio, and a salt official in Scutari. For discussion of the political context, see Romano, *Likeness*, 268.

31. *MC, Liber Stella*, reg. 24, f. 73 r–v, 1486 May 28.

32. Queller, *VP*, 113–40.

33. *CX, Miste*, reg. 15, f. 52r, 1455 May 2, summarized in Thiriet, *DAV*, II: no. 1503.

34. Mallett and Hale, 429–60; Ridolfi; Praga, "Organizzazione militare"; Pepper; Georgopoulou, 48–67.

35. In addition to the *Rulers of Venice* entries, see Kohl, *Records*, nos. 3051, 3298, and 4355.

36. Dandolo had previously served in a number of important posts, including ambassador to Hungary during the delicate period after King Louis's death; see Kohl, *Records*, nos. 2882, 2794, 3051, 3286.

37. For instance, when Venetian Albania was threatened, *provveditori* were sent to Dagno (Danj) from 1445 and to Croia (Kroja) from 1462.

38. The survey includes *SegV*, registers 4 and 6. Register 5 was omitted because it has no patronymics and overlaps chronologically with register 6. Within the sample, there were 2,214 positions total, of which 1,253 positions (56 percent) were filled by single-time officeholders; 568 positions (25 percent) were filled by people who held 2 offices; 249 positions (11 percent) were filled by 83 people who held 3 offices; 92 positions (4 percent) were filled by 23 people who held 4 offices; 45 positions (2 percent) were filled by 9 people who had 5 offices total; and 6 offices held by 1 person.

39. Del Torre, 223–26.

40. The sample consisted of 180 positions, filled by 164 men (11 men held 2 offices, 1 held 3 offices, and 1 held 4 offices). One hundred sixty-three of 180 positions were filled by men with prior experience, and 111 positions filled by those with experience outside of Venice.

41. Wright, "Minio," 16–18.

42. Borsari, "Bembo, Francesco."

43. Borsari, "Barbo, Pantaleone"; *ADC, Ducali e Lettere*, b. 1, reg. 5, f. 4r, 1409–11 for Duodo's judgeship.

44. Gullino, "Emo, Gabriele."

45. Other examples of this pattern in Zara and its region include Marco di Antonio Barbarigo, castellan of Novegrad (1497) and castellan in Zara (1504); Giovanni Battista di Girolamo Bondumier, castellan (1499) and treasurer (1503) in Zara; Sebastiano di Nicolò da Canal, castellan of Aurana (1474) and Novegrad (1480); Andrea di Nicolò Giustinian, castellan of Novegrad (1504) and treasurer of Zara (1508); Francesco di Pietro Orio, treasurer (1468) and count (1500) in Zara.

46. Other examples of this pattern from Corfu include Girolamo di Pietro Diedo, castellan (1438) and counselor (1451); Nicolò di Ludovico Memmo, captain (1500) and captain of the town (1511); Antonio di Giovanni da Ponte, castellan (1485) and then captain of the town (1516).

47. Other examples of this pattern from Crete include Andrea da Canal, judge (1384) and rector (1403) of Rettimo; Pietro Civran, rector of Canea (1412) and duke (1415); Nicolò di Francesco Cocco, counselor in Canea (1444), rector of Canea (1467), and captain (1472); Bernardo Donà, rector of Canea (1455) and duke (1466); Matteo di Marco Donà, rector of Canea (1421) and duke (1437); Marino di Francesco Garzoni, treasurer (1450) and duke (1484); Iacopo di Secondo Miani, treasurer (1441) and rector of Rettimo (1467); Gabriele di Nicolò Pizzamano, treasurer of Canea (1469) and rector of Rettimo (1495); Bernardino di Vinceslao da Riva, treasurer of Crete (1484),

counselor of Canea (1494), and rector of Rettimo (1521); Andrea di Pietro Zorzi, counselor of Canea (1480) and rector of Sitia (1487).

48. Bartolomeo di Andrea Barbaro served as a judge in Crete twice (1439, 1450). Pietro di Francesco Ferro served as treasurer and then castellan in Nauplion (1463, 1487). Marco di Nicolò Dandolo served as counselor in Negroponte twice (1443, 1449). Ottaviano Bon served as *podestà* of Nauplion twice (1397, 1403). Pietro di Filippo da Canal served as count of Sebenico twice (1471, 1480). Marco di Antonio Venier was treasurer of Sebenico twice (1472, 1477). Filippo di Lorenzo Barbarigo served as counselor in Modon twice (1438, 1450), as did Ludovico di Zaccaria Bredani (1438, 1449). Francesco di Giulio Bollani was count of Brazza twice (1496, 1520).

49. Giannasi. See chapter 6 of this volume for Capello's prosecution for corruption.

50. Ventura, "Barbarigo, Bernardo." See chapter 7 of this volume for his involvement on the uprising in Crete in the 1520s.

51. On the connections between branches of the Venetian *cà*, see Romano, *Patricians and Popolani,* 41–50; Crouzet-Pavan, *Sopra le acque,* I: 374–447; for family in Venetian politics, see Finlay, *Politics,* 81–82; Raines. For studies on specific Venetian families, see Borsari, "Ziani"; Benvenuti, "Zorzi"; Pozza, *Badoer;* Fees.

52. Lane, "Public Debt and Private Wealth"; Hocquet, "Capitalism marchand," 288–91; Doumerc, "Parti," 179–80; Judde de Larivière.

53. Stöckly, 267–310.

54. Doumerc, "Parti," 188–89; idem, "Dominio del mar," 152–54; Doumerc and Judde de Larivière, "Rôle du Patriciat."

55. Mueller, "Venetian Commercial Enterprise," 82–83.

56. Mueller, "Pubblico e privato."

57. Schmitt, "Commerce venitien"; idem, *Venezianische Albanien,* 367–97. Arbel has made a similar point about the Corner family's activities in Cyprus, see his "Reign of Caterina Corner."

58. The family of Pietro di Alvise Loredan, twice captain of the Gulf (1412, 1420) who received the submissions of Sebenico, Traù, Spalato, Curzola, Brazza, and Lesina, is a good example: both his father and grandfather had been captain-general of the sea, as were Pietro's son and grandson: Gullino, "Loredan, Pietro," 776. In another example, Andrea di Girolamo Bondumier served as castellan of Zara (1485); his brother Giovanni Battista di Girolamo held the same position (1498) and returned as treasurer (1503); and Giovanni Battista's son Bernardo was captain (1507); Barbaro, *Arbori,* II: f. 111. Girolamo di Quintino Tagliapietra served as castellan in Corfu (1445) and his son Quintino di Girolamo served as counselor there and died in office (1494).

59. Barbaro, *Arbori,* V: f. 450r.

60. Barbaro, *Arbori,* III: f. 297r.

61. Barbaro, *Arbori,* II: f. 201r; Carile, "Calbo, Giovanni." Barbaro gave Zanotto a fifth son, Andrea, but Carile found that the details of Andrea's life coincided almost exactly with those of Zanotto's son Alvise and concluded that Zanotto had four, not five sons. Zanotto was in office in Scutari in 1419, not after 1426 as Carile states: Valentini, *AAV,* XVII: 385.

62. Barbaro, *Arbori,* VI: f. 501r and f. 508r.

63. *Listine,* X: 297–98, 1463 Jan. 13. The same thing occurred when Leonardo Venier died while serving as count of Sebenico—his son, Marco, took his place: *Listine,* X: 30, 1454 April 4.

64. The *Rulers of Venice* database shows that 147 houses had at least one member elected to an office between 1460 and 1510. This figure complements Gullino, "Patriziato," 390, who found 142 houses registered in the *Balla d'Oro* from 1414 to 1443.

65. Pillinini, "Bollani, Candiano." For the Bollani on Crete, see McKee, *Uncommon Dominion,* 157.

66. Stöckly, 306, finds that the Diedo were tenth among the families that dominated captaincies, a position disproportionately large for their social status.

67. Barbaro, *Arbori,* III: f. 233r; Rossi, "Diedo, Antonio."

68. Rossi, "Diedo, Pietro."

69. Barbaro, *Nozze,* f. 18r–v; *AvC,* reg. 107, f. 46v; Barbaro, *Arbori,* I: f. 95r.

THREE · Public Office and Patrician Family Strategies

1. These restrictions were by no means limited to Venetian officials but were a regular feature of Italian *podestarie;* see Chambers and Dean, 49–50; Queller, *VP,* 184–86, gives the history of such prohibitions in a Venetian context. For specific prohibitions against eating with locals, except during weddings, in the *stato da mar,* see *Collegio, Commissioni, Formulari,* v. 6, f. 79v (Zara 1413), f. 86v (Arbe 1413); Ljubić, *Commissiones,* I: 6 (Traù 1441), 18 (Zara 1461) and 143 (Sebenico 1515); BL, Add Ms 20979, f. 3r (Veglia 1507); Maltezou, *Commissio,* 52 (Canea 1589). For prohibitions against accepting gifts while in office, see Queller, *VP,* 184; Sathas, II: 152 (Corfu 1406); and Bacchion, 36–38; *Collegio, Commissioni, Formulari,* v. 6, f. 79v (Zara 1413); Ljubić, *Commissiones,* I: 6 (Traù 1441), 18 (Zara 1461), and 143 (Sebenico 1515); BL Add Ms 20979, f. 3 (Veglia 1507); BL Add. Ms. 41659, f. 8r (Candia 1459); Maltezou, *Commissio,* 51 (Canea 1589); Hodgetts, 88–91. One of the duke of Crete's responsibilities was to oversee the auction of state properties; Leone Duodo's 1459 commission, BL Add. Ms. 41659, f. 12v, states that he could only conduct these auctions in the public square and nowhere else, limiting opportunities for favoritism. Regulations against marrying locals, or marrying while in office, do not appear as regularly. The commissions of the captain of Candia, duke of Crete, and rector of Canea forbid officers from marrying or acquiring property for a year after leaving office: Gasparēs, "Mētropolikē," 205; BL, Add. Ms. 41659, f. 25r; Maltezou, *Commissio,* 71. Marriages were also forbidden for the rector of Brazza: Jutronić, 283. Arbel, "Colonie," 972, states that in Cyprus, permission was sometimes granted for officials to marry locally while in office, suggesting that under normal circumstances such marriages were not allowed.

2. Gothein, 29. King, 436–37, summarizes his career as an officeholder and as a humanist; see also Girgensohn, II: 983–97; Witt, 458–62.

3. Cited and translated in King, 41, for his career see 374–76.

4. For the difficulties inherent in the position, see Cozzi, *RVEM,* I: 193; Major, 248; Muir, *Mad Blood,* 49–76; and Wright, "Minio," 1–235; Hodgetts, 152–74. Zorzi, "Gius-

dicenti e operatori," 523, makes a similar point on the difficulties facing Florentine territorial officials; see also Weissman, "Importance," 271.

5. Mueller, "Aspects," 36–38; Wright, "Minio," 38–40. Hodgetts, 186, notes that while the Venetian colonies were supposed to be self-supporting, and salaries paid from local revenues, this was rarely the case, and officials could petition for salary they had not received on their return to Venice. On the other hand, the Venetian state often made demands on officials' salaries during times of financial difficulty or suppressed them completely: after 1434, the state took 10 percent of salaries under 400 ducats and 15 percent of salaries above that figure, and then 30 percent and 40 percent of salaries, substantially decreasing the amount of money an official could expect from his post: Thiriet, *RV*, 194–95. Rectors could, though, petition for an exemption to the deduction and thus receive the whole salary.

6. For prohibitions against revoking or revising sentences, see *Collegio, Commissioni, Formulari*, v. 6, f. 90 r–v (Sebenico 1413); Ljubić, *Commissiones*, I: 7 (Traù 1441); Maltezou, *Commissio*, 120 (Canea 1589).

7. Ljubić, *Commissiones*, I: 146 (Sebenico 1515); DAZ, *Ducali e Terminazioni*, II, f. 136v, no. 976, 1482 June 28. The Florentine central government exercised a similarly strict control over their territorial rectors; the difference in the Venetian maritime state was one of distance. See Thiriet, *RV*, 188, on traveling distances within the empire; De Angelis, 174–82, on Florentine control of territorial rectors.

8. Chittolini, "Onore," 124.

9. Chambers and Dean, 17; Chittolini, "Onore," 107.

10. Chambers and Dean, 49; Zorzi, "Giusdicenti," 535–38.

11. Viggiano, "Aspetti politici," 488–89.

12. Viggiano, *Governanti*, 203; see also Hill, IV: 869–70; Benvenuti, *Zara*, 196. For the inclusion of the prohibition in individual commissions, see BL Add. Ms. 41659, f. 32r (Crete 1459); Ljubić, *Commissiones*, I: 22 (Zara 1461) and 146 (Sebenico 1515). Later prohibitions suggest that while speeches might have disappeared, other forms of celebration took their place: the *Dieci* in 1506 forbade the firing of guns during festivals or during the arrival of a rector without express mandate and save in cases of necessity of state: *CX, Miste*, reg. 31, f. 95r, 1506 Aug. 4. In 1589, the rector of Canea's commission forbids what had become a customary celebration of the rector's birthday as well as celebrations or festivals when he left office: Maltezou, *Commissio*, 93.

13. Venetian ceremonies of entry and exit closely mirror those seen in other Italian territorial states: Chambers and Dean, 179; Connell, "Commissario," 607–8; Chittolini, "Onore," 106. For descriptions of such ceremonies in the Venetian maritime state, see Benvenuti, *Zara*, 25 and 49; Cozzi, *RVEM*, I: 192–93; Georgopoulou, 216; Marmora, 249; Nikiforou-Testone; Iliadou, 499–500; Papadaki, *Cerimonie*.

14. BSR, "Statuta et leges civitatis cathari," Statuti 195, 338–39.

15. Georgopoulou, 74–101; Pozza, "Chiese veneziane"; Calabi.

16. Rizzi, 223–85; for fortifications in the southern part of the empire, see Georgopoulou, 55–73. The 1419 treaty with the Ottomans specified that the Ottomans would recognize Venetian dominion over all locations flying the insignia of San

Marco, indicating that the banner had a practical as well as ritual significance: Asonitis, "Relations," 283.

17. For the *loggie* of Dalmatian cities, see Pilo, 94–95, 122–23, 195. For the *loggia* of Corfu, see Nikiforou-Testone, 59–61; Karapidakis, *Civis Fidelis,* 55. For the *loggie* of Crete, see Georgopoulou, 84–90; Gerola, III: 35–36; for Nauplion, see Wright, "Wooden Towns," 173.

18. In some places, Venice took over an already existing public building for its rectors' residence, as was the case in Crete: Georgopoulou, 94–100. In Negroponte, Thiriet suggests, the Venetian state inherited a palace from the Ghisi. Sabalich, 289, has published a document showing that in 1421 Venice purchased the palace it had been renting from some Zarentine nobles; see also Benvenuti, *Zara,* 198; Pilo, 128, 212.

19. The Venetian state was careful to ensure that its representative live in a public building, not a private residence. In Patras, e.g., the Senate specified that its representative should live in "unam domum communis": Sathas, II: 213, 1408 Nov. 7. For examples of the prohibition against unauthorized repairs or building in individual rectors' commissions, see Ljubić, *Commissiones,* I: 150 (Sebenico 1515); Maltezou, *Commissio,* 184 (Canea 1589).

20. *CX, Miste,* f. 122r, 1489 July 4. The prohibition against sculpted coats of arms appears twice in Paulo Erizzo's 1489 commission as count of Cattaro: BL, Add 23712, f. 4v–5r and f. 9v; BL, Add 20979, f. 8r (Veglia 1507). The captain of Cyprus was subject to a similar regulation: he was forbidden from placing his coat of arms anywhere but in his own palace, and then he was limited to a painted coat of arms costing no more than 2 ducats: Hill, IV: 870. Again, Venetian officials were not unique: Italian *podestarie* regularly left coats of arms and insignia on buildings in cities where they had ruled: Chambers and Dean, 10.

21. For Dalmatian examples, see Ivančević, 112–13; Pilo, 91, 95–96, 105, 130, 208. For Cretan examples, see Georgopoulou, 54; Gerola, I: 111–12, 122, and 252–54. For Cyprus, see Von Wartburg, 68; Jeffrey, 110–11, 339–440.

22. Marković, 81; Olivieri, "Calbo, Marc'Antonio," notes that Antonio was well known for his intellectual and cultural interests in Dalmatia.

23. Marmora, 396.

24. One of the earliest prohibitions on family members came from the Great Council on June 14, 1258, ordering that neither the duke nor the counselors of Crete could bring with them sons, brothers, grandsons, or nephews: Cessi, *Deliberazioni,* II: 340. Hodgetts, 86–87, notes a similar prohibition for the castellans of Coron and Modon. The regulation was extended to all colonies in 1300: Thiriet, *DAV,* I: 79. The prohibition against accompanying family was repeated on February 28, 1319, and there was a failed attempt to revoke the law in 1319: *MC, Fronenis,* f. 33r, 1319 July 22. Thiriet, *RV,* 196, notes that in the fourteenth century, officials frequently received special permission to bring wives or children on their overseas postings.

25. Thiriet, *DAV,* II: no. 1001, 1402 Dec. 24 and no. 1348, 1434 July 4. An interesting exception to the regulation of giving offices to relatives came when the duke of Crete, Giovanni Pisani, was allowed to elect his *nipote* Andrea as a notary; see *Collegio, No-*

tatorio, reg. 12, f. 112v, 1479 Nov. 15. For the prohibition in individual commissions, see *Collegio, Commissioni, Formulari,* v. 6, f. 79v (Zara 1413), f. 86v (Arbe 1413); Ljubić, *Commissiones,* I: 7 (Traù 1441), 18 (Zara 1461), and 143 (Sebenico 1515); BL, Add. Ms. 41659, f. 8r–v, f. 22v (Candia 1459).

26. The regulation, repeated in a number of commissions, stated that officials could not wear mourning clothes for any relatives except parents or children, and even then only for eight days, see Ljubić, *Commissiones,* I: 10 (Traù 1441) and 143 (Sebenico 1515); Hill, IV: 869; Maltezou, *Commissio,* 92 (Canea 1589).

27. Finlay, *Politics,* 85–87. Despite the prohibition, close relatives did serve in the same regimes at the same time. For instance, brothers Bernardino and Domenico di Battista Vallaresso served on Corfu simultaneously, Bernardino as captain of the island (1494–1496) and Domenico as counselor (1493–1495). Their term of service followed their father's stint as *bailo* on the island (1488–1490).

28. For the Venetian patriciate and *terraferma* property, see Crouzet-Pavan, *Venice,* 101–11; idem, "Venise et le monde"; Pozza, "Proprietari fondiari"; Gullino, "Quando il mercante." Mueller, *Venetian Money Market,* 498, notes that after 1419, Venetians with estates in the *terraferma* paid taxes only in Venice. For the *stato da mar,* see Schmitt, *Venezianische Albanien;* Mueller, "Venetian Commercial Enterprise"; idem, "Pubblico e privato." A number of older studies of Venetian patrician families in the maritime state focus on particular regions or particular families: see, e.g., Borsari, "Ziani"; Benvenuti, "Zorzi"; Loenertz, *Ghisi*; idem, "Querini."

29. Francesco di Felise Bon served as treasurer and castellan of Arbe (1468) and count of Nona (1472) and in 1477 married a woman from Brazza. Alessandro di Luca Viaro was *bailo* of Durazzo (1512); while there, he married the widow of Nicolò Diedo of Durazzo. Andrea di Nicolò Baseggio served as count of Spalato (1510), and in 1523 his daughter married a man from the island of Cherso. Girolamo di Luca Caravello served as treasurer of Sebenico (1481), and his niece married a Nicolò da Sebenico during his term of office: Barbaro, *Nozze,* f. 15r, f. 32v, f. 78r, f. 426v. An interesting and perhaps atypical case of a Venetian official using a term of office to arrange a beneficial marriage for his son has been published and analyzed by Koumanoudi. Bartolomeo Querini, *bailo* of Negroponte (1372–1374) was convicted of using Venetian resources to force Nicolo dalle Carceri, duke of the Archipelago, to marry his daughter to Querini's son and then appropriating money and fortresses from Carceri.

30. Arbel, "Greek Magnates," 331; he gives the example of the Cypriot Zegno Synglitico, who married his granddaughter Maria to Francesco di Lorenzo Barbarigo, with a dowry of 21,000 ducats, more than five times the maximum for Venetians. McKee, *Uncommon Dominion,* 68, demonstrates the same phenomenon for fourteenth-century Crete, finding that Greek Cretan women usually had sizable dowries.

31. Romano, *Patricians and Popolani,* 55.

32. Fine, 603–4; Wright, "Testament," 1–21. Sources differ on the date of the Erizzo-Cernovich marriage; the most plausible is 1490, evidenced by the Senate's congratulation to Ivan/John Cernovich (Crnojević) on his son's marriage.

33. Paolo went on to serve as count of Zara (1493–1495); Isabetta's other brother, Giovanni Battista, served as count of Brazza (1504–1507) and married into the Al-

tavilla baronial family of Corfu: *AvC,* reg. 107, f. 123v; Barbaro, *Nozze,* f. 181v. After Zorzi's 1496 flight to Venice, he served as a commander in Ravenna, was arrested, escaped from prison, was recaptured, eventually pardoned, and left Venice for Ottoman territory in 1500; Wright, "Testament," 3–9, offers a detailed narration of these events based on Sanudo's *Diarii.* After Zorzi's departure from Venice, Isabetta and the couple's sons received several pensions and benefits: *Grazie,* reg. 26, f. f. 72v, 79r, and f. 120v, 1505 June 21, 1525 Aug. 7 and 1526 April 13.

34. *AvC, Cronaca,* reg. 106–7; Barbaro, *Nozze;* on Barbaro, see Ventura, "Barbaro, Marco." For a detailed analysis of the genre of Venetian *libri di famiglia,* see Betto, 35–52; Plebani, 94–95. A later manuscript at the Correr, *Ms Gradenigo* n. 72, "Donne Veneziane," also includes many of the marriages mentioned in the above sources.

35. Marriage certainly operated as a stabilizing factor among the Venetian patriciate, and Stuard, 12, finds marriage an important stabilizing factor in Ragusan politics in the same period, arguing that a friendship circle of aristocratic families who intermarried bore "the principal responsibility for obtaining political, social and economic consensus."

36. The marriage is noted in Barbaro, *Nozze,* f. 440v; idem, *Arbori,* VII: f. 225; see also *Listine,* VIII: 93–94, 1421 June 8; Pederin, "Wichtigen Ämte," 340; Benvenuti, *Zara,* 206. Chiara's will indicated she still owned unspecified properties in Zara in 1425, although the villages of Zemonico and Novegrad passed to the Venetian state: *Notarile Testamenti, Atti Matteo di Andronicus,* b. 54, n. 3, 1425 Aug. 2. After Tommaso's death, Chiara remarried Michele di Donato Giustinian: *AvC, Cronaca,* reg. 107, f. 369r and Barbaro, *Nozze,* f. 223v.

37. The Matafari clan was among Zara's nobility in 1283: Benvenuti, *Zara,* 201; for the family's wealth, see Raukar, *Zadar,* 306. Krekić, "Developed Autonomy," 196, summarizes Raukar's conclusions on the concentration of political power in the hands of a few families, including the Matafari, Begna, and Grisogono.

38. Praga, *Dalmatia,* 141. The Matafari never actually took control of the islands; in 1407, Lodovico Matafari successfully besieged the island of Pago and Ladislas gave him the right to hold the island in fief: Brunelli, 522–23.

39. *Listine,* VI: 12 and 70, 1409 Sept. 5 and 1410 March 29; Venice conceded to him the castle of Novegrad and the village of Zelminac for his lifetime and with the right to pass it to his legitimate male heirs. Venice's grant was the result of a compromise, as Ladislas had granted Novegrad to Guido Matafari before signing over his rights to Venice: Krekić, "Venezia e l'Adriatico," 80.

40. *Listine,* VI: 124 and 149, 1410 Nov. 8 and 1411 April 13.

41. Barbaro, *Nozze,* 440v; for Simone Begna's wealth, see Raukar, *Zadar,* 306. Francesco di Santo was an investor in Barbary galleys, *AvC,* reg. 178, f. 144r, 1444 Nov. 13. Simone Begna married a daughter of Paolo Contarini in 1423, Pietro di Simone Begna married the daughter of Francesco di Pietro Diedo in 1464, and Alvise di Simone Begna married the daughter of Giovanni di Daniele da Canal in 1463; Barbaro, *Nozze,* f. 104r, 122r, and 160r.

42. Santo di Francesco Venier, Simone's grandson, was a Venetian patrician and served as an *ufficiale sopra le Mercanzie del Levante* (1476), a *giudice del mobile* (1482),

podestà della Motta (1485), and as *giudice dell'esaminador* (1486). Pietro di Tomà Venier, Guido Matafari's grandson, was twice a ducal elector. The Matafari of Zara remained closely associated with the Venetian state: in 1482–1484, Zuan Matafari of Zara was commanding a galley in the Venetian fleet: Sanudo, *Vite,* I (1989): 254 and II: 427.

43. Girgensohn, II: 599–604, reconstructs Arimondo's career in some detail. Doumerc, "Parti," 185, states that the Arimondo were heavily invested in maritime trade, with a near monopoly on the Flanders galleys.

44. Brunelli, 515–16; Krekić, "Developed Autonomy," 196.

45. *AvC, Cronaca,* reg. 107, f. 2r; Barbaro, *Nozze,* f. 8v; *AvC, Balla d'Oro,* reg. 162, f. 7v, 1430 Aug. 31; *AvC, Balla d'Oro,* reg. 163, f. 13r, 1437 July 4 and 1441 May 17.

46. Pietro di Giacomo was count of Zara (1409); Pietro di Fantino was count of Durazzo (1407); Donato di Fantino was count of Scutari (1409) and *provveditore* in Albania (1412); Prosdecimo di Donato was count of Traù (1460); Ambrogio di Pietro was treasurer in Alessio (1447); Cristoforo di Nicolò was castellan of Aurana (1447); Nicolò di Donato was count of Cherso and Ossero (1467) and count of Sebenico (1483); Pietro di Nicolò was *podestà* of Antivari (1448) and captain of Zara (1471), and Francesco di Nicolò was castellan of Traù (1481), count of Arbe (1492), count of Lesina (1494), and count of Zara (1521).

47. Nicolò Arimondo was count of Pago in 1420 Nov. 14: *Listine,* VIII: 56. It is possible, but not certain, that this was the same Nicolò Arimondo who was count of Pola (in Istria) and was prosecuted for his actions in office in 1429: see Viggiano, "Note," 12.

48. HAC, *Enetokratia,* n. 5, f. 271r, 1442 Aug. 29.

49. HAC, *Enetikē Dioikēsis,* reg. 454, r. 2, f. 1r–v, 1454 Feb. 13.

50. *AvC, Cronaca,* reg. 107, f. 2r; Barbaro, *Nozze,* f. 9v.

51. Karapidakis, *Civis Fidelis,* 207–8; HAC, *Enetokratia,* reg. 5, f. 269r.

52. *AvC, Cronaca,* reg. 107, f. 295r; Barbaro, *Nozze,* f. 401v. The Salamon appear in Corfiote council lists from 1568 on: Karapidakis, *Civis Fidelis,* 279.

53. Barbaro, *Nozze,* f. 104v; "Donne Veneziane," f. 25v; Karapidakis, *Civis Fidelis,* 268.

54. Asonitas, "Introduzione," 65–67, reconstructs a case involving the De Gothis patrimony that treated the question of female succession; the same case appears in Mustoxidi, I: 694–96. In 1435, Rinaldo de Gothis died with no male heirs and two daughters, Philippa and Altadonna. Rinaldo had named Matteo and Adam San Ippolito as his daughters' legal representatives, and the San Ippolito then engaged in a lengthy legal battle with Rinaldo's brother Arsenio, who claimed his brother's fief as his own. In 1437, the Venetian *bailo* Giovanni Nani, basing his decision on the *Assises de Romanie,* affirmed Philippa and Altadonna's right to the property. Arsenio took his case to the *Quarantia* in Venice, which in 1453 affirmed Arsenio's right to the barony. Eventually, Arsenio agreed to give Altadonna (Philippa had died) a dowry of 1,200 ducats. In addition to marriage, Corfiote property passed to the Venetian state when a baron died without heirs, as happened in the case of Pierotto de Altavilla. The Corfiote treasury auctioned his lands off and used the money to invest in shares of the public debt: Thiriet, *RDS,* III: no. 2699, 1445 Aug. 13.

55. Marmora, 283–84.

56. Karapidakis, *Civis Fidelis,* 263–83, has published a list of all the cognomens appearing in Corfiote councils with their first and last date of appearance. For the fifteenth and first half of the sixteenth century, records exist from 1432, 1443, 1440, 1443, 1473, 1477–78, 1490, 1497, 1503, 1506–1508, 1520, and 1524. Venetian patrician cognomens included on the list are the *Arimondo* (1443), Barozzi (1433), Bernardo (1490), *Capello* (1524–1552), *Da Canal* (1524–1582), Darmer (1443–1524), *Da Molin* (1477–1549), *Malipiero* (1520–1588), Moro (1432), Mudazzo (1490), *Michiel* (1443), *Salamon* (1568–1572), *Trevisan* (1508), *Tron* (1555), and *Zorzi* (1503). Possession of a Venetian patrician cognomen is of course not evidence of membership in that patriciate, but in this case, the overlap between Venetian cognomens in the council lists and Venetian patricians who contracted marriages with Corfiotes, given in italics above, is striking.

57. *AvC, Cronaca,* reg. 107, f. 255r and f. 290r; *AvC, Balla d'Oro,* reg. 164, f. 300r; Barbaro, *Nozze,* f. 357v and f. 389v.

58. *AvC, Cronaca,* reg. 107, f. 343v; *AvC, Balla d'Oro,* reg. 164, f. 323r–v; Barbaro, *Nozze,* f. 425v; HAC, *Enetokratia,* reg. 103, no. 10, f. 4r–v.

59. Jacoby, *AR,* 264–65, discusses a case in 1471, when Venice acknowledged Cola de Gothis's right to pass his barony of Psorarce to his daughter Diana. Sathas, I: 268, indicates that the fief passed to Diana's daughter, Ludovica, who in turn married the Venetian patrician Girolamo Bragadin.

60. *AvC, Cronaca,* reg. 107, f. 180r; Barbaro, *Nozze,* f. 315v.

61. *ProvvF,* b. 1167, n. 8, f. 1r and 3r; *AvC, Cronaca,* reg. 107, f. 178v; Barbaro, *Nozze,* f. 315v.

62. *AvC, Cronaca,* reg. 107, f. 180v; HAC, *Enetokratia,* reg. 103, f. 4v and f. 10v. It is possible that the Malipiero contact with Corfu began with Marino Malipiero's 1386 position as Venetian *provveditore;* a second Malipiero, Michele, was *bailo* in 1409, but in a clan as large as the Malipiero it is difficult to determine the degree of relationship without a patronymic.

63. *AvC, Cronaca,* reg. 107, f. 77r; Barbaro, *Nozze,* 99v.

64. *AvC, Cronaca,* reg. 107, f. 2r; *AvC, Balla d'Oro,* reg. 162, f. 154r, 1438 Oct. 29; *AvC, Balla d'Oro,* reg. 163, f. 155v, 1441 Dec. 4; Barbaro, *Nozze,* f. 9v, f. 99v, f. 245r–v, f. 449v. For the San Ippolito, see Jacoby, *AR,* 260–62. *ProvvF,* 1167, n. 8, f. 1r, lists two San Ippolito among the islands' barons: Adam and Andrea.

65. Jacoby, *AR,* 261.

66. Asonitis, "Relations," 285.

67. Arbel, "Cypriot Nobility," distinguishes those considered to be nobles from those with an elevated social status and concludes that the Greek element in the former group was limited.

68. Arbel, "Greek Magnates," 329.

69. Arbel, "Greek Magnates," 336, n. 86; Barbaro, *Nozze,* f. 358v.

70. Schmitt, "Commerce venitien," 891–93; idem, *Venezianische Albanien,* 383–86.

71. McKee, *Uncommon Dominion,* 72–83.

72. Gullino, "Cocco, Niccolò."

73. *AvC, Balla d'Oro,* reg. 163, f. 32v, 1461 June 27.

74. Chojnacki, "Kinship Ties and Young Patricians."

75. *AvC, Balla d'Oro,* reg. 163, f. 354r, 1436 Nov. 17.

76. Tucci, "Patrizio veneziano mercante," 17.

77. Karapidakis, *Civis Fidelis,* 185 and 281; *AvC, Cronaca,* reg. 107, f. 322r; *AvC, Balla d'Oro,* reg. 164, f. 295r; Barbaro, *Nozze,* f. 411v.

78. The Tron family's presence on Crete is documented first in 1390, when Jana Tron was recorded as a communal debtor: *ADC, Atti Antichi,* b.11, reg. 11, f. 25r. Donato Tron was among the island's feudatories at the turn of the fifteenth century: *ADC, Libri Pheudatorum,* b. 23, reg. 3, u.p. (1398–1401). In 1414, Gabriele di Michele Tron was a witness to a petition in the ducal court: *ADC, Atti Antichi,* b. 22, u.p. Elena Tron, widow of Nicolò, was among the feudatories in 1453–1455, as was Bartolommeo di Nicolò in 1490: *ADC, Libri Pheudatorum,* b. 23, reg. 7 and reg. 9, u.p.

79. O'Connell, "Venetian Patriciate."

80. McKee, *Uncommon Dominion,* 129 and 234, n. 139 and n. 140, lists 54 successful and 5 unsuccessful candidates that appear in the *AvC, Raspe* registers between 1361 and 1427. Using the same registers, and including feudatories from Rettimo and Canea as well as Candia, I arrived at a total of 98 petitions. In addition to those petitions listed by McKee, see *AvC, Raspe,* reg. 3643, I, f. 96v and II, f. 54v, f. 66r, f. 91r; *AvC, Raspe,* reg. 3644, I, f. 50v, f. 58v–59r, f. 72v and II, f. 7v; *AvC, Raspe,* reg. 3645, I, f. 11r and II, f. 37v, f. 47r–v, f. 51r, 73r–v; *AvC, Raspe,* reg. 3646, I, f. 15r, f. 23r, f. 27v, f. 43v, f. 46v, f. 50r–v, f. 55v–56r, f. 114r–v and II, f. 17r–v, f. 22v–23r, f. 111v; *AvC, Raspe,* reg. 3647, I, f. 44v–45r and II, 37v, f. 76v, f. 97v, f. 86r. From 1427 through the end of the fifteenth century, there are another 125 petitions: see O'Connell, "Venetian Patriciate."

81. One indication of the lacunae in the Tron of Candia's documented presence in the Venetian patriciate is the impossible genealogy presented in Barbaro, *Arbori,* VII: f. 145r, in which he has Nicolò, a member of the Great Council in 1298, fathering seven sons who reached adulthood a century after their father, from the 1380s to 1420s.

82. *AvC, Raspe,* reg. 3645, II, f. 47r, 1402 Dec. 14.

83. *AvC, Raspe,* reg. 3648, I, f. 58r, 1431 Oct. 29.

84. *AvC, Cronaca,* reg. 107, f. 322v; Barbaro, *Nozze,* f. 411r.

85. *AvC, Ballo d'Oro,* reg. 162, f. 134v, 1422 Aug. 20.

86. *Collegio, Notatorio,* reg. 5, f. 176v, 1422 July 24. The case gives no patronymic, so it is impossible to state definitively that the Michele Tron in question is the same person.

87. *AvC, Balla d'Oro,* reg.163, f. 387v, 145? April 21; the precise year was illegibly smudged.

88. *AvC, Balla d'Oro,* reg. 163, f. 387v, 1457 Dec. 1. The connection to Crete persisted into the 1540s, as Filippo di Priamo Tron was referred to as "Da Candia": Grendler, "Leaders," 66.

89. Barbaro, *Nozze,* f. 122r, with an incorrect date of 1490.

90. *AvC, Balla d'Oro,* reg. 162, f. 9, 1435 Nov. 18; *AvC, Raspe,* reg. 3648, II, f. 37r–39v, 1439 Jan. 7, 9, and Feb. 25.

91. *AvC, Raspe,* reg. 3649, I, f. 46(a)r–v, 1444 March 20; *AvC, Raspe,* reg. 3649, II, f. 104r–v, 1450 July 10.

92. *Collegio, Notatorio,* reg. 7, f. 45v, 1442 April 19; *Grazie,* reg. 25, f. 64r, 1442 July 8.

93. *AvC, Raspe,* reg. 3649, II, f. 101r, 1450 May 29, also found in *Quarantia Criminale, Parti,* b. 18, f. 85r.

94. *Grazie,* reg. 25, f. 64r–v, 1442.

95. *Grazie,* reg. 25, f. 50r and 114r, 1442 and 1444.

96. *S Misti,* reg. 53, f. 149r–v, 1420 Aug. 9. Finlay, *Politics,* 227–51, describes the activities of the Tron in Venetian councils; the Luca he discusses was a grandson of the Luca under consideration here.

97. *CX, Miste,* reg. 15, f. 24v, 1454 Oct. 31, summarized in Thiriet, *DAV,* II: no. 1497; see also *Listine,* VI: 141, 1411 Feb. 12, where the Senate allowed Marino Caravello and Iacopo de Rippa, "who were well-informed" on Cattaro, to sit for the relevant discussion.

98. Returnees could not vote and could only speak on matters of their own competence: Finlay, *Politics,* 39. The captain of Crete's commission indicates that suggesting revisions in administration was part of that duty: see Gasparēs, "Mētropolikē," 205. One returning rector was so enthusiastic about this duty that the Senate transferred his numerous proposals to the *Collegio* so their consideration would not hold up other Senate business: *S Mar,* reg. 18, f. 97v, 1515 Sept. 15. For some examples of returning officials' proposals in the Senate, see Kohl, *Records,* nos. 476, 3328, 3347; Sathas, II: 81–85; Sathas, III: 54–55, 95–97; Valentini, *AAV,* nos. 1276, 1290, 1300.

99. Cozzi, "Politica del diritto," 71; the complaint from Cattaro is published in *Listine,* IX: 142–43.

FOUR · Imperial Justice

1. Cozzi, *RVEM,* I: 198; Cozzi, "Politica del diritto," 52; Mueller, "Aspects," 34; Cozzi, *RVEM,* I: 193; Valentini, "Stabilimenti," 223–25; Viggiano, "Considerazioni"; idem, "Aspetti politici"; idem, *Governanti;* Grubb, *Firstborn,* 136–48; Bouwsma, 56; and Thiriet, *RV,* 195–203.

2. For justice in advice literature, see Tatio, 17; Giannotti, I: 128–30; Viggiano, "Interpretazione della legge," 121; Arbel, "Résistance ou collaboration?" 137; Thiriet, *RV,* 235. Patricians about to serve in territorial offices carried the sword that symbolized the republic's justice: Muir, *Civic Ritual,* 114.

3. Muir, "Was There Republicanism?" 137–67; idem, "Sources of Civil Society," 392–400. For further studies emphasizing the negotiation inherent in medieval and early modern justice systems and their use as a venue in which to pursue individual interests, see Astaria, 52–53; Brown, *Unjust Seizure,* 6–7; Kagan, 136; Smail, 3–24.

4. *AvC, Raspe,* reg. 3645, I, f. 64v, 1397 May 16; see McKee, *Uncommon Dominion,* 75–83, for the Calergi on Crete.

5. Thiriet, *RV,* 243; Jacoby, *AR,* 9; Cozzi, "Politica del diritto," 31–34.

6. McKee, *Uncommon Dominion,* 28.

7. Cozzi, "Politica del diritto," 32; Jacoby, *AR,* 224–35.

8. The judge's oath is published in Gerland, 93–98; see also Santschi, "Aspects de la justice," 307; McKee, *Uncommon Dominion,* 27–30.

9. Santschi, "Aspects de la justice"; and idem, "Quelques aspects du statut."

10. Maltezou, "Byzantine 'Consuetudines,'" 277.

11. Jacoby, "From Byzantium to Latin Romania," 1–45.

12. *ADC, Ducali e Lettere,* b. 1, reg. 8, u.p., 1421 July 11.

13. McKee, *Uncommon Dominion,* 69–70.

14. The capitularies of the judges and officers of the night are published in Gerland, 92–107. Because the majority of surviving records from Crete are from the city of Candia, it is not clear when the separate magistracies of officers of the night, the five of the peace, and the judges *di proprio, di petizion,* and *di prosopo* were established in Canea and Rettimo. It seems that by the early fifteenth century in Canea the courts *di petizion* and *di proprio* were operating separately from those in Candia. In 1420, the Venetian Senate heard a proposal to give a salary to the "judges *di petizion* of Canea," *S Misti,* reg. 53 f. 58v, 1420 Feb. 3, edited in Noiret, *DI,* 271. In 1438, there was an appeal from Emmanuel Grasso, scribe of the judges *di proprio* in Canea, *AvC, Raspe,* reg. 3648, II, f. 23r, 1438 June 10. In both Canea and Rettimo, the rectors and their counselors appear prominently in cases which were appealed, and it is possible that these men took over some judicial functions which in Candia were handled by the judges *di petizion* and *di proprio.*

15. *S Misti,* reg. 18, f. 18r–v, 1339 March 3, published in Kohl, *Records,* no. 244; the Senate recognized that the men sent from Venice to serve on the courts *di proprio* and *di petizion* would be joining three locally elected judges. Judges were originally elected for terms of no more than two years: *MC, Liber Novella,* f. 177r, 1381 Oct. 3. But by 1415 their term in office had been shortened to six months: *S Misti,* reg. 51, f. 60r, 1415 Aug. 19. Even using a term of two years, and including the members of the court *di prosopo* and two substitute judges, the judicial system as designed meant seven or eight men every two years needed to be elected. From 1437 to 1490, seven new judges every two years would mean at least 186 new appointments. The Venetian election registers list only 106 appointments, a significant gap.

16. *ADC, Memoriali,* b. 30, f. 9v–10r, 1390 July 19, published in Santschi, *Régestes des arrêts civils,* no. 1294.

17. The 1354 conflict of Michele Corner and Nicolò Sagredo over the village of Scallani was judged by the duke, his counselors, and a council of twelve Venetian nobles: *S Misti,* reg. 26, f. 3v, 1354 July 15, discussed in Thiriet, *RV,* 267. In a second example, Jacobo Grimani brought a complaint to the rector's court in Rettimo that the *villani* belonging to his recently purchased lands had fled; his case was decided by the rector and several "*milites, sapientes*" of Crete: *AvC, Raspe,* reg. 3644, II, f. 25r–v and f. 51r, 1388 March 11 and 1389 Nov. 12. The reference's terminology is unclear: the *savi agli ordini* of Venice were sometimes referred to as *sapientes* of Crete, but the reference to *milites* suggests that these are military colonists, feudatories in the area.

18. Jacoby, *AR,* 186–235 and 258–70; Cozzi "Politica del diritto," 31–42; Asonitis, "Introduzione."

19. Cozzi, *RVEM,* I: 188.

20. Cozzi, *RVEM,* I: 188–90; Jacoby, *AR,* 195–211; idem, "Consolidation"; Major, 254.

21. Sathas, III: 2, 1412 Feb. 23; Sathas, III: 130, 1416 March 6; Sathas, III: 225–26, 1421 June 17; discussed in Jacoby, *AR,* 185–211.

22. "Secundum leges et consuetudines Imperii Romanie," cited and discussed in Jacoby, *AR,* 208–11.

23. Jacoby, *AR,* 258; see also Asonitis, "Introduzione"; Karapidakis, *Civis Fidelis,* 52–58.

24. *DVL,* II: 207 for text, Jacoby, *AR,* 259, for analysis.

25. Bacchion, 36 and 51–53; Karapidakis, *Civis Fidelis,* 58. For the division between Greek and Latin in the council, see chapter 5.

26. Cozzi, "Politica del diritto," 39–40; Hill, III: 766–72. As was the case on Negroponte, the Venetian counselors used their authority to position themselves as the supreme judicial authorities on the island, mediating in property disputes even before the official assumption of power in 1489; see *Capi X, Lettere Spedite,* b. 4, f. 116r, 1485 May 14.

27. Cozzi, *RVEM,* I: 195–201.

28. *Listine,* VI: 8, 1409 Sept. 5; Cozzi, "Politica del diritto," 63–64; Benvenuti, *Zara,* 198 and 206. The Zarentines had wanted to constrain the Venetian count to agree with three Zarentine counselors, but the Senate ruled that when there was disagreement, the count would decide for himself.

29. *Listine,* VI: 99, Cozzi, "Politica del diritto," 64; Schmitt, "Monumento," 44–46; Valentini, "Stabilimenti," 223–24.

30. In Sebenico, there were four consulting judges and also a council of fifteen that at times heard judicial cases: Pederin, "Šibenik," 817; *S Misti,* reg. 43, f. 156v–57r, 1396 Oct. 6, published in Kohl, *Records,* no. 3506; see also *AvC, Raspe,* reg. 3648, II, f. 93v, 1441 Aug. 12, where a sentence of banishment given by Sebenico's council of fifteen is overturned in Venice. In Spalato, the *capitoli* said that the Venetian count had sole jurisdiction in criminal cases, although civil cases would be judged according to the statutes and customs of Spalato and there were local judges as well: Cozzi, "Politica del diritto," 65–66; Pederin, "Spalato," 329. In Cattaro there were three locally elected judges, in Scutari there were four locally elected judges competent to hear cases under ten *hyperperi,* and Drivasto and Antivari also had local judges able to decide cases under ten *hyperperi.* These local judges had a consultative role; Dulcigno in 1406 requested that local judges "should be able to sit on the bench with the rector and give their opinions, but the rector will remain free to proceed and decide as he sees fit": *Listine,* V: 70, 1406 March 11.

31. Cozzi, "Politica del diritto," 59.

32. Cozzi, "Politica del diritto," 81; Viggiano, "Aspetti politici," 473–505.

33. See Ljubić, *Commissiones,* I: 9 (Traù 1441) and 147 (Sebenico 1515). In Corfu, if the *bailo* himself acted against the Corfiote privileges, he was fined: Lunzi, 255. The Senate made a strong connection between officials' respect for the privileges and the population's contentment, observing that the better the privileges are observed, the better populated the island will be: *S Mar,* reg. 12, f. 119r, 1487 Aug. 31, cited in Lunzi, 468.

34. *Listine,* VIII: 46–47, cited in Ortalli, "Curzola," 208.

35. Muir, *Mad Blood,* 57.

36. *Listine,* VI: 71, 1410 March 31; Benvenuti, *Zara,* 30; Cozzi, *RVEM,* I: 200.

37. Jacoby, *AR*, 199–201, 214, 258–60.

38. Valentini, "Lo statuto," 45–47, n. 96. The lords of Crnojević, the brothers Durasin and Kojcin and their nephew Stefano were granted similar privileges in their territory of Upper Zeta.

39. They had jurisdiction over simple assault, and they were competent to hear civil cases valued at up to 10 *hyperperi:* Gerland, 103; O'Connell, "Castellan."

40. *ADC, Missive e Responsive,* b. 8, reg. 5, u.p., 1491 May 12.

41. *ADC, Missive e Responsive,* b. 8, reg. 5, f. 74v, 1489 Feb. 13.

42. Both series are now held in the *Archivio di Duca di Candia* in the Venetian state archives: Tiepolo, IV: 1008–9. Santschi has published some of the *Sentenze* records in *Régestes des arrêts civils.*

43. Viggiano, "Conflittualità giudiziarie," 107–50.

44. Santschi, *Régestes des arrêts civils,* no. 1843, 1399 Dec. 2; the ducal court decided, on the basis of the castellan of Malvesin's report, that since this road was new and the older road had always been sufficient for the region's inhabitants, Corner was justified.

45. *ADC, Missive e Responsive,* b. 8, reg. 5, f. 74v, 1489 Feb. 10. For another example of conflict over water rights, see *ADC, Missive e Responsive,* b. 8, reg. 2, f. 15v, 1450 May 30, published in Thiriet, *DAV,* II: Appendix 324, for a conflict between the bishop of Cheronisso and Marco Abramo, feudatory of Astrachi, over access to the river which divided their property.

46. *ADC, Memoriali,* ser. I, b. 32, reg. 42, f. 2r, 1443 Oct. 15. In a similar example, the ducal court heard an appeal from the court *di proprio* between Pietro Zorzi and his sister Agnes over the taxes owed on the estate of their father, Graciano, deciding that Pietro was responsible for 22 ducats, or two-thirds, of the taxes due, and Agnes should pay the remaining third: *ADC, Memoriali,* b. 32, reg. 42, f. 3r–v, 1443 Oct. 22.

47. *ADC, Missive e Responsive,* b. 8, reg. 2, f. 14v, f. 17r, f. 20v, and f. 23r, 1450 July 31. In another example, Fantin Dandolo accused the villagers of Belvedere of damaging his animals: *ADC, Missive e Responsive,* b. 8, reg. 5, u.p., 1491 May 16.

48. *ADC, Missive e Responsive,* b. 8, reg. 5, f. 78v, 1489 March 9.

49. *ADC, Missive e Responsive,* b. 8, reg. 5, f. 72r, 1489 Feb. 6.

50. *ADC, Missive e Responsive,* b. 8, reg. 2, f. 24v, 1450 Aug. 19. For further examples of feudatories' powers over their *villani,* see *ADC, Missive e Responsive,* b. 8, reg. 2, f. 18r, 1450 June 6, where Tito Gradenigo insisted that some of his *villani* living on Pietro Bon's land return to his property; *ADC, Missive e Responsive,* b. 8, reg. 5, f. 103r, 1489 May 28, where Jacopo Dandolo, a feudatory of Bonifacio, successfully petitioned to have some of his peasants' exemptions from the *angarie* revoked; and *ADC, Missive e Responsive,* b. 8, reg. 5, u.p., 1491 May 16, where Francesco Dandolo introduced a case against his *villani* for poaching and having damaged his animals.

51. *ADC, Missive e Responsive,* b. 8, reg. 2, f. 23r, 1450 Aug. 8.

52. *ADC, Missive e Responsive,* b. 8, reg. 2, f. 22r, 1450 Aug. 11. It is unclear if Giorgio was related to the Manusso Casanello referenced earlier in chapter 4.

53. Santschi, *Régestes des arrêts civils,* no. 845, 1375 Oct. 21.

54. *ADC, Ducali e Lettere,* b. 1, reg. 12, f. 15v, 1424 July 5. Zorzi da Porto, castellan of Belvedere, also presented evidence when Zanachi Franco appealed to the ducal court, *ADC, Ducali e Lettere,* b. 1, reg. 12, f. 9r, 1424 Aug. 10.

55. *S Mar,* reg. 9, f. 116v, 1471 Oct. 11; also in *ADC,* b. 50 bis, f. 81r; published in Noiret, *DI,* 519. The cases in question had to be appealed directly to Venice because they were considered criminal matters; orators requested the right to appeal sentences to the regime in Candia when the case was a civil matter, regardless of the existence of a prison sentence, and the Senate agreed and also expanded the ducal court's competence, giving it jurisdiction in all appeals under 800 *hyperperi.*

56. Thiriet, *RV,* 240; see Vlassi for a list of judicial expenses from Cefalonia.

57. *MC, Liber Regina,* f. 117r, 1472 Sept. 27: Leo Querini of Crete managed to have his and his brothers' case heard in Venice in the first instance, despite the rules against this, by complaining in the Great Council that he had remained in Venice, "at great expense," in order to solicit the introduction of his case.

58. Cozzi, "Politica del diritto," 69. Most of the recent scholarship on the important role of appeals deals primarily with the *terraferma;* see Viggiano, *Governanti,* for an excellent summary and interpretation of judicial practice in the Veneto; see also Mazzacane; Knapton, "Istituzioni centrali"; idem, "Consiglio dei Dieci"; idem, "Tribunali veneziani"; and Grubb, *Firstborn,* 136–48. Both Knapton's bibliographical note in *RVEM,* I: 349–53, and Viggiano's *Governanti* offer more comprehensive bibliographies.

59. The *Avogaria* was one of the oldest magistracies in Venice and was formed to safeguard constitutional and legal practices in Venice, and it absorbed the examination of appeals from subjects; according to Viggiano, it also acted as a defender of local privilege. As defined in 1349, and redefined in 1468, the *Avogaria* was responsible for criminal cases, proofs of nobility, the review of rectors' judicial acts, and, if necessary, the discipline of corrupt or incompetent rectors. They were specifically given the right to hear appeals from subjects in 1407: Gullino, "Evoluzione," 348, although this was a confirmation of a privilege they had already been practicing, as earlier appeals from the *stato da mar* demonstrate. The *auditori nuovi* were created in December 1410, joining the *auditori di sentenze (vecchi)* in hearing civil appeals, and their duties were modified in June 1418; see Viggiano, *Governanti,* 51–177; his "Considerazioni," 15–48; Lopez, "Auditori nuovi," 259–316.

60. Cozzi, "Politica del diritto," 114–16; Finlay, *Politics,* 68–73, discusses the courts of the *Quarantia;* see also Lopez, "Alcune magistrature minori," 37–67. For cases from Crete heard in the Minor Council, see *AvC, Raspe,* reg. 3645, I, f. 50v, 1396 June 28; *AvC, Raspe,* reg. 3646, II, f. 78v–79r, 1415 March 5; *AvC, Raspe,* reg. 3647, I, f. 7r–v, f. f. 78r–v, f. 81v, and f. 82r, 1417 July 7, 1420 May 24, Aug. 1 and Aug. 20; *AvC, Raspe,* reg. 3647, II, f. 22v, 1423 Jan. 9; *AvC, Raspe,* reg. 3649, I, f. 96r and f. 102r–v, 1445 Oct. 15 and 1446 Jan. 10. For cases heard in the *giudici di petizion,* see *ADC, Ducali e Lettere,* b. 1, reg. 3, f. 3v, 1402 Aug. 30 and *ADC, Ducali e Lettere,* b. 2, reg. 18, f. 30r, 1442 Jan. 8.

61. Cozzi and Viggiano have both documented the struggle between the *Avogaria di Comun* and the *Dieci* in the late fifteenth century; see Cozzi, "Authority and the Law"; and Viggiano, *Governanti,* 51–146. The *Dieci* sometimes intervened on an infor-

mal basis; see for instance a case where the *Dieci* urged Zaccaria Calbo, rector of Canea, to return damages taken from Jacobo Giustinian even though his case was officially inappellable: *Capi X, Lettere Spedite,* b. 1, r. 2, f. 320, 1474 Nov. 7.

62. *AvC, Raspe,* reg. 3651, II, f. 10r, 1461 July 24.

63. *AvC, Raspe,* reg. 3647, I, f. 96r, 1421 May 20.

64. *Quarantia Criminale, Parti,* reg. 20, f. 23r–v, 1490 April 2; *AvC, Raspe,* reg. 3657, f. 36v, 1490 April 28.

65. For a detailed analysis of this conflict, see Viggiano, *Governanti,* 51–177.

66. Lopez, "Auditori nuovi," 264 and 276–77.

67. *AvC, Raspe,* reg. 3653, f. 133v, 1473 Jan. 7. See also *AvC, Raspe,* reg. 3656, f. 212v–213r, 1489 April 24.

68. *CX, Miste,* reg. 19, f. 140r, 1479 July 9; *CX, Criminali,* b. 1, reg. 4, u.p., 1505 May 8.

69. *Auditori Nuovi,* b. 184 and b. 185; Tiepolo, IV: 995–96. The fragmentary nature of this source precludes any definitive statement of the proportion of appeals to the two magistracies. For examples of *auditori* cases on inheritance from the *ADC,* see *Missive e Responsive,* b. 8, reg. 1, no. 1, 1417 April 20; *Ducali e Lettere,* b. 2, reg. 18, f. 17r–v, 1441 Nov. 8; *Ducali e Lettere,* b. 2, reg. 19, f. 7v and f. 8v, 1443 July 25 and Aug. 31; *ADC, Ducali e Lettere,* b. 2, reg. 27, u.p., 1473 Jan. 8; *Ducali e Lettere,* b. 2, reg. 29, f. 79r, 1477; *Missive e Responsive,* b. 8, reg. 5, f. 73r, 1488 Feb. 7. For property disputes, see *Ducali e Lettere,* b. 1, reg. 10, f. 17v–18, f. 20r–v, and f. 61v–62r, 1423 Jan. 18, Feb. 28 and 1424 Feb. 19; *Ducali e Lettere,* b. 2, reg. 18, f. 9v, 1441 Aug. 26. For *auditori* cases from Zara, see DAZ, *Ducali e Terminazioni,* I, f. 45r, no. 105, and f. 121r no. 402, 1430 May 23 and 1452 March; DAZ, *Ducali e Terminazioni,* II, f. 83r, no. 769, f. 117r, no. 883, f. 120r, no. 910, f. 123v, no. 934, 1469 Feb. 6, 1477 Jan. 30, 1477 Sept. 13, and 1479 May 19. Pederin, "Spalato," 334, states that few appeals made it to Venice because of the slowness of the appeals process; as a commercial city, people chose arbitration because they wanted to resolve things quickly. Viggiano, in "Considerazioni," 22, notes the frequent involvement of the *auditori* in inheritance disputes on the *terraferma.*

70. A survey of the *Avogaria di Comun*'s correspondence to rectors from 1455 to 1456 (*AvC, Lettere ai Rettori,* b. 3583, reg. 2) carries out this observation. The number of letters from most locations of the *stato da mar* varies between one and twelve: Arbe (6), Zara (4), Sebenico (2), Spalato (2), Durazzo (7), Curzola (4), Scutari (3), Drivasto (1), Cattaro (4), Corfu (9), Modon/Coron (12), Negroponte (1). In contrast, there are a total of thirty-six letters for Crete: Canea (8), Rettimo (7), Sitia (1), and Candia (20).

71. *MC, Liber Leona,* f. 80v, 1395 Feb. 7.

72. Gullino, "Evoluzione," 348.

73. Viggiano, *Governanti,* 31; *CX, Miste,* reg. 8, f. 84r and 86r, 1403 July 18 and 26, published in Thiriet, *DAV,* II: nos. 1032 and 34; discussed in Thiriet, *RV,* 238–39.

74. *MC, Liber Regina,* f. 164r, 172r, 1477 May 20.

75. *S Mar,* reg. 16, f. 153r, 1507 July 16.

76. *MC, Liber Leona,* f. 41v, 1390 May 29.

77. *ADC, Ducali e Lettere,* b. 2, reg. 27, f. 6r, 1472 Aug. 21.

78. Valentini, "Stabilimenti," 223; Pederin, "Venezianische Verwaltung," 128.

79. *Grazie,* reg. 25, f. 10v, 1440 July 29; *Grazie,* reg. 23, f. 92r, 1434 Oct.; *Grazie,* reg. 25, 39r, 1441 Sept.; *Grazie,* reg. 25, f. 57r, 1442 March; *Grazie,* reg. 25, f. 61r, 1442 April; *Grazie,* reg. 25, f. 51r, 1442 May. For more on the *Grazie* records, see later in chapter 5. For the outcome of Michele Silvestro of Traù's appeal, see *Collegio, Notatorio,* reg. 7, f. 47v, 1442 May 17.

80. *Grazie,* reg. 25, f. 43v, 1441; *Grazie,* reg. 25, f. 58r, 1442 March.

81. *Grazie,* reg. 22, f. 8v, 1424 March 24; *Grazie,* reg. 23, f. 10v, 1431 July 22; *Grazie,* reg. 23, f. 43v, 1432 Dec. 23; *Grazie,* reg. 24, f. 56r, 1439 July; *Grazie,* reg. 24, f. 59r, 1439 Aug. 8; *Grazie,* reg. 25, f. 113r, 1442 Sept.; *Grazie,* reg. 25, f. 68v, 1444 March.

82. For subjects' desire to appeal to Venice from the *terraferma,* see Viggiano, *Governanti,* 51–146; Cozzi, "Politica del diritto," 114–121; Grubb, *Firstborn,* 136–48; and Muir, "Was There Republicanism?" 137–67.

83. *AvC, Raspe,* reg. 3647, I, f. 71v, 1419 Dec. 15; *AvC, Raspe,* reg. 3657, f. 36v, 1490 April 28.

84. *ADC, Ducali e Lettere,* b. 1, reg. 3, f. 8v–9r and f. 21v, 1403 Jan. 13 and Nov. 22, summarized in Thiriet, *Duca di Candia,* nos. 26, 106–7, 130, 165–66, 168, 182, and 186.

85. *ADC, Ducali e Lettere,* b. 1, reg. 18, f. 32v, 1441 June. In another case, Maria, wife of Jacobo Trevisan, appeared before the *Quarantia* to defend Jacobo's sale of some land in Sitia belonging to her: *ADC, Missive e Responsive,* b. 8 reg. 5, f. 87v, 1488 Aug. 30.

86. DAZ, *Ducali e Terminazioni,* I, f. 74v–75r, no. 218, 1438 Nov. 28.

87. Cozzi, *RVEM,* I: 196.

88. *AvC, Raspe,* reg. 3646, f. 91v, 1415 Aug. 2. For a similar example from Coron, see *Auditori Nuovi,* b. 185, r. 2, u.p., 1461 March.

89. *ADC, Ducali e Lettere,* b. 2, reg. 26, f. 21r, 1465 Oct.

90. *Capi X, Lettere dei Rettori,* b. 286, f. 336r–v, 1596 May 29, published and analyzed by Lambrinós, "Rivalités économiques et sociales."

91. *AvC, Raspe,* reg. 3657, f. 216r, 1493 Feb. 28.

92. *AvC, Raspe,* reg. 3651, II, f. 84r, 1460 April 28.

93. BSR, Statuti Mss 286, 1427 Dec. 4. See also *AvC, Raspe,* reg. 3650, f. 36v–37r, 1457 June 5, for an appeal from Antivari against a rector's decision that had not respected their statutes.

94. *AvC, Raspe,* reg. 3647, II, f. 22r, 1424 Jan. 12. See chapter 3 for Arimondo's family connections to Dalmatia.

95. *AvC, Raspe,* reg. 3648, I, f. 38r, 1430 July 7; *AvC, Raspe,* reg. 3649, I, f. 20r, 1446 Nov. 18; *AvC, Raspe,* reg. 3649, II, f. 31r, 1447 April 19; *AvC, Raspe,* reg. 3650, f. 15v, 1451 July 28; *AvC, Raspe,* reg. 3650, f. 47v, 1457 Sept. 26; *AvC, Raspe,* reg. 3650, f. 63v, 1458 April 13; *AvC, Raspe,* reg. 3652, f. 12v, 1466 June 10; *AvC, Raspe,* reg. 3655, f. 40v–41r, 1480 July 12; *AvC, Raspe,* reg. 3655, f. 115r, 1482 July 19; *AvC, Raspe,* reg. 3656, f. 12v, 1483 Oct. 29; *AvC, Raspe,* reg. 3656, f. 57v, 1485 March 18; *AvC, Raspe,* reg. 3658, f. 143r, 1497 June 2.

96. *Quarantia Criminale, Parti,* b. 19, f. 71r, 1476 Nov. 7.

97. *AvC, Raspe,* reg. 3656, f. 63r–v, 1485 May 11.

98. *S Misti,* reg. 24, f. 48v, 1347 Nov. 8.

99. *AvC, Raspe,* reg. 3648, II, f. 30r, 1438 Sept. 29.

100. *AvC, Raspe,* reg. 3648, II, f. 23r, 1438 June 10. The rector of Sitia Ruggiero Zorzi's condemnation of Nicolò Cocco, a former notary of the Cretan chancellery, was overturned in 1410; see Thiriet, *DAV,* II: no. 1150.

101. *AvC, Raspe,* reg. 3649, f. 26r, 1443 July 30.

102. *AvC, Raspe,* reg. 3646, f. 101r–v, 1411 May 19.

103. Valentini, *AAV,* no. 1873, 1414 June 8.

104. *AvC, Raspe,* reg. 3643, II, f. 16v–17r, 1372 March 12. Nicolò Griego also was sent to prison for a year because he, in league with Minotto, advanced false testimony against Venier. In another example, captain of Crete Vito Trevisan's condemnation against Antonio of Rome was overturned, and unusually, the *avogadori* proposed that Trevisan return Antonio's money out of his own pocket, as well as paying a 200 *hyperperi* fine: *AvC, Raspe,* reg. 3644, I, f. 45v, 1382 Aug. 19.

105. Four of his sentences of banishment were revoked, a condemnation for murder was overturned on the basis of the perpetrator's insanity, and his decision about the disposition of some ecclesiastical prebends was reversed: *AvC, Raspe,* reg. 3647, I, f. 109v–110r, 1421 Oct. 3; *AvC, Raspe,* reg. 3647, II, f. 22v, 1423 Jan. 9; *AvC, Raspe,* reg. 3648, I, f. 17r and f. 37r–v, 1429 Feb. 18 and 1430 June 16: *AvC, Raspe,* reg. 3648, II, f. 49r, 1439 Sept. 15; *AvC, Raspe,* reg. 3651, II, f 54r–54v, 1463 Sept. 1. For Mudazzo's prosecutions for corruption, see chapter 6.

106. Valentini, *AAV,* no. 1449, 1409 June 28.

107. *Quarantia Criminale, Parti,* b. 20, f. 12v, 1490 Jan. 8. See also *AvC, Raspe,* reg. 3649, I, f. 11r, 1442 Oct. 7; *AvC, Raspe,* reg. 3649, I, f. 56v, 1444 July 17, also in *Quarantia Criminale, Parti,* b. 18, f. 36r–v.

108. *AvC, Raspe,* reg. 3648, II, f. 43r, 1439 March 24 and April 13.

109. *AvC, Raspe,* reg. 3646, II, f. 110v–111r, 1416 July 13.

110. *Collegio, Notatorio,* reg. 5, f. 176v, 1422 July 24.

111. *AvC, Raspe,* reg. 3653, f. 51r–v, 1470 Aug. 1. See also *AvC, Raspe,* reg. 3646, II, f. 32v–33r, 1413 July 9; *AvC, Raspe,* reg. 3647, I, f. 26v, 1418 Jan. 5. For the legal precedents, see Thiriet, *RV,* 238.

112. *AvC, Raspe,* reg. 3657, f. 12v and 130v, 1489 Aug. 4 and 1492 April 13. For other examples of cases with problems of testimony, see *AvC, Raspe,* reg. 3646, I, 33r, 1407 Oct. 4; *AvC, Raspe,* reg. 3649, I, f. 102–102v, 1446 Jan. 10.

113. *AvC, Raspe,* reg. 3658. f. 205r–v, 1498 Dec. 14.

114. *AvC, Raspe,* reg. 3650, f. 2v and 6r, 1451 March 31.

115. For instance, a large proportion of the letters in *AvC, Lettere ai Rettori,* b. 3583, are requests from the *Avogaria* to rectors for documents or information in pending cases.

116. *ADC, Missive e Responsive,* b. 8, reg. 1, no. 11, 1417 May 8.

117. *ADC, Missive e Responsive,* b. 8, reg. 8, f. 102r, 1526 April 19. In 1543, the count of Traù wrote asking that his sentence against a forger be approved and that the *Dieci* not allow any appeals: *Capi X, Lettere dei Rettori,* b. 281, f. 215r, 1543 April 22.

118. For the typical career path of *avogadori,* see Viggiano, "Disciplina dei Rettori," 186–88, where he demonstrates that eighty-two of the *avogadori* elected between 1440 and 1490 were between fifty and sixty years old, and that 45 percent of the *avogadori* also occupied an important office in the *dominio* during the same period.

119. Girolamo di Alvise Donà was first an *auditor nuovo* (1471) and then *podestà* in Pirano (1475) and count of Traù (1482). Orsato di Donato Giustinian was an *auditor nuovo* (1448) before becoming *bailo* of Cyprus (1452). Antonio di Luca Dolfin served twice in the *Quarantia* (1440, 1443) and then went abroad as rector of Fitilei (1445), as count of Pago (1449), and *provveditore* of Dagno (1454). Luca di Marco Zeno was an *auditor vecchio* (1463), *avogador* (1483), captain of Crete (1492), and captain of Padova (1498).

120. Gullino, "Foscarini, Nicolò." Benedetto di Francesco Trevisan was an *auditor* (1470), *podestà* of Vicenza (1474) and Treviso (1477), and lieutenant in Friuli (1482) before his first term as *avogador* (1483). He was then captain of Verona (1484), returned to the *Avogaria* (1486), and was captain of Crete (1487) and *podestà* of Padova (1491).

121. Gullino, "Cocco, Niccolò." Antonio di Marco Erizzo served on the *Quarantia* (1454), as counselor in Modon and Coron (1456), as *provveditore* in Dagno (1464), and in the *Avogaria* twice (1470, 1489); see Gullino, "Erizzo, Antonio." Pietro di Francesco Falier was on the *Quarantia* (1438), count of Pago (1441), an *auditor nuovo* (1448), consul in Tunis (1453), and on the *Avogaria* (1471). Alvise di Marino Lando began his career as an *auditor nuovo* (1467), served as count of Traù (1470), and returned to the *Avogaria* three times (1479, 1480, and 1483). Antonio di Alvise Calbo was an *auditor nuovo* (1474), count of Sebenico (1486), captain of Bergamo (1495), and then *avogador* (1489); see Olivieri, "Calbo, Marc'Antonio." Girolamo di Francesco Zorzi served as an *auditor vecchio* (1469), castellan on Corfu (1473), treasurer of Pago (1482), and then as *avogador* (1488).

122. Pillinini, "Bollani, Candiano."

123. Luca Tron was count of Traù (1421), count of Zara (1430), duke of Crete (1439), *avogador* (1443), *podestà* of Padova (1444), and *avogador* again (1446). Fantin Viaro was captain of Vicenza (1420), captain of Crete (1427), captain of Verona (1435), captain of Padova (1437), and lieutenant of Friuli (1440) before serving as an *avogador* (1441); he then returned to Crete as captain (1443). Delfino Venier was captain of Crete (1428), *podestà* of Brescia (1434), *avogador* (1442), captain of Crete again (1443), and *avogador* again (1449).

124. The Zaccaria Bembo mentioned here is not the same man profiled by Spiazzi, "Bembo, Zaccaria."

125. Pillinini, "Bollani, Domenico"; Gullino, "Donà, Andrea;" Gullino, "Emo, Pietro."

126. Rossi, "Diedo, Antonio." Bernardo introduced a total of three cases which overturned sentences of Diedo's, one for confiscating some goods of the Grimani brothers against the form of their father's will, *AvC, Raspe,* reg. 3650, I, f. 5v, 1451 April 14, and two against Diedo's sentences of banishment, *AvC, Raspe,* reg. 3650, I, f. 17r and f. 73r, 1451 Dec. 11 and 1453 June 22.

127. Diedo joined an ongoing prosecution of some Jews of Candia for the alleged crucifixion of lambs, *AvC, Raspe,* reg. 3650, I, f. 74r, 1453 July 14; *AvC, Raspe,* reg. 3650, II, f. 9v, 1454 July 7.

128. *AvC, Raspe,* reg. 3650, II, f.11v–12v, f. 19r, f. 26v, f. 46r, f. 50r, 1454 June 21, 26–27, 1454 Sept. 10, 1455 Jan. 10, 1455 Aug. 7 and 1455 Sept. 4.

129. *AvC, Raspe,* reg. 3650, II, f. 47r, 1455 Aug. 12. For a case that Diedo and Vitturi prosecuted together, see *AvC, Raspe,* reg. 3650, II, f.11v–12r, 1454 June 21 and 26. In another example, Tomà Duodo began his career as a judge in Crete, returned as duke (1443), and was elected to the *Avogaria* after his return to Venice (1449). In the same time span, his brother Vittore was a counselor in Candia (1438) and his nephew Nicolò followed him to the island as a judge (1445) and returned as treasurer (1451). Tomà had several of his sentences overturned by the *Avogaria* and then went on to prosecute several cases originating in Crete; see *AvC, Raspe,* reg. 3649, I, f. 102r–v, 1446 Jan. 10; *AvC, Raspe,* reg. 3649, II, f. 31r and 33v–34r, 1447 April 19. For cases he prosecuted, see: *AvC, Raspe,* reg. 3649, II, f. 54v and f. 72v, 1448 June 19 and 1449 Feb. 19; *AvC, Raspe,* reg. 3650, I, f. 74r, 1453 July 14; *AvC, Raspe,* reg. 3650, II, f. 9v, 1454 July 7.

130. Mocenigo's correspondence is in *ADC, Ducali e Lettere,* b. 2, reg. 18.

131. *AvC, Raspe,* reg. 3649, I, f. 56v, 1447 July 17; also in *Quarantia Criminal, Parti,* b. 18, f. 36r–v.

132. *ADC, Ducali e Lettere,* b. 1, reg. 3, f. 22v, 1404 July 30, summarized in Thiriet, *Duca di Candia* no. 109; *Grazie,* reg. 22, 62v, 1426 Feb. 2; *ADC, Ducali e Lettere,* b. 2, reg. 19, f. 34v, 1444 July 28.

133. *Grazie,* reg. 25, f. 134r, 1445 March 19; *Grazie,* reg. 22, f. 24v, 1424 Sept. 6. Nicolò Grimani's fine was cut from 500 to 50 *hyperperi,* and Zuanne Agnati's sentence for sodomy was cut from 50 *hyperperi* to 10 *hyperperi: Grazie,* 25, f. 26r.

134. *Grazie,* reg. 25, f. 4v, 1440 May 8.

135. *Grazie,* reg. 24, f. 65r, 1439 Aug.

136. *Grazie,* reg. 25, f. 68v, 1442 Sept.

137. *Grazie,* reg. 25, f. 73v and 113r, 1442 Oct. and 1444 May.

FIVE · Negotiating Empire

1. Chittolini, "Private"; see also Weissman, "Taking Patronage Seriously"; Briquet.

2. Molho, "Patronage and the State," 238; see also idem, "Cosimo de Medici."

3. Essential beginning points to the extensive literature on this theme include Kent, *Rise of the Medici;* Rubenstein; Klapisch-Zuber, "Kin, Friends, and Neighbors."

4. On the ties of neighborhood in Florence, see Weissman, *Ritual Brotherhood;* Kent and Kent, *Neighbours and Neighbourhood;* Eckstein. On Florentine—and especially Medici—patronage relationships with territorial clients, see the contributions of Fabbri, Salvestrini, R. Black, and Milner in *Florentine Tuscany;* Connell, "Clientelismo"; idem, "Changing Patterns."

5. Romano, "Quod sibi fiat Gratia"; idem, *Patricians and Popolani,* 123–31. My description of the *grazia* approval process closely follows that of Romano, *Patricians and Popolani,* 124; and Mor's introduction to the *Cassiere della Bolla Ducale,* lxxvi–lxxx.

6. Romano, *Patricians and Popolani,* 126.

7. *S Mar,* reg. 18, f. 149v–150r, 1516 Dec. 16. Cateruzza's cousins, Marino Barozzi and his wife Isabella, had received permission in 1503 to extend their home and had paid 4 soldi annually to maintain their privilege. Marino and Cateruzza had obtained the

space for the kitchen in 1513, also at a fee of 4 soldi per year, and in 1516 they appeared before the Senate asking for permission to build the kitchen. It is possible that the state's concern over the Loredan kitchen stemmed from its proximity to the fortifications of Rettimo. This is not the only construction permit that appears in the *grazia* records, although others have more overt economic purposes. Marco Chachossi of Corfu received permission to build a shop to sell wine on communal lands, *Grazie,* reg. 25, f. 64r, 1442 Aug.; Cressi di Donato Zadolini of Zara received permission to build an olive mill on his property: DAZ, *Ducali e Terminazioni,* II, f. 13v, no. 832, 1472 Feb. 3.

8. See, e.g., *Grazie,* reg. 22, f. 15v, f. 28r, f. 72r–v; *Grazie,* reg. 23, f. 9r, f. 13v, f. 20v; *Grazie,* reg. 24, f. 60v, 65r; *Grazie,* reg. 25, f. 1v, f. 4v, f. 10v, f. 12r, f. 56v, f. 64r, f. 67r, f. 72v, f. 73v–74v, f. 114r–v, f. 118v; *S Mar,* reg. 6, f. 195r, 1460 Aug. 1; *S Mar,* reg. 8, f. 66r and 67v, 1466 March 22 and 24; *S Mar,* reg. 10, f. 96, 1476 Sept. 23; *S Mar,* reg. 12, f. 22r, 1484 Sept. 10.

9. *PSM, Misti,* b. 3, n. 7, letter of 1498 Feb. 6. Weissman, "Importance," 275–78, points to the importance of debt and credit networks within the constellation of obligations and friendships that defined a Renaissance Florentine's world.

10. *PSM, Misti,* b. 3, n. 7, letters dated 1494 April 5, 1486 Feb. 10, 1497 Jan. 11 and Feb. 6. Venier left Cambio 60 gold ducats in his will; see *PSM, Misti,* b. 3, u.p., 1501 Nov. 22. On the Cambio and their position in Spalatine society, see Gligo et al., *Zlatna Knjiga,* 76 and 202; Raukar, "Fiorentini," 679; Pederin, "Spalato," 333.

11. *PSM, Misti,* b. 3, n. 7, letter dated 1494 April 5.

12. One of the few instances that record a nonofficial acting as a sponsor was when Dionysio Giustinian acted as the *plezius* of Davide Doymo of Sebenico for a *grazia: Grazie,* reg. 25, f. 69r. While Giustinian held no official position, he and his sister both married into Sebenican families: Barbaro, *Nozze,* f. 223v.

13. See the inventory in Mor, xc–xcv, which documents the successive losses to the series; see also Mueller, *Procuratori,* 283, n. 83, for difficulties in the documentation of *grazie.*

14. *Grazie,* reg. 21, f.12r–24r, March 1409–March 1410. There were 134 entries total in this period, 16 from the *stato da mar,* 14 from Crete. It is possible that the residents of the *stato da mar*'s prominence in the *grazia* records is a function of their distance from the centers of power, and thus the need to record privileges and favors.

15. *Grazie,* reg. 22, f. 1r–8r, 22 Oct. 1423–Oct. 1424. There were 256 entries total, 26 from the *stato da mar* and 17 from Crete.

16. *Grazie,* reg. 23, f. 22v–47v, March 1432–March 1433. There were 237 total entries, 24 from the *stato di mar* and 21 from Crete. *Grazie,* reg. 24, f. 50r–70r. There were 212 total entries, 30 from the *stato da mar,* 19 from Crete. *Grazie,* reg. 25, f. 28r–50v, March 1441–March 1442. There were 231 total entries, 26 from the *stato da mar* and 13 from Crete.

17. Simone Matafari received a *grazia* absolving him of some duties on foreign wines: DAZ, *Ducali e Terminazioni,* I, no. 116, f. 47r, 1431 Dec. 2. Nicolò di Simone Begna petitioned for money owed to his father in 1443 and was able to write directly to the *auditori nuovi* when he was involved in a dispute over the ownership of the vil-

lage of Goriza: DAZ, *Ducali e Terminazioni,* I, no. 273, f. 87r, 1443 March 15, and *Auditori Nuovi,* reg. 185, b. 2, u.p., 1461 April 30. The Venetian government also intervened in favor of Zoilo Grisogono in a dispute over his hereditary right to the village of Caschienichi, worth 30 ducats: DAZ, *Ducali e Terminazioni,* II, no. 854, f. 106v, 1474 July 29. Lodovico Matafari, who owed 100 ducats to the treasury in Zara, was absolved of his debt by *grazia,* and Giovanni di Alvise Matafari received a position in the local militia: DAZ, *Ducali e Terminazioni,* II, f. 108r, nos. 860 and 861, 1475 June 6 and Sept. 2. Zuanne Gradenigo in 1483 received an income from some property near Zara: Pederin, "Venezianische Verwaltung," 140. Zuanne's sons were offered positions as *stipendarii* in 1517, in addition to payments from Cherso and Ossero: *S Mar,* reg. 18, f. 157r–v, 1517 Jan. 27.

18. For his services to the Venetian state, Perozzo di Altavilla received a pension of 24 ducats annually: Valentini, *AAV,* no. 1044. Vaxili de San Ippolito distinguished himself fighting against the Genoese and received permission to build in the *borgo* of the city: *Grazie,* reg. 25, f. 100v, 1443 Nov. In 1464, Michele de Gothis received the valuable concession of a Corfiote fief consisting of the revenues from the gypsies on the island: Jacoby, *AR,* 263; Soulis, "Gypsies," 157, 164–65. Leonardo de Gothis was captain of the island before his 1489 death: Sanudo, *Vite,* II: 61.

19. DAZ, *Ducali e Terminazioni,* II, f. 99r, no. 827, 1472 April 27.

20. *Listine,* VII: 59, 1412 Dec. 30.

21. For his many acts of loyalty to Venice, Jurich received 150 lire annually, and Daniele, his son, was captain of Sebenico in 1429: *Listine,* VIII: 64–65 and 140.

22. *Grazie,* reg. 23, f. 10r, 1431 July 22.

23. *MC, Liber Leona,* f. 65r, 1392 Nov. 24.

24. Kohl, *Records,* no. 3329, 1393 April 15.

25. *Listine,* VI: 255, 1412 April 28.

26. Pederin, "Venezianische Verwaltung," 107–9, lists many of these subsidies, including those to Simone Detrico and Tommaso de Petrizio. Detrico and his heirs also received a position in the Zarentine treasury and permission to import horses: DAZ, *Ducali e Terminazioni,* I, f. 156r, no. 153, 1434 June 18; DAZ, *Ducali e Terminazioni,* II, f. 102r and f. 100r, nos. 838 and 868, 1473 May 12 and 1474 April 4. In Durazzo, Venice granted Rascho Dukagini the office of captain of the city: *Grazie,* reg. 25, f. 118v, 1444 July 4. In Cyprus, Hannibale and Matteo Paleologo received 200 ducats a year from the treasury of Cyprus for themselves and their heirs: *Grazie,* reg. 26, f. 112r, 1516 Feb. 16.

27. Valentini, "Amministrazione," 849.

28. Mueller, *Venetian Money Market,* 389–94.

29. Thiriet, *DAV,* II: no. 885, 1387 Sept. 18.

30. *Grazie,* reg. 26, f. 120r, 1501 April 3.

31. For scribes and chancellors, see DAZ, *Ducali e Terminazioni,* I, f. 72r, no. 207, 1437 Aug. 28; *Grazie,* reg. 26, f. 48r, f. 71r, f. 77r, and f. 84v, 1504 Jan. 13, 1511 Sept. 28, 1515 Sept. 12, and 1521 Aug. 22. For military posts, see Imhaus, *Minoranze orientali,* 275–77; *Grazie,* reg. 22, f. 61r, 1425 Nov. 6; *Grazie,* reg. 23, f. 6r, 1431 March 26; *Collegio, Notatorio,* reg. 6, f. 165r, 1436 Aug. 2; *S Mar,* reg. 1, f. 211r, 1444 Feb. 14; *Grazie,* reg. 25, f. 118v, 1444 July 4; *ADC, Missive e Responsive,* b. 8, reg. 2, u.p., 1455 April 16; *ADC, Ducali e*

Lettere, b. 2, reg. 24, u.p., 1461 March 14; *S Mar,* reg. 8, f. 67v, 1466 March 22; and *Grazie,* reg. 26, f. 11r, f. 30r, f. 44r, f. 48r, f. 70r, f. 79r, f. 85v, f. 88r, f. 92v, f. 97v, f. 98v, f. 110v, f. 122r.

32. *Grazie,* reg. 25, f. 113r, 1444 April 4.

33. To offer just one example, the Da Porto clan, feudatories of long standing on Crete, obtained a number of *grazie:* Giorgio received two *grazie,* one for the castellany of Belvedere and one for debt relief, and Antonio da Porto's debts to the commune were forgiven in 1466; see *S Misti,* reg. 45, f. 69r, 1401 April 15; *S Mar,* reg. 2, f. 134r, 1446 March 31; and *S Mar,* reg. 8, f. 67v, 1466 March 22, all published in Noiret, *DI,* 116, 413, and 501.

34. *Collegio, Notatorio,* reg. 6, f. 165r, 1436 Aug. 2.

35. On the Calergi family and its marriages, see Thiriet, *RV,* 130–39; McKee, *Uncommon Dominion,* 74–83. In 1294, Alexis Calergi received significant concessions in return for his help in ending a rebellion against Venice: Borsari, *Dominio veneziano,* 54–66. In the fourteenth century, the Calergi received a number of cash loans repayable in wheat: Mueller, *Venetian Money Market,* 405. In 1407, Matteo di Giorgio Calergi received an annual pension of 400 *hyperperi: Liber Commemorali,* X: 67, 1407 Dec. 18. Zuanne Calergi received permission to participate in offices on Crete: *Grazie,* reg. 24, f. 70r, 1440 March 9. Zuanne Calergi was rewarded for his loyalty during the Sifi Vlastos conspiracy: *CX, Miste,* reg. 17, f. 163r, 1472 May 23.

36. *Grazie,* reg. 25 f. 64r, 1442 June 2; *S Mar,* reg. 4, f. 13v, 1450 Dec. 6. On the Ialina family's marital connections with Veneto-Cretans, see McKee, *Uncommon Dominion,* 73; on the gradual definition of the Cretan nobility, see Papadaki, "Krētikē eugéneia," 305–18; Lambrinós, "Exélixē."

37. Jacoby, "Venice, the Inquisition"; *Grazie,* reg. 23, f. 81v and 92v, 1434 Aug. 1 and Dec. 5.

38. *MC, Liber Novella,* f. 101v–102r, 1364 June 9 and 16; *Collegio, Secreti,* f. 111v–12r, 1364 July 28, summarized in Thiriet, *DAV,* II: nos. 754 and 758. Karapidakis, *Civis Fidelis,* 60, suggests that on Corfu, the practice of *grazia* created a growing mentality among Corfiotes that loyalty to Venice resulted in the maintenance of or access to privileges.

39. *S Misti,* reg. 32, f. 87v and f. 103v, 1367 Oct. 3 and 1368 Jan. 3; *MC, Liber Leona,* f. 23v, 1388 May 3.

40. *S Misti,* reg. 35, f. 85v, 1376 Feb. 14.

41. Fine, 422; Schmitt, *Venezianische Albanien,* 245–51; Božić, 69.

42. Božić, 69; *Listine,* V: 49.

43. Valentini, *AAV,* n. 1447, 1409 June 26.

44. For examples of such challenges, see Valentini, *AAV,* nos. 1450, 1457, 1873, and 2032.

45. The result was a cadastral survey and register of concessions, published in Valentini, *AAV,* vol. 8; see also Božić; and Schmitt, *Venezianische Albanien,* 270.

46. Manoussacas, *Sēphē Vlastou,* 8–16, for the historiography of the planned rebellion. Zinkeisen, IV: 623–24, includes the idea of naming the displaced Byzantine emperor king of the island. Manoussacas, *Sēphē Vlastou,* 7–8 and 19–21, sees Vlastos's

conspiracy as an attempt to form a free Greek state, a successor to Byzantium, and Maltezou, "Historical," 25, also says that it is possible such motivations inspired the rebels.

47. *CX, Miste,* reg. 16, f. 108v–109r, 1463 Dec. 29, published in Manoussacas, *Sēphē Vlastou,* 130–32.

48. *CX, Miste,* reg. 20, f. 43r–43v, 1481 Jan. 30, published in Manoussacas, *Sēphē Vlastou,* 149–51.

49. *CX, Miste,* reg. 16, f. 22r and 42v, 1461 Feb. 11–13 and Nov. 12, published in Manoussacas, *Sēphē Vlastou,* 115–16 and 122–23.

50. *CX, Miste,* reg. 16, f. 30r–v, 1461 June 19 and 22, published in Manoussacas, *Sēphē Vlastou,* 117–20.

51. For Venetian religious policy on Crete, see Maltezou, "Historical," 26–29; Tomadakis; Fedalto, I: 377–414. For an introduction to the literature on the Council of Florence/Ferrara and its reception in Venice and among Greeks, see Gill; Hussey; Setton, *Papacy,* II: 39–81; Geanakoplos, "Council," 84–111; and Lock, 193–239.

52. *S Mar,* reg. 4, f. 132v, 1452 June 26, published in Noiret, *DI,* 436 and in Fedalto, III: 246. The Senate conformed Paulopolus's election: *S Mar,* reg. 4, f. 136v, 1452 June 20, published in Fedalto, III: 247.

53. Vacalopolous, 272–83.

54. *ADC, Ducali e Lettere,* b. 2, reg. 19, f. 30r, 1444 June 12.

55. *Collegio, Notatorio,* reg. 8, f. 176v, 1453 Jan. 10.

56. *CX, Miste,* reg. 14, f. 155r, 1453 May 23; Manoussacas, *Sēphē Vlastou,* 89.

57. The relevant documents are published in Manoussacas, *Sēphē Vlastou,* 135–43 and 149–51; see also Jacoby, "Agent juif."

58. The administration of Lima's reward was a long and complicated process, because while he had been promised the protopapacy when it became vacant, Lima refused to leave Rettimo to serve in his new post. The *Dieci* also ordered the regime to investigate Lima and determine the veracity of his information, but they were apparently satisfied with the result; see Manoussacas, *Sēphē Vlastou,* 84–85, and the documents published on 111–13 and 146–55 as well as Thiriet, *DAV,* II: no. 1510.

59. *CX, Miste,* reg. 16, f. 69v, 1462 July 28, published in Manoussacas, *Sēphē Vlastou,* 127–28.

60. *CX, Miste,* reg. 17, f. 106v, 1470 Aug. 28.

61. Manoussacas, *Sēphē Vlastou,* 92–93; see Cozzi, "Authority and the Law," 293–95, for this practice in the Venetian territories as a whole.

62. *ADC, Ducali e Lettere,* reg. 23, u.p., 1454 Oct. 1; *CX, Miste,* reg. 17, f. 163r, 1472 May 23, published in Manoussacas, *Sēphē Vlastou,* 145–46; Corner, BMV It VI 286 (5985) f. 47v; *ADC, Missive e Responsive,* b. 8, reg. 2, u.p., 1455 June 20, published in Manoussacas, *Sēphē Vlastou,* 113–14, and summarized in Thiriet, *DAV,* II: no. 1511.

63. *ADC, Ducali e Lettere,* reg. 23, u.p., 1454 Oct. 1.

64. *CX, Miste,* reg. 16, f. 34r, 1461 June 23, published in Manoussacas, *Sēphē Vlastou,*121, and summarized in Thiriet, *DAV,* II: no. 1594.

65. *CX, Miste,* reg. 15, f. 56v–57r, 1455 June 11, reported in a letter sent June 12: *ADC, Missive e Responsive,* b. 8, reg. 2, u.p.

66. For instance, in *Grazie,* reg. 25, 1440–42, a little more than one-half of the entries pertaining to Crete dealt with debt (fourteen out of twenty-three).

67. *S Misti,* reg. 40, f. 89v, 1387 Aug. 30, published in Noiret, *DI,* 14.

68. *Grazie,* reg. 25, f. 114v, 1444 June 6.

69. *MC, Liber Leona,* f. 110r, 1400 June 1.

70. DAZ, *Ducali e Terminazioni,* I, f. 41r, no. 97, 1427 Nov. 21.

71. *ADC, Ducali e Lettere,* b. 1, reg. 6, 1409 Sept. 4 and 1410 Aug. 2, 4, and 28, summarized in Thiriet, *DAV,* II: nos. 1108, 1154–55, and 1159.

72. *S Misti,* reg. 40, f. 51v, 1386 Dec. 11, published in Noiret, *DI,* 9.

73. The debt situation is discussed in detail in Starr, 84–86. For further amnesties, see *S Misti,* reg. 40, f. 51v and f. 89v, 1386 Dec. 11 and 1387 Aug. 30 and *S Misti,* reg. 40, f. 137v, 1388 Dec. 24; *MC, Liber Leona,* f. 106r, 1400 June 1; *S Misti,* reg. 45, f. 72r and f. 89v, 1401 April 19 and June 21; *Grazie,* reg. 21, f. 10r, 1409 Feb. 11; *Grazie,* reg. 21, f. 12v, 1409 March 27; *S Misti,* reg. 49, f. 67r, 1411 Nov. 13, summarized in Noiret, *DI,* 9, 17, and 23, 116–17, 212.

74. *S Misti,* reg. 51, f. 73r, 1415 Oct. 3 and f. 80v–81v, 1415 Nov. 1, the latter published in Noiret, *DI,* 239–42.

75. *S Misti,* reg. 51, f. 137r and 149v, 1416 June 11 and 30, published in Noiret, *DI,* 244–45.

76. In the final vote, there were forty-eight for, forty against, and seven abstentions.

77. *S Misti,* reg. 51, f. 154v and f. 156r, 1416 Aug. 21 and Aug. 29, published in Noiret, *DI,* 245–47.

78. *AvC, Raspe,* reg. 3647, I, f. 53v–55v, 1419 March 3.

79. *ADC, Missive e Responsive,* b. 8, reg. 1, letter 5, 1417 April 21, summarized in Thiriet, *DAV,* II: no. 1221 (incorrectly dated April 22).

80. *S Misti,* reg. 51, f. 92v, 1418 May 28, summarized in Noiret, *DI,* 264–65.

81. *S Misti,* reg. 53, f. 145r, f. 146r and 149r, 1420 July 30, Aug. 1 and 9.

82. *S Misti,* reg. 53, f. 275r–v, 1421 March 13, incorrectly summarized in Noiret, *DI,* 287.

83. *S Misti,* reg. 54, f. 148v, 1423 Sept. 26, published in Noiret, *DI,* 297. The prohibition applied throughout the maritime state, as the same decree was received in Zara: DAZ, *Ducali e Terminazioni,* I, f. 29v–30r, no. 70, 1423 Oct. 7.

84. *S Mar,* reg. 1, f. 76v, 1442 Jan. 15; *S Mar,* reg. 8, f. 1, 1465 Jan. 8, published in Noiret, *DI,* 401 and 493–94.

85. *S Mar,* reg. 4, f. 90v–91r, 1451 Oct. 14, published in Noiret, *DI,* 435.

86. DAZ, *Ducali e Terminazioni,* II, f. 118r, no. 393, 1454 Oct. 15.

87. *S Mar,* reg. 6, f. 129r, 1459 May 25; published in Noiret, *DI,* 457. For further *grazie* offering debt relief, see *S Mar,* reg. 8, f. 57v, f. 68r, f. 124r, f. 138r, f. 140r, and f. 168r, 1466 March 22 and April 10, 1467 April 28, Aug. 25, and Sept. 8, 1468 May 6; *S Mar,* reg. 9, f. 64r, 1470 Oct. 22; *Collegio, Notatorio,* reg. 12, f. 126v, 1480 June 10; *CX, Miste,* reg. 21, f. 198r, 1483 Jan. 28; *S Mar,* reg. 14, f. 158r, 1498 May 18; *S Mar,* reg. 15, f. 98v, 1501 Sept. 14; *S Mar,* reg. 16, f. 166r, 1507 Aug. 4; *S Mar,* reg. 20, f. 147v–148r, 1524 Sept. 27; and *S Mar,* reg. 20, f. 188v–189r, 1525 Sept. 27.

88. In addition to Papadia-Lala's extensive analysis in *Thesmos,* see *Listine,* VI: 8,

1409 Sept. 5; Arbel, "Colonie," 971; idem, "Urban Assemblies," 212; Bacchion, 52–53; Benvenuti, *Zara,* 206–8; Karapidakis, *Civis Fidelis,* 58–59; McKee, *Uncommon Dominion,* 49–52; Pederin, "Venezianische Verwaltung," 113; Praga, *Dalmatia,* 152–53; Thiriet, *RV,* 203–11.

89. DAZ, *Ducali e Terminazioni,* I, f. 77r, no. 230, 1440 Sept. 16; *CX, Miste,* reg. 15, f. 58v, 1455 June 27.

90. DAZ, *Ducali e Terminazioni,* II, f. 78r, no. 760, 1469 Nov. 10.

91. *Grazie,* reg. 26, f. 122r–v, f. 125r, 1501 April 3, 1507 April 3, 1514 Oct. 17, 1515 July 27.

92. *Grazie,* reg. 21, f. 73v, 1414 April 3.

93. *Grazie,* reg. 24, 51r, 1439 April 12. In a second example from Zara, Giovanni de Aurana's privilege was extended to his heirs as well: DAZ, *Ducali e Terminazioni,* I, f. 72r, no. 206, 1438 Jan. 23.

94. *Grazie,* reg. 25, f. 72v, 1442.

95. DAZ, *Ducali e Terminazioni,* I, f. 125v–126r, no. 417, 1453 July 1.

96. Papadia-Lala, *Thesmos,* for the distinctions among councils; for Corfu, see HAC, *Enetokratia,* reg. 5, n. 3. Karapidakis, *Civis Fidelis,* 207, points to the distinction between Greek and Latin but states that it gradually lost any ethnic or religious significance.

97. Thiriet, *RDS,* III: no. 2491, 1439 March 9.

98. Thiriet, *RDS,* III: nos. 2694 and 2717; idem, *RV,* 401; Sathas, IV: 187–89.

99. *MC, Liber Spiritus,* f. 9r–v and f. 140r–v, 1326 Sept. 16 and 1344 Aug. 31; *S Misti,* reg. 51, f. 40r–v, f. 58r, and f. 160v–161r, 1415 June 21, Aug. 19, and 1416 Aug. 29; *S Misti,* reg. 53, f. 41v–42r, 1420 Jan. 9; *S Misti,* reg. 54, f. 31r, 1422 May 17, partially published in Noiret, *DI,* 234–37, 249–252, 270–71, and 292. A second set of deliberations provided room for negotiations, saying the regime could give offices by *grazia* "when they saw fit," and in tacit recognition of the practice, that those who received office by *grazia* at least had to present themselves in Venice for the *Signoria*'s approval: *MC, Liber Spiritus,* f. 166r–v, 1350 Feb. 14; *MC, Liber Novella,* f. 165r, 1359 June 30. The council eventually authorized the award of *grazie* to "good and honest citizens": *MC, Liber Novella,* f. 177r, 1381 Oct. 3. The Venetian Senate used *grazie* to award other offices on Crete, appointing the overseer of armaments in Candia in 1387, a state prosecutor for the island in 1388, the director of the arsenal in 1400, and one of the more important judgeships in 1409 by *grazia: Collegio, Notatorio,* reg. 2, f. 92v, 1387 Sept. 18; *MC, Liber Leona,* f. 19v, 1388 May 3; *S Misti,* reg. 45, f. 16v, 1400 June 5, published in Noiret, *DI,*106–7; and *ADC, Ducali e Lettere,* b. 1, reg. 4, f. 99r, 1409 July 3.

100. *S Mar,* reg. 3, f. 119v–120, 1449 May 16, copy in *ADC,* b. 50 bis, reg. 6, f. 47r–47v, published in Noiret, *DI,* 423–24.

101. *Collegio, Notatorio,* reg. 8, f. 123v, f. 165v, and f. 177v, 1450 Oct. 7, 1452 July 23, and 1453 Jan. 10; *Collegio, Notatorio,* reg. 9, f. 47r, 1455 May 9; O'Connell, "Sinews of Rule." Nicolò Avonal was most likely related to the Pietro Avonal mentioned earlier in chapter 5.

102. *CX, Miste,* reg. 15, f. 40v–41r, 1455 April 11. These regulations are discussed in the context of Venetian politics in Romano, *Likeness,* 268–69, and in the context of their *terraferma* applications in Law, "Stato veneziano," 284–98, and Queller, *VP,* 34.

103. *S Mar,* reg. 5, f. 97r, 1455 June 12, published in Noiret, *DI,* 447.

104. *S Mar,* reg. 12, f. 108v, 1487 March 22.

105. *S Mar,* reg. 13, f. 35r–36r, 1490 Aug. 27; *S Mar,* reg. 14, f. 196r–v, 1499 Aug. 30; *S Mar,* reg. 15, f. 102v–106r, 1501 Sept. 15; *S Mar,* reg. 15, f. 150r–151r, 1502 Sept. 20, all published in Ploumidēs, *Presveies,* 14–18, 22, and 30–44.

106. Bacchion, 51–55.

107. Sathas, II: 213, 1408 Sept. 5.

108. Sathas, III: 32, 1413 Sept. 11, discussed in Bacchion, 53.

109. Sathas, I: 113, 1422 May 7; discussed in Bacchion, 53–55, and Karapidakis, *Civis Fidelis,* 60.

110. Papadia-Lala, *Thesmos;* Karapidakis, *Civis Fidelis.*

111. Sathas, III: 465–67, 1440 May 11, discussed in Bacchion, 58.

112. Karapidakis, *Civis Fidelis,* 60; Sathas, V: 225–26, 1489 July 30.

113. HAC, *Enetokratia,* reg. 1, f. 8r–v.

114. Sathas, III: 194, 1418 Feb. 22.

115. Sathas, III: 308–10, 1426 July 13.

116. Božić, 96.

117. Božić, 134.

118. Božić, 76–77.

119. Božić, 79; *S Misti,* reg. 53, f. 135v, 1421 May 15.

120. *Grazie,* reg. 21, f. 2v–3r, 1407 Oct. 13.

121. Arbe: *Listine,* VI: 48–50 and *Listine,* IX: 137–39, 265–67, 294–300, and 336–44, 1410 Jan. 6; 1441 March 23; 1448 Feb. 26; 1449 March 30; 1450 March 22. Corfu: Sathas, II: 149–52; III: 31–33; I: 112–14 and I: 465–72, 1406 July 26; 1411 Sept. 11; 1422 May 7; and 1440 May 11. Crete: 1416 Aug. 29 and 1449 May 16; published in Noiret, *DI,* 246 and 423–24. Drivasto: 1401 Aug. 4; 1403 May 7; 1421 May 10; 1442 Aug. 5; 1443 May 17; 1447 Feb. 2; Valentini, "Stabilimenti," 199–200. Durazzo: 1401 Oct. 7; 1408 April 9; 1416 April 10; 1417 April 17; 1423 July 16; 1439 May 1; 1440 Oct. 28; Valentini, "Stabilimenti," 199–200. Negroponte: 1412 Feb. 23; 1415 Feb. 4; 1418 Jan. 5; 1426 July 13; 1430 July 25; published in Sathas, III: 1–2, 125–27, 189–90, 306–13, 388–91. Pago: 1410 June 12; 1412 April 29, 1415 May 16; 1417 Dec. 20; 1441 March 2; 1442 Sept. 14; 1445 July 28; 1450 Nov. 23; published in *Listine,* VI: 99–101, 258–59; *Listine,* VII: 201–3, 239–40; *Listine,* IX: 136–37, 162–64, 223–25, 363–66. Scutari: 1401 Jan. 14; 1421 April 5; 1422 April 6; 1425 Aug. 5; Valentini, "Stabilimenti," 199; Sebenico: 1412 Feb. 23; 1413 Nov. 3; 1414 Aug. 7; 1417 Dec. 20, 1422 May 10; 1450 March 15; published in *Listine,* VII: 81–82, 133–34, 164–69, 239; *Listine,* VIII: 167–71; *Listine,* IX: 322–27, 354–55. Traù: 1421 Aug. 2, published in *Listine,* VIII: 105–9. Zara: 1410 March 31; 1422 March 27; 1422 April 7; 1450 May 11; published in *Listine,* VI: 71–74; *Listine,* VIII: 147–51, 153–56; *Listine,* IX: 346–52.

122. Valentini, "Stabilimenti," 201.

123. In Negroponte at the same time the *Assises of Romanie* were compiled, the regime created a volume of all the ducal bulls (*sub bulli dogali*) and letters, obliging administrators to follow them strictly: Jacoby, *AR,* 206–7. In Dalmatia, ducal letters and the responses to delegations are collected in chancelleries: for Arbe, see *Ducal Registrum litterarum communis Arbi 1504,* "Libro Maromano della universita di Arbe,"

BSR, Statuti Mss 637; in Zara, see DAZ, *Ducali e Terminazioni*, vols I–III; for Crete, *ADC, Ducali e Lettere Ricevute.*

124. Sathas, III: 426 and 432, 1435 July 21 and 1436 Nov. 20.

125. *CX, Miste*, reg. 25, f. 119r, 1492 April 11.

126. *Listine*, VI: 7 and 71, 1409 Sept. 5 and 1410 March 31. In September of 1409, Venice responded to a list of petitions from the "representatives of the community of Zara," but in 1410, a delegation from the commoners of Zara arrived, saying that the previous delegation had represented only the nobility and demanding that their own petitions be heard separately.

127. DAZ, *Ducali e Terminazioni*, II, f. 89r, no. 792, 1470 May 23.

SIX · Syndics, Prosecutions, and Scandal

1. Chambers and Dean, 48.

2. Queller, *VP;* Chojnacki, "Review," 600; Kohl, "Review."

3. Muir, "Review," 289; see also idem, "Was There Republicanism?" 152–59; Waquet.

4. Chittolini, "Private," 51.

5. For the role of gossip and public speech as a form of resistance, see Wickham; in the Venetian context, see Horodowich, "Gossiping Tongue," and Finlay, *Politics*, 153.

6. Venier's relevant correspondence can be found in *PSM, Misti*, b. 3, nos. 1, 8, 9, 16–19; *S Mar*, reg. 12, f. 87v, 1486 Aug. 11.

7. *PSM, Misti*, b. 3, n. 5.

8. Sanudo, *Vite dei Dogi*, II: 564.

9. *Collegio, Commissioni, Formulari*, reg. 6, f. 94r, states that the count of Spalato received 600 ducats in salary; Venier's accounts, in *PSM, Misti*, b. 3, n. 3, indicate that he expected to receive 600 ducats as well, and he added an entry to the *Libro d'Oro* of Spalato declaring as much: Gligo et al., *Zlatna Knjiga*, 318. On Sept. 29, 1455, the Great Council had ruled that officials would extend their terms of service by one-third without any corresponding raise in salary: Gullino, "Evoluzione," 350; see Thiriet, *RV*, 195, for earlier measures taxing salaries. The original term of office was twenty-four months, which was then extended to thirty-two months.

10. *PSM, Misti*, b. 3, no. 3; see also nos. 1 and 4. Venier received a letter, now much damaged, from Doge Agostino Barbarigo dated April 14, 1488, reprimanding him for his refusal to give Fantino Coppo the money owed to him from his time in office, amounting to 1,241 lire; the *Dieci* took up the matter in 1488; see *Capi X, Lettere Spedite*, b. 5, f. 95, 1488 Sept. 25.

11. Sanudo, *Diarii*, III: 39, suggests that Da Canal's chancellor had fled to avoid either testifying against Da Canal or to avoid prosecution himself. The case can be followed in Sanudo, *Diarii*, III: 68, 466, 486, 505.

12. Sanudo, *Diarii*, III: 509, 762, and 801; *S Terra*, reg. 13, f. 146v, 1500 Sept. 19.

13. Sanudo, *Diarii*, III: 813–14, *S Terra*, reg. 13, f. 149v–150r, 22 Sept. 1500; see also Queller, *VP*, 179.

14. Sanudo, *Diarii*, III: 1488 and 1573.

15. Sanudo, *Diarii*, IV: 252.

16. *S Misti,* reg. 43, f. 122r, 1396 April 6, discussed in Dudan, *Sindicato,* 78–79. For the longer interval, see *S Misti,* reg. 53 f. 146r, 1420 Aug. 1, where the prologue to the syndics' commission states that while usually syndics are sent every five years but recently had not been sent for seven years. For syndication in other Italian city-states, see Jones, 410.

17. Many of the commissions of fifteenth-century syndics are published: *S Misti,* reg. 41, f. 78v, 1390 May 26; *S Misti,* reg. 43, f. 122r–v, 1396 April 6, published in Noiret, *DI,* 34 and 76–78; 1401 Jan. 30, published in Sathas, II: 56–59; *MC, Liber Leona,* f. 148v, 1405 Feb. 12, published in Iorga, I: 146; *S Misti,* reg. 47, f. 184r–186r, 1408 April 18, published in Noiret, *DI,* 186–68, and in Sathas, II: 198–205; 1413 July 17, published in Sathas, III: 16–22; *S Misti,* reg. 53 f. 166r–173r, 1420 Sept. 2, published in Noiret, *DI,* 278–86, and in *Listine,* VIII: 37–38; 1425 July 12: Sathas, III: 292–93; 1430 July 25, published in Sathas, III: 381–91; *S Mar,* reg. 2, f. 176r–v, 1446 Sept. 21, published in Noiret, *DI,* 415–16.

18. DAZ, *Sindika Avogadora,* f. 6r, 1461 May 5, includes a list of complaints from the community of Traù and the syndics' responses, which were for the most part noncommittal.

19. The syndics' role on the *terraferma* and their connection with other Venetian magistracies has been analyzed extensively; see Lopez, "Auditori nuovi"; idem, "Alcune magistrature"; Cozzi, "Authority and Law," 293–345; Knapton, "Tribunali veneziani," 151–70; Viggiano, "Considerazioni"; idem, "Aspetti politici," 473–505; idem, "Interpretazione della legge," 121–31; idem, *Governanti,* 147–68. For the *stato da mar,* see Thiriet, *RV,* 195–203, and Dudan, *Sindicato.*

20. Thiriet, *RDS,* III: no. 2731, 1446 Sept. 21.

21. *S Misti,* reg. 48, f. 136v and f. 155r, 1410 May 3.

22. Thiriet, *DAV,* II: nos. 1062–63.

23. *CX, Miste,* reg. 13, f. 63v–65r and f. 70v–73r, 1447 April 12–13, May 28, and June 5; see also Gullino, "Donà, Andrea"; Queller, *VP,* 194; Romano, *Likeness,* 201–3.

24. Thiriet, *RDS,* III: no. 3066, 1458 Sept. 4. Erizzo had served as counselor in Coron previously (1444).

25. *Listine,* IX: 314–15, 1449 Dec. 16; Schmitt, "Chiave," 35–38.

26. Corner was elected in January of 1444 and entered his regimen in June of that year; in April of 1445 elections began for Corner's successor. Giovanni Falier was elected in April 1445, but there is no evidence he took office, and the Antivarian petition of 1449 indicates that Andrea Venier took Corner's place. Venier was elected castellan in Scutari in December of 1441; by July of 1448 he was serving as a *provveditore* in Albania during the Skanderbeg conflict: *Listine,* IX: 274–75, 1448 July 29. For Dolfin in Antivari, see Schmitt, *Venezianische Albanien,* 471.

27. *AvC, Raspe,* f. 99r, 1450 May 11. Iacopo and Girolamo Dolfin are both listed in the *SegV* as sons of Vittore; it seems, however, that they were not brothers; see Barbaro, *Arbori,* III: f. 256 and f. 268.

28. Knapton, "Condanna penale." Querini's case was one of a group of prosecutions against castellans in the 1470s: Queller, *VP,* 179. For official misconduct and the line between "legal" and "illegal" actions elsewhere in Italy, Chabod's essays "Stipendi nominali" and "Usi e abusi" remain a useful starting point.

29. DAZ, *Sindika Avogadora*, f. 6r, 1461 May 5.

30. The documents are published in *DVL*, II: 208; 1387 Jan. 8; the *capitoli* forbade rectors from demanding the use of residents' boats, horses, or goods and from accepting or demanding meat, fish, chickens, or wheat. See Queller, *VP*, 196, on this topic more generally.

31. *S Misti*, reg. 51, f. 60v, 1415 Aug. 19, published in Noiret, *DI*, 238–39.

32. Sathas, III: 459–60; 1439 Aug. 1.

33. *AvC, Raspe*, reg. 3645, I, f. 13r, 1393 Dec. 18; Queller, *VP*, 177. For Dandolo's full career and his sister's marriage into Veneto-Cretan society, see Girgensohn, II: 727.

34. *AvC, Raspe*, reg. 3653, f. 19v, 1469 June 12.

35. *AvC, Raspe*, reg. 3644, II, f. 64r–v, 1389 Sept. 28. Contarini was fined 90 *hyperperi* and had to pay the expenses of the special *provveditore* sent to review all of his decrees.

36. Queller, *VP*, 199; Foscolo was fined 200 lire and excluded from further offices on Corfu.

37. *AvC, Raspe*, reg. 3650, I, f. 5v, 1450 April 14.

38. *CX, Miste*, reg. 25, f. 81r, 1491 Oct. 19; Sanudo, *Vite*, II: 650; Queller, *VP*, 195.

39. *CX, Miste*, reg. 19, f. 168r–170v, 1479 May 5–26; Sanudo, *Vite*, I: 147–48; Malipiero, 122; Fine, 600; Gullino, "Da Lezze, Antonio." Schmitt, *Venezianische Albanien*, 622–28. Antonio was son of the Benedetto da Lezze referenced earlier in chapter 6.

40. *AvC, Raspe*, reg. 3647, I, f. 82r, 1420 Aug. 20. The *ROV* entry incorrectly lists Antonio Michiel as the rector of Canea for this year: it was in fact Michele Trevisan.

41. For cases where officials were tried but found to be innocent, see *Quarantia Criminale, Parti*, b. 19, f. 18r, 1475 Oct. 20; *AvC, Raspe*, reg. 3656, f. 32v–33r, 1484 April 28.

42. *S Misti*, reg. 42, f. 122v, 1393 Aug. 5, the Senate voted to order Andrea Bembo, the current *bailo* of Negroponte, and his counselor Antonio Bollani to investigate the conduct of the previous *bailo*. Emo and his two counselors, Antonio Michiel and Eustacchio Cocco, were all prosecuted, *S Misti*, reg. 42, f. 153r–154r, 1394 Feb. 6. Emo and Michiel were convicted, but Cocco narrowly escaped sentencing.

43. Queller, *VP*, 176–77, for the law and its application.

44. *AvC, Raspe*, 3647, f. 11r, 1417 July 30; published in Valentini, *AAV*, no. 2198.

45. Schmitt, *Venezianische Albanien*, 376.

46. Barbaro, *Arbori*, IV: f. 77, 95, 100, 105–6; Kohl, *Records*, nos. 3545, 3506, 3500, 3499, and 3472; Gambino.

47. Schmitt, *Venezianische Albanien*, 376; Valentini, *AAV*, nos. 2723, 3008, 3070, 3333.

48. Pietro's service as counselor of Candia is not listed in *ROV*; see *AvC, Raspe*, reg. 3646, f. 38v, 1408 March 1.

49. *AvC, Raspe*, reg. 3646, II, f. 110v, 1416 July 13; Thiriet, *DAV*, II: 1212.

50. *ADC, Missive e Responsive*, b. 8, n. 1, f. 9r, 1417 May 10; Thiriet, *DAV*, II: 1224.

51. *AvC, Raspe*, reg. 3647, I, f. 111r–v, 1421 Oct. 15. The *avogadori* agreed and restored Nicola to his position.

52. *S Misti*, reg. 54, f. 33r, 1422 June 2; Thiriet, *DAV*, II: 1843, 1422 June 2–8.

53. *S Misti*, reg. 54, f. 58r, 1422 Oct. 12; summarized in Thiriet, *DAV*, II: no. 1858. The Senate vote on proceeding against Diedo was sixty-eight then seventy-four in favor, thirty-seven then thirty-eight against, and thirty-five then twenty-seven unsure.

54. For the matter of the dowry, see *AvC, Lettere Rettore,* reg. 3583, u.p., 1425 March 28.

55. Stöckly, 305–8.

56. Romano, *Likeness,* 144.

57. Schmitt, *Venezianische Albanien,* 458.

58. There were three Giorgio Loredans in the fifteenth century, so without patronymics it is difficult to determine the exact relationships between the officeholders: Gullino, "Loredan, Giorgio."

59. *AvC, Raspe,* reg. 3646, 81r; 1410 May 15; See also Queller, *VP,* 177, Schmitt, *Venezianische Albanien,* 392; Valentini, *AAV,* nos. 1452, 1553.

60. Kohl, *Records,* no. 3246, 1391 June 16.

61. *AvC, Raspe,* reg. 3646, II, f. 7v–9r, 1412 Aug. 9.

62. *AVC, Raspe,* reg. 3646, II, f. 8v.

63. *S Misti,* reg. 59, f, 15r, 1433 Nov. 6.

64. Loenertz, "Querini."

65. *AvC, Raspe,* reg. 3646, f. 107v–108v, 1416 June 1; Valentini, *AAV,* no. 2021; Schmitt, *Venezianische Albanien,* 391–92; Queller, *VP,* 199.

66. *AvC, Raspe,* reg. 3646, f. 112r–v, 1416 Aug. 7.

67. The Nani were among the original colonists of the island in 1212; members of the Nani appear in the Candiote Great Council in the fourteenth century: McKee, *Uncommon Dominion,* 44–47, 159, 179.

68. *AvC, Raspe,* reg. 3645, I, f. 33v–34v, 1402 March 16; summarized in Queller, *VP,* 190.

69. Giannasi. Capello was from the Santa Maria Mater Domini branch of the family; Barbaro, *Arbori,* II: f. 249.

70. *S Misti,* reg. 59, f. 17r, 1433 Nov. 24; Queller, *VP,* 178.

71. Mueller, "Pubblico e privato," 85–89.

72. *AvC, Raspe,* reg. 4648, f. 20r–v, 1438 May 12, cited and discussed in Mueller, "Pubblico e privato," 87–88.

73. The Sagredo were among the colonists sent in 1211 as well as in the Cretan Great Council in 1358: McKee, *Uncommon Dominion,* 179–81. They also were listed among the landholders of the island in 1453 and 1490: *ADC, Libri Pheudatorum,* b. 23, reg. 7, f. 51r, f. 61v, f. 86r, f. 103v, f. 138v, f. 169v, f. 198r; *ADC, Libri Pheudatorum,* b. 23, reg. 7, f. 26r, f. 52r, f. 92v, f. 111r, f. 186r.

74. The precise dates of the rectors' terms are difficult to reconstruct, as the data on 1430s offices only comes from the manuscript BMV It VII 198 (8383) f. 193r, which is not always accurate on dates. This list of officeholders has Mudazzo elected in 1426, and then has Luca Contarini and Pietro Darmer both elected in 1432. It is possible that Luca Contarini held the office from 1430 to 1432, or it is possible that no successor to Mudazzo was elected until 1432. For the prosecutions, see *S Misti,* reg. 58, f. 155r, f. 189v, and f. 206v (copy), 1432 Nov. 10, 1433 March 19 and April 23; *S Misti,* reg. 59, f. 27v, 1434 Feb. 16, summarized in Noiret, *DI,* 356–58, and Queller, *VP,* 193–94. Sanudo, *Vite,* I (1999): 115–16 and 596–97 also mentions the affair.

75. *AvC, Raspe,* reg. 3649, II, f. 33r; 1447 May 15.

76. *AvC, Raspe,* reg. 3649, II, f. 113r, 1450 Dec. 8.

77. *S Mar,* reg. 3, f. 182v, 1450 April 23.

78. Barbaro, *Nozze,* f. 268r.

79. Sagredo does not appear in *ROV* as elected to a post, but he appears in *Listine,* X: 297, 1464 Jan. 13, as the count of Lesina; he is gravely ill and receives permission for his son, Albano, to take his place as count. For his prosecution, see *AvC, Raspe,* reg. 3652, f. 99r, 1468 Nov. 24.

80. Zorzi, "Florentines," 112–13, states that the possibility of reprisals was one of the reasons the system of syndication became obsolete in Florence at the beginning of the fifteenth century.

81. *MC, Liber Novella,* f. 157r, 1376 March 16.

82. *AvC, Raspe,* reg. 3646, f. 52r, 1414 March 9.

83. *Collegio, Notatorio,* reg. 5, f. 19r and f. 26v, 1414 Oct. 22 and 1415 March 5, summarized in Thiriet, *DAV,* II: nos. 1195 and 1197, but where he reads "Querini" I read Civrano. In 1452, the *Quarantia* reiterated this principle when overturning syndic Antonio Gradenigo's condemnation of Micheletto Scludi, saying that "quia proprio ipsos casus fuerant alias condemnatus per regimen Crete et . . . syndici non possint se impedire de specialibus personis": *AvC, Raspe,* reg. 3650, I, f. 49v, 1452 Nov. 6.

84. Noiret, *DI,* 378–85; Thiriet, *RDS,* III: no. 2470, 1438 May 13.

85. *AvC, Raspe,* reg. 3645, II, f. 65v, 1403 Nov. 10; also in *Collegio, Notatorio,* reg. 3, f. 114r, summarized in Thiriet, *DAV,* II: no. 1042.

86. *AvC, Raspe,* reg. 3645, II, f. 71r, 1404 May 26.

87. *AvC, Raspe,* reg. 3646, f. 80r, 1415 March 19.

88. *AvC, Raspe,* reg. 3646, f. 86r, 1415 June 12.

89. *AvC, Raspe,* reg. 3650, f. 63v, 1456 April 6.

90. *AvC, Raspe,* reg. 3650, f. 64r, 1456 April 9.

91. *AvC, Raspe,* reg. 3652, f. 80v, 1467 Nov. 14.

92. *AvC, Raspe,* reg. 3648, II, f. 91v, 1441 Aug. 1. Biagio was the grandfather of Girolamo di Mosè Venier.

93. *AvC, Raspe,* reg. 3649, II, f. 91v, 1449 Nov. 18.

94. *AvC, Raspe,* reg. 3646, II, f. 93v, 1415 Sept. 16.

95. In the first round of voting, there were sixteen in favor, eight against, and ten unsure. In the second round of voting on January 3, there were first eleven in favor, five against, and sixteen unsure, and then fourteen in favor, six against, and twelve unsure. In the third council, January 13, there were nineteen in favor, six against, and seven unsure.

96. *AvC, Raspe,* reg. 3646, II, f. 100v, 1416 April 8.

SEVEN · Fault Lines of Empire

1. Tenenti, "Sense of Space," 30; see Finlay, "Crisis and Crusade," for more general reactions.

2. Gilbert, 274; see also Chambers, Pullan, and Fletcher, 70, for Domenico Morosini's proposal to limit high offices to deserving nobles to curtail bribery and corruption.

3. Sanudo, *Diarii,* VIII: 374.

4. For the war on the *terraferma,* see Finlay, *Politics,* 163–81; Gilbert. For the maritime state, see Doumerc, "Adriatique," 274–82; for rebellions on Cyprus, see Aristidou, "Venetian Rule," 40–41; idem, *Anékdota,* vols. 1–3; for Nauplion, see Wright, "Minio," 139–69.

5. Del Torre; Ventura, *Nobiltà,* 121–88; Muir, *Mad Blood,* xx–xxv; Doumerc, "Adriatique," 274.

6. Both Gabelić and Papadia-Lala publish a number of key documents from Venetian and local archives. In addition to Gabelić's work, the rebellion at Lesina is discussed from a pro-Venetian standpoint by Praga, *Dalmatia,* 167–69, and by Zaninović.

7. Bracewell, 20–21; Praga, *Dalmatia,* 165. The incursions can be followed in Sanudo, *Diarii,* III: 1292 and 1618; IV: 325–28, 368, 708, 742–44; V: 82, 90, 120, 194, and 217.

8. In the second decade of the sixteenth century, there was a widespread, sharp dip in the price of wheat across Europe; Spooner and Braudel, 464 and 474; see also Brummett, 135, and Setton, *Papacy,* III: 81. Grain prices in Friuli fell precipitously during the decade: Muir, *Mad Blood,* 135–51. There were also shortages—e.g., in 1504 a ship was forced to discharge its grain in Candia, and in 1510 Cyprus, usually a grain exporter, had to import from Syria and Egypt: Sanudo, *Diarii,* V: 354, 824, 973; X: 105; XI: 265.

9. In September of 1510, the count of Zara heard rumors of Ottomans approaching and put guards in nine locations but wrote to Venice asking for funding. Orators from Traù came to Venice in March 1514 complaining about the damages they had suffered at the hands of the Turks and suggesting it would be good to give the neighboring *sanzachi* leaders presents: Sanudo, *Diarii,* XI: 315 and XVIII: 101; Setton, *Papacy,* III: 45 and 57.

10. *Capi X, Lettere dei Rettori,* b. 274, f. 43r, 1501 July 22.

11. *Capi X, Lettere dei Rettori,* b. 274, f. 79r, 1501 July 2. Alessandro's brother Sebastiano di Alvise Contarini was count of Cattaro in the same period; the Venetian state instructed him to keep his eyes open for rebels and other suspicious happenings as well as to remain alert against an Ottoman advance: *Capi X, Lettere dei Rettori,* b. 275, f. 78r–v, 1501 Nov.

12. *Capi X, Lettere dei Rettori,* b. 274, f. 81r–v, 1506 March 15.

13. Luzzato, 215–27; Mallett and Hale, 473–74; Gilbert, 283–85; Finlay, *Politics,* 165–75.

14. Spalato and Traù also reported attacks, and the governor of Traù requested fifty horsemen from Venice, stating that the local treasury was empty: Sanudo, *Diarii,* X: 76, 207. For other incursions, see Sanudo, *Diarii,* IX: 549; X: 343 and 406; XII: 22.

15. *CX, Miste,* reg. 15, f. 146v, 1458 March 8.

16. Cited in Cervelli, *Machiavelli e la crisi,* 47.

17. For Pasqualigo's report, see Ljubić, *Commissiones,* I: 115–23; for Venice's warning to Zara, see *CX, Miste,* reg. 33, f. 124r, 1510 Aug. 7; for Hungary and the League of Cambrai, see Setton, *Papacy,* III: 55 and 70.

18. Doumerc, "Adriatique," 277–81. Sanudo reported that in March of 1511, the *Sig-*

noria received letters from Zara, Spalato, and Sebenico narrating the "turbation of Dalmatia" and the most recent Ottoman raids: Sanudo, *Diarii,* XII: 34.

19. *CX, Miste,* reg. 33, f. 112r–114r, 1511 Feb. 4; *CX, Miste,* reg. 34, f. 59r, 1511 March 11.

20. *Listine,* IX: 79–80 and 141–42, 1435 Aug. 13 and 1441 May 7; Ventura, *Nobiltà,* 152–53.

21. *CX, Miste,* reg. 33, f. 112r–114r, 1511 Feb. 4, and *CX, Miste,* reg. 34, f. 59r, 1511 March 11.

22. *Capi X, Lettere dei Rettori,* b. 280, f. 16r–17r, 1511 Oct. 24–29; *CX, Miste,* reg. 34, f. 109r–v, 1511 July 18; *Capi X, Lettere dei Rettori,* b. 280, f. 16r–17r, 1511 Oct. 24–29.

23. *Capi X, Lettere dei Rettori,* b. 275, f. 81r–v, 1512 Dec. 15; *Capi X, Lettere dei Rettori,* b. 274, f. f. 85r–v, 1511 Oct. 18. According to Orio, the population of Arbe was protesting his banishment of Agostino Hermoro and his brother to Venice for ten years.

24. Gabelić, 553.

25. Da Molin's letter of May 28, 1510, is reported in Sanudo, *Diarii,* X: 527–28.

26. Sanudo, *Diarii,* X: 545. The actual letter has not been preserved.

27. Sanudo, *Diarii,* X: 624.

28. Sanudo, *Diarii,* X: 624.

29. Giovanni Navagero was elected as a syndic and *provveditore* July 25, 1510, received his commission on Aug. 10, 1510, and ordered to leave within a week or pay 500 ducats on Sept. 9 1510: Gabelić, 635–39; Sanudo, *Diarii,* X: 694 and 819.

30. Gabelić, 637.

31. Gabelić, 644.

32. Gabelić, 625–26.

33. Ivetić, "Storiografie," 124–28; Raukar, *Zadar,* 302.

34. Gabelić, 552. In addition to Gabelić's work, the rebellion at Lesina is discussed, from a pro-Venetian standpoint, by Praga, *Dalmatia,* 167–69, and by Zaninović.

35. Ventura, *Nobiltà,* 150–68.

36. For Giustinian's complete career, see Gullino, "Giustinian, Sebastiano"; for his family, see Barbaro, *Arbori,* VII: 473–76. Rawdon Brown offers a laudatory portrait of Giustinian's career in *Four Years,* I: 6–29.

37. Sanudo, *Diarii,* VIII: 267. Alvise Giustinian, Sebastian's brother and the *podestà* of Capodistria, sent a letter defending his brother against those who criticized him: Sanudo, *Diarii,* IX: 332; Gullino, "Giustinian, Sebastiano," 293.

38. Sanudo, *Diarii,* XIV: 522. On July 27 the four men Giustinian had sent from Zara arrived in Venice, among whom was the chancellor of Zara. He lost his office and was forever banned from chancelleries of Dalmatia: Sanudo, *Diarii,* XV: 453. Giustinian's progress can also be tracked in Marc'Antonio Michiel's *Chronicle,* excerpted in Ljubić, *Commissiones,* I: 137–38.

39. Sanudo, *Diarii,* XIV: 599. According to Sanudo's summary of Giustinian's letter, Giustinian closed by complaining that although he had done many great things in Dalmatia, the *Signoria* had never thanked him.

40. Sanudo, *Diarii,* XIV: 604; see also Ventura, *Nobiltà,* 161, n. 130, for corrections to the published version.

41. Gabelić, 641.

42. Gabelić, 645, 1512 July 21.
43. Gabelić, 647–49, 1512 July 21 and 22.
44. Gabelić, 555, and 648, 1512 Sept. 28; Sanudo, *Diarii,* XV: 155–57, Sept. 1512.
45. Sanudo, *Diarii,* XV: 372.
46. Sanudo, *Diarii,* XV: 348.
47. Sanudo, *Diarii,* XVI: 597.
48. Sanudo, *Diarii,* XVIII: 322.
49. Miani was first investigated, together with six other former officials, for having taken money from the *Rason Vecchie,* but none of the men were convicted: Sanudo, *Diarii,* XIV: 96.
50. Sanudo, *Diarii,* XVI: 10, 270, 406, and XVIII: 372.
51. Sanudo, *Diarii,* XVIII: 485; XIX: 34.
52. Sanudo, *Diarii,* XIX: 48, 63, 71, 76.
53. Gabelić, 628.
54. Sanudo, *Diarii,* XVIII: 439–40.
55. Gabelić, 651.
56. Gabelić, 651–55.
57. Gabelić, 656–57.
58. Gabelić, 652–54.
59. Gabelić, 629.
60. Maltezou, "Historical," 18; Ploumidēs, *Venetokratoúmenes,* 13; Tenenti, "Venezia e la pirateria."
61. *S Mar,* reg. 9, f. 117r, 1471 Oct. 11, published in Noiret, *DI,* 520. Malipiero, 109, mentions that the islanders were terrified of Turkish attacks in 1475, and they all fled to the mountains, leaving the coasts virtually deserted.
62. Sanudo, *Diarii,* VII: 568–70.
63. Ploumidēs, *Venetokratoúmenes,* 43.
64. Sanudo, *Diarii,* VII: 568–70.
65. *ADC, Missive e Responsive,* b. 8, reg. 7, u.p., 1513 Aug. 20; 1523–24 in Ploumidēs, *Venetokratoúmenes,* 90.
66. Sanudo, *Diarii,* XXXVI: 213.
67. *S Mar,* reg. 17, f. 66r, 1509 Nov. 21; *S Mar,* reg. 18, f. 71r, 1515 March 7; *S Mar,* reg. 19, f. 77v, 1518 Aug. 17; see also Mueller, "Aspects," 38.
68. *ADC, Missive e Responsive,* b. 8, reg. 6, u.p., 1508 Dec.
69. TeBrake, *Plague of Insurrection,* 9.
70. Sanudo, *Diarii,* I: 639–40; Malipiero, 705–6. Malipiero reports that Polani, the elder of the two, made himself vice-rector.
71. Sanudo, *Diarii,* I: 934. The *Dieci* condemned them to one year in prison and banned them from holding office in Crete for ten years. Chambers and Dean, 47, describe similar fights and struggles between competing authorities in Manuta.
72. 1526 May 5: *ADC, Missive e Responsive,* b. 8, reg. 8, f. 104v.
73. 1525 June 24: *ADC, Missive e Responsive,* b. 8, reg. 8, f. 45r–v.
74. *ADC, Missive e Responsive,* b. 8, reg. 6, u.p., 1509 July 17, published in Papadia-Lala, *Agrotikés tarachés,* 181–83. Paulo Nomico protested that this official had de-

manded exorbitant fees and pledges from him and had confiscated his animals, reducing him to poverty, and had had his soldiers "deliver [Nomico's] wife into [the *provveditore*'s] hands."

75. *ADC, Missive e Responsive,* b. 8, reg. 6, u.p., 1510 Jan. 14.

76. *ADC, Missive e Responsive,* b. 8, reg. 7, u.p., 1512 July 3, published in Papadia-Lala, *Agrotikés tarachés,* 183–84.

77. *S Mar,* reg. 18, f. 68v–69r, 1515 Feb. 19; *ADC, Missive e Responsive,* b. 8, reg. 7, u.p., 1514 Sept. 10, published in Papadia-Lala, *Agrotikés tarachés,* 187–88; Sanudo, *Diarii,* XVIII: 413–14, 417, and 420–21.

78. Gullino, "Giustinian, Sebastiano," 294; Sanudo, *Diarii,* XVIII: 478.

79. Sanudo, *Diarii,* XXVIII: 479; XXIX: 362.

80. Sanudo, *Diarii,* XXXIV: 301–2; *S Mar,* reg. 20, f. 87v–88v, 1523 July 18; Papadia-Lala, *Agrotikés tarachés,* 64–75.

81. *CX, Comuni,* filze 5, f. 125r, 1523, published in Papadia-Lala, *Agrotikés tarachés,* 194–95, and discussed on 59–63. Massolo had requested a *grazia* through the normal channels, but it had not received enough votes in the Great Council, so he appealed to the *Dieci.*

82. *CX, Comuni,* filze 5, f. 125r, 1523, published in Papadia-Lala, *Agrotikés tarachés,* 195–96.

83. *CX, Comuni,* filze 5, f. 125r, 1523, published in Papadia-Lala, *Agrotikés tarachés,* 195–96.

84. Sanudo, *Diarii,* XXXIV: 30; Hemmerdinger-Iliadou, "Crète," 564. Trevisan himself was no stranger to the island: he had visited on his way to act as ambassador to Cairo in 1515 and married a woman from the Mudazzo clan who brought him 3,000 ducats a year as a dowry.

85. Sanudo, *Diarii,* XXXIV: 57–58; *CX, Miste,* reg. 46, f. 142r, 1523 Dec. 9, published in Papadia-Lala, *Agrotikés tarachés,* 197–98.

86. Sanudo, *Diarii,* XXXIV: 57–58; *CX, Comuni,* filze I, f. 179r, 1525 July 29, published in Papadia-Lala, *Agrotikés tarachés,* 198–99, and discussed 77–83.

87. *ADC, Missive e Responsive,* b. 8, reg. 8, f. 45v–46r, 1525 June 28. The previous captain of the island, Tomà Mocenigo, had emphasized the importance of repairing the fortifications in his report to the *Signoria: Collegio, Relazioni,* reg. 61, I, f. 30r, 1525 July 25.

88. *ADC, Missive e Responsive,* b. 8, reg. 8, f. 47r, f. 49r, and f. 55v, 1525 July 1, 10, and 15.

89. When the feudator Iacopo Gradenigo died of plague, the peasants at Ierapetra, on the southeast coast, began to "disturb the peace," and the regime in Candia ordered the governor of Sitia to ride to the southern coast and restore order in Ierapetra: *ADC, Missive e Responsive,* b. 8, reg. 8, f. 4r, 1524 Oct. 26.

90. *ADC, Missive e Responsive,* b. 8, reg. 8, f. 110r–v, 1526 June 21, published in Papadia-Lala, *Agrotikés tarachés,* 201, 202, 204.

91. *ADC, Missive e Responsive,* b. 8, reg. 8, f. 110r–v, 1526 June 21, published in Papadia-Lala, *Agrotikés tarachés,* 201.

92. *CX, Comuni,* filze 5, f. 125r, 1523.

93. Sanudo, *Diarii,* XLVI: 425.

94. The relevant part of the chronicle is published in Papadia-Lala, *Agrotikés tarachés,* 169–70; see also her discussion of the relationship between the manuscript and historical events, 1–5.

95. Papadia-Lala, *Agrotikés tarachés.* There is a wide literature on European peasant uprisings in this period; useful works that emphasize rural communities' resistance to landlords' demands are TeBrake, Mullett, Mollat and Wolff, Bercé, and Hanawalt. See Bak, 78–80; Molnar, 82–83, and Setton, *Papacy,* III: 158 for parallels with the 1514 peasant revolt in Hungary.

96. *ADC, Missive e Responsive,* b. 8, reg. 8, f. 33r, 1527 Oct. 19; *CX, Secreti,* reg. 2, f. 3r–v, 1527 April 27, published in Papadia-Lala, *Agrotikés tarachés,* 205–6.

97. Sanudo, *Diarii,* XXVI: 36–37; he wrote in 1517 that Corner had spent five years on the island; for his marriage, see Barbaro, *Nozze,* f. 53r and 83r.

98. Sanudo, *Diarii,* XLVI: 425–28, two letters written Nov. 9 and 27, 1527. It is likely, although not definite, that this Andrea Calergi was related to Corner through marriage.

99. Papadia-Lala, *Agrotikés tarachés,* 120–29; *Capi X, Lettere dei Rettori,* b. 285, f. 23r, 1528 April 2, and *Capi X, Lettere dei Rettori,* b. 285, f. 30r, 1528 July 24, published in Papadia-Lala, *Agrotikés tarachés,* 217–18.

100. *Capi X, Lettere dei Rettori,* filza 28, f. 144r, 1528 July 5, published in Papadia-Lala, *Agrotikés tarachés,* 216; *Capi X, Lettere dei Rettori,* b. 285, f. 24r, 1528 April 6, and for the progression of the appeal in later decades, see f. 42r and f. 44r.

101. *Capi X, Lettere dei Rettori,* b. 285, f. 26r–27v and f. 28r, 1528 April 9, 14, 15, and May 6; *Capi X, Lettere dei Rettori,* filza 28, f. 318r, 1528 Nov. 7, published in Papadia-Lala, *Agrotikés tarachés,* 207–12, 214–15, and 220. Some of the returnees were caught and hung in Rettimo, but others escaped into the mountains of Sfakia.

102. *Capi X, Lettere dei Rettori,* b. 285, f. 25r–v, 1528 April 16, published in Papadia-Lala, *Agrotikés tarachés,* 213–15.

103. *Capi X, Lettere dei Rettori,* b. 285, f. 25r–v, 1528 July 24, published in Papadia-Lala, *Agrotikés tarachés,* 218–20.

104. 1528 Jan. 6: *ADC, Missive e Responsive,* b. 8, r. 9, f. 36v; 1527 April 27: *CX, Secreti,* reg. 2, f. 3r.

105. Gleason.

106. Doumerc, "Dominio del mar," 164–78.

107. Brown, *Calendar of State Papers, Venetian series,* vol 2, n. 707.

108. Cozzi, *RVEM,* II: 44; Tenenti, "Sense of Space," 29; Pujeau.

109. Maltezou, "Historical," 20; Knapton, *RVEM,* II: 380–84; Bacchion, 99–100 for reforms in Corfu.

110. Chambers, Pullan, and Fletcher, 32.

111. Ljubić, *Commissiones,* I: 148.

112. Ljubić, *Commissiones,* II: 72.

113. Ljubić, *Commissiones,* II: 52.

114. Setton, *Papacy,* III: 469.

WORKS CITED

Archival Sources

Archivio di Stato, Venezia (ASV)

Archivio di Duca di Candia (ADC)

Ducali e Lettere, buste 1, 2, 4

Missive e Responsive, busta 8

Atti Antichi, busta 11

Libri Pheudatorum, busta 23

Memoriali, buste 30, 32

Scritture Politiche Varie, buste 50, 50 bis

Auditori Nuovi

Buste 184, 185

Avogaria di Comun (AvC)

Cronaca Matrimoni, reg. 107

Balla d'Oro, reg. 162–65, 169

Prove di età, 178

Lettere ai Rettori, buste 3582–83

Raspe, reg. 3643–3662

Capi di Dieci (Capi X)

Lettere dei Rettori, buste 274–75, 281, 285–86

Lettere Spedite, buste 1, 4, 5

Cassiere della Bolla Ducale

Grazie, reg. 22, 23, 24, 25, 26

Collegio

Commissioni, reg. 6

Notatorio, passim

Relazioni, reg. 61

Secreti, reg. 3

Consiglio di Dieci (CX)

Comuni, filze 1, 5

Criminali, busta 1

Miste, passim

Secreti, reg. 2

Maggior Consiglio (MC)
Deliberazioni, reg. *Fronenis, Spiritus, Novella, Leona, Ursa, Regina,* and *Stella*
Miscellanea codici
Serie I, 17–23: Marco Barbaro, *Arbori de' patritii veneti,* eighteenth-century copy with additions
Procuratori di San Marco (PSM)
De Citra, reg. 82
Misti, b. 3
Provveditori sopra Feudi (ProvvF)
Buste 1075, 1076
Quarantia Criminale
Parti, buste 18–20
Segretario alle Voci
Misti, reg. 1–9
Senato (S)
Misti, reg. 46–60
Mar, reg. 1–25
Terra, reg. 13
Notarile Testamenti
Atti Matteo di Andronicus, b. 54
Biblioteca Marciana di Venezia (BMV)
Anon. *'Reggimenti' dalla republica Veneta, sec XV–XVII,* It VII 198 (8383)
Barbaro, Marc'Antonio. *Libro di Nozze Patrizie,* It VII 156 (8492)
Dolfin, Zorzi. *Chronica.* It VII 794 (8503)
Corner, Andrea. *Historia di Candia,* It VI 286 (5985)
Museo Civico Correr, Venice (MCC)
Ms Gradenigo 72, "Donne Veneziane"
Državni Arhiv Zadar (DAZ)
Ducali e Terminazioni, reg. 1–3.
Sindika Avogadora
Historical Archives of Corfu (HAC)
Enetokratia, reg. 1, 5, 95, 103, 109
Enetikē Dioikēsis, reg. 133, 454
British Library (BL)
Add. Mss. 8603, 8604, 20979, 23712, 24897, 41659
Biblioteca del Senato di Roma (BSR)
Statuti Mss 286, 637
Statuti 195

Published Primary Sources

Brown, Rawdon, ed. *Calendar of State Papers and Manuscripts Relating to English Affairs, Existing in the Archives and Collections of Venice, and in Other Libraries of Northern Italy.* Vol. 2. London: Longman Green, 1865.

Cessi, Roberto. *Deliberazioni del Maggior Consiglio de Venezia.* Vol. 2 Accademia dei Lincei. Bologna: N. Zanichelli, 1934.

Chrysostomides, J., ed. *Monumenta Peloponnesiaca: Documents for the History of the Peloponnese in the 14th and 15th Centuries.* Camberley: Porphyrogenitus, 1995.

Favaro, Elena, ed. *Cassiere della Bolla Ducale, Grazie-Novus Liber, 1299–1305.* Venice: Il Comitato Editore, 1962.

Gerland, Ernst. *Das Archiv des Herzogs von Kandia im K. Staatsarchiv zu Venedig.* Strasbourg: Karl J. Trübner, 1899.

Giannotti, Donato. *Opere Politiche,* ed. Furio Diaz. Milan: Marzorati, 1974.

Gligo, Vedran, Marin Berket, Vladimir Rismondo, and Ljerka Šimunković, ed. *Zlatna Knjiga Grada Splita (Libro d'oro della comunita di Spalato).* Biblioteka Knjiga Mediterana 14. Split: Književni Krug, 1996.

Iorga, Nicolae. *Notes et extraits pour servir à l'histoire des croisades au XVe siècle.* Vols. 1 and 3. Paris: E. Leroux, 1899–1902.

Kohl, Benjamin G., ed. *The records of the Venetian Senate on disk, 1335–1400.* New York: Italica Press, 2001.

Kohl, Benjamin G., Andrea Mozzato, and Monique O'Connell, eds. *Rulers of Venice, 1332–1524.* Online Database published by the Renaissance Society of America, in press.

Ljubić, Sime, ed. *Commissiones et relationes venetae.* Monumenta spectantia historiam Slavorum meridionalium. Zagreb: Sumptibus Academiae Scientiarum et Artium, 1876.

———, ed. *Listine o odnošajih izmedju Južnoga slaventsva i Mletačke Republike.* Vols. 4–10, Monumenta spectantia historiam Slavorum meridionalium. Zagreb: Knjizharnici Fr. Zhupana, 1872–1893.

Malipiero, Domenico. "Annali veneti dall'anno 1457 al 1500." *Archivio Storico Italiano* 7 (1843–44): 5–720.

Maltezou, Chryssa, ed. *Commissio del doge di Venezia al rettore di Canea 1589; Ire debeas in rettorem Caneae.* Graecolatinas Nostra no 4. Venice: Hellenic Institute, 2002.

Marmora, Andrea. *Della historia di Corfu descritta.* Venice: Presso il Curti, 1672.

Morosini, Antonio. *The Morosini Codex.* 2 vols., ed. John R. Melville-Jones, Michele Pietro Ghezzo, and Andrea Rizzi. Padova: Unipress, 1999.

Morosini, Paolo. "Defensio venetorum ad Europae principes contra obtrectatores." In *Bibliotheca Manuscripta ad S. Marci Venetiarum, Codices Mss Latini,* ed. Giuseppe Valentinelli, 3, 189–230. Venice: Ex Typographia Commercii, 1870.

Noiret, Hippolyte, ed. *Documents inédits pour servir a l'histoire de la domination Vénitienne en Crète de 1385 à 1485.* Paris: Thorin & fils, 1892.

Ploumidēs, Georgios. *Presveies Krētōn pros tē Venetia, 1487–1558.* Ioannina: Panepistemiou Ioanninon, 1986.

Predelli, Riccardo, ed. *I libri commemoriali della Republica di Venezia: Regestri.* Vol 3. Venice: Monumenti storici publicati dalla Deputazione veneta di storia patria, 1883.

Ratti Vidulich, Paola, ed. *Duca di Candia, Bandi (1313–1329).* Fonti per la storia di Venezia. Venice: Il Comitato Editore, 1965.

Santschi, Elisabeth, ed. *Régestes des arrêts civils et des mémoriaux (1363–1399) des archives du Duc de Crète.* Venice: Istituto Ellenico, 1976.

Sanudo, Marino. *I diarii di Marino Sanuto.* Bologna: Forni Editore, 1969.

———. *De origine, situ et magistratibus urbis Venetae, ovvero, La Città di Venetia (1493–1530)*, ed. Angela Caracciolo Aricò. Milan: Cisalpino–La Goliardica, 1980.
———. *Le Vite dei Dogi (1474–1494).* Vols. I and II, ed. Angela Caracciolo Aricò. Padova: Editrice Antenore, 1989–2001.
———. *Le Vite dei Dogi (1423–1457).* Transcription Chiara Frison. Vol. 1A, ed. Angela Caracciolo Aricò. Venice: La Malcontenta, 1999.
Sathas, Konstantin, ed. *Documents inédits relatifs à l'histoire de la Grèce au Moyen Age.* Paris: Maisonneuve, 1880–90.
Tafel, G. L., and G. M. Thomas, ed. *Urkunden fur Alteren Handels und Staatsgeschichte der Republik Venedig mit Besonderer Beziehung auf Byzanz und die Levante.* Fontes rerum austriacarum, Diplomataria et acta, XII–XIV. Vienna, 1856–57.
Tatio, Giovanni. *L'imagine del rettore della bene ordinata città.* Venice: Appresso Gabriel Giolito di Ferrarii, 1573.
Thiriet, Freddy, ed. *Délibérations des assemblées vénitiennes concernant la Romanie.* Paris and The Hague: Mouton, 1966–68.
———, ed. *Duca di Candia: ducali e lettere ricevute (1358–1360, 1401–1405).* Fonti per la storia di Venezia: Sez. I, Archivi pubblici. Venice: Comitato per la pubblicazione delle fonti relative alla storia di Venezia, 1978.
———, ed. *Régestes des délibérations du Sénat de Venise concernant la Romanie.* Paris and The Hague: Mouton, 1958–61.
Thomas, G. M., and Riccardo Predelli, ed. *Diplomatarium Veneto-Levantinum, sive acta et diplomata res venetas, Graecas atque Levantis illustrantia.* Venice: Deputazione veneta di storia patria, 1880–99.
Valentini, Giuseppe, ed. *Acta Albaniae Veneta Saeculorum XIV et XV.* Archivio di Stato di Venezia. Milan-Palermo: Typis P.I.M.E., 1967–81.

Secondary Sources

Abernethy, David. *The Dynamics of Global Dominance: European Overseas Empires, 1415–1980.* New Haven: Yale University Press, 2000.
Arbel, Benjamin. "Colonie d'oltremare." In *Storia di Venezia. Il Rinascimento. Società ed economia,* ed. Alberto Tenenti and Ugo Tucci, V: 947–85. Rome: Enciclopedia Italiana, 1996.
———. "The Cypriot Nobility from the Fourteenth to the Sixteenth Century: A New Interpretation." In *Latins and Greeks in the Eastern Mediterranean after 1204,* ed. Bernard Hamilton, Benjamin Arbel, and David Jacoby, 175–96. London: Frank Cass, 1989.
———. *Cyprus, the Franks, and Venice, 13th–16th Centuries.* Variorum Collected Studies Series. Burlington, Vt.: Ashgate, 2000.
———. "Greek Magnates in Venetian Cyprus: The Case of the Synglitico Family." *Dumbarton Oaks Papers* 49 (1995): 325–39.
———, ed. *Intercultural Contacts in the Medieval Mediterranean: Studies in Honor of David Jacoby.* London: Frank Cass, 1996.
———. "The Reign of Caterina Corner (1473–1489) as a Family Affair." *Studi Veneziani* 26 (1993): 67–85.

———. "Résistance ou collaboration? Les Chypriotes sous la domination vénitienne." In *Etat et colonisation au Moyen Age et à la Renaissance,* ed. Michel Balard, 131–44. Lyon: La Manufacture, 1989.

———. "A Royal Family in Republican Venice: The Cypriot Legacy of the *Corner della Regina.*" *Studi Veneziani* 15 (1988): 131–52.

———. *Trading Nations: Jews and Venetians in the Early Modern Eastern Mediterranean.* Leiden: Brill, 1995.

———. "Urban Assemblies and Town Councils in Frankish and Venetian Cyprus." In *Cyprus, the Franks, and Venice, 13th–16th Centuries,* 203–13. Burlington, Vt.: Ashgate, 2000.

———. "Venetian Cyprus and the Muslim Levant, 1473–1570." In *Cyprus, the Franks and Venice 13th–16th centuries,* 159–85. Burlington, Vt.: Ashgate, 2000.

Arbel, Benjamin, Bernard Hamilton, and David Jacoby, eds. *Latins and Greeks in the Eastern Mediterranean after 1204.* London: Frank Cass, 1995.

Aristidou, Ekaterini C., ed. *Anékdota éngrapha tēs Kypriakēs historías apó to Kratikó Archeío tēs Venetías.* Nicosia: Kentron Epistēmonikōn Ereunōn, 1990–1999.

———. "Venetian Rule in Cyprus." In *Cyprus: Jewel in the Crown of Venice,* ed. Vassos Karageorghis, Loukia Loizou Hadjigavriel, and Chryssa A. Maltezou, 33–46. Nicosia: The Anastasios G. Leventis Foundation and the Leventis Municipal Museum of Nicosia, 2003.

Armesto, Felipe Fernandez. *Before Columbus: Exploration and Colonization from the Mediterranean to the Atlantic, 1229–1492.* Philadelphia: University of Pennsylvania Press, 1987.

Asdrachas, Spyros. "L'économie rurale dans les îles ionieenes pendant la domination vénitienne. Une equisse générale." In *Venezia e le Isole Ionie,* ed. Chryssa Maltezou and Gherardo Ortalli, 233–40. Venice: Istituto veneto di scienze, lettere ed arti, 2005.

———. "Rendita feudale e rendita fondiaria a Corfù all'epoca della dominazione veneziana." In *Levante Veneziano. Aspetti di storia delle Isole Ionie al tempo della Serenissima,* ed. Massimo Costantini and Aliki Nikiforou, 21–38. Rome: Bulzoni Editore, 1996.

Ashtor, Eliyahu. *Levant Trade in the Later Middle Ages.* Princeton: Princeton University Press, 1983.

———. "Spice Prices in the Near East in the 15th century." In *Studies on the Levantine Trade in the Middle Ages,* 26–41. London: Variorum Reprints, 1978.

———. "The Venetian Supremacy in Levantine Trade: Monopoly or Pre-Colonialism?" *Journal of European Economic History* 3 (1974): 5–53.

Asonitis, Spyros. "L'introduzione delle Assise di Romania in Corfù." In *Levante Veneziano. Aspetti di Storia delle Isole Ionie al tempo della Serenissima,* ed. Massimo Costantini and Aliki Nikiforou, 59–76. Rome: Bulzoni Editore, 1996.

———. "Relations between the Venetian *Regimen Corfou* and the Albanians of Epirus (14th–15th centuries)." In *The Mediaeval Albanians,* ed. Charalampos Gasparēs, 271–91. Athens: National Hellenic Research Foundation, Institute for Byzantine Research, 1998.

Astarita, Tommaso. *Village Justice: Community, Family, and Popular Culture in Early Modern Italy.* Baltimore: The Johns Hopkins University Press, 1999.

Babinger, Franz. "Le vicende veneziane nella lotta contro i Turchi durante il secolo XV." In *Storia della civiltà veneziana,* ed. Vittore Branca, II: 143–53. Florence: Sansoni, 1979.

Bacchion, Eugenio. *Il dominio Veneto su Corfù (1386–1797).* Venice: Edizioni Altino, 1956.

Bak, Janos. "The Late Medieval Period, 1382–1526." In *A History of Hungary,* ed. Peter Suger, 54–83. Bloomington: Indiana University Press, 1990.

Balard, Michel. "L'amministrazione genovese e veneziana nel Mediterraneo orientale." In *Genova, Venezia, il Levante nei secoli XII–XIV. Atti del convegno internazionale di studi, Genova-Venezia, 10–14 marzo 2000,* ed. Gherardo Ortalli and Dino Puncuh, 201–28. Venice: Istituto veneto di scienze, lettere ed arti and il società ligure di storia patria, 2001.

———. "Etat del la recherche sur la Latinocratie en Méditerranée orientale." In *Ploúsioi kai phtōchoi: stēn koinōnia tēs Hellēnolatinikēs anatolēs. Diethnés sympósio,* ed. Chryssa Maltezou, 17–36. Venice: Istituto Ellenico, 1998.

———, ed. *Etat et colonisation au moyen âge et à la renaissance.* Lyon: La Manufacture, 1989.

———. *La Romanie génoise: XIIe–début du XVe siècle.* 2 vols. Genoa: Atti della Società Ligure di Storia Patria, 1978.

Balard, Michel, and Alain Ducellier, eds. *Coloniser au moyen âge.* Paris: Armand Colin, 1995.

———, eds. *Le partage du monde: échanges et colonisation dans la Méditerranée médiévale.* Paris: Publications de la Sorbonne, 1998.

Banks, Kenneth. *Chasing Empire across the Sea: Communications and the State in the French Atlantic, 1713–1763.* Montreal: McGill–Queens University Press, 2002.

Barkey, Karen. *Bandits and Bureaucrats: The Ottoman Route to State Centralization.* Ithaca and London: Cornell University Press, 1994.

Benton, Lauren A. *Law and Colonial Cultures: Legal Regimes in World History, 1400–1900.* Studies in Comparative World History. Cambridge: Cambridge University Press, 2002.

———. "Legal Spaces of Empire: Piracy and the Origins of Ocean Regionalism." *Comparative Studies in Society and History* 47, no. 4 (2005): 700–24.

Benvenuti, Angelo de. *Storia di Zara dal 1409 al 1797.* Milan: Fratelli Bocca Editori, 1944.

———. "Gli Zorzi di Venezia nella storia della Dalmazia e del Friuli." *Rivista Dalmatica* 28 (1957): 3–18.

Bercé, Yves-Marie. *Revolt and Revolution in Early Modern Europe: An Essay on the History of Political Violence,* trans. Joseph Bergin. Manchester: Manchester University Press, 1987.

Bertelé, Tommaso. "Badoer, Giacomo." *DBI* 5 (1963): 109–13.

Betto, Bianca. "Linee di politica matrimoniale nella nobilta veneziana fino al XV secolo. Alcune note geneologiche e l'esempio della famiglia Mocenigo." *Archivio Storico Italiano* 139 (1981): 3–64.

Borsari, Silvano. "Barbo, Pantaleone." *DBI* 6 (1964): 253–54.

———. "Bembo, Francesco." *DBI* 8 (1966): 115–17.

———. *Il dominio veneziano a Creta nel XIII secolo.* Naples: Fausto Fiorentino Editore, 1963.

———. "Una famiglia veneziana del medioevo: Gli Ziani." *Archivio Veneto* 109, no. 145 (1978): 27–72.

———. "I veneziani delle colonie." In *Storia di Venezia. La formazione dello Stato Patrizio,* ed. Giorgio Cracco, Girolamo Arnaldi, and Alberto Tenenti, III: 127–58. Rome: Enciclopedia Italiana, 1996.

Bouwsma, William James. *Venice and the Defense of Republican Liberty: Renaissance Values in the Age of the Counter Reformation.* Berkeley: University of California Press, 1968.

Božić, Ivan. "Le système foncier en Albanie vénitienne au XVe siècle." *Studi Veneziani* 5–6 (1963–64).

Bracewell, Catherine Wendy. *The Uskoks of Senj: Piracy, Banditry, and Holy War in the Sixteenth-Century Adriatic.* Ithaca: Cornell University Press, 1992.

Braudel, Fernand. *The Mediterranean and the Mediterranean World in the Age of Philip II,* trans. Sian Reynolds (1st U.S.) ed. New York: Harper & Row, 1972.

———. "Prices in Europe from 1450 to 1750." In *Cambridge Economic History of Europe,* ed. E. E. Rich and C. H. Wilson, IV: 378–486. Cambridge: Cambridge University Press, 1967.

Briquet, Jean Louis. "Clientelismo e processi politici." *Quaderni Storici: Clientelismi* 97, no. 1 (1998): 9–30.

Brown, Alison. "The Language of Empire." In *Florentine Tuscany: Structures and Practices of Power,* ed. William J. Connell and Andrea Zorzi, 32–47. Cambridge: Cambridge University Press, 2000.

Brown, Patricia Fortini. *Venice and Antiquity: The Venetian Sense of the Past.* New Haven: Yale University Press, 1996.

Brown, Rawdon. *Four Years at the Court of Henry VIII. Selections of Despatches written by the Venetian ambassador Sebastian Giustinian and addressed to the Signory of Venice.* 2 vols. London: Smith, Elder, 1854.

Brown, Warren. *Unjust Seizure: Conflict, Interest, and Authority in an Early Medieval Society.* Ithaca: Cornell University Press, 2001.

Brummett, Palmira J. *Ottoman Seapower and Levantine Diplomacy in the Age of Discovery.* Albany: State University of New York Press, 1994.

Brunelli, Vitaliano. *Storia della citta di Zara. Dai tempi piu remoti sino al 1409 compilata sulle fonti e integrata da tre capitoli sugli usi e costumi.* Trieste: LINT, 1974.

Budak, Neven. "Urban Elites in Dalmatia, 1350–1450." In *Città e sistema adriatico alla fine del medioevo. Bilanci degli studi e prospettive di ricerca. Convegno di Studi, Padova 4–5 aprile 1997,* ed. Michele Pietro Ghezzo, 181–200. Venice: Società Dalmata di Storia Patria, 1997.

Bullard, Melissa Meriam, S. R. Epstein, Benjamin G. Kohl, and Susan Mosher Stuard. "Where History and Theory Interact. Frederic C. Lane on the Emergence of Capitalism." *Speculum* 79, no. 1 (2004): 88–119.

Burkholder, Mark, ed. *Administrators of Empire.* An Expanding World: The European Impact on World History, vol. 22. Brookfield, Vt.: Ashgate Publishing, 1998.

Bushnell, Amy Turner. "Gates, Patterns, and Peripheries: The Field of Frontier Latin America." In *Negotiated Empires: Centers and Peripheries in the Americas, 1500–1820,* ed. Christine Daniels and Michael Kennedy, 15–28. New York: Routledge, 2002.

Calabi, Donatella. "Città e territorio nel dominio da mar." In *Storia di Venezia. Dal Rinascimento al Barocco,* ed. Gaetano Cozzi and Paolo Prodi, VI: 943–77. Rome: Enciclopedia Italiana, 1994.

Canny, Nicholas. *The Origins of Empire.* The Oxford History of the British Empire, ed. William Roger Lewis. Oxford: Oxford University Press, 1998.

Carile, Antonio. "Calbo, Giovanni (Detto Zanotto)." *DBI* 16 (1973): 478–79.

———. "Partitio terrarum Imperii Romaniae," *Studi Veneziani* 7 (1965): 125–305.

Cervelli, Innocenzo. *Machiavelli e la crisi dello stato veneziano.* Napoli: Guida Editore, 1974.

Cessi, Roberto. *Storia della Repubblica di Venezia.* Milan-Messina: G. Principato, 1944.

———. "Venezia e l'acquisto di Nauplia e d'Argo." *Nuovo Archivio Veneto* 30 (1915): 147–73.

Chabod, Federico. "Stipendi nominali e busta paga effetiva dei funzionari dell'amministrazione milanese alla fine del Cinquecento." In idem, *Carlo V e Suo Impero,* 281–398. Turin: Einaudi, 1985.

———. "Usi e abusi nell'amministratione dello Stato di Milano a mezzo il Cinquecento." In idem, *Carlo V e Suo Impero,* 451–522. Turin: Einaudi, 1985.

Chambers, David. "Merit and Money: The Procurators of St. Mark and Their *Commissioni.*" *Journal of the Warburg and Courtauld Institutes* 60 (1997): 23–88.

Chambers, David, and Trevor Dean. *Clean Hands and Rough Justice: An Investigating Magistrate in Renaissance Italy.* Ann Arbor: University of Michigan Press, 1997.

Chambers, David, Brian Pullan, and Jennifer Fletcher, eds. *Venice: A Documentary History, 1450–1630.* Oxford: Blackwell, 1992.

Chittolini, Giorgio. "Cities, 'City-States,' and Regional States in North-Central Italy." *Theory and Society* 18 (1989): 689–706.

———. "Civic Religion and the Countryside in Late Medieval Italy." In *City and Countryside in Late Medieval and Renaissance Italy: Essays Presented to Philip Jones,* ed. Trevor Dean and Chris Wickham, 93–108. London: Hambledon Press, 1990.

———. *La Crisi degli ordinamenti comunali e le origini dello stato del Rinascimento.* Bologna: Il Mulino, 1979.

———. "The Italian City-State and Its territory." In *City States in Classical Antiquity and Medieval Italy,* ed. Kurt Raaflaub, Anthony Molho, Julia Emlen, 589–602. Ann Arbor: University of Michigan Press, 1991.

———. "L'onore dell' officiale." In *Florence and Milan: Comparisons and Relations. Acts of Two Conferences at Villa I Tatti 1982–1984,* ed. Nicolai Rubinstein, Sergio Bertelli, and Craig Hugh Smyth, I: 101–35. Florence: La Nuova Italia Editrice, 1989.

———. "The 'Private,' the 'Public,' the State." In *The Origins of the State in Italy, 1300–1600*, ed. Julius Kirshner, 34–61. Chicago: University of Chicago Press, 1996.

Chojnacki, Stanley. "La formazione della nobiltà dopo la Serrata." In *Storia di Venezia. La formazione dello Stato Patrizio*, ed. Giorgio Cracco, Girolamo Arnaldi, and Alberto Tenenti, III: 641–725. Rome: Enciclopedia Italiana, 1996.

———. "Identity and Ideology in Renaissance Venice: The Third Serrata." In *Venice Reconsidered: The History and Civilization of an Italian City State, 1297–1797*, ed. John Martin and Dennis Romano, 263–94. Baltimore: The Johns Hopkins University Press, 2000.

———. "In Search of the Venetian Patriciate: Families and Factions in the Fourteenth Century." In *Renaissance Venice*, ed. J. R. Hale, 47–90. London: Faber and Faber, 1973.

———. "Kinship Ties and Young Patricians in Fifteenth Century Venice." *Renaissance Quarterly* 32, no. 2 (1985): 240–70.

———. "Nobility, Women and the State: Marriage Regulation in Venice, 1420–1535." In *Marriage in Italy 1300–1600*, ed. Trevor Dean and Kate Lowe, 128–51. Cambridge: Cambridge University Press, 1998.

———. "Political Adulthood in Fifteenth Century Venice." *American Historical Review* 91 (1986): 798–801.

———. "Review of *The Venetian Patriciate*." *Journal of Modern History* 60, no. 3 (1988): 599–602.

———. "Social Identity in Renaissance Venice: The Second Serrata." *Renaissance Studies* 8 (1994): 341–58.

Cochrane, Eric, and Julius Kirshner. "Deconstructing Lane's Venice." *Journal of Modern History* 47, no. 2 (1975): 321–34.

Cohn, Samuel. *Creating the Florentine State: Peasants and Rebellion, 1348–1434*. Cambridge: Cambridge University Press, 1999.

———. *Lust for Liberty: The Politics of Social Revolt in Medieval Europe, 1200–1425. Italy, France, and Flanders*. Cambridge: Harvard University Press, 2006.

Connell, William J. "Changing Patterns of Medicean Patronage: The Florentine Dominion during the Fifteenth Century." In *Lorenzo il Magnifico e il suo mondo*, ed. Gian Carlo Garfagnini, 87–107. Florence: Olschki Editore, 1994.

———. "Clientismo e stato territoriale: Il potere fiorentino a Pistoia nel XV secolo." *Società e Storia* 14, no. 153 (1991): 523–43.

———. "Il commissario e lo stato territoriale fiorentino." *Ricerche Storiche* 18 (1988): 591–617.

———. "The Humanist Citizen as Provincial Governor." In *Florentine Tuscany: Structures and Practices of Power*, ed. William J. Connell and Andrea Zorzi, 144–64. Cambridge: Cambridge University Press, 2000.

Connell, William J., and Andrea Zorzi, ed. *Florentine Tuscany: Structures and Practices of Power*. Cambridge: Cambridge University Press, 2000.

Costantini, Massimo. *Una Repubblica nata sul mare: navigazione e commercio a Venezia*. Venice: Marsilio, 2005.

Coureas, Nicolas. "Economy." In *Cyprus: Society and Culture 1191–1374*, ed. Chris Schabel and Angel Nicolaou Konnari, 103–57. Leiden: Brill, 2005.

Cozzi, Gaetano. "Authority and the Law in Renaissance Venice." In *Renaissance Venice,* ed. J. R. Hale, 293–345. London: Faber and Faber, 1973.

———. "Cultura politica e religione nella publica storiografia Veneziana del 500." *Studi Veneziani* 5–6 (1963–64): 215–94.

———. "Domenico Morosini e il *De bene instituta re publica.*" *Studi Veneziani* 12 (1970): 405–58.

———. "La politica del diritto nella Repubblica di Venezia." In *Stato, società e giustizia nella repubblica veneta (sec. XV–XVIII),* ed. Gaetano Cozzi, 15–152. Rome: Jouvence,1980.

Cozzi, Gaetano, and Michael Knapton. *La Repubblica di Venezia nell'età moderna.* 2 vols. Storia d'Italia, 12. Turin: UTET, 1986.

Cracco, Giorgio. "Badoer, Albano." *DBI* 5 (1963): 90–91.

Crouzet-Pavan, Elisabeth. *'Sopra le acque salse.' Espaces, pouvoir et societé à Venise à la fin du moyen âge.* 2 vols. Rome: Istituto storico italiano per il Medio Evo, 1992.

———. *Venice Triumphant: The Horizons of a Myth.* Trans. Lydia G. Cochrane. Baltimore: The Johns Hopkins University Press, 2002.

———. "Venise et le monde communal: recherches sur les podestats vénitiens." In *I podestà dell'Italia comunale,* ed. Jean-Claude Maire Vigueur, I: 259–88. Rome: Istituto storico italiano per il Medio Evo, 2000.

Da Mosto, Andrea. *L'Archivio di stato di Venezia.* 2 vols. Rome: Biblioteca d'Arte Editrice, 1937.

Dávid, Geza. "Administration in Ottoman Europe." In *Süleyman the Magnificent and His Age: The Ottoman Empire in the Early Modern World,* ed. Metin Kunt and Christine Woodhead, 71–90. New York: Longman, 1995.

De Angelis, Laura. "Territorial Offices and Officeholders." In *Florentine Tuscany: Structures and Practices of Power,* ed. William Connell and Andrea Zorzi, 165–82. Cambridge: Cambridge University Press, 2000.

De Vivo, Filippo. "The Diversity of Venice and Her Myths." *The Historical Journal* 47, no. 1 (2004): 169–77.

Del Torre, Giuseppe. *Venezia e la terraferma dopo la guerra di Cambrai: fiscalità e amministrazione (1515–1530).* Milan: Franco Angeli, 1986.

Doumerc, Bernard. "L'Adriatique du XIIIe–XVIIe siècle." In *Histoire de l'Adriatique,* ed. Pierre Cabanes, 203–311. Paris: Seuil, 2001.

———. "La crise structurelle de la marine vénitienne au XVe siècle: le problème du retard des *mude.*" *Annales ESC* 40, no. 3 (1985): 605–23.

———. "Il dominio del mar." In *Storia di Venezia. Il Rinascimento. Politica e cultura,* ed. Alberto Tenenti and Ugo Tucci, IV: 113–80. Rome: Enciclopedia Italiana, 1996.

———. "Le parti de la mar à Venise à la fin du XVe siècle: une étude de prosopographie." In *Oriente e Occidente tra medievo ed età moderna, Studi in onore di Geo Pistarino,* ed. Laura Balletto, I: 177–90. Genoa: G. Brigati, 1997.

———. "La Tana au XV siècle: comptoir ou colonie?" In *Etat et colonisation au moyen âge et à la renaissance,* ed. Michel Balard, 251–66. Lyon: La Manufacture, 1989.

Doumerc, Bernard, and Claire Judde de Larivière, "Le Rôle du Patriciat dans la Gestion des galères marchandes à Venise au début du seizième siècle," *Studi Veneziani* n.s. 36 (1998): 57–84.

Doyle, Michael W. *Empires*. Ithaca: Cornell University Press, 1986.

Ducellier, Alain. "L'Adriatique du IVe au XIIe siècle." In *Histoire de l'Adriatique*, ed. Pierre Cabanes, 141–99. Paris: Seuil, 2001.

———. *La Façade Maritime de l'Albanie au Moyen Age. Durazzo et Valona du XIe au XVe siècle*. Thessaloniki: Institute for Balkan Studies, 1981.

Dudan, Bruno. *Il diritto coloniale veneziano e le sue basi economiche*. Rome: Anonima Romana Editoriale, 1933.

———. *Il dominio veneziano di Levante*. Bologna: Nicola Zanichelli, 1938.

———. *Sindicato d'oltremare e di terraferma*. Rome: Foro Italiano, 1935.

Dursteler, Eric. *Venetians in Constantinople: Nation, Identity, and Coexistence in the Early Modern Mediterranean*. Baltimore: The Johns Hopkins University Press, 2006.

Eckstein, Nicholas. *The District of the Green Dragon: Neighbourhood Life and Social Change in Renaissance Florence*. Florence: Olschki Editore, 1995.

Elliott, J. H. *Empires of the Atlantic World: Britian and Spain in America 1492–1830*. New Haven: Yale University Press, 2006.

———. "A Europe of Composite Monarchies." *Past and Present* 137 (1992): 48–71.

Fedalto, Giorgio. *La Chiesa Latina in Oriente*. 3 vols. Verona: Mazziana, 1973.

Fees, Irmgard. *Ricchezza e potenza nella Venezia medioevale: la famiglia Ziani*. Rome: Il Veltro, 2005.

Fincati, Luigi. "La perdita di Negroponte, luglio 1470." *Nuovo Archivio Veneto* 32 (1886): 267–307.

Fine, John V. A., Jr. *The Late Medieval Balkans: A Critical Survey from the Late Twelfth to the Ottoman Conquest*. Ann Arbor: University of Michigan Press, 1987.

Finlay, Robert. "Crisis and Crusade in the Mediterranean: Venice, Portugal, and the Cape Route to India (1498–1509)." *Studi Veneziani* n.s. 28 (1994): 45–90.

———. *Politics in Renaissance Venice*. New Brunswick, N.J.: Rutgers University Press, 1980.

———. "The Venetian Republic as a Gerontocracy: Age and Politics in the Renaissance." *Journal of Medieval and Renaissance Studies* 8 (1978): 157–78.

Gabelić, Andro. *Ustanak hvarskih pučana (1510–1514): izvori, tokovi, dometi* [The Rebellion of Hvar's Plebeians]. Spilt: Književni Krug, 1988.

Gallina, Marino. "L'affermarsi di un modello coloniale: Venezia e il levante tra due e trecento." *Thesaurismata* 23 (1993): 14–39.

———. *Una società coloniale del trecento: Creta fra Venezia e Bisanzio*. Venice: Deputazione Editrice, 1989.

Gambino, F. "Gradenigo, Iacopo." *DBI* 58 (2002): 330–32.

Gasparēs, Charalampos. "Mētropolitikē exousia kai Axiōmatoúchoi tōn apoikiōn: O kapitános Krētēs (14os–15os aiōnes)." *Symmeikta* 12 (1998): 171–214.

Geanakoplos, Deno J. "The Council of Florence (1438–1439) and the problem of Union between the Byzantine and Latin Churches." In *Byzantine East and Latin*

West: Two Worlds of Christendom in the Middle Ages and Renaissance, 84–111. Oxford: Blackwell, 1966.

———. *Greek Scholars in Venice: Studies in the Dissemination of Greek Learning from Byzantium to Western Europe.* Cambridge: Harvard University Press, 1962.

Georgopoulou, Maria. *Venice's Mediterranean Colonies: Architecture and Urbanism.* Cambridge: Cambridge University Press, 2001.

Gerola, Giuseppe. *Monumenti veneti nell'isola di Creta.* 4 vols. Venice: Istituto veneto di scienze, lettere ed arti, 1905–1917.

Giannasi, Laura. "Cappello, Andrea." *DBI* 18 (1975): 737–38.

Gilbert, Felix. "Venice in the Crisis of the League of Cambrai." In *Renaissance Venice,* ed. J. R. Hale, 274–92. London: Faber and Faber, 1973.

Gill, Joseph. *The Council of Florence.* Cambridge: Cambridge University Press, 1959.

Girgensohn, Dieter. *Kirche, Politik und adelige Regierung in der Republik Venedig zu Beginn des 15. Jahrhunderts.* 2 vols. Göttingen: Vandenhoeck & Ruprecht, 1999.

Gleason, Elisabeth. "Confronting New Realities: Venice and the Peace of Bologna, 1530." In *Venice Reconsidered: The History and Civilization of an Italian City State, 1297–1797,* ed. John Martin and Dennis Romano, 168–84. Baltimore: The Johns Hopkins University Press, 2000.

Goffman, Daniel, and Christopher Stroop. "Empire as Composite: The Ottoman Polity and the Typology of Dominion." In *Imperialisms: Historical and Literary Investigations, 1500–1900,* ed. Balachandra Rajan and Elizabeth Sauer, 129–45. New York: Palgrave, 2004.

Gothein, Percy. "Zaccaria Trevisan." *Archivio Veneto* 21 (1937): 1–59.

Grendler, Paul. "Leaders of the Venetian State, 1540–1609: A Prosopographical Analysis." *Studi Veneziani* 19 (1990): 35–86.

———. "The 'Tre Savii sopra Eresia' 1547–1605: A Prosopographical Study." *Studi Veneziani* 3 (1979): 283–340.

Grivaud, Gilles. "Sur quelques contradictions sur l'administration vénitienne à Chypre (1473–1570)." *Thesaurismata* 20 (1990): 185–205.

Grubb, James. "Alla ricerca delle prerogative locali: la cittadinanza a Vicenza 1404–1509." *Civis* 24 (1984): 17–32.

———. *Firstborn of Venice: Vicenza in the Early Renaissance State.* Baltimore: The Johns Hopkins University Press, 1988.

———. "Memory and Identity: Why Venetians Didn't Keep Ricordanze." *Renaissance Studies* 8, no. 4 (1994).

———. "When Myths Lose Power: Four Decades of Venetian Historiography." *Journal of Modern History* 58 (1986): 43–94.

Gullino, Giuseppe. "Cocco, Niccolò." *DBI* 26 (1982): 519–50.

———. "Da Lezze, Antonio." *DBI* 31 (1985): 746–48.

———. "Donà, Andrea." *DBI* 40 (1991): 706–9.

———. "Emo, Gabriele." *DBI* 42 (1993): 625–28.

———. "Emo, Pietro." *DBI* 43 (1993).

———. "Erizzo, Antonio." *DBI* 43 (1993): 156–58.

———. "Erizzo, Nicolo." *DBI* 43 (1993): 172–74.

———. "L'evoluzione constituzionale." In *Storia di Venezia. Il Rinascimento. Politica e cultura,* ed. Alberto Tenenti and Ugo Tucci, IV: 345–78. Rome: Enciclopedia Italiana, 1996.

———. "Foscarini, Nicolò." *DBI* 49 (1997): 400–2.

———. "Le frontiere navali." In *Storia di Venezia. Il Rinascimento. Politica e cultura,* ed. Alberto Tenenti and Ugo Tucci, IV: 13–111. Rome: Enciclopedia Italia, 1996.

———. "Giustinian, Sebastiano." *DBI* 57 (2001): 290–96.

———. "Loredan, Giorgio." *DBI* 65 (2005): 758–60.

———. "Loredan, Pietro." *DBI* 65 (2005): 775–79.

———. "Il Patriziato." In *Storia di Venezia. Il Rinascimento. Politica e cultura,* ed. Alberto Tenenti and Ugo Tucci, IV: 379–413. Rome: Enciclopedia Italiana, 1996.

———. "Quando il mercante costruì la villa: le proprietà dei Veneziani nella Terraferma." In *Storia di Venezia. Dal Rinascimento al Barocco,* ed. Gaetano Cozzi and Paolo Prodi, VI: 875–924. Rome: Enciclopedia Italiana, 1994.

Hanawalt, Barbara. "Peasant Resistance to Royal and Signorial Impositions." In *Social Unrest in the Late Middle Ages,* ed. Francis X. Newman, 23–48. Binghamton: Center for Medieval and Early Renaissance Studies, 1986.

Hemmerdinger-Iliadou, Démocratie. "La Crète sous la domination vénitienne et lors de conquête turque (1322–1684) d'après les pélerins et les voyageurs. Renseignements nouveaux au peu connus." *Studi Veneziani* 9 (1967): 535–625.

Hill, George. *A History of Cyprus.* Vols. 3 and 4. Cambridge: Cambridge University Press, 1948.

Hocquet, Jean Claude. "Capitalism marchand et classe marchand à Venise au temps de la renaissance." *Annales ESC* 34, no. 2 (1979): 279–304.

———. *Le sel et la fortune de Venise.* 2 vols. Villeneuve-d'Ascq: Publications de l'Université de Lille, 1978.

Hodgetts, Christine A. "The Colonies of Coron and Modon under Venetian Administration 1204–1400." Ph.D. thesis, University of London, 1974.

Horden, Peregrine, and Nicholas Purcell. *The Corrupting Sea: A Study of Mediterranean History.* Oxford: Blackwell, 2000.

Horodowich, Elizabeth. "The Gossiping Tongue: Oral Networks, Public Life and Political Culture in Early Modern Venice." *Renaissance Studies* 19, no. 1 (2005): 22–45.

———. "The New Venice: Historians and Historiography in the 21st Century Lagoon." *History Compass* 2 (2002): 1–27.

Hussey, J. M. *The Orthodox Church in the Byzantine Empire.* Oxford: Clarendon Press, 1986.

Iliadou, Démocratie. "La Crète sous la domination vénitienne et lors de la conquéte turque (1322–1684)." *Studi Veneziani* 15 (1973): 451–585.

Imhaus, Brünehilde. "Chypre et Venise: entre liens commerciaux et stratégies politiques." In *Cyprus: Jewel in the Crown of Venice,* ed. Vassos Karageorghis, Loukia Loizou Hadjigavriel, and Chryssa A. Maltezou, 21–30. Nicosia: The Anastasios G. Leventis Foundation and the Leventis Municipal Museum of Nicosia, 2003.

———. *Le minoranze orientali a Venezia, 1300–1510.* Rome: Il Veltro, 1997.

Inalcik, Halil. *The Ottoman Empire: The Classical Age, 1300–1600*, trans. Norman Itzkowitz and Colin Imber. New York: Praeger, 1973.

Ivančević, Radovan. "Trogirska Loža: Templum Iuris et Ara Iustitiae (1471)" [In Croatian with Italian summary]. In *Rana Renesansa u Trogiru*, 91–115. Split: Književni Krug, 1997.

Ivetić, Egidio. "Dalmazia e Slavi negli studi di Roberto Cessi." *Archivio Veneto* ser. V, 164 (2005): 125–44.

———. *Oltremare: l'Istria nell'ultimo dominio veneto.* Venice: Istituto veneto di scienze, lettere ed arti, 2000.

———. "Storiografie nazionali e interpretazioni della Dalmazia medievale." In *Venezia e la Dalmazia anno mille, secoli di vicende comuni*, ed. Nedo Fiorentin, 95–133. Regione del Veneto: Canova, 2000.

Jacoby, David. "Un agent juif au service de Venise: David Maurogonato de Candie." *Thesaurismata* 9 (1972): 68–96.

———. *Byzantium, Latin Romania and the Mediterranean.* Variorum Collected Studies Series. Aldershot: Ashgate, 2001.

———. "Changing Economic Patterns in Latin Romania: The Impact of the West." In *The Crusades from the Perspective of Byzantium and the Muslim World*, ed. Angeliki E. Laiou and Roy Parviz Mottahedeh, 197–233. Washington, D.C.: Dumbarton Oaks, 2001.

———. "Citoyens, sujets et protégés de Venise et de Gênes en Chypre du XIIIe au XVe siècle." In *Recherches sur la Méditerranée orientale du XIIe au XVe siècle: peuples, sociétés, économies*, 159–88. London: Variorum Reprints, 1979.

———. "La colonisation militaire vénitienne de la Crète au XIII siècle." In *Le partage du monde: échanges et colonisation dans la Méditerranée médiévale*, ed. Michel Balard and Alain Ducellier, 297–313. Paris: Publications de la Sorbonne, 1998.

———. "La consolidation de la domination de Venise dans la ville de Négrepont (1205–1390): Un aspect de sa politique coloniale." In *Bizanzio, Venezia e il mondo franco-greco. Atti di colloquio internazionale organizzato nel centenario della nascita di Raymond Joseph Loenertz, o.p.*, ed. Chryssa Maltezou and Peter Schreiner, 151–87. Venice: Istituto Ellenico di Studi Bizantini e Postbizantini, Centro Tedesco di Studi Veneziani, 2002.

———. "Encounter of Two Societies: Western Conquerors and Byzantines in the Peloponnesus after the Fourth Crusade." *American Historical Review* 78 (1973): 873–906.

———. *La Féodalité en Grèce médiévale: Les* Assises de Romanie, *sources, application et diffusion.* École pratique des hautes études. VI section. Documents et recherches sur léconomie des pays byzantins, islamiques, et slaves, et leurs relations commerciales au Moyen Age, 10. Paris: Mouton, 1971.

———. "From Byzantium to Latin Romania: Continuity and Change." In *Latins and Greeks in the Eastern Mediterranean after 1204*, ed. Benjamin Arbel, 1–45. London: Frank Cass, 1989.

———. "Quelques aspects de la vie juive en Crète dans la première moitié du XVe siècle." In *Pepragména tou 3. Diethnoús Krētologikoú Synedriou, Réthymnon 1971*, ed. Georgios I. Kourmoules and M. I. Manoussacas, II: 108–17. Athens: [s.n.], 1973.

———. *Recherches sur la Méditerraneé orientale du XIIe au XVe siècle: peuples, sociétés, économies.* London: Variorum Reprints, 1979.

———. "Social Evolution in Latin Greece." In *A History of the Crusades. The Impact of the Crusades on Europe,* ed. Norman P. Zacour and Harry W. Hazard, VI: 177–222. Madison: University of Wisconsin Press, 1989.

———. *Trade, Commodities and Shipping in the Medieval Mediterranean.* Variorum Collected Studies Series. Aldershot: Ashgate, 1997.

———. "La Venezia d'oltremare nel secondo duecento." In *Storia di Venezia. L'età del Comune,* ed. Giorgio Cracco and Gherardo Ortalli, II: 263–99. Rome: Enciclopedia Italiana, 1995.

———. "Venice, the Inquisition, and the Jewish community of Crete." *Studi Veneziani* 12 (1970): 127–44.

Jeffrey, George. *A Description of the Historic Monuments of Cyprus.* London: Zeno Publishers, 1918. Reprint, 1983.

Jones, Philip *The Italian City State: From Commune to Signoria.* Oxford: Clarendon Press, 1997.

Judde de Larivière, Claire. "L'abandon de la navigation de ligne: les enjeux d'un processus économique (Venise, fin XVe–debut XVIe siècle)." *Studi Veneziani* n.s. 47 (2004): 121–31.

Jutronić, Andre. "I conti (rettori), rapprensentanti veneti, presso il commune di Brac (Brazza) le loro lettere al consiglio dei dieci a Venezia." *Studi Veneziani* 7 (1965): 379–423.

Kagan, Richard. *Lawsuits and Litigants in Castile, 1500–1700.* Chapel Hill: University of North Carolina Press, 1981.

Karapidakis, Nicolas. "Administration et mileûx administratifs en crète vénitienne XVI siècle." Ph.D. thesis, University of Paris, 1983.

———. *Civis Fidelis: l'avènement et l'affirmation de la citoyenneté corfiote (XVIème–XVIIème siècles).* Frankfurt am Main/New York: P. Lang, 1992.

———. "La formazione di un ceto di potere a Corfù." In *Venezia e le Isole Ionie,* ed. Chryssa Maltezou and Gherardo Ortalli. Venice: Istituto veneto di scienze, lettere ed arti, 2005.

———. "Narrazione e concetti della storiografia greca sul periodo del dominio veneziano." In *Italia-Grecia: temi e storiografie a confronto,* ed. Chryssa Maltezou and Gherardo Ortalli, 113–25. Venice: Istituto Ellenico, 2001.

Kastritsis, Dimitris J. *The Sons of Bayezid: Empire Building and Representation in the Ottoman Civil War of 1402–1413.* Leiden: Brill, 2007.

Kent, Dale. *The Rise of the Medici: Faction in Florence, 1426–1434.* Oxford: Oxford University Press, 1978.

Kent, F. W., and Dale Kent. *Neighbours and Neighbourhood in Renaissance Florence: The District of the Red Lion in the Fifteenth Century.* New York: J. J. Augustin, 1982.

Khoury, Dina Rizk. "Administrative Practice between Religious Law *(Shari'a)* and State Law *(Kanun)* on the Eastern Frontiers of the Ottoman Empire." *Journal of Early Modern History* 5, no. 4 (2001): 305–30.

King, Margaret L. *Venetian Humanism in an Age of Patrician Dominance.* Princeton: Princeton University Press, 1986.

Kitromilides, Paschalis. "Bridges to the Renaissance and the Enlightenment: The Assimilation of Italian Culture as a Problem in Greek Historiography." In *Italia-Grecia: temi e storiografie a confronto,* ed. Chryssa Maltezou and Gherardo Ortalli, 37–46. Venice: Istituto Ellenico, 2001.

Klapisch-Zuber, Christiane. "Kin, Friends, and Neighbors: The Urban Territory of a Merchant Family in 1400." In *Women, Family, and Ritual in Renaissance Italy,* 68–93. Chicago: University of Chicago Press, 1985.

Knapton, Michael. "La condanna penale di Alvise Querini, ex-rettore di Rovereto (1477): solo un altra smentita del mito di Venezia?" *Atti dell'Accademia Roveretana degli Agiati* a. 238, s. VI, 28 (1988): 303–32.

———. "Il Consiglio dei Dieci nel governo della terraferma: un ipotesi interpretiva per il secondo 400." In *Venezia e la terraferma attraverso le relazioni dei rettori. Atti del Convegno,* ed. Amelio Tagliaferri, 237–60. Trieste: Giuffre, 1981.

———. "Le istituzioni centrali per l'amministrazione ed il controllo della terraferma." In *Venezia e le Istituzioni di Terraferma,* ed. Gherardo Ortalli, 35–56. Bergamo: Assessorato alla Cultura, 1988.

———. "Nobiltà e popolo e un trentennio di storiografia veneta." *Nuova Rivista Storica* 82 (1998): 167–92.

———. "Tribunali veneziani e proteste padovane nel secondo quattrocento." In *Studi Veneti offerti a Gaetano Cozzi,* 151–71. Vicenza: Il Cardo, 1992.

Kohl, Benjamin G. "Review of *The Venetian Patriciate.*" *Speculum* 63 no. 3 (1988): 707–9.

Koumanoudi, Marina. "'Contra deum, jus, et justitiam': The Trial of Bartolomeo Querini, Bailo and Captain of Negroponte." In *Bizanzio, Venezia e il mondo franco greco. Colloquio internazionale nel centenario della nascita di Raymond Joseph Loenertz,* ed. Chryssa Maltezou and Peter Schreiner, 235–89. Venice: Istituto Ellenico, 2000.

Krekić, Bariša. "Developed Autonomy: The Patricians in Dubrovnik and Dalmatian Cities." In *Città e sistema adriatico alla fine del medioevo. Bilanci degli studi e prospettive di ricerca. Convegno di Studi, Padova 4–5 aprile 1997,* ed. Michele Pietro Ghezzo, 185–215. Venice: Società Dalmata di Storia Patria, 1997.

———. "Venezia e l'Adriatico." In *Storia di Venezia. La formazione dello Stato Patrizio,* ed. Giorgio Cracco, Girolamo Arnaldi, and Alberto Tenenti, III: 51–85. Rome: Enciclopedia Italiana, 1996.

Lambrinós, Kostas. "E exélixē tēs Krētikēs eugéneias stous prōtous aiōnes tēs Venetokratias." *Thesaurismata* 26 (1996): 206–24.

———. "Rivalités économiques et sociales dans un village crétois fin du 16e siècle" [In Greek with French summary]. In *Enthymēsis Nikoláou M. Panagiōtakē,* ed. Athanasios Markopoulos, Stephanos Kaklamanēs, Giannēs Mauromatēs, 379–96. Irakleion: Vikelaia Dēmotikē Vivliothēkē, 2000.

Lane, Frederic C. *Andrea Barbarigo, Merchant of Venice, 1418–1449.* New York: Octagon Books, 1967.

———. "At the Roots of Republicanism." *American Historical Review* 71 (1966): 403–20.

———. "Family Partnerships and Joint Ventures." In *Venice and History: The Collected Papers of Frederic C. Lane,* 36–55. Baltimore: The Johns Hopkins University Press, 1966.

———. "The Mediterranean Spice Trade: Further Evidence of its Revival in the Sixteenth Century." *American Historical Review* 45, no. 3 (1940): 581–90.

———. "Public Debt and Private Wealth, Particularly in Sixteenth Century Venice." In *Histoire économique du monde mediterraneen. Mélanges en l'honneur de Fernand Braudel,* I: 317–25. Toulouse, 1973. Reprint, *Profits from Power: Readings in Protection Rent and Violence-Controlling Enterprises.* Albany: State University of New York Press, 1979.

———. *Venice, A Maritime Republic.* Baltimore: The Johns Hopkins University Press, 1973.

———. *Venice and History: The Collected Papers of Frederic C. Lane.* Baltimore: The Johns Hopkins University Press, 1966.

Law, John Easton. "Lo stato veneziano e le castellanie di Verona." In *Venice and the Veneto in the Early Renaissance,* 277–98. Burlington, Vt.: Ashgate, 2000.

———. "Verona and the Venetian State in the Fifteenth Century." *Bulletin of the Institute of Historical Research* 52, no. 125 (1979): 9–22.

Lock, Peter. *The Franks in the Aegean, 1204–1500.* New York: Longman, 1995.

Loenertz, R. J. *Les Ghisi, dynastes vénitiens dans l'Archipel, 1207–1390.* Florence: Olschki Editore, 1975.

———. "De quelques îles grèques et leurs seigneurs vénitiens aux XIV et XV siècles." *Studi Veneziani* 14 (1972): 3–35.

———. "Les Querini, comtes dí Astypalee, 1413–1537." *Orientalia Christiana Periodica* 30 (1964): 385–97.

Lopez, Carlo Ceferino. "Di alcune magistrature minori Veneziane." *Studi Veneziani* 1 (1977): 36–67.

———. "Gli auditori nuovi e il dominio di terraferma." In *Stato, società e giustizia nella repubblica Veneta,* ed. Gaetano Cozzi, 259–313. Rome: Jouvence, 1980.

Lopez, Roberto. "Il principio della guerra veneto-turca nel 1463." *Archivio Veneto* ser. V, 15 (1934): 45–131.

Lunzi, Ermanno. *Della condizione politica delle Isole Ionie sotto il dominio Veneto.* Venice: Tip. De Commercio, 1858.

Luzzatto, Gino. *Storia economica di Venezia dall'XI al XVI secolo.* Venice: Centro internazionale delle Arti e del Costume, 1961.

Madden, Thomas F. *Enrico Dandolo and the Rise of Venice.* Baltimore: The Johns Hopkins University Press, 2003.

Magnante, Giannina. "L'acquisto dell'isola di Cipro da parte della repubblica di Venezia." *Archivio Veneto* ser. V, 5 (1929): 78–133.

Major, Alain. "L'administration vénitienne à Négreponte (fin XIVe–XVe siècle)." In *Coloniser au moyen âge,* ed. Michel Balard and Alain Ducellier, 246–58. Paris: Armand Colin, 1995.

Mallett, Michael, and J. R. Hale. *The Military Organization of a Renaissance State: Venice, c. 1400 to 1617*. Cambridge: Cambridge University Press, 1984.

Maltezou, Chryssa. "Byzantine 'Consuetudines' in Venetian Crete." *Dumbarton Oaks Papers* 49 (1995): 269–80.

———. "The Historical and Social Context." In *Literature and Society in Renaissance Crete*, ed. David Holton, 17–48. Cambridge: Cambridge University Press, 1991.

Maltezou, Chryssa, and Gherardo Ortalli, ed. *Italia-Grecia: temi e storiografie a confronto. Atti del convegno di studi, Istituto Ellenico di Studi Bizantini e post-Bizantini di Venezia*. Venice: Istituto Ellenico, 2001.

Manoussacas, Manoussos. *Hē en Krētē Synōmosia tou Sēphē Vlastou, 1453–1454, kai ē néa Synōmotikē kinēsis tou 1460–1462* [The Conspiracy of Sifi Vlastos (1453–1454) and the New Conspiratorial Movement of 1460–1462]. Athens: Didaktorikē Diatribē, 1960.

———. "L'isola di Creta sotto il dominio veneziano: problemi e richerche." In *Venezia et il Levante fino al secolo XV*, ed. Agostino Pertusi, I: pt. 2, 473–514. Florence: Olschki Editore, 1973.

Marković, Predrag. "L'architecture renaissance en Croatie." In *La Renaissance en Croatie*, ed. Alain Erlande-Brandenburg and Miljenko Jurković, 71–110. Zagreb: Musée national de la Renaissance and Galerie Klovićevi dvori, 2004.

Mas Latrie, Louis. "Documents nouveaux servant de preuves à la histoire de l'île de Chypre sous les princes de la maison de Lusignan." *Mélanges historiques* 4 (1882): 343–619.

———. *Histoire de l'île de Chypre sous le regne des princes de Lusignan*. Paris, 1852–61. Reprint, Famagusta: Editions l'Oiseau, 1970.

McKee, Sally. "Greek Women in Latin Households of Fourteenth Century Crete." *Journal of Medieval History* 19 (1993): 229–49.

———. "Households in Fourteenth Century Venetian Crete." *Speculum* 70 (1995): 27–67.

———. "The Revolt of San Tito." *Mediterranean Historical Review* 9 (1994): 173–204.

———. *Uncommon Dominion: Venetian Crete and the Myth of Ethnic Purity*. Philadelphia: University of Pennsylvania Press, 2000.

McNeal, Edgar H., and Robert Lee Wolff. "The Fourth Crusade." In *The Later Crusades*, ed. Harry W. Hazard and Robert Lee Wolff (*A History of the Crusades*, vol. 2), 163–86. Madison: University of Wisconsin Press, 1969.

Melville-Jones, John R. *Venice and Thessalonica, 1423–1430: The Venetian Documents*. Archivio del litorale adriatico, 7. Padua: Unipress, 2002.

Meserve, Margaret. "News from Negroponte: Politics, Popular Opinion, and Information Exchange in the First Decade of the Italian Press." *Renaissance Quarterly* 59 (2006): 440–79.

Molho, Anthony. "Cosimo de Medici: Pater patriae or padrino?" *Stanford Italian Review* 1 (1979): 5–33.

———. "Patronage and the State in Early Modern Italy." In *Klientelsysteme im Europa der Frühen Neuzeit*, ed. Antoni Mazack, 233–42. Munich: Oldenbourg, 1988.

Mollat, Michel, and Philippe Wolff. *The Popular Revolutions of the Late Middle Ages.* Lyton Seels. London: Allen & Unwin, 1973.

Molnar, Miklos. *A Concise History of Hungary,* trans. Anna Magyar. Cambridge: Cambridge University Press, 2001.

Monfasani, John. *Byzantine Scholars in Renaissance Italy: Cardinal Bessarion and Other Emigrés.* Aldershot: Ashgate, 1995.

Mor, Carlo Guido. "Introduzione." In *Cassiere della Bolla Ducale, Grazie–Novus Liber, 1299–1305,* ed. Elena Favaro, i–xcv. Venice: Il Comitato Editore, 1962.

Mozzato, Andrea. "Problems and Possibilities of Constructing a Research Data Bank. The Venetian Case." *Storia di Venezia* 2 (2004): 1–38.

Mueller, Reinhold C. "Aspects of Venetian Sovereignty in Medieval and Renaissance Dalmatia." In *Quattrocento Adriatico: Fifteenth-Century Art of the Adriatic Rim; Papers from a Colloquium Held at the Villa Spelman, Florence, 1994,* ed. Charles Dempsey, 29–56. Bologna: Nuova Alfa Editoriale, 1996.

———. "Effetti della guerra di Chioggia (1378–1381) sulla vita economica e sociale di Venezia." *Ateneo Veneto* 19 (1981): 27–42.

———. "Espressioni di status sociale a Venezia dopo la serrata del Maggior Consiglio." In *Studi Veneti offerti a Gaetano Cozzi,* 53–61. Venice: Il Cardo, 1992.

———. "Greeks in Venice and 'Venetians' in Greece: Notes on Citizenship and Immigration in the Late Middle Ages." In *Ploúsioi kai phtōchoi: stēn koinōnia tēs Hellēnolatinikēs anatolēs. Diethnés sympósio,* ed. Chryssa Maltezou, 167–80. Venice: Istituto Ellenico, 1998.

———. "L'imperialismo monetario veneziano nel Quattrocento." *Società e Storia* 8 (1980): 277–97.

———. "The Jewish Moneylenders of Late Trecento Venice: A Reconsideration." *Mediterranean Historical Review* 10 (1995): 20–35.

———. *The Procuratori di San Marco and the Venetian Credit Market.* New York: Arno Press, 1977.

———. "The Procurators of San Marco in the Thirteenth and Fourteenth Centuries: A Study of the Office as a Financial and Trust Institution." *Studi Veneziani* 12 (1971): 105–220.

———. "Pubblico e privato nel dominio veneziano delle isole Greche a metà Quattrocento: Il caso dei Giustinian." In *Venezia e le Isole Ionie,* ed. Chryssa Maltezou and Gherardo Ortalli, 71–100. Venice: Istituto veneto di scienze, lettere ed arti, 2005.

———. "A Venetian Commercial Enterprise in Corfu, 1440–42." In *Money and Markets in the Palaeologan Era,* ed. N. G. Moschonas, 81–94. Athens: Institute for Byzantine Research, 2003.

———. *The Venetian Money Market: Banks, Panics and the Public Debt, 1200–1500.* Vol. 2. Baltimore: The Johns Hopkins University Press, 1997.

Muir, Edward. *Civic Ritual in Renaissance Venice.* Princeton: Princeton University Press, 1981.

———. *Mad Blood Stirring: Vendetta and Factions in Friuli during the Renaissance.* Baltimore: The Johns Hopkins University Press, 1993.

———. "Review of *The Venetian Patriciate.*" *Renaissance Quarterly* 41, no. 2 (1988): 288–91.

———. "The Sources of Civil Society in Italy." *Journal of Interdisciplinary History* 29, no. 3 (1999): 379–406.

———. "Was There Republicanism in the Renaissance Republics?" In *Venice Reconsidered: The History and Civilization of an Italian City-State, 1297–1797,* ed. John Martin and Dennis Romano, 137–67. Baltimore: The Johns Hopkins University Press, 2000.

Mullett, Michael A. *Popular Culture and Popular Protest in Late Medieval and Early Modern Europe.* London: Croom-Helm, 1987.

Mustoxidi, Andreas. *Delle Cose Corciresi.* Corfu: Nella tipografia del governo, 1848.

Nicol, Donald MacGillivray. *Byzantium and Venice: A Study in Diplomatic and Cultural Relations.* Cambridge: Cambridge University Press, 1988.

Nikiforou-Testone, Aliki. "The Transformation of the Urban Landscape in Public Ceremonies during the Venetian Occupation." In *Corfu: History, Urban Space and Architecture, 14th–19th centuries,* ed. Ennio Concina and Aliki Nikiforou-Testone, 59–70. Corfu: Cultural Society of Korkyra, 1994.

Noli, Fan Stylian. *George Castrioti Scanderbeg, 1405–1468.* New York: International Universities Press, 1947.

O'Connell, Monique. "The Castellan in Local Administration in Fifteenth Century Venetian Crete." *Thesaurismata* 33 (2004): 161–77.

———. "Sinews of Rule: The Politics of Officeholding in Fifteenth-Century Venetian Crete." *Renaissance Studies* 15 (2001): 256–71.

———. "The Venetian Patriciate in the Mediterranean: Legal Identity and Lineage in Fifteenth Century Venetian Crete," *Renaissance Quarterly* 57 (2004): 466–93.

Olivieri, Achille. "Calbo, Marc'Antonio." *DBI* 16 (1973): 480–82.

———. "Canal, Alvise." *DBI* 14 (1974): 635–36.

———. "Cappello, Vincenzo." *DBI* 18 (1975): 827–30.

Ortalli, Gherardo. "Entrar nel Dominio: le dedizioni delle città alla Repubblica Serenissima." In *Società, economia, istituzioni. Elementi per la conoscenza della Repubblica Veneta,* I: 49–62. Verona: Cierre Edizioni, 2002.

———. "Il ruolo degli statuti tra autonomie e dipendenze: Curzola e il dominio veneziano." *Rivista Storica Italiana* ser. V, 98 (1986): 195–220.

———. *Venezia e Creta: atti del convegno internazionale di studi Iraklion-Chania, 30 settembre–5 ottobre 1997.* Venice: Istituto veneto di scienze, lettere ed arti, 1998.

Pagden, Anthony. *Lords of All the World: Ideologies of Empire in Spain, Britain and France c. 1500–c. 1800.* New Haven: Yale University Press, 1995.

———. *Peoples and Empires: A Short History of European Migration, Exploration, and Conquest, from Greece to the Present.* New York: The Modern Library, 2001.

Paladini, Filippo Maria. "Storia di Venezia e retorica del dominio adriatico. Venezianità e imperialismo (1938–1943)." *Ateneo Veneto* 38 (2000): 253–98.

Papadaki, Aspasia. "Axiōmata stē Venetokratoúmenē Krētē katá to 160 kai 170 aiōna." *Krētika Chronica* 26 (1986): 99–136.

———. *Cerimonie religiose e laiche nell'isola di Creta durante il dominio veneziano,* trans. Giorgio Pelidis. Quaderni della Rivista di bizantinistica, 9. Spoleto (Perugia): Fondazione Centro italiano di studi sull'alto Medioevo, 2005.

———. "E Krētikē eugéneia stēn koinōnia tēs Venetokratoúmenēs Krētēs." In *Ploúsioi kai phtōchoi: stēn koinōnia tēs Hellēnolatinikēs anatolēs. Diethnés sympósio,* ed. Chryssa Maltezou, 305–18. Venice: Istituto Ellenico, 1998.

———. "La storia di Creta sotto il dominio veneto: il punto di vista della storiografia greca." In *Narrazione e concetti della storiografia greca sul periodo del dominio veneziano,* ed. Chryssa Maltezou and Gherardo Ortalli, 71–82. Venice: Istituto Ellenico, 2001.

Papadia-Lala, Anastassia. *Agrotikés tarachés kai exegérseis stē Venetokratoúmenē Krētē (1509–1528). E epanástasē tou Geōrgiou Gadanoléou-Lyssogiōrgē* [Agrarian Disturbances and Uprisings in Venetian Crete (1509–1528): The "Rebellion" of Georgios Gadanoleou-Lyssogiorges]. Athens: Didaktorikē Diatribē, 1983.

———. *Ho thesmos tōn astikōn koinotētōn ston ellēniko chōro kata tēn periodo tēs venetocratias (13os–18os ai.): mia synthetikē prosengisē* [L'istituzione delle comunità cittadine in territorio greco durante il periodo della dominazione veneziana (XIII–XVIII sec.): un approccio sintetico. In Greek with English summary]. Venice: Istituto Ellenico, 2004.

———. "La 'venetocrazia' nel pensiero greco. Storicità, realtà, prospettive." In *Italia-Grecia: temi e storiografie a confronto,* ed. Chryssa Maltezou and Gherardo Ortalli, 61–70. Venice: Istituto Ellenico, 2001.

Pederin, Ivan. "Appunti e notizie su Spalato nel Quattrocento." *Studi Veneziani* 21 (1991): 323–409.

———. "Commercio, economia, pesca, arti e mestieri in Arbe nel Quattrocento." *Archivio Storico Italiano* 147, no. 2, alt no 540 (1989): 215–49.

———. "Il mito di Venezia nella storiografia e letturatura Croata secoli XV–XIX." In *Mito e antimito di Venezia nel bacino adriatico,* ed. Sante Graciotti, 41–63. Rome: Il Calamo, 2001.

———. "Šibenik (Sebenico) nel basso Medioevo fino al 1440." *Archivio Storico Italiano* 149, no. 4, alt. no. 550 (1991): 811–85.

———. "Die Venezianische Verwaltung Dalmatiens und Ihre Organe." *Studi Veneziani* 12 (1986): 99–162.

———. "Die Wichtigen Ämter der Venezianischen Verwaltung in Dalmatien und der Einfluss Venezianischer Organe auf die Zustände in Dalmatien." *Studi Veneziani* 20 (1990): 305–55.

Pepper, Simon. "Fortress and Fleet: The Defence of Venice's Mainland Greek Colonies in the Late Fifteenth Century." In *War, Culture, and Society in Renaissance Venice: Essays in Honour of John Hale,* ed. Cecil H. Clough, Michael Mallett, and David Chambers, 29–56. London: Hambledon Press, 1993.

Perdue, Peter C. *China Marches West: The Qing Conquest of Central Eurasia.* Cambridge: Harvard University Press, 2005.

Pertusi, Agostino. "Per la storia di Dulcigno nei secoli XIV–XV e dei suoi statuti cittadini." *Studi Veneziani* 15 (1973): 213–71.

Piergiovanni, Vito. "Lo statuto: lo specchio normativo della identità cittadine." In *Gli*

Statuti dei Comuni e delle Corporazioni in Italia nei Secoli XIII–XVI, ed. Senato della Reppublica, 13–19. Rome: Edizioni de Luca, 1995.

Pillinini. "Bollani, Candiano." *DBI* 11 (1969): 287–89.

———. "Bollani, Domenico." *DBI* 11 (1969): 290–91.

Pilo, Giuseppe Maria. *Per trecentosettantasette anni. La gloria di Venezia nelle testimonianze artistiche della Dalmazia.* Venice: Edizioni della Laguna, 2000.

Plebani, Tiziana. "Vite di donne nei libri di famiglia veneziani." *Mélanges de l'École française de Rome* 113, no. 1 (2001): 91–106.

Ploumidēs, Georgios. *Hoi Venetokratoúmenes Hellēnikés chōres metaxy tou deutérou kai tou tritou Tourkovenetikoú polémo* [I paesi Greci sotto il dominio Veneziano tra la seconda e la terza guerra Turco-Veneziano, in Greek with Italian summary]. Ioannina: Panepistemion Ioanninon, 1974.

Pozza, Marco. *I Badoer: una famiglia veneziana dal X al XIII secolo.* Padua: Aldo Francisci, 1982.

———. "Le chiese veneziane intitolate a San Marco nell'Oriente mediterraneo nei secoli XII e XIII." In *San Marco: aspetti storici e agiografici. Atti del Convegno internazionale di studi, Venezia, 26–29 aprile 1994*, ed. Antonio Niero, 611–26. Venice: Marsilio, 1996.

———. "I proprietari fondiari in terraferma." In *Storia di Venezia. L'età del Comune*, ed. Giorgio Cracco and Gherardo Ortalli, II: 661–80. Rome: Enciclopedia Italiana, 1995.

Praga, Giuseppe. *History of Dalmatia.* Trans. Edward Steinberg and ed. Franco Luxardo. Pisa: Giardini, 1993.

———. "L'organizzazione militare della Dalmazia nel quattrocento e la costruzione di castel Cippico vecchio di Traù." *Archivio storico per la Dalmazia* 20 (1935–36): 462–77.

Pujeau, Emmanuelle. "La Préveza (1538) entre idéologie et histoire." *Studi Veneziani* 51 (2006): 155–204.

Queller, Donald E. *The Venetian Patriciate: Reality versus Myth.* Urbana: University of Illinois, 1986.

Queller, Donald E., and Thomas F. Madden. *The Fourth Crusade: The Conquest of Constantinople.* 2nd [rev.] ed. Philadelphia: University of Pennsylvania Press, 1997.

Radding, Cynthia. *Landscapes of Power and Identity: Comparative Histories in the Sonoran Desert and the Forests of Amazonia from Colony to Republic.* Durham: Duke University Press, 2005.

Raines, Dorit. "Office Seeking, Broglio, and the Pocket Political Guidebooks in Cinquecento and Seicento Venice." *Studi Veneziani* 22 (1991): 137–94.

Raukar, Tomislav. "I fiorentini in Dalmazia nel secolo XIV." *Archivio Storico Italiano* 153, no. 4 (1995): 657–80.

———. *Zadar u XV stoljeću: ekonomski razvoj i društveni odnosi* [Zadar in the Fifteenth Century: Economic Development and Social Relations, in Croatian with English summary]. Institut za hrvatsku povijest, 6. Zagreb: Sveučilište, Centar za povijesne znanosti, 1977.

Ravegnani, Giorgio. "La conquista veneziana di Corfù." In *Venezia e le Isole Ionie*, ed.

Chryssa Maltezou and Gherardo Ortalli, 101–12. Venice: Istituto veneto di scienze, lettere ed arti, 2005.

———. "La conquista veneziana di Creta e la prima organizzazione militare dell'isola." In *Venezia e Creta,* ed. Gherardo Ortalli, 33–35. Venice: Istituto veneto di scienze, lettere ed arti, 1998.

———. "La Romània veneziana." In *Storia di Venezia. L'età del Comune,* ed. Giorgio Cracco and Gherardo Ortalli, II: 183–231. Rome: Enciclopedia Italiana, 1995.

Richard, Jean. "Chypre du protectorat a la domination vénetienne." In *Venezia e il Levante fino al secolo XV,* ed. Agostino Pertusi, I: pt. 2, 657–78. Florence: Olschki Editore, 1973.

———. "Une économie coloniale? Chypre et ses ressources agricoles au Moyen Age." *Byzantinische Forschungen* 5 (1977): 331–52.

Ridolfi, Maddalena. *Venezia e la difesa del Levante: da Lepanto a Candia 1570–1670.* Venice: Arsenale, 1986.

Rizzi, Alberto. *I Leoni di San Marco: il simbolo della Repubblica veneta nella scultura e nella pittura.* Venice: Arsenale, 2001.

Romano, Dennis. *The Likeness of Venice: A life of Doge Francesco Foscari 1373–1457.* New Haven: Yale University Press, 2007.

———. *Patricians and Popolani: The Social Foundations of the Venetian Renaissance State.* Baltimore: The Johns Hopkins University Press, 1987.

———. "'Quod sibi fiat Gratia': The Adjustment of Penalties and the Exercize of Influence in Early Renaissance Venice." *Journal of Medieval and Renaissance Studies* 13 (1983): 251–68.

Romano, Dennis, and John Martin. "Reconsidering Venice." In *Venice Reconsidered: The History and Civilization of an Italian City State, 1297–1797,* ed. John Martin and Dennis Romano, 1–38. Baltimore: The Johns Hopkins University Press, 2000.

Rösch, Gerard. "Il gran guadagno." In *Storia di Venezia. L'eta del Comuné,* ed. Giorgio Gracco and Gherardo Ortalli, II: 233–63. Rome: Enciclopedia Italiana,1991.

Rossi, Franco. "Diedo, Alvise." *DBI* 39 (1991): 756–59.

———. "Diedo, Andrea." *DBI* 39 (1991): 759–60.

———. "Diedo, Antonio." *DBI* 39 (1991): 761–64.

———. "Diedo, Pietro." *DBI* 39 (1991): 779–81.

Rubenstein, Nicolai. *The Government of Florence under the Medici (1434–1494).* Oxford: Clarendon Press, 1997.

Ruggiero, Guido. *Violence in Early Renaissance Venice.* New Brunswick, N.J.: Rutgers University Press, 1980.

Sabalich, Giuseppe. *Guida archelogica di Zara.* Zadar: Leone Woditzka, 1897.

Salvadori, Patrizia. "Gli ufficiali estrinseci fiorentini e Lorenzo dei Medici." *Annali della Scuola Normale Superiore di Pisa. Quaderni: Gli officiali negli stati italiani del Quattrocento,* ser. IV, 1 (1997): 213–24.

Santschi, Elisabeth. "Aspects de la justice en Crète vénitienne d'après les Memoriali du XIV siècle." *Krētika Chronica* 24 (1972): 294–324.

———. *La notion de de 'feudum' en Crète vénitienne, XIIIe–XVe siècles.* Montreux: Ganguin and Laubscher, 1976.

———. "Quelques aspects du statut des non-libres en Crète au XIVe siècle." *Thesaurismata* 9 (1972): 104–36.

Schmitt, Oliver Jens. "'La chiave per l'Adriatico': Albania e Venezia nella percezione reciproca alla fine del medioevo." In *Venezia, l'altro e l'altrove: aspetti della percezione reciproca,* ed. Suzanne Winter, 23–55. Rome: Edizioni di storia e letteratura, 2006.

———. "Le commerce vénitien dans l'Albanie Vénitienne: méchanismes et conjonctures d'un espace économique au XVe siècle." *Anuario de Estudios Medievales* 33, no. 2 (2003): 881–903.

———. "Un monumento dell'Albania medievale: gli statuti di Scutari." In *Statuti di Scutari della prima metà del secolo XIV con le addizioni fino al 1469,* ed. Lucia Nadin, 25–45. Rome: Viella, 2002.

———. *Das venezianische Albanien (1392–1479).* Südosteuropäische Arbeiten. Vol. 110. Munich: R. Oldernburg Verlag, 2001.

Schmitt, Oliver Jens, and G. Saint-Guillain. "Actes inédits concernant Venise, ses possessions albanaises et ses relations avec Skanderbeg entre 1464 et 1468." *Turcica* 31 (1999): 247–312.

Setton, Kenneth Meyer. "The Catalans and Florentines in Greece, 1380–1462." In *A History of the Crusades: The Fourteenth and Fifteenth Centuries,* ed. Harry W. Hazard, III, 225–77. Madison: University of Wisconsin Press, 1969–1989.

———. *The Papacy and the Levant, 1204–1571.* 4 vols. Philadelphia: American Philosophical Society, 1976.

Šimunković, Ljerka. "La politica linguistica della Serenissima verso i possedimenti 'di là da mar': il caso della Dalmazia." In *Mito e antimito di Venezia nel bacino adriatico (secoli XV–XIX),* ed. Sante Graciotti, 95–104. Rome: Il Calamo, 2001.

Smail, Daniel Lord. *The Consumption of Justice: Emotions, Publicity, and Legal Culture in Marseille, 1264–1423.* Ithaca: Cornell University Press, 2003.

Soulis, George C. "The Gypsies in the Byzantine Empire and the Balkans in the Late Middle Ages." *Dumbarton Oaks Papers* 15 (1961): 143–65.

Stahl, Alan M. "Office-holding and the Mint in Early Renaissance Venice." *Renaissance Studies* 6 (1994): 404–15.

———. "A Prosopography of Medieval Venetian Mint Officials." *Medieval Prosopography* 21 (2000): 41–131.

———. *The Venetian Tornesello: A Medieval Colonial Coinage.* New York: American Numismatic Society, 1985.

Starr, Joshua. "Jewish Life in Crete under the Rule of Venice." *Proceedings of the American Academy for Jewish Research* 12 (1942): 54–114.

Stöckly, Doris. *Le système de l'Incanto des galées du marché à Venise (fin XIIIe–milieu XVe siècle).* New York: Brill, 1995.

Stuard, Susan Mosher. *A State of Deference: Ragusa/Dubrovnik in the Medieval Centuries.* Philadelphia: University of Pennsylvania Press, 1992.

Subrahmanyam, Sanjay. *The Portuguese Empire in Asia, 1500–1700: A Political and Economic History.* New York: Longman, 1993.

———. "Written on Water: Designs and Dynamics in the Portuguese *Estado da*

India." In *Empires: Perspectives from Archeology and History,* ed. Terence D'Altroy, Susan Alcock, Kathleen Morrison, and Carla Sinopoli, 42–69. Cambridge: Cambridge University Press, 2001.

TeBrake, William H. *A Plague of Insurrection: Popular Politics and Peasant Revolt in Flanders, 1323–1328.* Philadelphia: University of Pennsylvania Press, 1993.

Tenenti, Alberto. "I corsari in Mediterraneao all'inizio del Cinquecento." *Rivista Storica Italiana* 72 (1960): 234–87.

———. "La politica veneziana e l'Ungheria all'epoca di Sigismondo." In *Venezia e il senso del mare: storia di un prisma culturale dal XIII al XVIII secolo,* 309–31. Milan: Guerini e associati, 1999.

———. "The Sense of Space and Time in the Venetian World of the Fifteenth and Sixteenth Centuries." In *Renaissance Venice,* ed. J. R. Hale, 17–46. London: Faber and Faber, 1973.

———. "Il senso dello stato." In *Storia di Venezia. Il Rinascimento. Politica e cultura,* ed. Alberto Tenenti and Ugo Tucci, IV: 311–44. Rome: Enciclopedia Italiana, 1996.

———. "Venezia e la pirateria nel Levante." In *Venezia et il Levante fino al secolo XV,* ed. Agostino Pertusi, I: pt. 2, 708–71. Florence: Olschki Editore, 1973.

Thiriet, Freddy. "La condition paysanne et les problèmes de l'exploitation rurale en

———. "Sui dissidi sorti tra il Comune de Venezia e i suoi feudatori di Creta nel Trecento." *Archivio Storico Italiano* 114 (1956): 699–712.

———. "A propos de la seigneurie des Venier sur Serigo." *Studi Veneziani* 12 (1970): 199–212.

———. *La Romanie Vénitienne au Moyen Age. Le Développement et l'exploitation du domaine colonial vénitien.* Paris: Bibliothéque des écoles françaises d'Athénes et de Rome, 1959.

Tiepolo, Maria Francesca, et al. "Archivio di Stato di Venezia." In *Guida generale degli Archivi di Stato Italiani,* ed. Maria Francesca Tiepolo, IV: 859–1148. Rome: Ministero per I beni Culturali e Ambientali, 1994.

Tilly, Charles. *Coercion, Capital, and European States, AD 990–1990.* Oxford: Basil Blackwell, 1990.

Todesco, Maria Teresa. "Andamento demografico della nobiltà veneziani allo specchio delle votazioni nel Maggior Consiglio (1297–1797)." *Ateneo Veneto* 27 (1989): 119–64.

Tomadakis, Nicolaos. "La politica religiosa di Venezia a Creta verso i cretesi ortodossi dal XIII al XV secolo." In *Venezia et il Levante fino al secolo XV,* ed. Agostino Pertusi, II: 783–800. Florence: Olschki Editore, 1973.

Topping, Peter. "The Morea 1364–1460." In *The Fourteenth and Fifteenth Centuries,* ed. Harry W. Hazard, III: 141–66. Madison: University of Wisconsin Press, 1975.

Tournoy, G. "Diedo, Francesco." *DBI* 39 (1991): 769–74.

Tucci, Ugo. "Il patrizio veneziano mercante e umanista." In *Mercanti, nave, monete nel Cinquecento veneziano,* 15–43. Bologna: Il Mulino, 1981.

Vacalopolous, Apostolos. "Flight of the Inhabitants of Greece to the Aegean Islands, Crete and Mane during the Turkish Invasions of the 14th-15th Century." In *Charanis Studies,* ed. Angeliki Laiou-Thomadakis. New Brunswick, N.J.: Rutgers University Press, 1980.

Valentini, Giuseppe. "Appunti sul regime degli stabilimenti veneti in Albania nel secolo XIV e XV." *Studi Veneziani* 8 (1966): 195–265.

———. "Dell'amministrazione veneta in Albania." In *Venezia e il Levante fino al secolo XV*, ed. Agostino Pertusi, I: pt. 2, 843–910. Florence: Olschki Editore, 1973.

———. *Lo statuto personale in Albania all'epoca di Skanderbeg. Appunti dagli archivi della Repubblica Veneta.* Rome: Shêjzat, 1967.

Ventura, Angelo. "Barbarigo, Bernardo." *DBI* 6 (1964): 59–61.

———. "Barbaro, Marco." *DBI* 6 (1964): 112–13.

———. "Bembo, Bernardo." *DBI* 8 (1966): 103–6.

———. "Bragadin, Lorenzo." *DBI* 13 (1971): 681–84.

———. "Il Dominio di Venezia nel Quattrocento." In *Florence and Venice: Comparisons and Relations*, ed. Nicolai Rubenstein, Sergio Bertelli, and Craig Hugh Smyth, I: 167–90. Florence: La Nuova Italia, 1979.

———. *Nobiltà e popolo nella societa veneta del 400 e 500*. Bari: Laterza, 1964.

Verlinden, Charles. *The Beginnings of Modern Colonization*, trans. Yvonne Freccero. Ithaca: Cornell University Press, 1970.

Viggiano, Alfredo. "Aspetti politici e giurisdizionali dell'attività dei rettori veneziani nello 'stato da terra' del Quattrocento." *Società e Storia* 65 (1994): 473–505.

———. "Considerazioni su gli auditori novi-sindaci e l'amministrazione della giustizia civile: conflittualità sociali et intervento statale nel primo secolo della terraferma veneta." *Studi Veneziani* 21 (1991): 15–48.

———. "La disciplina dei rettori nello stato Veneto del'400." *Annali della Scuola Normale Superiore di Pisa, ser. IV, Quaderni: Gli officiali negli stati italiani del Quattrocento* 1 (1997): 181–90.

———. *Governanti e governati: legittimità del potere ed esercizio dell'autorità sovrana nello stato veneto della prima età moderna.* Treviso: Fondazione Benetton Edizioni Canova, 1993.

———. "Interpretazione della legge e mediazione politica: note sull'avogaria di comun nel secolo XV." In *Studi Veneti offerti a Gaetano Cozzi*, 121–31. Venice: Il Cardo, 1992.

———. "Note sull'amministrazione veneziana in Istria nel secolo XV." *Acta Histriae* 3 (1994): 5–20.

———. "Tra Venezia e Creta. Conflittualità giudiziarie, identità sociali e memorie familiari nello stato da mar del Quattrocento." In *Venezia e Creta*, ed. Gherardo Ortalli, 107–50. Venice: Istituto Ellenico, 1998.

Vilfan, Sergij. "Towns and States at the Juncture of the Alps, the Adriatic, and Pannonia." In *Cities and the Rise of States in Europe, A.D. 1000–1800*, ed. Charles Tilly and Wim P. Blockmans, 44–59. Boulder: Westview Press, 1994.

Vlassi, Despina E. "La tariffa delle spese giudiziarie pubblicata a Cefalonia nel 1511." *Studi Veneziani* 7 (1983): 233–52.

Von Wartburg, Marie-Louise. "Vestigia Leonis: Art and Architecture in Cyprus under Venetian Rule." In *Cyprus: Jewel in the Crown of Venice*, ed. Vassos Karageorghis, Loukia Loizou Hadjigavriel, and Chryssa A. Maltezou, 57–73. Nicosia: The Anastasios G. Leventis Foundation and the Leventis Municipal Museum of Nicosia, 2003.

Waquet, Jean-Claude. *Corruption: Ethics and Power in Florence, 1600–1770,* trans. Linda McCall. University Park: The Pennsylvania State University Press, 1992.

Weissman, Ronald. "The Importance of Being Ambiguous: Social Relations, Individualism, and Identity in Renaissance Florence." In *Urban Life in the Renaissance,* ed. Susan Zimmerman and Ronald Weissman, 269–80. Newark: University of Delaware Press, 1989.

———. *Ritual Brotherhood in Renaissance Florence.* New York: Academic Press, 1982.

———. "Taking Patronage Seriously: Mediterranean Values and Renaissance Society." In *Patronage, Art and Society,* ed. F. W. Kent and Patricia Simons, 25–45. Oxford: Clarendon Press, 1987.

Wickham, Chris. "Gossip and Resistance among the Medieval Peasantry." *Past and Present* 160 (1998): 3–24.

Witt, Ronald. *In the Footsteps of the Ancients: The Origins of Humanism from Lovato to Bruni.* Leiden: Brill, 2000.

Wright, Diana G. "Bartolomeo Minio: Venetian Administration in 15th-Century Nauplion." *Electronic Journal of Oriental Studies* 3, no. 5 (2000): 1–235.

———. "The First Venetian Love Letter? The Testament of Zorzi Cernovich." *Electronic Journal of Oriental Studies* 9, no. 2 (2006): 1–20.

———. "The Wooden Towns of the Stato da Mar: Medieval Construction in Nauplion." *Studi Veneziani* 40 (2000): 169–77.

Yotopoulou, Elly. "Alcune considerazioni sulle classe sociale corfiotte e sulla politica veneta nei loro confronti in base a quanto risulta dalle fonti e in modo particulare dai testi delle ambasciate." In *Levante Veneziano. Aspetti di Storia delle Isole Ionie al tempo della Serenissima,* ed. Massimo Costantini and Aliki Nikiforou, 97–122. Rome: Bulzoni Editore, 1996.

Zaninović, Marin. "Relazioni fra Hvar (Lesina) e Venezia: Note." *Archivio Veneto* ser. V, 134, no. 169 (1990): 129–37.

Zannini, Andrea. "L'impiego pubblico." In *Storia di Venezia. Il Rinascimento. Politica e cultura,* ed. Alberto Tenenti and Ugo Tucci, IV: 415–63. Rome: Enciclopedia Italiana, 1995.

Zinkeisen, J. W. *Geschite des Osmanischen Reiches in Europa.* Vol. 4. Hamburg: F. Perthes, 1856.

Zorzi, Andrea. "The Florentines and Their Public Offices in the Early Fifteenth Century: Competition, Abuses of Power, and Unlawful Acts." In *History from Crime,* ed. Edward Muir and Guido Ruggiero, 110–34. Baltimore: The Johns Hopkins University Press, 1994.

———. "Giusdicenti e operatori di giustizia nello stato territoriale fiorentino del XV secolo." *Ricerche Storiche* 19 (1989): 517–52.

———. "The 'Material Constitution' of the Florentine Dominion." In *Florentine Tuscany: Structures and Practices of Power,* ed. William J. Connell and Andrea Zorzi, 6–31. Cambridge: Cambridge University Press, 2000.

INDEX

Page numbers in *italics* indicate maps and tables.